8TH ADVANCED ARCHITECTURE CONTEST

DESIGN FOR LIVING

Global contest to rethink our habitat from the body to the city

CONTENT

Carles Enrich Studio, IN FLOW Canyelles, 2017

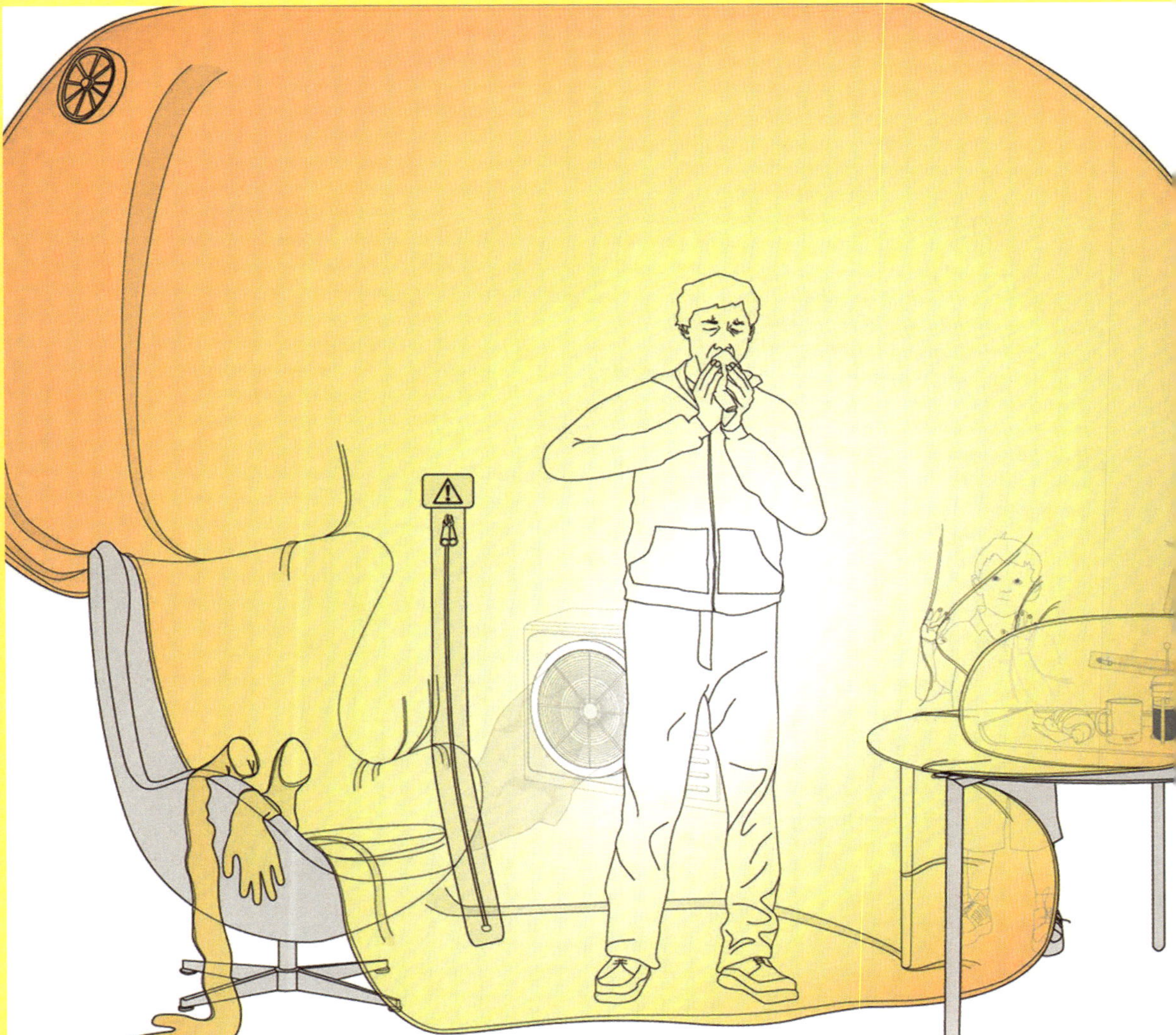

Domestic Isolation Unit. MAP Architects / David A. Garcia © 2010

The Institute for Advanced Architecture of Catalonia calls its **8th Advanced Architecture Contest** as a global reflection to rethink human habitats, at a time when the fight for life and climate allows us to consider how we would like to live in the coming decades.

The objective is for students and professionals from all over the world to propose how to design our living environment, at whichever scale most interests them to promote and protect human life: how to rethink our bodies, how to design the objects that surround us, how to redesign the homes that we inhabit, what functions they must incorporate, how to grow communities or re-naturalize public spaces, how to reinvent our cities taking advantage of digital communications in times of confinement and broadly how we define our relationships with others in a time of changes.

In these ways we want to inspire reflection on how we can accelerate our future using design in order to respond to the health, energy, food, production, environmental or social challenges of the coming years.

We like to think that each person's life begins at home, which is the center of their universe and the origin of their social interactions. In times of crisis like the present, we have been confined to our homes and they have become microcities where we live, work and rest, connected to the world through information networks. So, after this experience, how do you imagine the future for our living environment?

The contest encourages participants to propose a design related to their way of life, at the scale that most interests them from our bodies to the city, anywhere in the world, and that reflects different cultural, environmental, economic or social conditions.

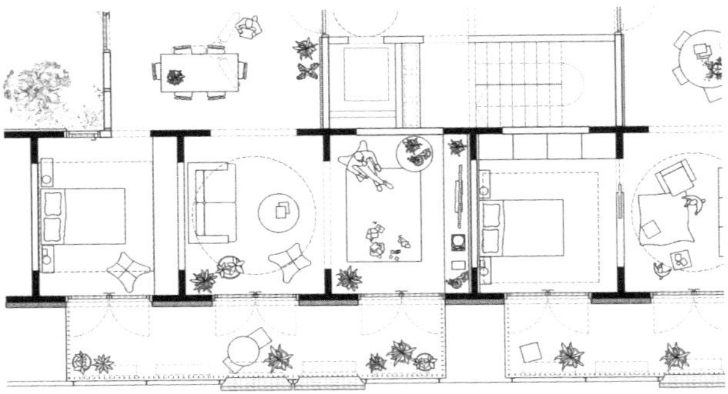

Impsol Housing in Sant Adrià del Besós. © Carles Enrich Studio 2018

Japanese Bedroom
Interior, 1882

How we live,
Media House Project
Laura Cantarella 2001

Benny Lam, Subdivided Flats, 2012

Saami Family in Norway, Circa 1900

Tan Handan,
Hong Kong apartment,
2020

Standard, Bathroom, 1903

Ray Eames and Charles Eames (Photo: Vicente Guallart) Case Study House 8, 1949

RULES & DELIVERY

ELIGIBILITY

The competition is opened to students and professionals.

There is no age limit; the projects may be carried out be individually or in groups, with no restriction on the number of members of the team.

RESTRICTIONS

The following will not be eligible to take part in the competition:

- Any individual or organization related to the promoting organization, such as meers of the advisory committee or sponsored researchers, and anyone professionally associated with the promoter;
- Members of the Competition Jury and organizing Staff, or any person to whom a member of the jury acts as director, supervisor or adviser;
- Any person directly or indirectly involved in the summary of the Competition.

DOCUMENTS & GRAPHIC MATERIALS REQUIRED

Write a brief description (max 200 words) that outlines key concepts around proposals or changes for our living habitats at the time for the fight for life and climate

Graphic description: Site plans, floor plans, elevations, sections, perspective drawings, photographs of physical or digital models and axonometric drawings at any scale and descriptive texts explaining the project are allowed. The descriptive texts must be in English.

Format:

The proposals should be presented on three (3) DIN A-3 panels and comply with the following format:

Each panel will be presented in PDF format. The size of each file must not exceed 1MB.

The same panels will also be presented in a JPG format and maximum dimensions of 1920px by 1080px. The size of each file will not have to exceed 1MB.

Video (optionary): You have the option to submit a 1 minute (maximum) video to explain in, a few words, the key concepts of your proposal. Please use English subtitles even if you are speaking English. (It is not mandatory to speak in the video, you may also use text, images, animation etc). To submit the video: First upload the video to YouTube, then login in to your competition profile page and paste the YouTube link to the video section of the submission.

INTERNATIONAL JURY

Melat Assefa
Adis Abebba
Consultant World Bank,
Fab Academy Graduate

Ali Basbous
Beirut
Founder Build by Associative Data

Donald Bates
Melbourne
Co-founder Lab Architecture Studio, Chair of Architectural Design Melbourne School of Design

Caroline Bos
Amsterdam
Co-founder UN Studio

Lucas Cappelli
Barcelona
Member Board of Trustee IAAC

Aziza Chaouni
Fez / Toronto
Professor at Faculty of Architecture, Landscape and Design in Toronto, Founder Aziza Chaouni Projects

Hernan Diaz Alonso

Los Angeles

Director SCI-Arc, Founder HAD-X

Tomas Diez

Barcelona

Director IAAC's Fab Lab Barcelona, Fab City Global Instigator

Julio Gaeta

Mexico

Co-founder Gaeta Springall Arquitectos, Director Fabrica de Ciudad, CDMX

Anna Gener

Barcelona

CEO Savills Aguirre Newman

Vicente Guallart

Barcelona / Moscow

Founder Guallart Architects, Director HSE's Shukhov Lab

Daniel Ibañez

Boston

Harvard GSD, Co-director MAEBB IAAC

INTERNATIONAL JURY

Beno Juarez
Lima
President Fab Lab Peru

Lydia Kallipoliti
New York
Assistan Profesor The Cooper Union

Petr Kudryavtsev
Moscow
CEO Citymakers

Anupama Kundoo
Auroville / Berlin
Founder Anupama Kundoo Architects

Xavier Marcet
Barcelona
IAAC President Board of Trustees, President Lead to Change

Areti Markopoulou
Barcelona
Academic Director IAAC

Xavier Matilla
Barcelona
Chief Architect Barcelona City Council

Nuria Moliner
Barcelona
Architect, Researcher, Communicator

Farshid Moussavi
London
Founder Farshid Moussavi Architecture, Professor GSD Hardvard

Mu Shao Hui
Shenzhen
Deputy Chief Planner. UPDIS Urban Planning Design Institute Shenzhen

Willy Muller
Barcelona
Founder WMA, Director Urban Sciences Lab IAAC

Florencia Pita
Los Angeles
Founder Florencia Pita & co, Professor at SCI-Arc

INTERNATIONAL JURY

Nadya Peek

Seattle

Assistant Professor, Human Centered Design & Engineering. University of Washington, Phd MIT Center for Bits

Nasrine Seraji

Paris

Founder Atelier Seraji

Sherry Lassiter

Cambridge (USA)

President Fab Foundation

Fiona Raby

New York

University Professor of Design and Social Inquiry, The New School

Carlo Ratti

Torino / Cambridge

Founder Carlo Ratti Associati, Director MIT's Senseable City Lab

Michael Rojkind

Mexico

Founder Rojkind Arquitectos

Marcela Sabino
Rio de Janeiro
Head of Innovation, Museum of Tomorrow, Foresight Strategist

Luby Springall
Mexico
Co-founder Gaeta Springall Arquitectos

Oscar Tomico
Barcelona
Head Studies of the degree in Industrial Design Engineering, Elisava

RESULTS OF THE 8TH ADVANCED ARCHITECTURE CONTEST

The 8th edition of the Advanced Architecture Contest has been organized under the title Design for Living. On July 15th 2020 deadline to receive projects was closed, having received 193 proposals from 80 countries. The organization made a first selection of 126 projects that have been included in this publication, with 36 of those being qualified as finalists.

The international jury submitted their votes with the following results:

OT Oscar Tomico, **PK** Petr Kudryavtsev, **JG** Julio Gaeta, **LS** Luby Springall, **CB** Caroline Bos, **MS** Marcela Sabino, **MR** Michel Rojkind, **NS** Nasrine Seraji, **FM** Farshid Mousavi, **XM** Xavier Matilla, **AM** Areti Markopoulou, **NM** Nuria Moliner, **VG** Vicente Guallart, **TD** Tomas Diez, **LK** Lydia Kallipoliti, **MA** Melat Asefa, **XM** Xavier Marcet, **BJ** Beno Juarez, **NP** Nadya Peek, **MS** Mu Shao Hui, **LC** Lucas Cappelli, **DB** Donald Bates, **WM** Willy Muller, **DI** Daniel Ibañez, **CR** Carlo Ratti, **AC** Aziza Chaouni, **AB** Ali Basbous

JURORS CODE	OT	PK	JG	LS	CB
694QMUZRL					
355X8OELJ					
317VN4EB5					
6681643SA					
578K7KLX					
687WT2DJ					
690IF1QA5					
665DODZ1M					
43246C9B9					
666WHC3QN	2				
205G97F78					
5957O58PV	1				4
357AX7RC1			5	5	
6789BA9Y8					
6999WXMOI					
245X2R9A6					
399GBH1T8			4	3	
468ASK9BF		2			
137PATJSN	3	1			
27006PZAI					
4454TA47Y	5			1	
122JHG8MU					
6200EJWA8			3	4	
480QFQC0J					
629MO1UVX					
193EVRMT9					
272JFWT77					3
5948TN1BO					1
14295YWKB			1	2	
546XT7EY8		4			5
369ULY8QE		5	2		
688GNKUEP		3			2
551I0ISUK					
619AA610I					
723Q55363					
411OU1YYI	4				

MS	MR	NS	FM	XM	AM	NM	VG	TD	LK	MA	XM	BJ	NP	MS	LC	DB	WM	DI	CR	AC	AB	TOTAL
	4					2								4	1				3			14
								4													2	6
			4																			4
											3				4							7
		5									5				2			2				14
3				1						2												6
	5				4	4		1				2				2	4					22
5						5				3		3	2									20
														3								3
																						5
														5				1			4	20
			5	3										1								9
			1													4						5
													3									3
			2				2						5							1		17
																						2
					3	1		2	3	4						1						18
																	3					9
					2				4			1	1			3			5		3	19
																						7
				2																		2
		2		4			5				2							4	2			19
										1			4						4			9
		3						5														11
	2	4						3												2		12
2					1							4					2			3		15
		1																		4		14
4	3		3			3	1		5			5			3	5		5	1	5	1	51
							3				4										5	17
									1													1
1	1						4		2	5	1						5					19
														2								2
				5	5										5		1	3				23

WALL-E

Aramis Corullo, Paula Casia, Gellaine Burgos, Althea Poblete & Angelo Landicho

SELECTED WORKS
2020

FIRST PRIZE 369ULY8QE

RE LİFE CYCLE

WHEN DEATH CREATES ETERNAL LİVİNG

Suwapat Rodprasert
Pongpol Punjawaytegul
Thailand

The purpose of this project is to design the structure that promotes new living system in which beneficial to all living , death and the earth Looking towards the idea of closed loop self-sustainable system (based on cradle-to-cradle templates), instead of considering death as the end of human life cycle, turning it to become aesthetically valuable traces that support daily routine. The design take advantage of fundamental metabolisms process to convert dead body into a temporal renewable energy for dwelling and respectively, provides nourishment for upcoming nature to grow. As a result, death creates life.

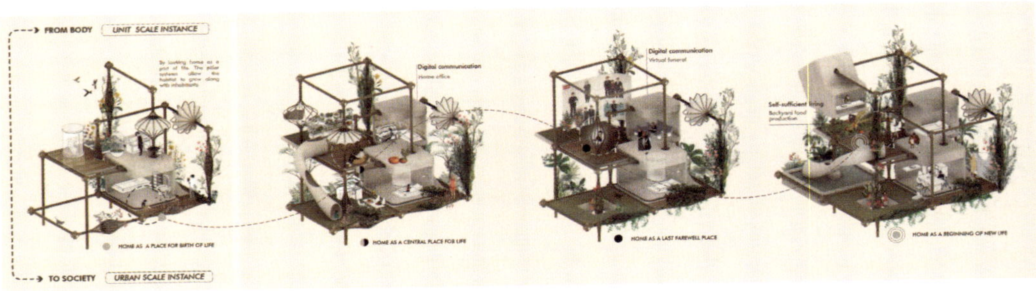

RECONNECTING LIFE AND DEATH

"Relife-Life-Cycle" system is created to manage how people handle death and in turn, how they live to honor both the earth and the departed for eternity

369ULY8QE
A
B
C
D
E
F
STRUCTURAL ADAPTATION
A PREPARING STATE
B DECOMPOSITION STATE
C WIND TURBINE
D RAIN COLLECTOR
E SHADING DEVICE
F CULTIVATION PLANTER

SECOND PRIZE 4110U1YYI

REDEFİNİNG "REFUGEE"

IN AN AUTONOMOUS SHATİLA

Yvonne Asiimwe
Cyprus

The project proposes methods in which refugee camps can become self sufficient entities with an unique identity by looking at and overwhelmingly crowded example -Shatila- a refugee camp that was meant to accommodate hundreds of Palestinian refugees within Beirut but later became permanent and over-populated with approximately 10.000-22.000 new residents.
With the ongoing pandemic in mind, one wonders how those in such conditions would live through an unanticipated lockdown.

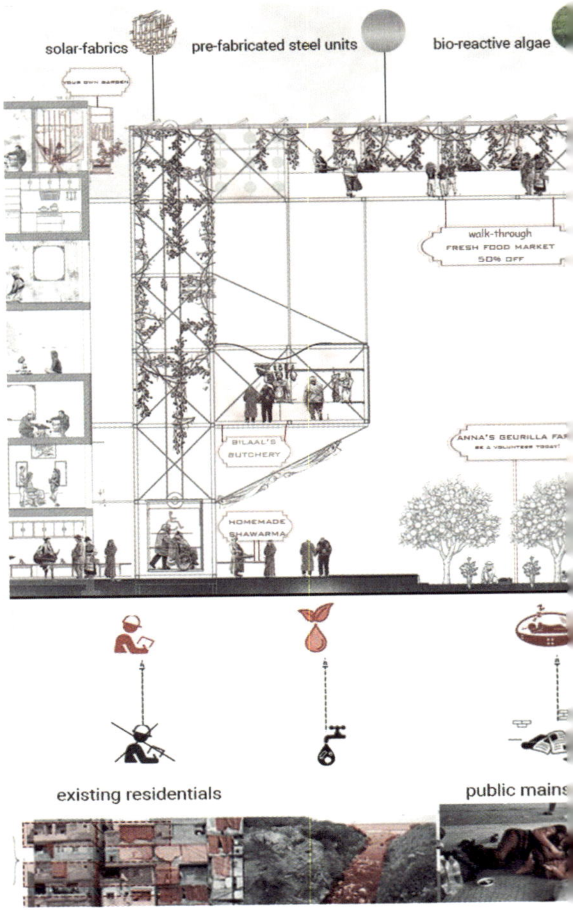

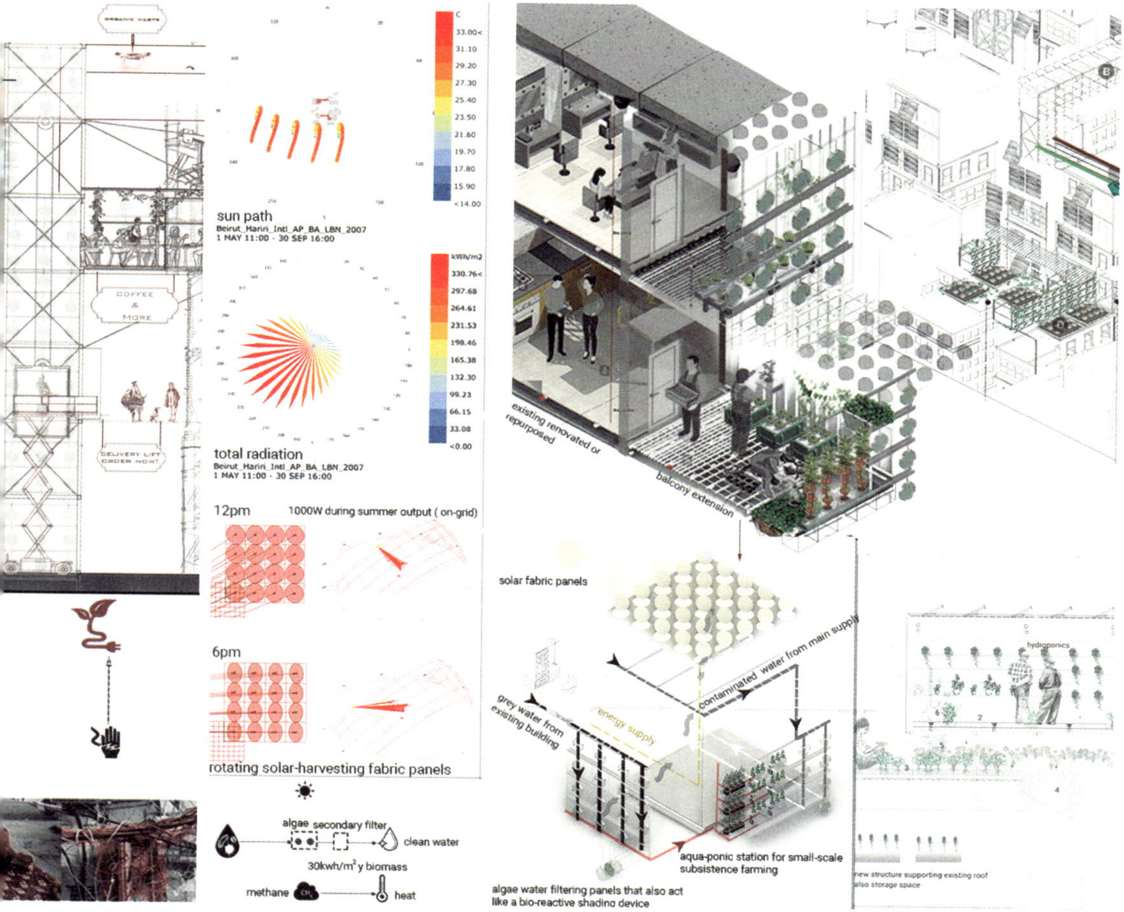
COFFEE & MORE
DELIVERY LIFT ORDER NOW!
sun path
Beirut_Hariri_Intl_AP_BA_LBN_2007
1 MAY 11:00 - 30 SEP 16:00
C
33.00<
31.10
29.20
27.30
25.40
23.50
21.60
19.70
17.80
15.90
<14.00
total radiation
Beirut_Hariri_Intl_AP_BA_LBN_2007
1 MAY 11:00 - 30 SEP 16:00
kWh/m2
330.76<
297.68
264.61
231.53
198.46
165.38
132.30
99.23
66.15
33.08
<0.00
12pm
1000W during summer output (on-grid)
6pm
rotating solar-harvesting fabric panels
algae secondary filter
clean water
30kwh/m² y biomass
methane
heat
existing renovated or repurposed
balcony extension
solar fabric panels
contaminated water from main supply
grey water from existing building
energy supply
aqua-ponic station for small-scale subsistence farming
algae water filtering panels that also act like a bio-reactive shading device
hydroponics
new structure supporting existing roof also storage space

proposal
proposal
proposal
private pockets
existing
W.C
kiosk
KIOSK
EXISTING
indoor nursery
removable lift
REMOVABLE LIFT
A
B
A

NERO

B

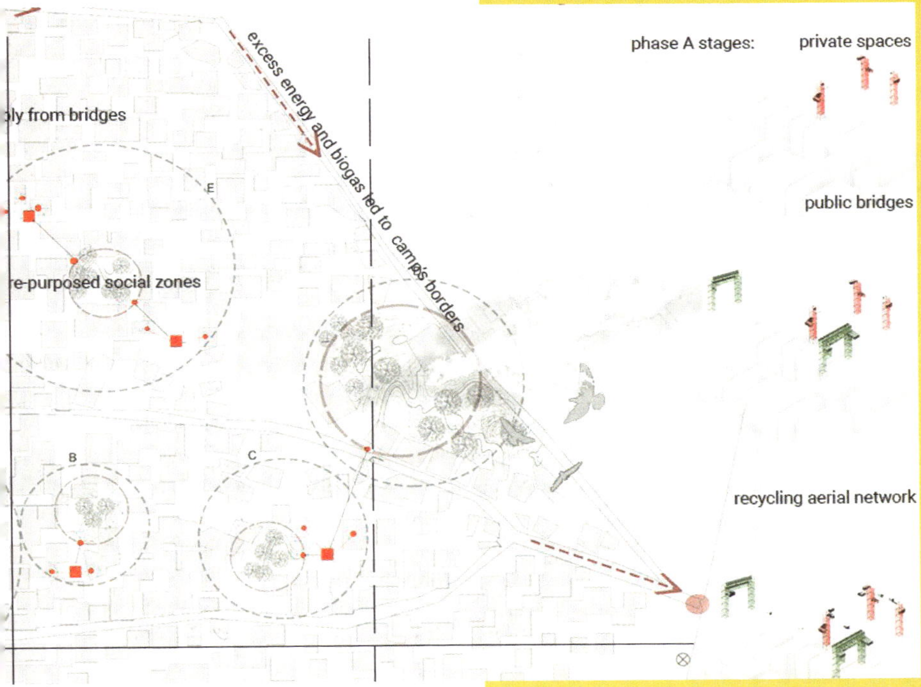

This will be the beginning of a pedestrianized Shatila in order to host activities like guerrilla farming and expand the existing street-markets

THİRD PRIZE 43246C9B9

WALL-E

TRANSFORMİNG WASTE İNTO A FLOATİNG CİTY TO RESTORE THE SUNKEN KİNGDOM OF BİNUANGAN

Aramis Corullo
Paula Carmela Casia
Angelo Landicho
Althea Poblete
Gellaine Marie Burgos
Philippines

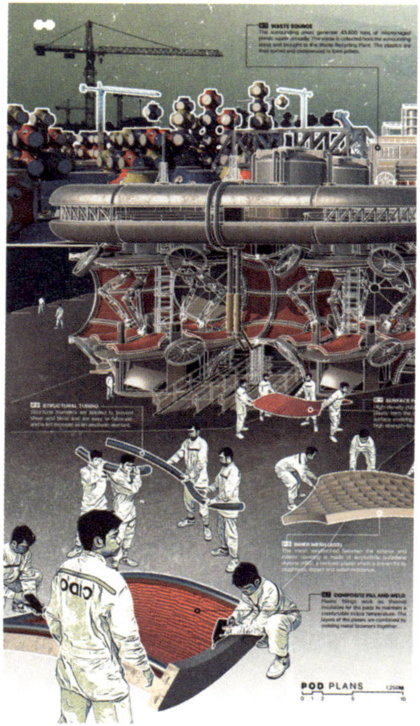

The Philippines ranks third in the world as the biggest ocean polluter of plastic. Wall-E's main idea is to find life in the middle of a wasteland. It's named after a series of walls that connect and provide foundation for the settlements in the area. These sunken fortifications now serve as the walkways to connect to the people to their homes. However, Binuangan village has to problems: their land is slowly sinking into the ocean and the lack of proper water treatment and solid waste management. Despite these alarming problems the locals refuse to leave their homes as fishing is their main source of livehood. To address these environmental issues Wall-E proposes amphibious pods made from recycled plastic waste. The future presents us an opportunity to transform our coastal habitats into resilient cost-effective and mass-produced alternatives which positively impact our environment.

3,800 tons of mismanaged
collected from the surrounding
cycling Plant. The plastics are
pellets.
3D PRINTING FACTORY
There are four automated printers in a single factory pod to produce four panels simultaneously. The recycled plastic pellets are melted and converted into a 5 mm filament that goes into the large format 3D printers.
SCHWARZ P SURFACE
The Schwarz P surface was chosen as the overall form of the pod to facilitate air and light circulation due to its high porosity. Its minimal surface allows the design to lessen material usage in non-crucial areas. The shape also enables the creation of a mesh or lattice when joined together for great shock absorption and impact resistance.
FACTORY TRANSFER
Pellets are carried to the printing facility through lifts. One pod requires 21,883 kg of recycled plastic to form its mass.
SURFACE PANEL (HDPE)
High-density polyethylene (HDPE), the most abundant plastic from the collected waste, is used to create the surface covering. HDPE is a lightweight plastic with a high strength-to-density ratio which allows it to float.
SPACE-SAVING FURNITURE
To maximize the use of space, the use of retractable, foldable, as well as multi-functional furniture was considered.
EVAPORATIVE OFF-GRID TOILET
To minimize the use of water and electricity, a pod uses an evaporative off-grid toilet that uses evaporates most of the sewage waste.
between the exterior and
de of acrylonitrile butadiene
plastic which is known for its
ater-resistance.
OMPOSITE FILL AND WELD
fillings work as thermal
rs for the pods to maintain a
table indoor temperature. The
f the panels are combined by
g metal fasteners together.
TANK
KITCHEN
DINING AREA
TOILET
PERSONALIZED AREA
ENTRY
WORK / STUDY
LAUNDRY
SHOWER
LIVING AREA
OPEN TO BELOW
WALK-IN CLOSET
SHOWER
SLEEPING AREA

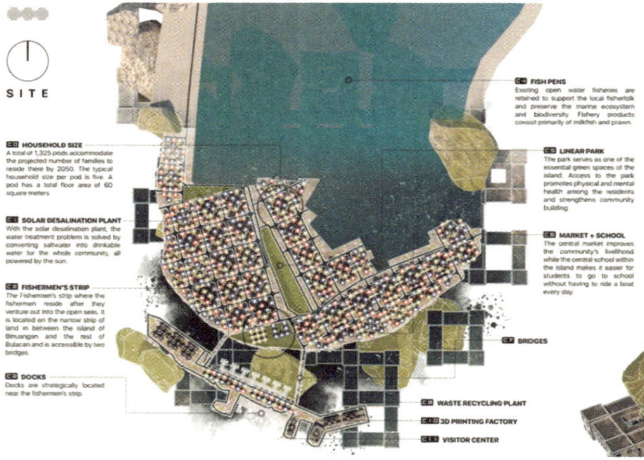

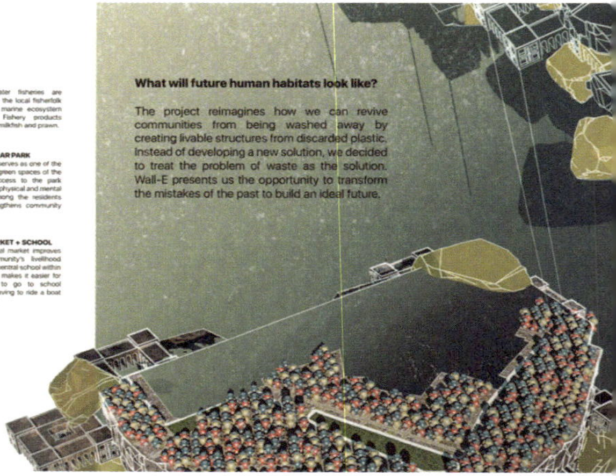

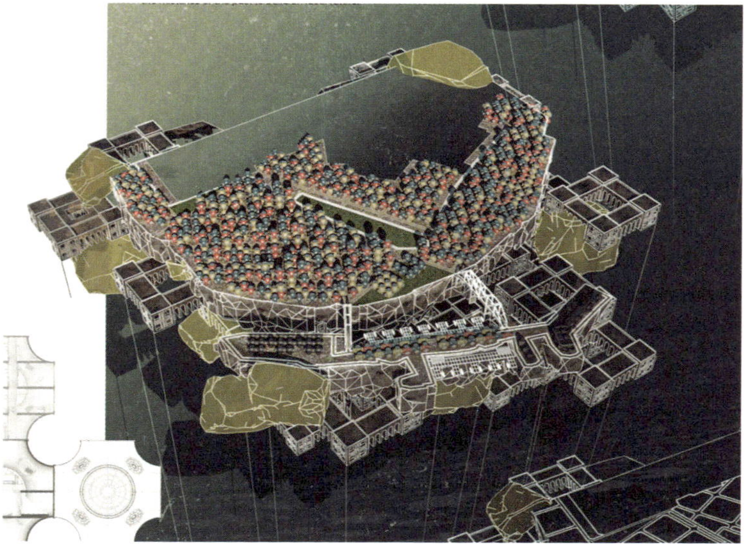

What will future human habitats look like? The project reimagines how we can revive communities from being washed away by creating livable structures from discarded plastic

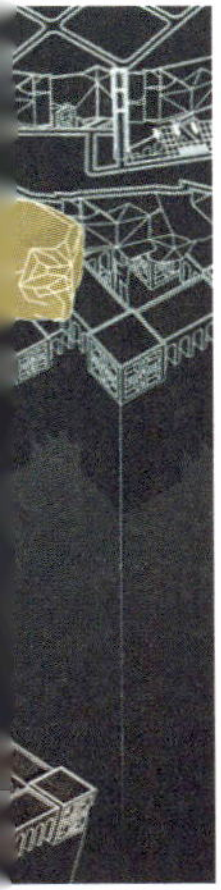

43246C9B9

Algal Bloom
Leonardo Zanatta

SELECTED WORKS
2020

HONORABLE MENTİON

357AX7RC1

SOUL OF ABOBE

PROTOTYPE HABİTAT FOR MARGİNALİZED PEOPLE

Hasib Sarowar
Shoheli Akter
Bangladesh

The corridor of their habitat is a life for them and it will also increase the risk of being attacked how to post covid-19. Since human beings don't leave without Souls, the soul (corridor) has been reconstituted and replaced in the body (habitat). Which will give them New Hope of survival.

Self Quarantine Space

Flexibility in cluster development and Section of a collective Community

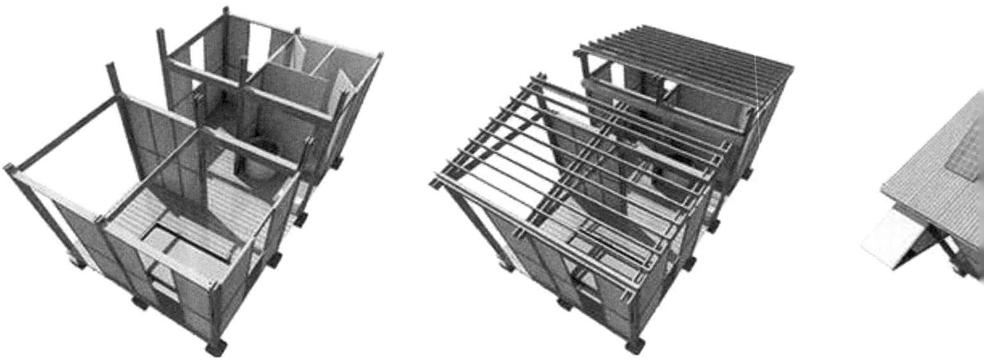

Flexibility in cluster development and section of a collective community

HONORABLE MENTION 666WHC3QN

HOUSE OF WASTE

Deepika Raghu
Lilett Ricaurte
Andrea Destasio
India

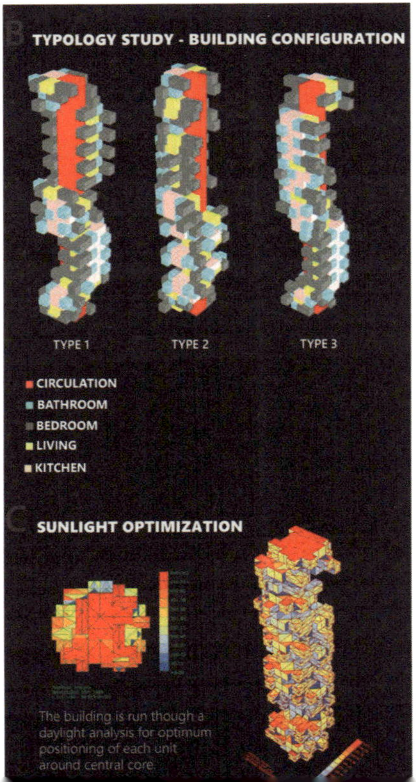

The project proposes new ideas for a recalibrated lifestyle where multiple forms of decomposition act as agents for producing and recycling waste within a household. Some processes are more time and labour intensive while others are faster, automated processes. It seeks to envision an alternate future within the paradigm of what can actually be done. By growing your own food, creating energy from your organic waste and being able to dispose of your waste easily, this project shows the possibilities of this new lifestyle, coupling it with convenience for the inhabitants of the space.

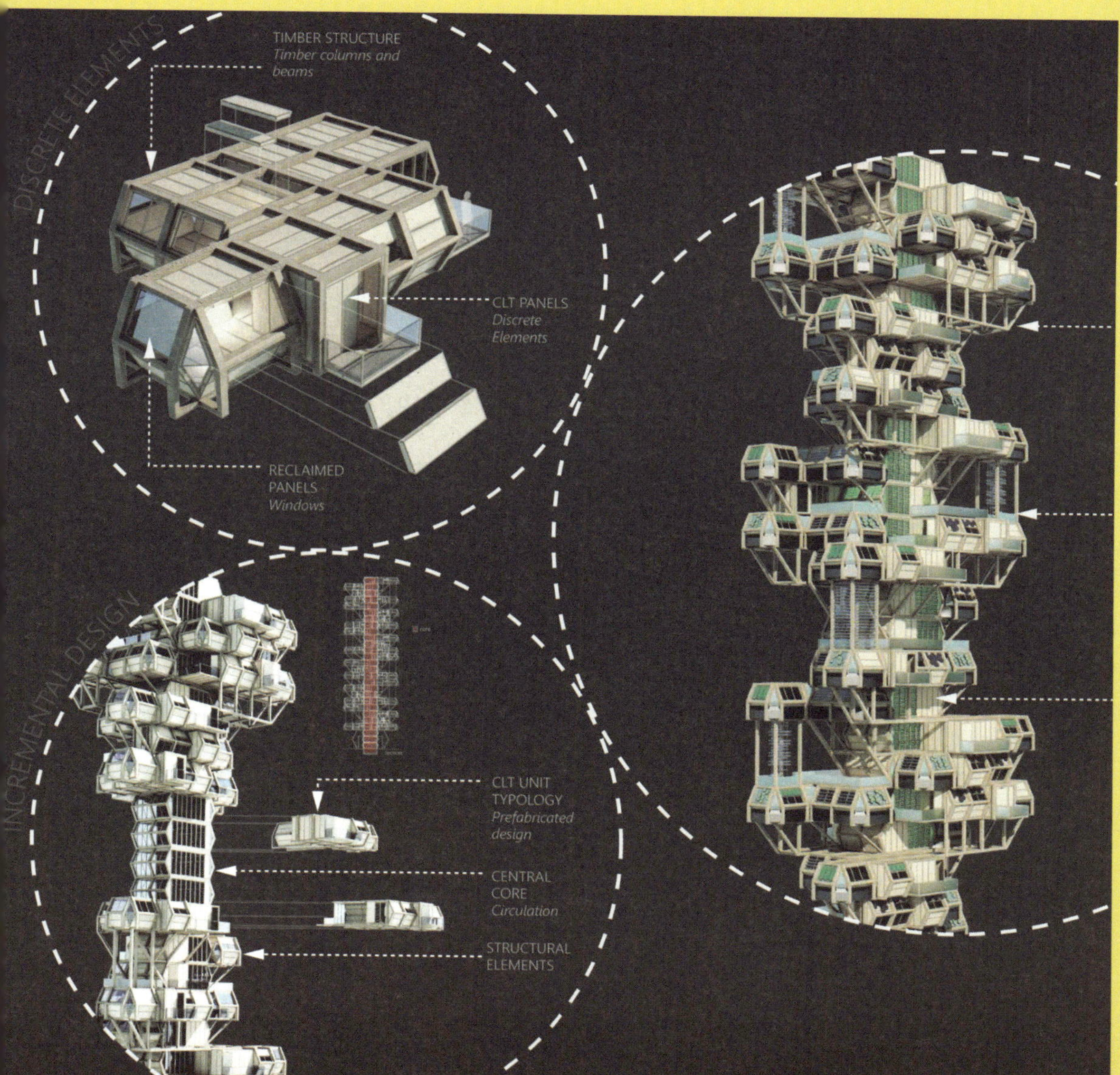
DISCRETE ELEMENTS
TIMBER STRUCTURE
Timber columns and beams
CLT PANELS
Discrete Elements
RECLAIMED PANELS
Windows
INCREMENTAL DESIGN
CLT UNIT TYPOLOGY
Prefabricated design
CENTRAL CORE
Circulation
STRUCTURAL ELEMENTS

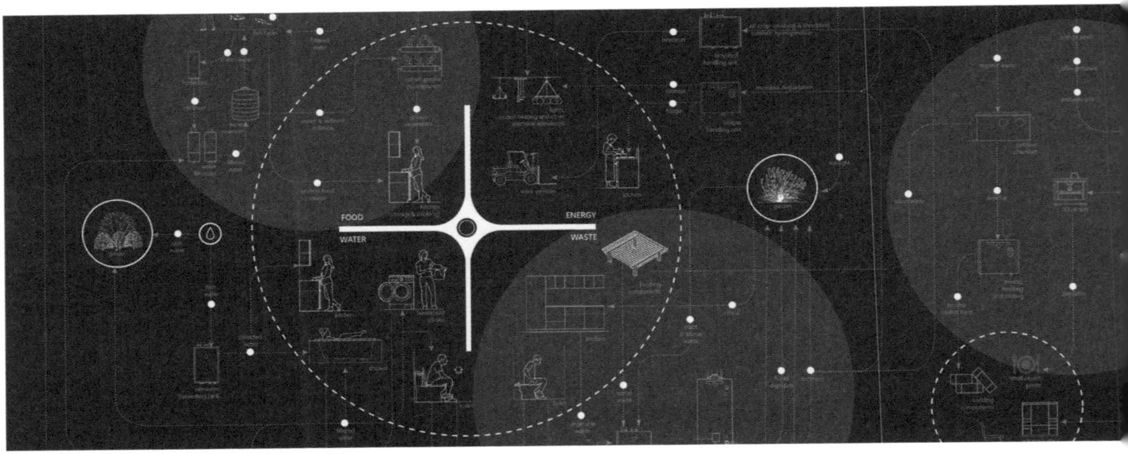

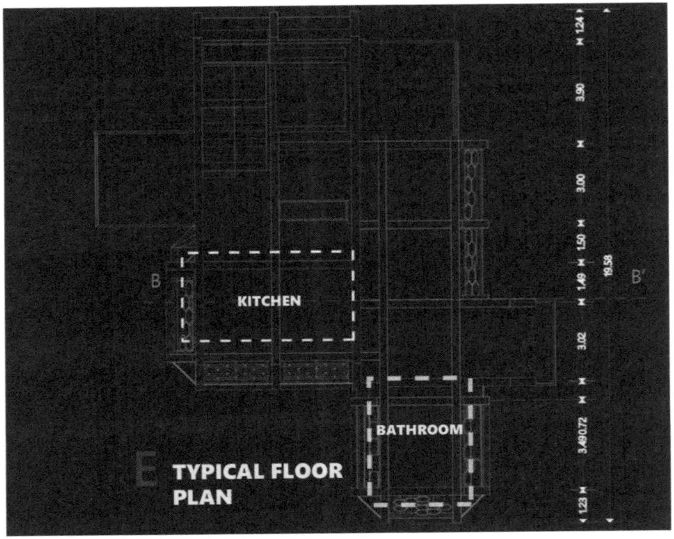

Circular system network

666WHC3QN

D WASTE-CONSCIOUS LIVING

The project proposes new ideas for a recalibrated lifestyle where multiple forms of decomposition act as agents for producing and recycling waste within a household. Some processes are more time and labour intensive while others are faster, automated processes. It seeks to envision an alternate future within the paradigm of what can actually be done. By growing your own food, creating energy from your organic waste and being able to dispose of your waste easily, this project shows the possibilities of this new lifestyle, coupling it with convienience for the inhabitants of the space.

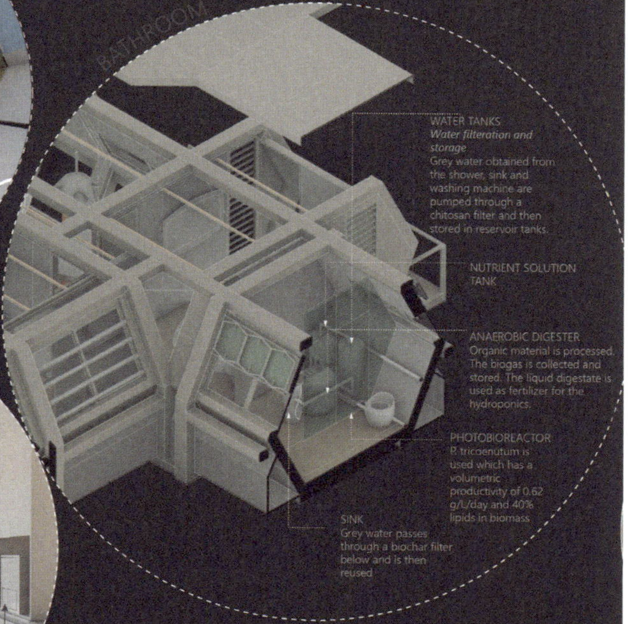

-ORGANIC WASTE DISPOSAL AND COLLECTION SYSTEM
Automatic recycling machine and automatic sorts, processes, shreds, the waste material and identifys the package by barcode marking of the bin. (this process requires limited intervention from the inhabitants)

- COMPOST BIN/SHREDDER
Two chamber design to break down the food within 10-12 days. (this process requires user intervention)

- 3D PRINTER
For small-object printing such as cups, spoons or plates from biopolymers produced from the household organic waste which is processed.

HONORABLE MENTION

122JHG8MU

AMAZON LIVING

Michael Daw
Great Britain

Amazon Living explores a world after Coronavirus, fear of deadly viruses has forced the isolation of all individuals. One of the few corporations to profit from Coronavirus, Amazon continues to develop their methods of supplying everything needed for living direct to your home through their new Amazon Living pods. The pods are designed around the human needs, the utility interface, a wall of vending type units are installed onto an entire wall of the pod. The delivery infrastructure, a mass of wires, pipes, ducts and chutes cover the towers plugging into the pods delivering anything the inhabitants may need.

▲

Aerial view showing the high density living towers

HONORABLE MENTION

629M01UVX

ARCHITECTURE CREATED FOR NATURE

Natalia Winnicka
Barcelona

The purpose of this project is to show that with both a new perspective on architecture for nature and a common known way of building, lost and poor spaces in the cities and towns have the potential to be revitalized with greenhouses and urban agriculture techniques.
This type of architecture intends to focus on energy reduction, making use of nature's cycles and balancing agrarian and urban functions.
The purpose of the Urban Green-houses is not only to act as a sustainable solution to the current issues in cities but to connect people with nature and is the new WAY/DESIGN for LIVING.

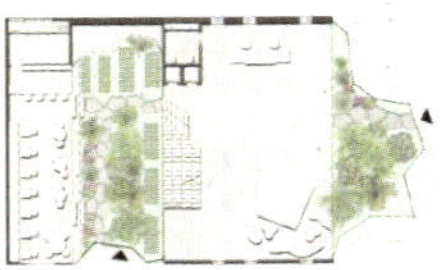

LEVEL 0
Floor plan

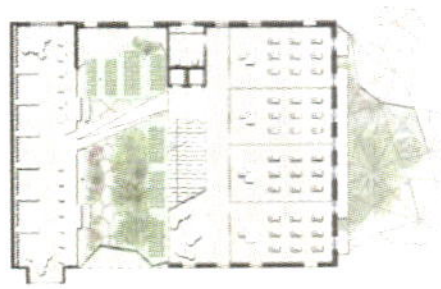

LEVEL 1
Floor plan

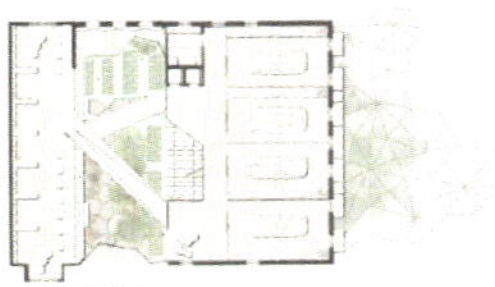

LEVEL 2
Floor plan

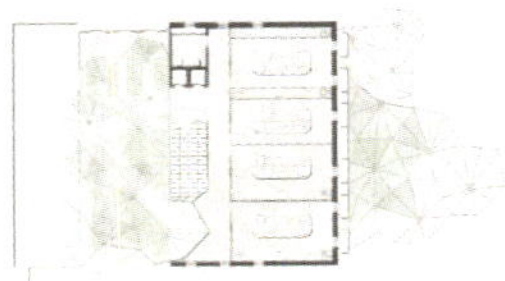

LEVEL 3
Floor plan

Interior Garden. Visualization.

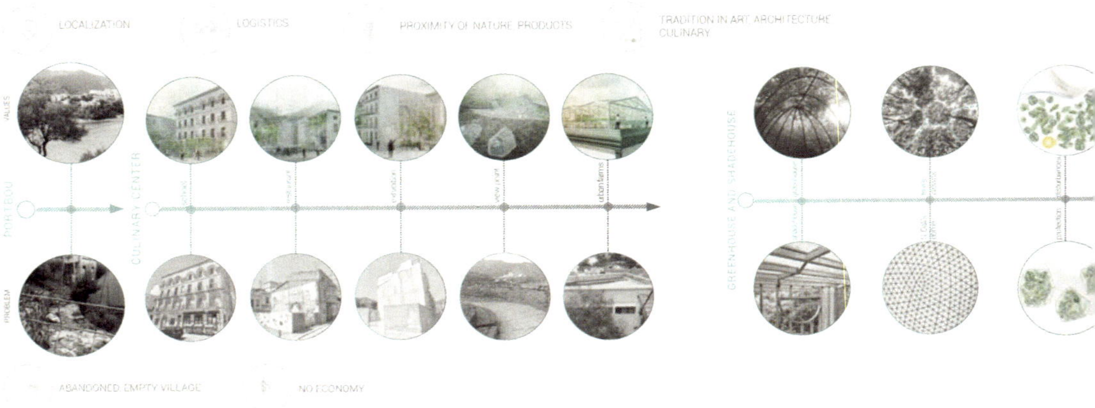

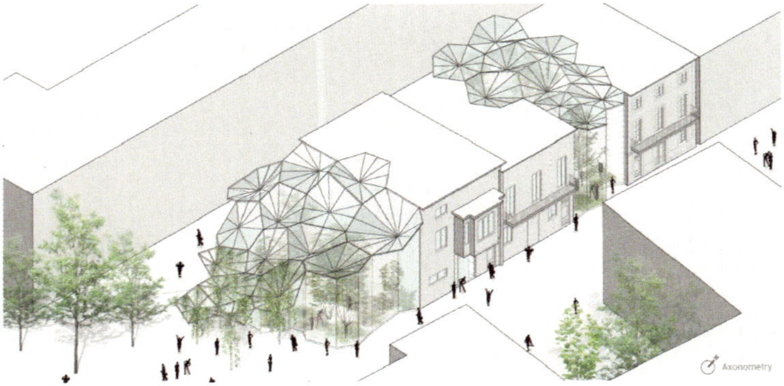

Rooftop urban gardens ▶

HONORABLE MENTION

619AA6101

THE LIVING RIG ISLAND

Yangchuan Tian
China

Named Living Rig Island, the reimagined offshore island, evolves from discarded aging mega infrastructure found in the middle of the Gulf of Mexico to an island network that supports a new water economy. Rethinking and transforming the experience and relationship between humans and the ocean, this project treats the symbiotic collaboration of ocean farms and green machines as new forms of ocean industry that are ready to emerge.

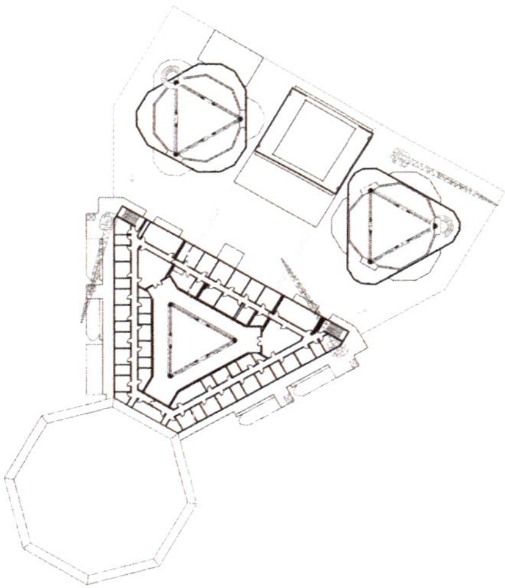

PLAN A

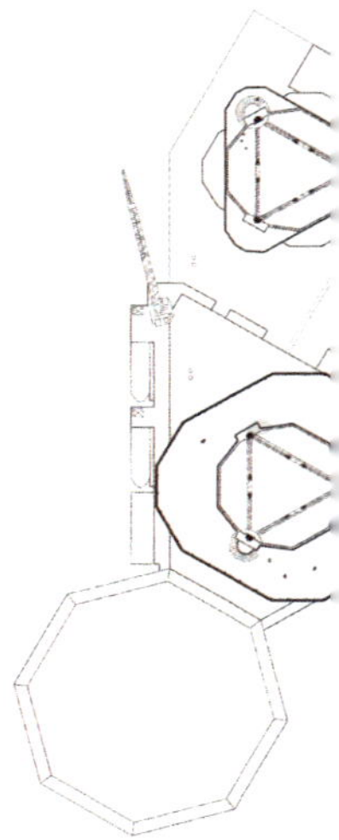

PLAN B

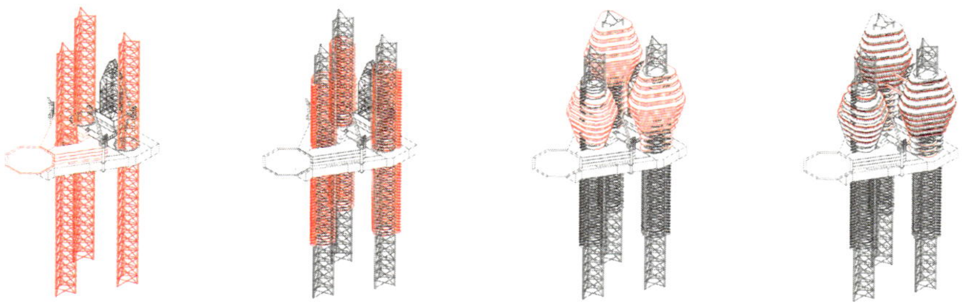

1. EXISTING STRUCTURE MAINTAINED
NEW TRUSS LEGS ADDED

2. SPIRAL CIRCULATION AND SUPPORT RAILS

3. GROW SPACES AND COMMUNAL SPACES

4. SKY PATH AND SAFETY RAILS

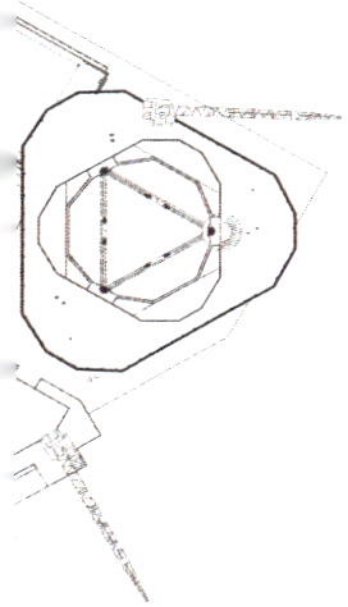

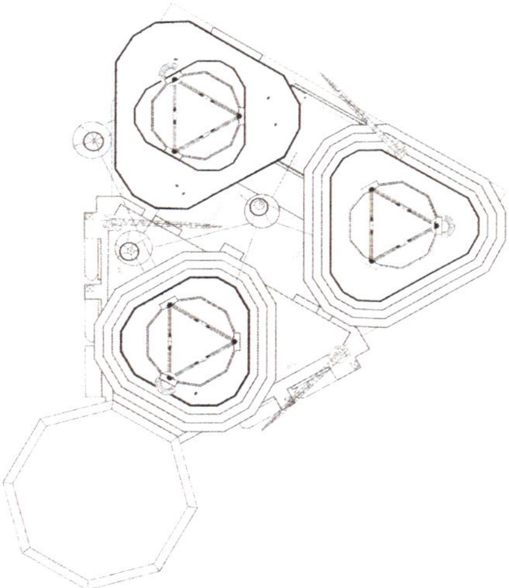

PLAN C

APTURE BALLONS, CONTROL
ND ECOLOGICAL NESTS

◀ **Architecture design and development**

HONORABLE MENTION 137PATJSN

ALGAL BLOOM

Leonardo Zanatta
Brasil

When used in conjunction with bioreactors, microalgae is up to 400 times more effective than a tree at removing CO2 from the atmosphere, one kg of algae requires about 1.8kg of carbon dioxide, which is converted into biomass and oxygen. Now imagine if we could scale up this process and use algae at an urban scale. Not only would it sequester carbon dioxide and boost hyper-local oxygen levels but also dissipate the pollution layer that traps heat over the city, decreasing local temperatures.

Turning cities into comfortable, clean and self-sustainable habitats

HONORABLE MENTION

399GBH1T8

WHAT İF WE COULD GET A SECOND CHANCE?

Agata Holdemajer
Katarzyna Krawczyk
Poland

We decided to look at a future from a global perspective but create a proposal for the future development of habitation for the Happy People Estate in Warsaw. This neighborhood is an example of characteristic housing-landscape in Poland, and it accumulates all the aspects that are not meeting the needs of XXI century housing. There is a need to re-define the whole structure of living within a city from the scale of a single apartment, infrastructure, and the way we commute to the holistic organization of cities. We propose the re-densification of existing housing units and creating a vertical structure to create new places to live and work.

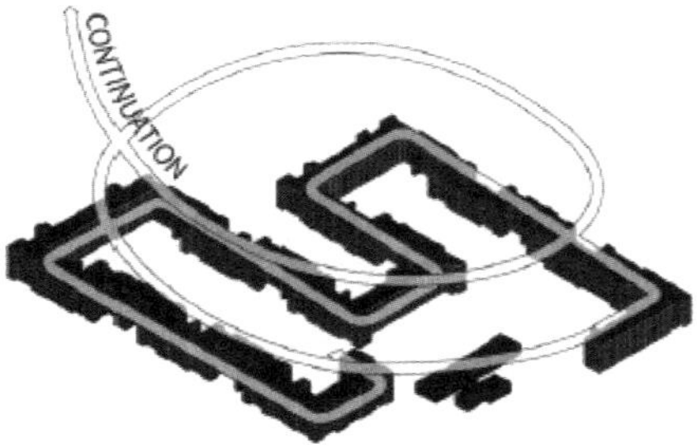

Vertical continuation of the idea of Linear Continous

The gradual dev
vertical

POLAND

WARSAW

ɔf the

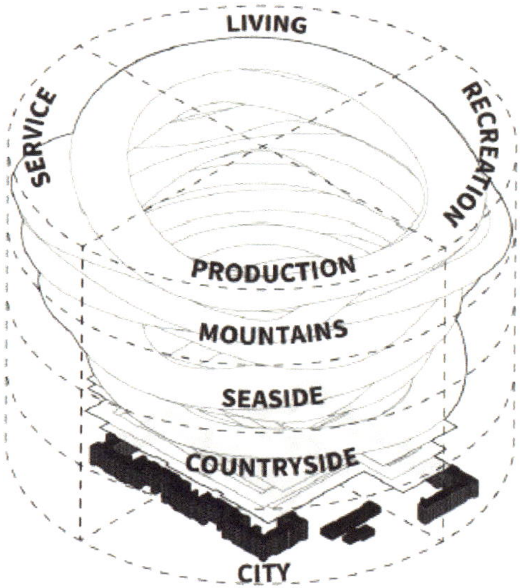

Vertical divisions of functions and horizontal divisions of landscapes

PY POEPLE
ESTATE

The idea of extending the linear communication of galleries and connection seaside with mountains are both referring to the primary Hansen's works and the idea of Linear Continuous System

HONORABLE MENTİON

688GNKUEP

THE USELESS VİLLAGE

Daniel Martínez
Pablo Bris Marino
Felix Bendito Muñoz de Cuerva
Spain

Home in the productive period is a rest place, a refuge after working or studying. The limits of the home are inside of those of the house. There is an exchange between the productive rhythm and our personal rhythm. When we became senior citizens, home is a place of isolation and protection from the city. The house is a wall that protect our home from the city. In the present situation, when we became dependent, nursing home is the only option. No house, no home.

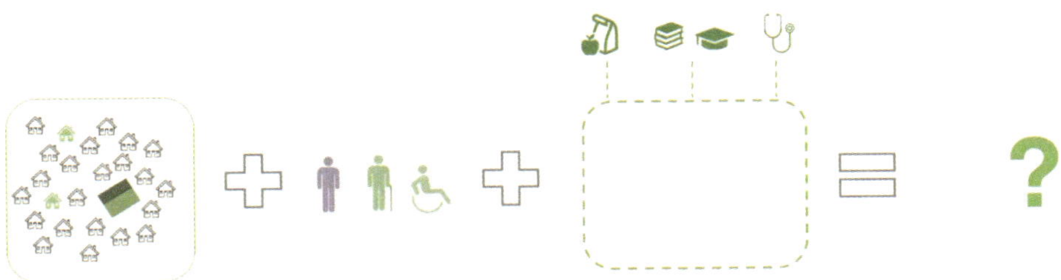

"Just as industrializati-on created the working class, AI create a new unworking class"
Y. Harari, Homo Deus

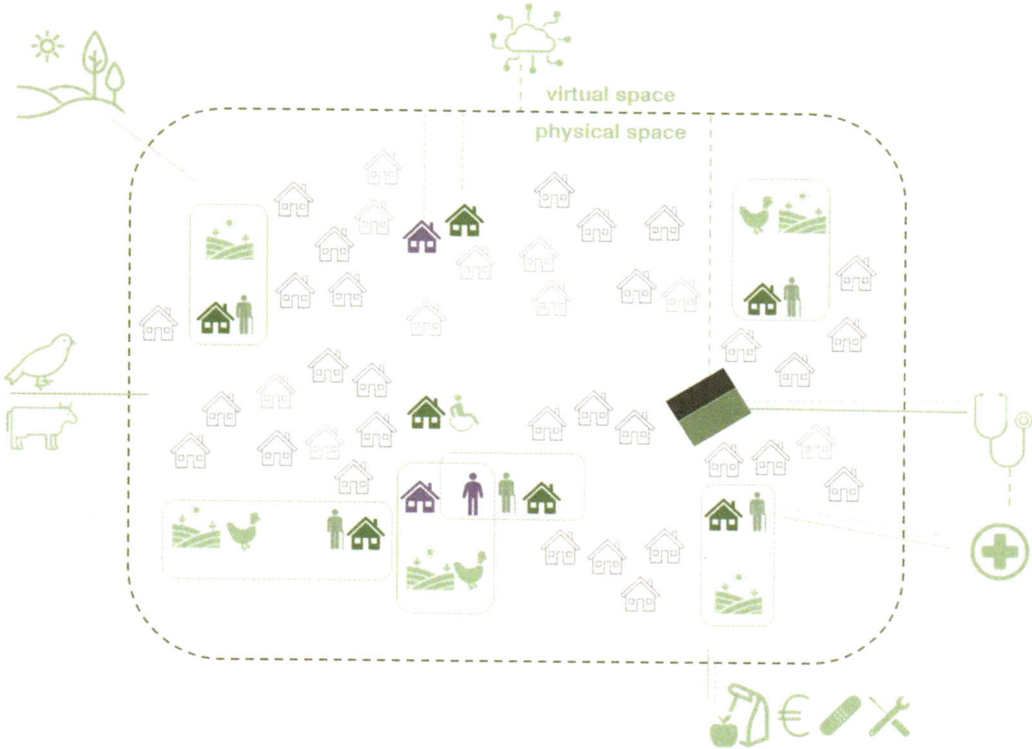
virtual space
physical space

HONORABLE MENTİON

14295YWKB

URBAN DRONEPORT

DRONE LOGİSİTİCS İN URBAN ENVİRONMENT

Saul Ajuria Fernández
Barcelona

This work aims to design a building and a new infrastructure network that allows the transport of goods with drones in urban areas. For this competition it was decided to locate the project within the South node of the M-30 road in Madrid, characterized by being a disused urban vacuum that has many potential users of the new delivery network in its range of action. The project is designed to be adapted easily to other cities as it is shown in the images below. The Urban Droneport is based on a process architecture, which optimizes the system's operation and contributes to boost all aspects for the development of the new infrastructure.

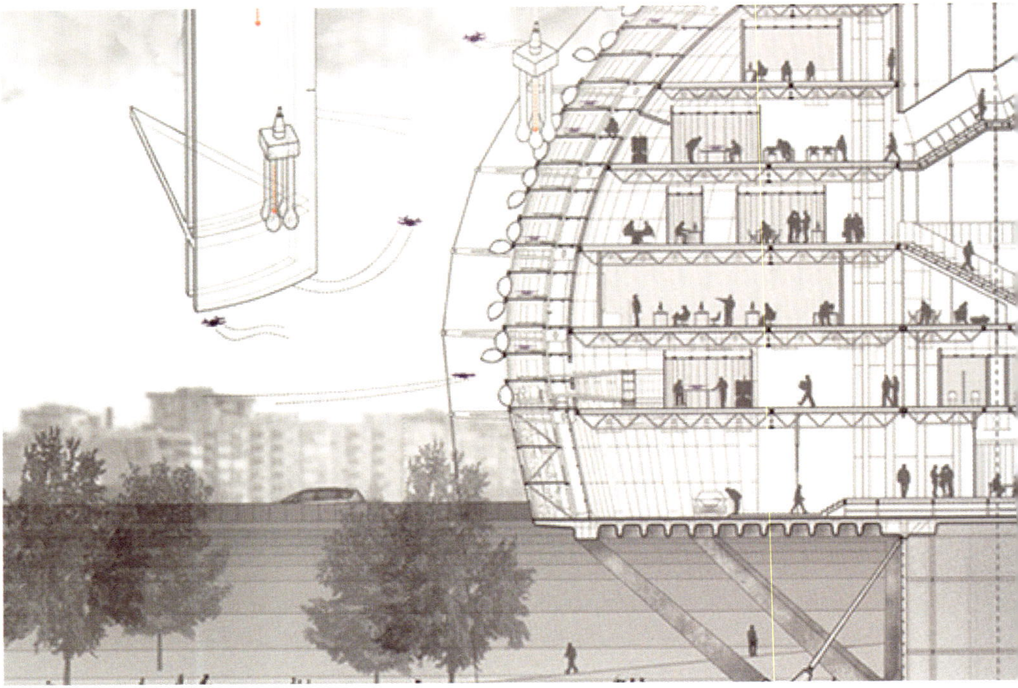

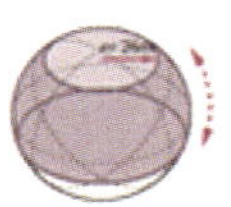

1. Spherical volumetry

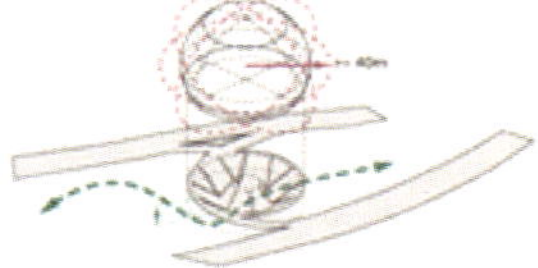

2. Connect the ground floor.

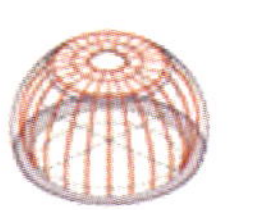

3. Structure on the outside.

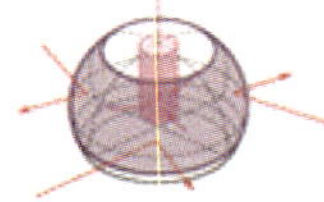

4. Insulation from the outside.

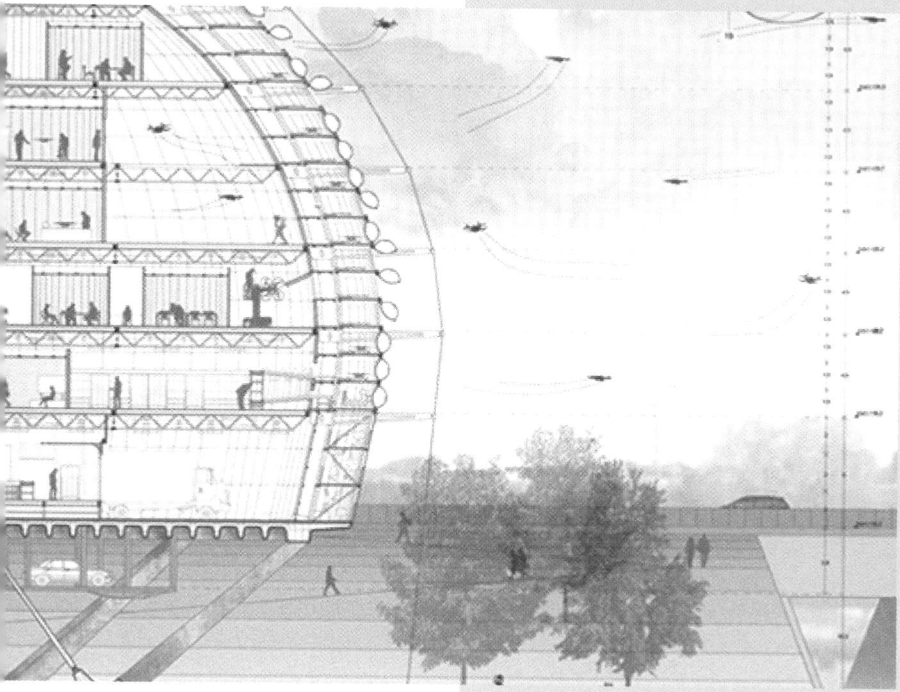

◀ **Process and program axonometric**

HONORABLE MENTION

694QMUZRL

SLUM İSOLATİON COMMUNİTY

Zihao Wu
Zihan Xue
China

The new crown epidemic has made mankind profoundly aware that they will continue to fight against diseases and climate in the future and the habitat environment will definitely change. Faced with the epidemic, humans have choose home isolation to control the spread of the cirus. However, poorer slums have problems of crowded population, poor sanitation and negative living environment, which make the virus spread quickly. Our project aims to improve the lifestyle of slums. In the future, living units made with advanced technology can provide people with a hygienic living environment and isolated spaces to prevent the spread of viruses.

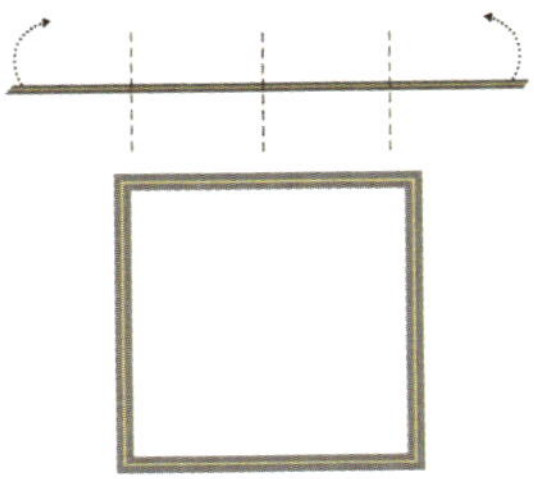

MARESK

Composition:
Vertical Community&Floating Nature

Translation:
The Framework

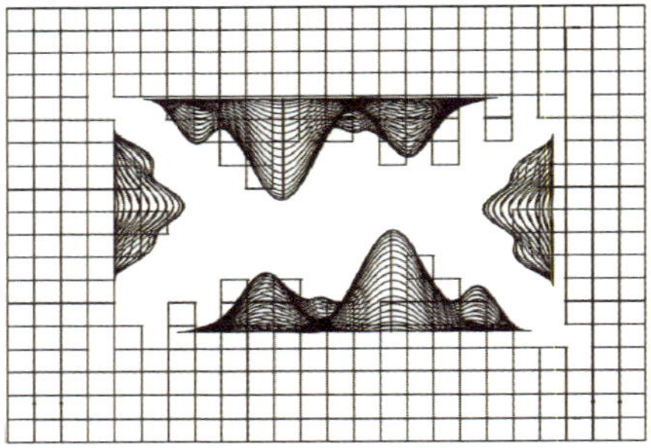

Concept diagrams

694QMUZRL

HONORABLE MENTİON

690IF1QA5

FOREST EMBASSY

A BOTTON-UP SOCİAL ALGORİTHM TOWARDS REWİLDİNG

Ariel Bintang
Andrew Tjio
Australia

'Forest Embassy' seeks to systemize the occupation of the countryside through a holocentric modification of mundane activities to rewild environments while maintaining economic productivity. Borneo will be used as the project's case study to be a bottom-up alternative towards Indonesia's hasty decision to build a top-down capital city in the Palm Oil ridden island. 'Forest Embassy' is essentially a social algorithm. A growing library of 'new normal' activities with the underlying goal of rewilding anthropocentric spaces will be generated and published by-and-to the public. The reviewed library of activities will guide how every individual -from farmers to the president- can contribute in their effort to rewild their environments.

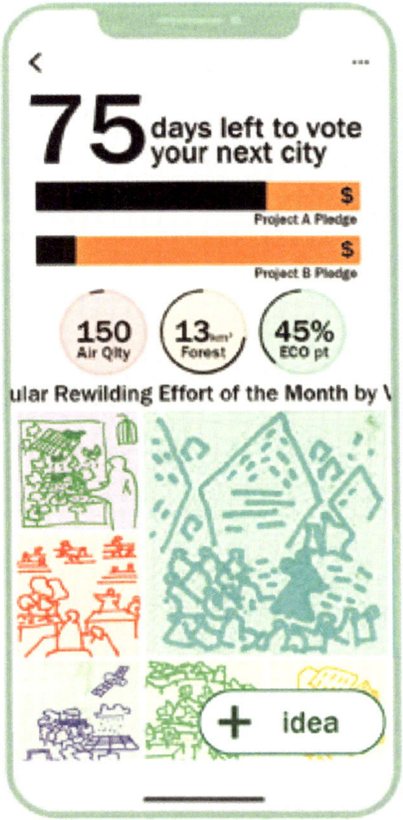
75 days left to vote your next city
$
Project A Pledge
$
Project B Pledge
150 Air Qlty
13 Forest
45% ECO pt
ular Rewilding Effort of the Month by V
+ idea

Locality : Kutai
Govt Spending 50% Budget
Corrupt Suspect
23 years to complete reforestation
dent announces Malaysian Partnersh

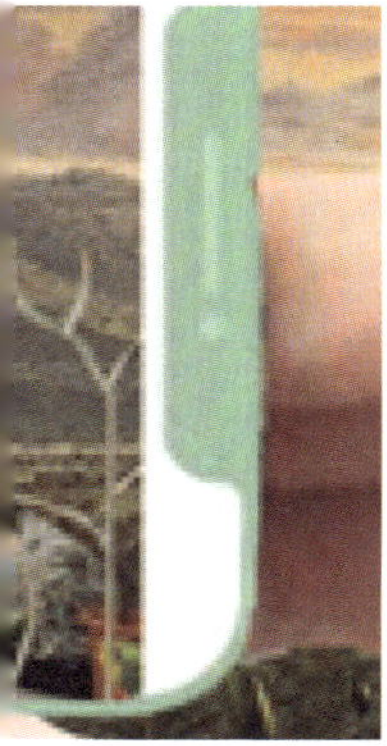

Case Study
Sidomulyo, Kutai Timur

HONORABLE MENTİON

546XT7EY8

RE-FORESTİNG

A STRATEGY FOR PRODUCTİVE VİLLAGES

Simon Feather
Great Britain

Tree diseases have become a major anxiety across the world, and it is unclear how climate change will affect our forests and the ecosystems they support. With prospect of so much more tree-planting in the coming years we need ways to achieve a broader range of objectives from tree planting to help solve the climate crisis, improve our ecology whilst generate timber production for use within our buildings. I think that architects and designers should have input into what we plant within our commercial forests, as they will ultimately be the ones designing with them once they are ready for harvest. My Project 'Re-foresting' is a set of nine productive model villages located along the M62, and within the 'Northern Forest'.

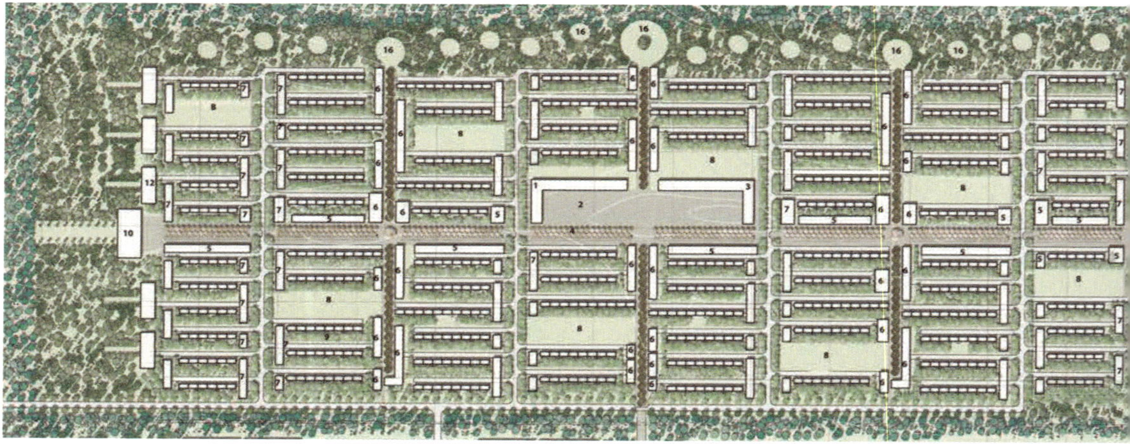

The project aims to promote the use of locally grown timber and revitalise the UK's timber industry.

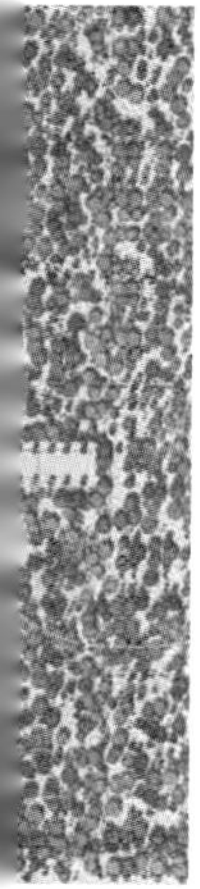

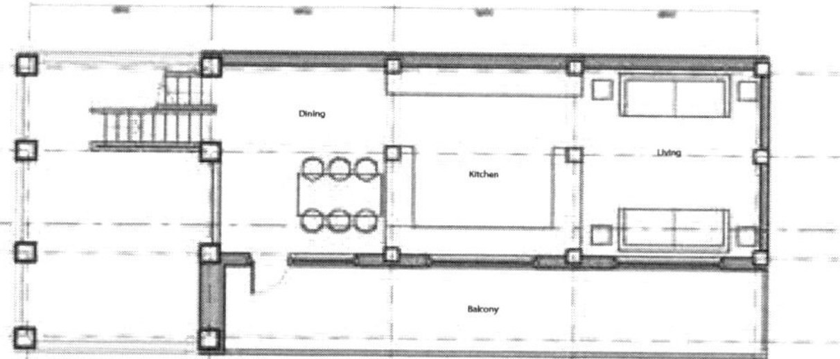

Third Floor Plan
1:100

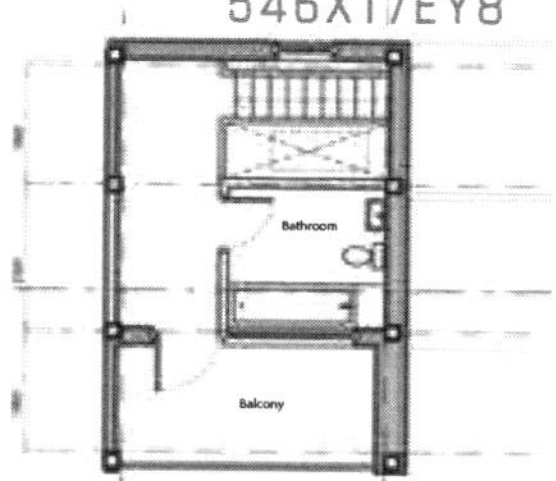

Sixth Floor Plan
1:100

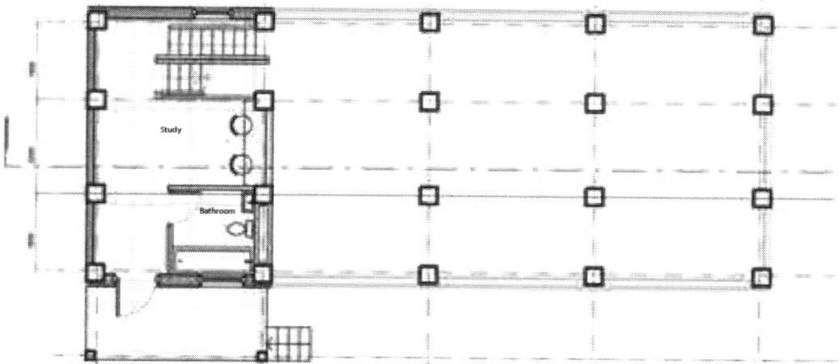

Second Floor Plan
1:100

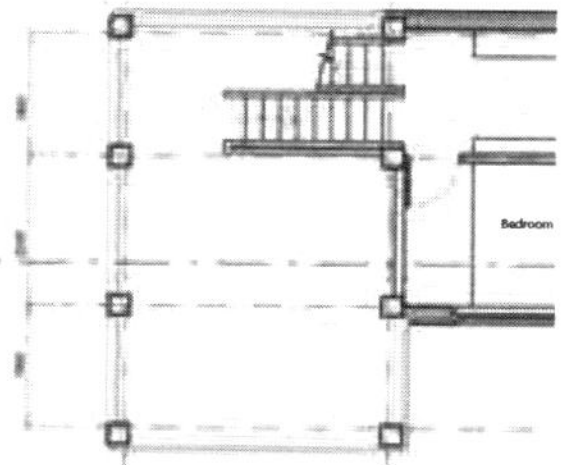

Fifth Floor Plan
1:100

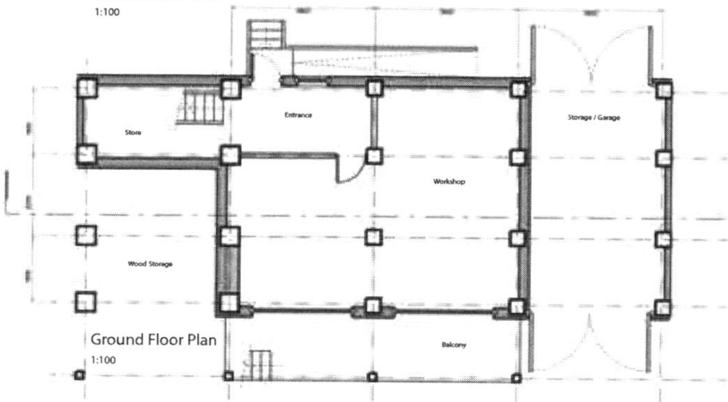

Ground Floor Plan
1:100

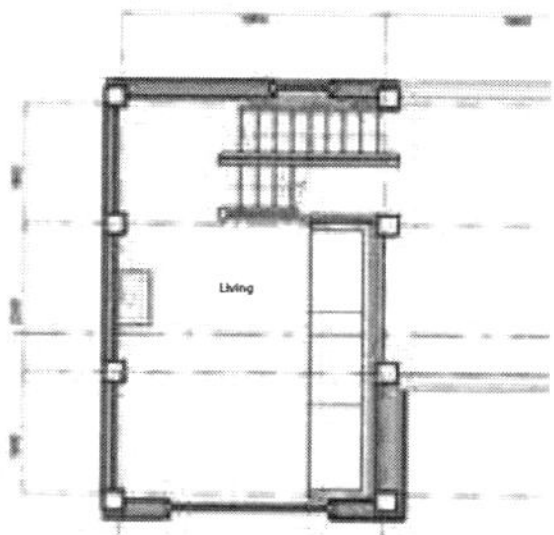

Fourth Floor Plan
1:100

Green Hub
Sun Yuan

SELECTED WORKS
2020

FINALIST 5948TN1B0

COEXİST: A DİALOGUE TOWARD CHANGE

Sadia Sharmin
Imran Hasan
Bangladesh

The present global crisis generates alternative queries which suggest that existing knowledge and strategy are not enough to shape future environments. One standard scheme or solution would not e applicable in different socio-cultural and climatic contexts. As this is not a problem-solving competition, we do not focus on the end outcome (solution). Rather, we focus on the process that brings us closer to the aspirations of individuals and their right to the city to visualize future habitats.

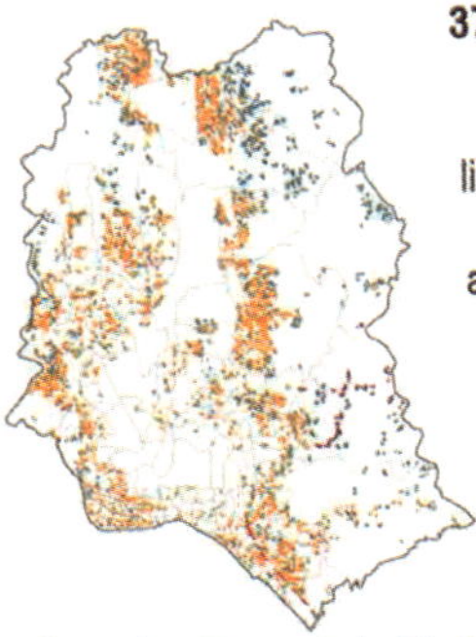

37.4% Dhaka population (4 million) lives in **5.1%** of the city area termed as "Basti".

CITY

Informal settlements in Dhaka
Source: EO4SD Urban consortium 2017

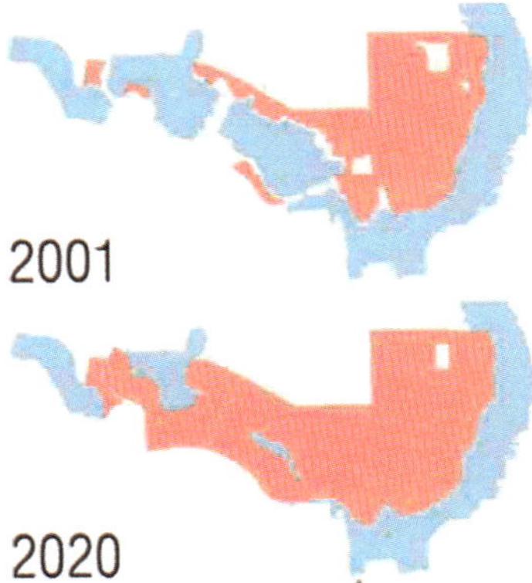

COMMUNITY

HOME

Self-organised pr
to a build structu

Aerial View of Karail Basti

Expansion of the settlement

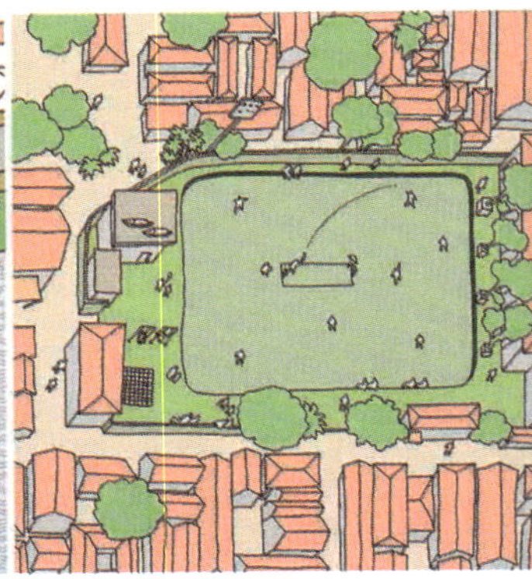

BODY

home_Adding soul

Amina
(tea-shop owner)

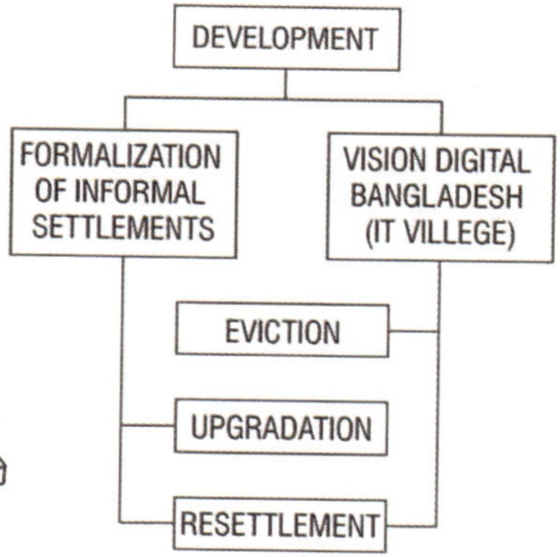

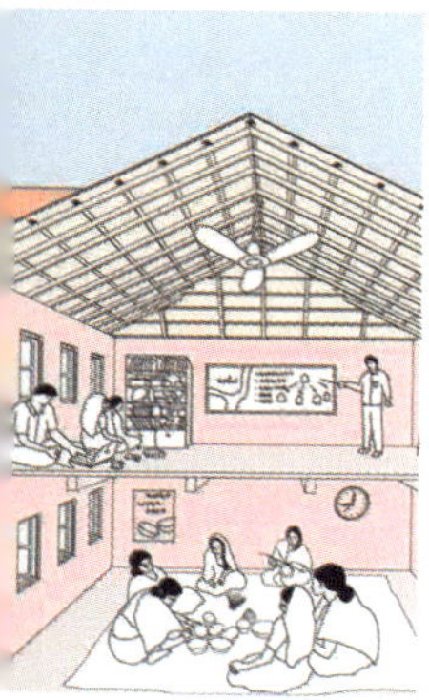

Rethink our habitat from the body to the city

FINALIST 272JFWT77

A FORMULA FOR THE COLLECTIVE

Paulina Sevilla
Mariana Martins
Brice Franquesa
Mexico

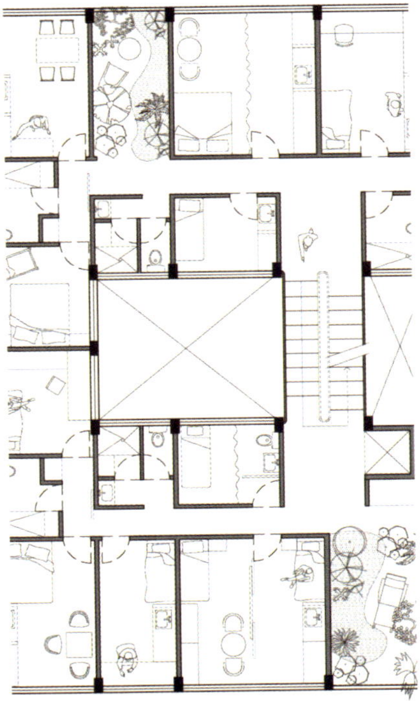

We believe that in the next few decades cities will be part of a reinvention and transformation process instead of the massive construction and growing that we witness today. There's no better place to imagine what this future could look like than Tlatelolco, one of the most emblematic collective housing projects in Mexico City. In Mexico, a big part of the population has no access to minimum decent housing - something that this pandemia made even more evident with the "stay at home" measure. This crisis context has demonstrated that we need to change our ways of living as individuals and as a society. It's urgent we think of an adaptation of housing in all scales, considering issues of equality, inclusion, flexibility, sustainability, security and recreation.

... IN FACT, ...

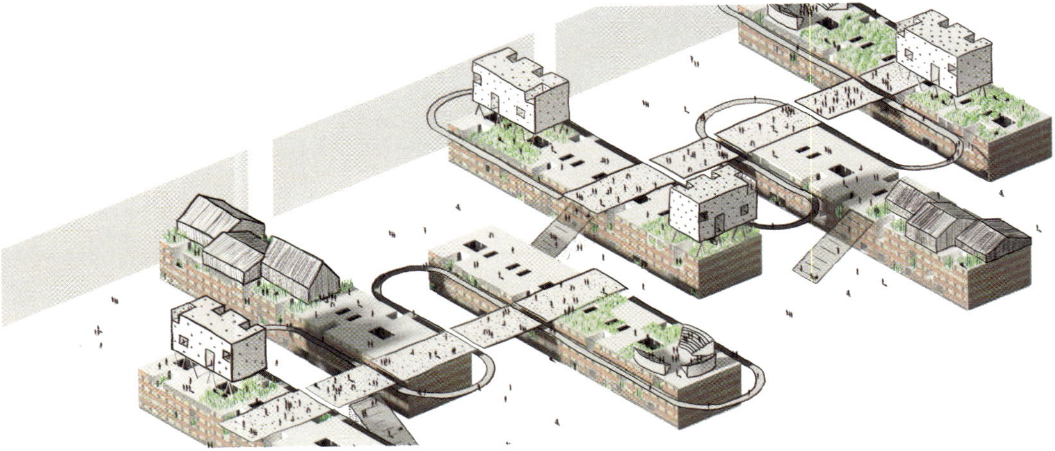

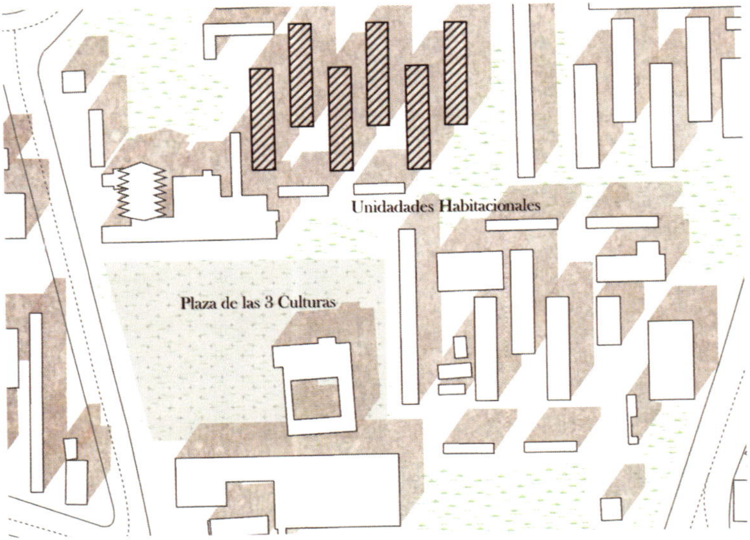

The individual prosperity depends on the collective successfulness

272JFWT77

FINALIST 6789BA9Y8

REPARKİNG

Isaque Davi Schafer
Ananda Rossi da Motta
Bruno Lorenz
Mateus Hillebrand
Brasil

Every construction embodies the values of an era. Thinking about the trend in which cars come to be seen as a service and not a good, in Reparking we project ourselves into a future where the parking buildings in the city of Porto Alegre become social housing. This is not just a functional issue, but also a subjective one. Reparking incorporates values and ideas of a future that we want to live. Instead of individualism, the community spirit. Rather than segregation, inclusion. After removing slabs and walls, we noticed the emergence of a structure that allows the manifestation of infinite possibilities for living. We foresee all parking lots in the city as a network, a system of decentralized housing that communicates with each other.

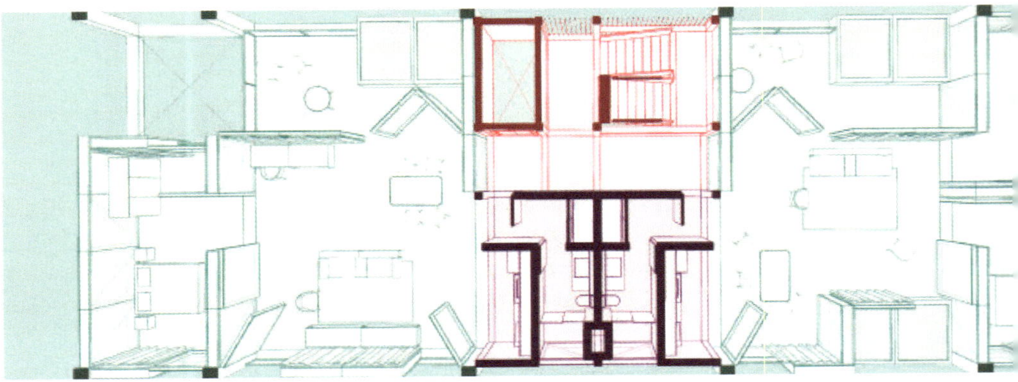

Parking buildings in the city of Porto Alegre become social housing

FINALIST 4454TA47Y

AQUA FARM CO-LIVING

Megan King
Australia

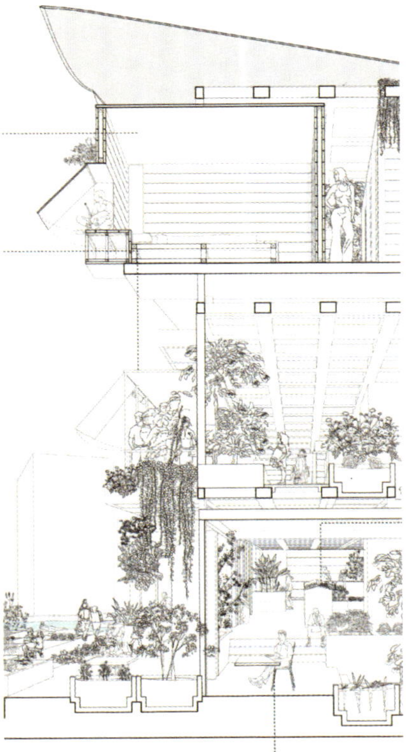

Eighty-five percent of Australia's population live in coastal areas. Rising sea levels and storm surges have had a significant impact on the coastline of Australia. As sea levels continue to rise, land mass subsequently will decrease, resulting in a shortage of usable land for residential use, agricultural production, and land productivity. The future poses the question; how can we as coastal communities live on water in such a way where both the community and our food production can thrive? Hydro-tecture is an architectural proposition designed to respond to this question: a farm and residential living, designed on water. Hydro-tecture takes a step away from the traditional means of separating food production, agriculture and residential living. It investigates how we might begin to blur the boundaries between these entities and in doing so, proposes that self-sufficiency for a community can be found in the hybrid. The design of Hydro-tecture farms proposes areas to encourage the overlap of functions, and 'blur the edges' between production and communal living.

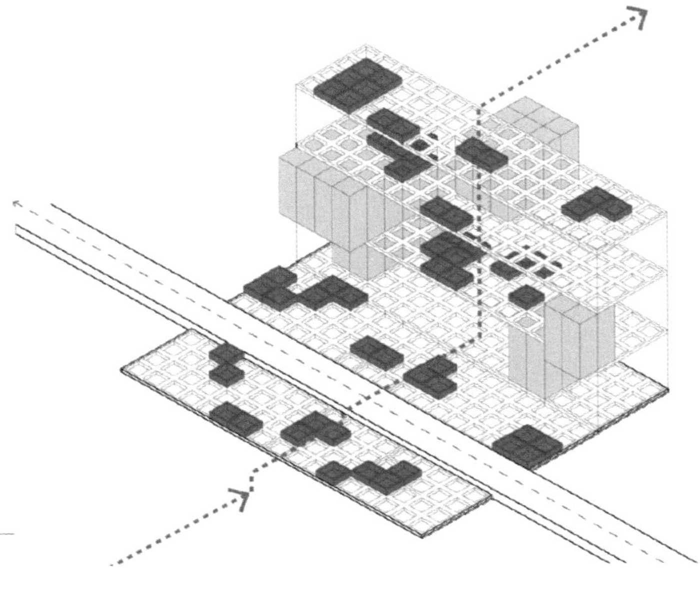

Aqua farm focuses on a series of crafted scenarios around food production, health benefits, social benefits, environmental benefits and economic benefits.

4454TA47Y

FINALIST 193EVRMT9

ETERNAL

Burcin Ayberk Ozdemir
Turkey

Modern society caused us to produce horizontal and vertical houses that cut, isolate, and protect us from the outside environment.As a result, perceptions between the user and the world were limited. To redefine user relationships. traditional relationships between the body, building and landscape, the project enables to encourage the future human body to move in space and to design and evaluate the life cycles of these users on their own. After establishing the Architectural Human Research Foundation, people are encouraged to explore their habitats and lifestyles. Users transmit the necessary algorithms to the MIT Alien robots in the installed factory. With this data, robots start to produce habitats according to the data, and this production coded to give each user the same cubic meter, so industrial futuristic and domestic processes are fused.

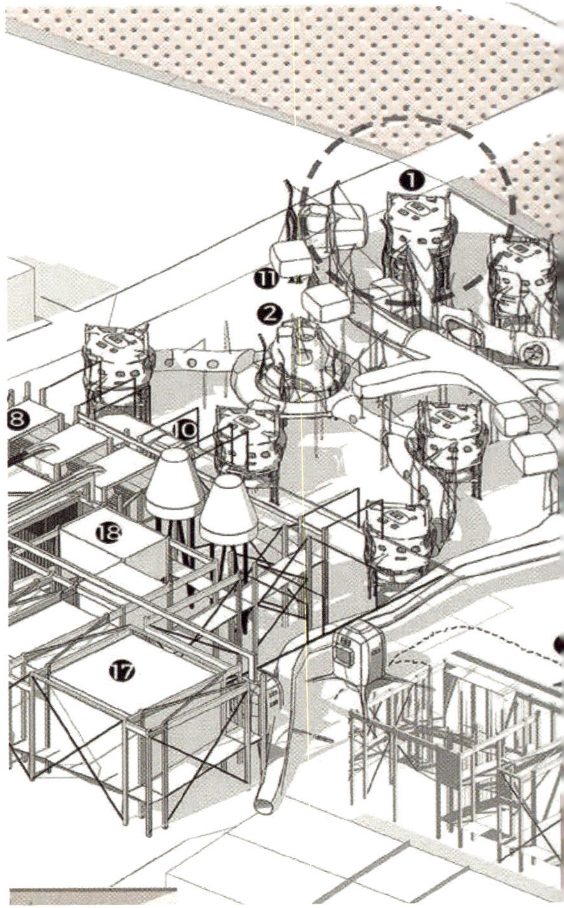

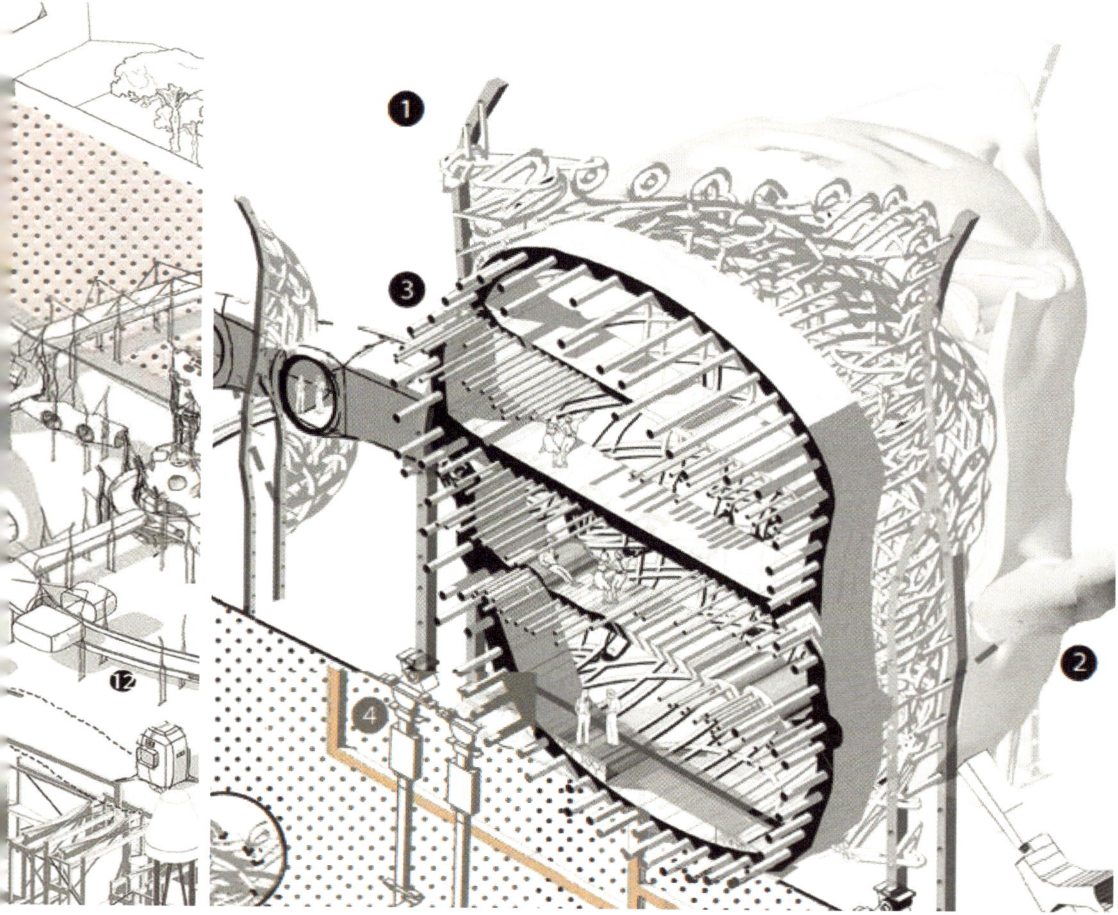
1
3
2
12
4

WHERE ?

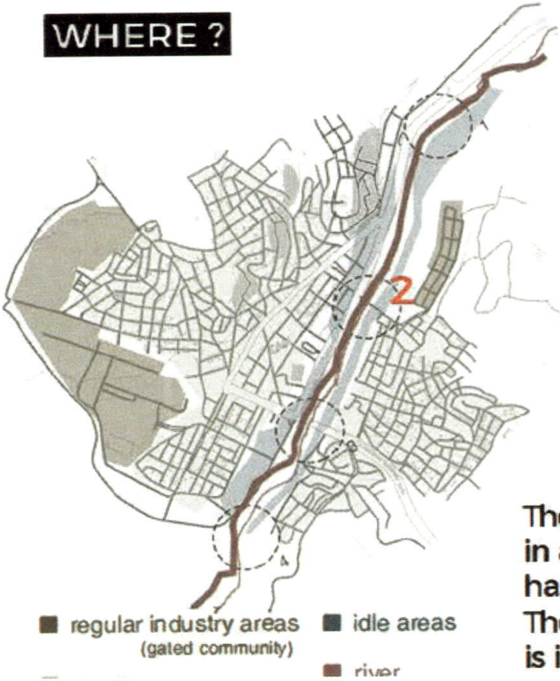

Çan County / Canakkale City
Typological Section

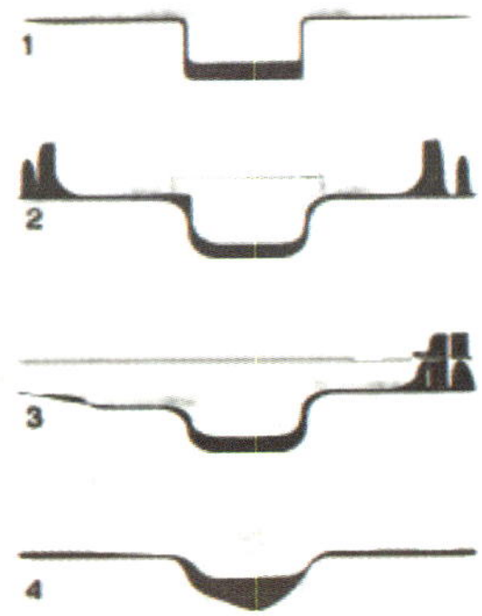

The project was established in area 2 and the project area has an idle area.
The back of the project area is in the industrial zone.

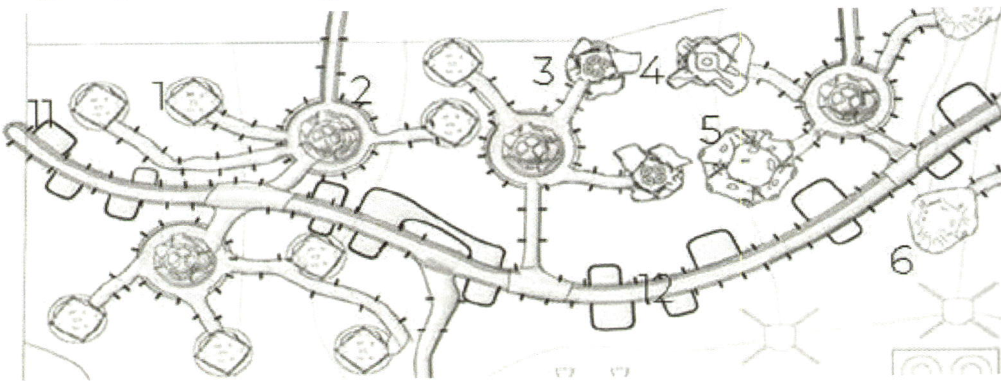

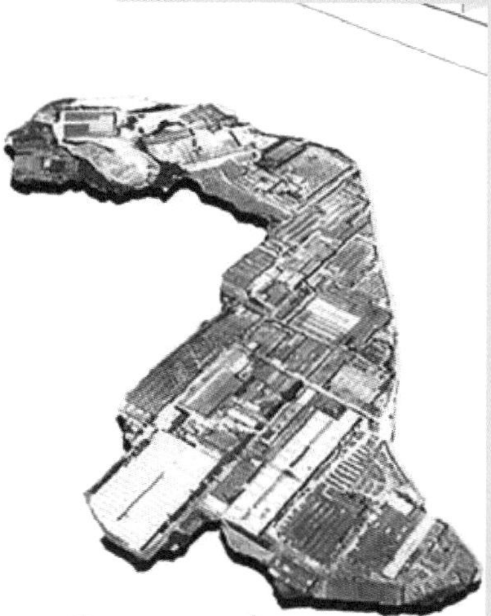

Çan-Turkey
Satellite View
(Urban Typology)

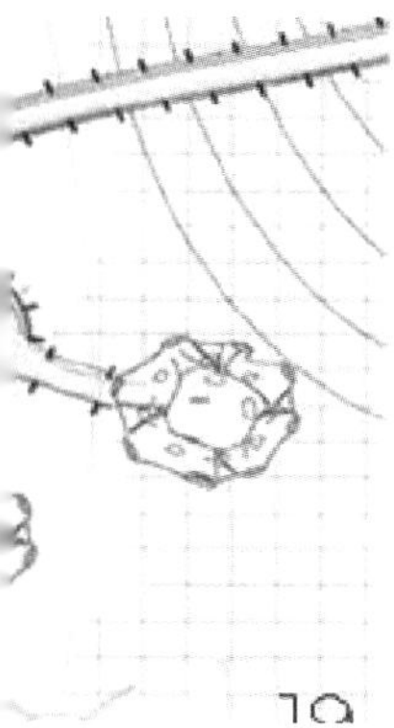

Site plan

FINALIST 687WT2DJ

LA BARCELONETA:

A SUSTAİNABLE NEİGHBOURHOOD

Anna Marco
Barcelona

The idea is to generate a neighbourhood that feels like a village within the big city, and its inhabitants can walk or bike everywhere.
To connect this town with the rest of the city, public transport is enforced as well as the big green metropolitan avenues at the urban edges of the peninsula.

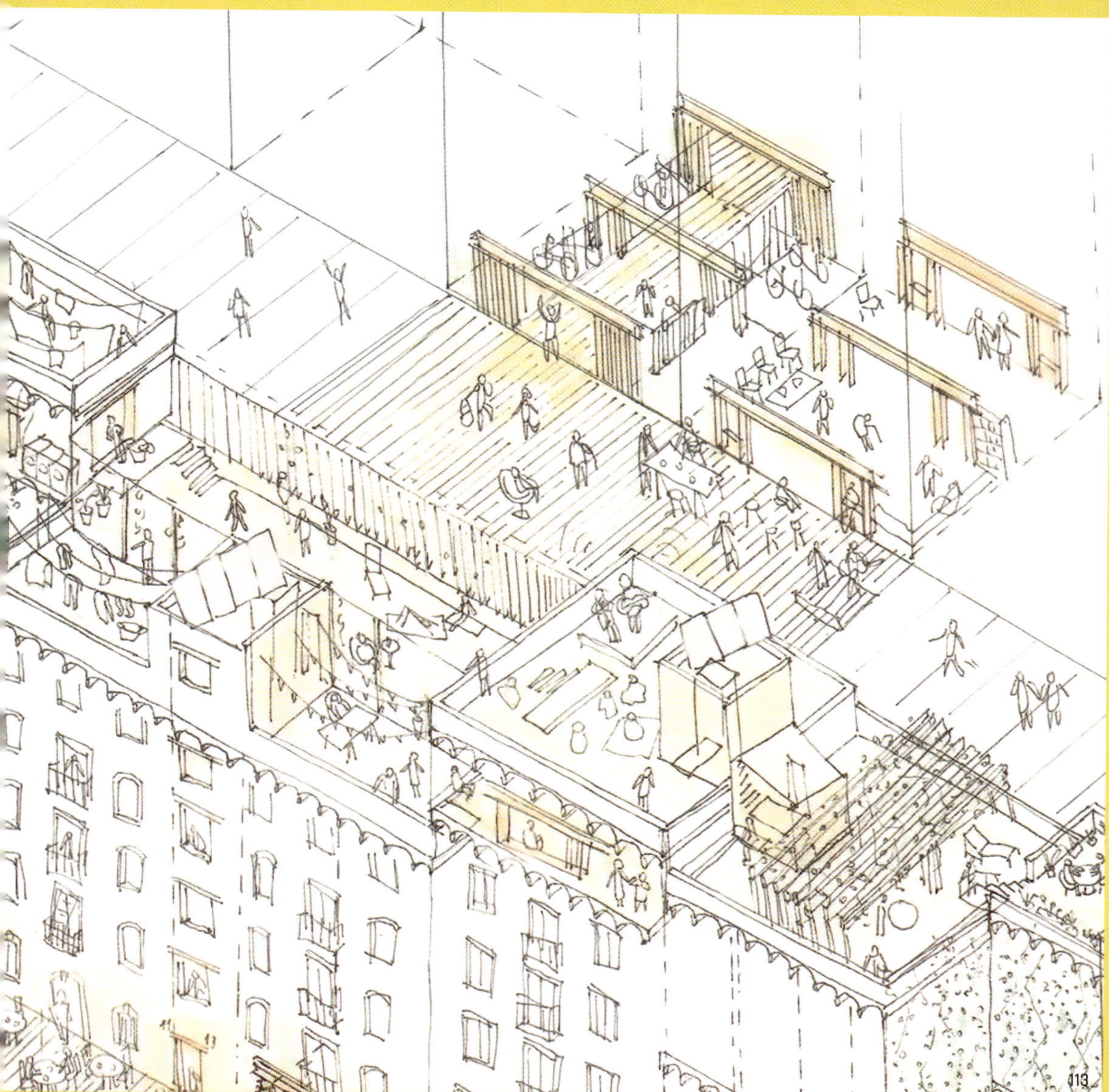

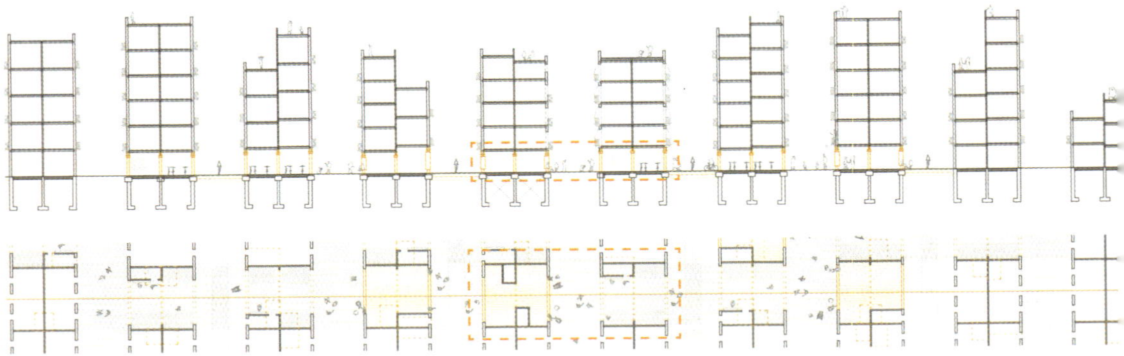

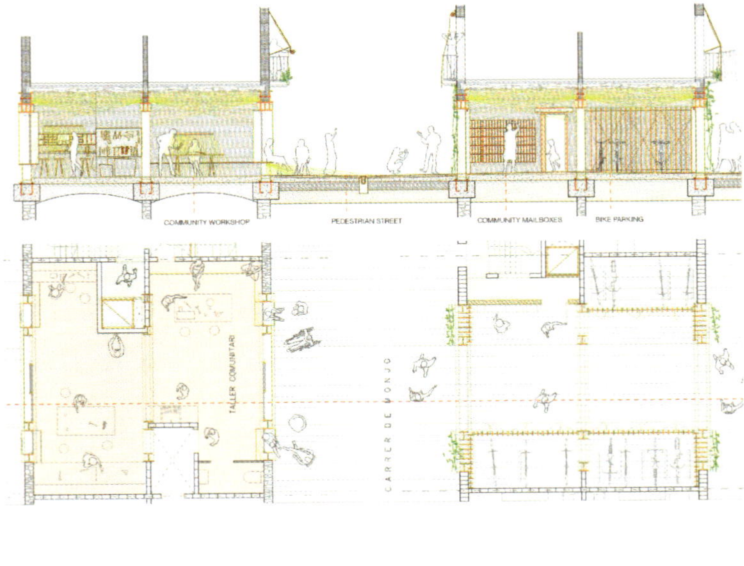

Adapting an existing dense district to the needs of the future

687WT2DJ

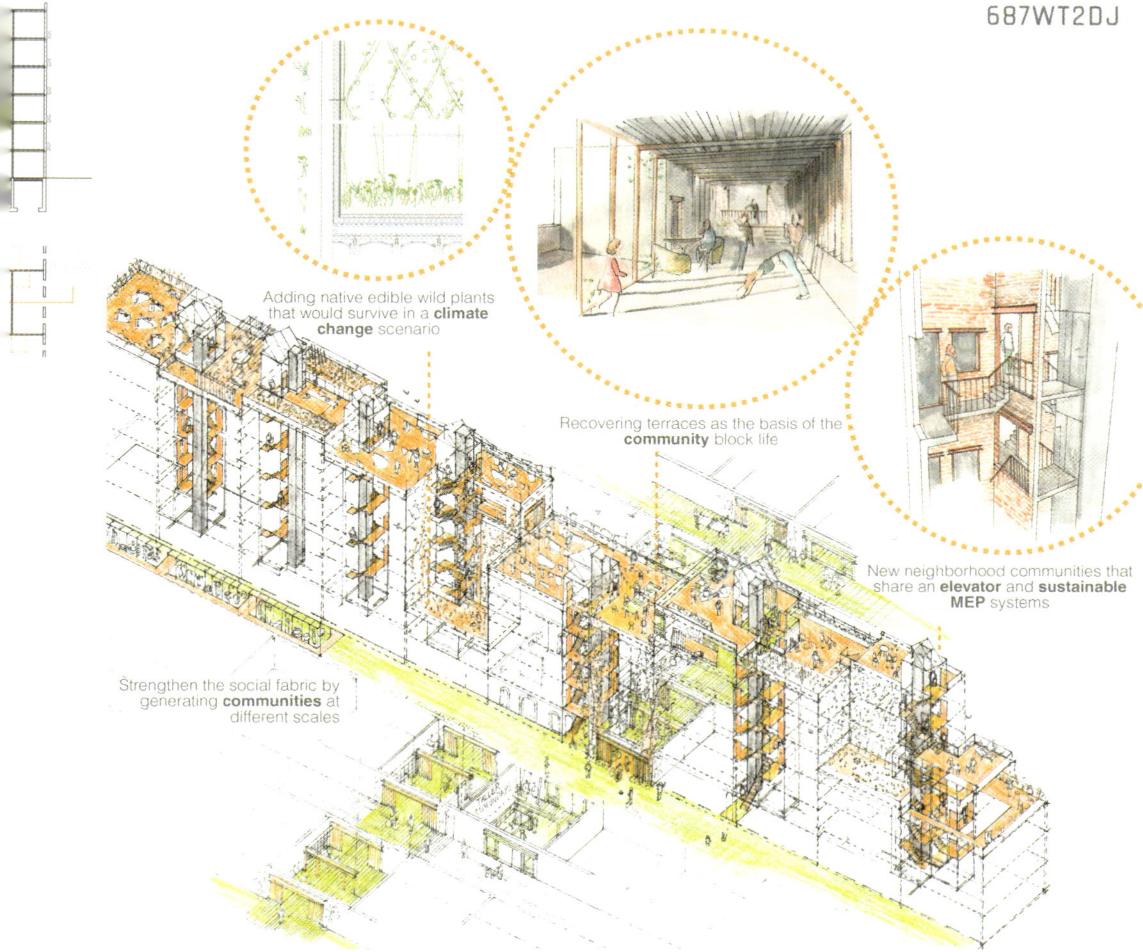
Adding native edible wild plants
that would survive in a **climate**
change scenario
Recovering terraces as the basis of the
community block life
New neighborhood communities that
share an **elevator** and **sustainable**
MEP systems
Strengthen the social fabric by
generating **communities** at
different scales

FINALIST 6200EJWA8

LET'S THİNK ABOUT TOMORROW

MichaL Kacprzyk
Poland
It's a conceptual design that attempts to predict the future. The assumption was to be a cure for the deteriorating climate. The building consists of reinforced concrete, steel, atainless construction based on natural gas and hydrogen. The building serves as scaffolding rack for residential modules. The flats are erected thanks to the ropes and hooks released from movable cranes located on the lattice. The apartment module has an area of 36.5m2. Steel construction, insulated with mineral wool and faced with galvanized sheet in any color. Modules can also be combined to increase space. Every second floor of the building contains an "green roof" type intensive evergreen vegetation. In the central part of the building there is also a skylight through which rainwater flows to the retention tank.

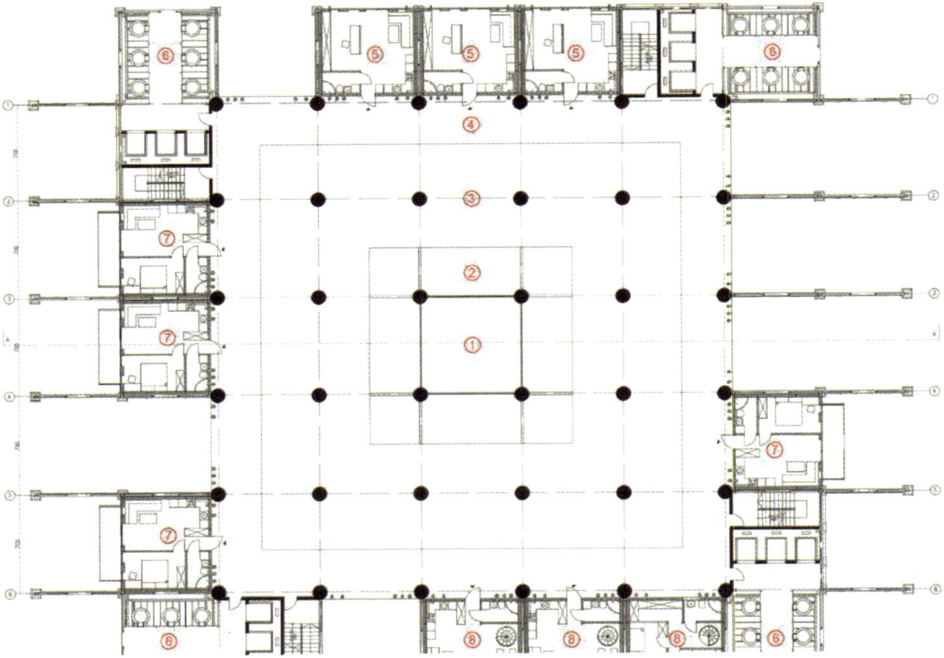

6
5
5
5
6
4
3
2
1
7
7
7
7
6
8
8
8
6

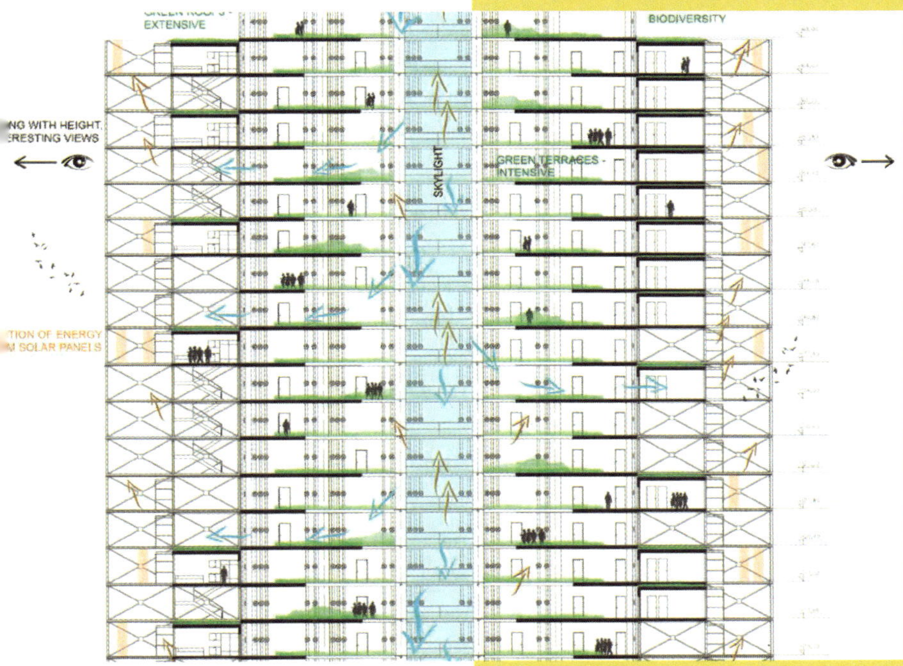

View of connecting buildings at different heights

FINALIST 355X80ELJ

GREEN HUB

CİTY RENWAL İN URBAN VİLLAGE

Sun Yuan
China

The project is located in Shenzhen, the special economic zone of China. I investigated the urban village, which has been a big issue during the urbanization. The site is located in Baishizhou, which is oppsite the famous sight "Window of the world". What impressed me most is that a young man told me that he never talked with his roomates even they had lived together for several months. I found that all the spaces in Baishizhou are used for living, leaving no space for plants, animals and so on. So my design deals with two things, one is living, the other is environment "Green Hub " is made up by units of 3x3 meters. Not all the space are used for living but neighbors can share public space, gardens and leisure place.

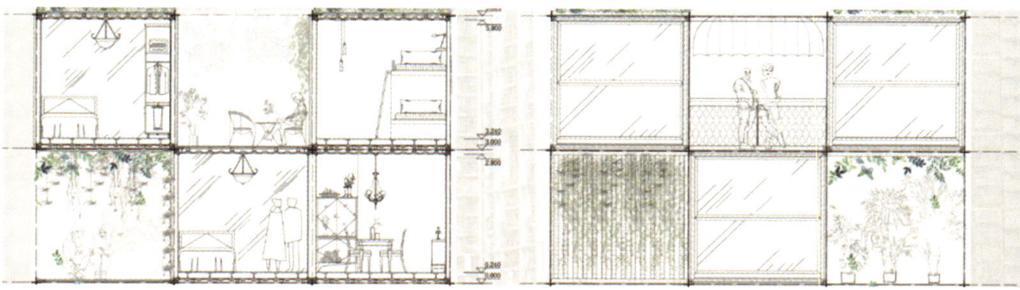

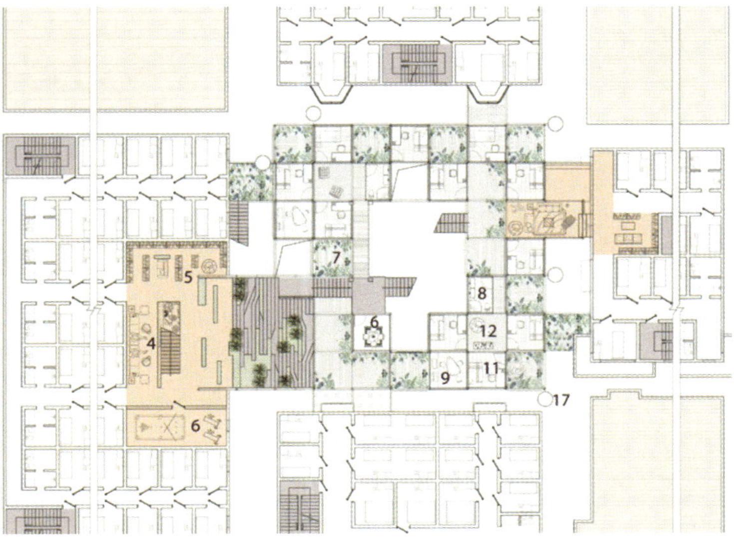

Site analysis: Baishizhou
A typical urban village in Shenzhen, China

INTERIOR CORRIDOR FOR BIRDS
STAIRCASE SYSTEM IN THE CORE
LIVING WITH BIRDS & PLANTS
RELAX IN A COOL PLACE AT NIGHT
N LIBRARY & KINDERGARTEN
GREENHOUSE
ORGANIC FOOD MARKET ON THE GROUND FLOOR
CLASSROOM & READING ROOM

FINALIST 665DODZ1M

FLUİD RESİLİENCE

Cecile Ngoc Suong Perdu
Vietnam

The Mekong Delta is one of the most productive, dense and vulnerable zones in the world. Its architecture has reflected the region's ability to adapt increasingly violent floods; higher demands for food, land use dispute and a need for climate adapted buildings. The design attempts to answer three challenges: climate change and the role of water, the land battle between food and housing and most recently Covid and social distancing.

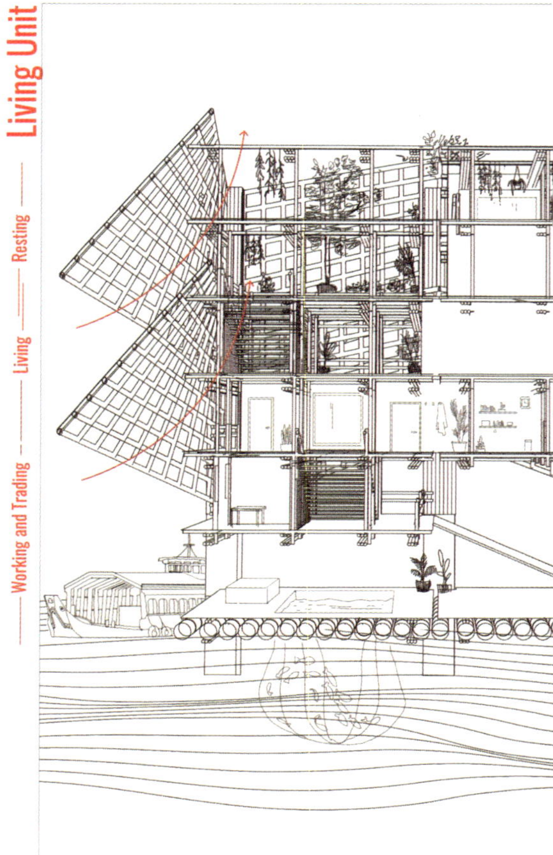

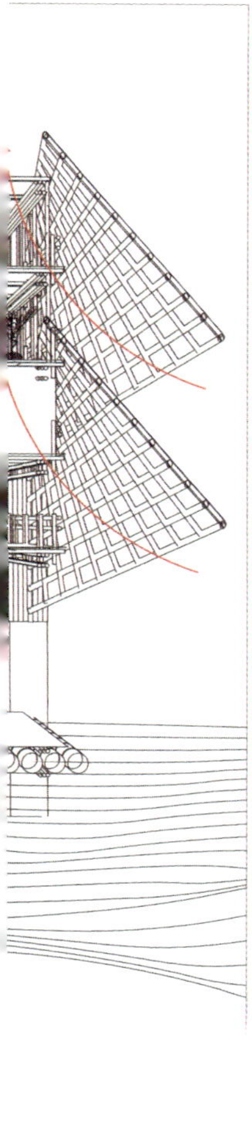

Isolation Unit — Quarters + outdoors space — Medical control and supply deposit

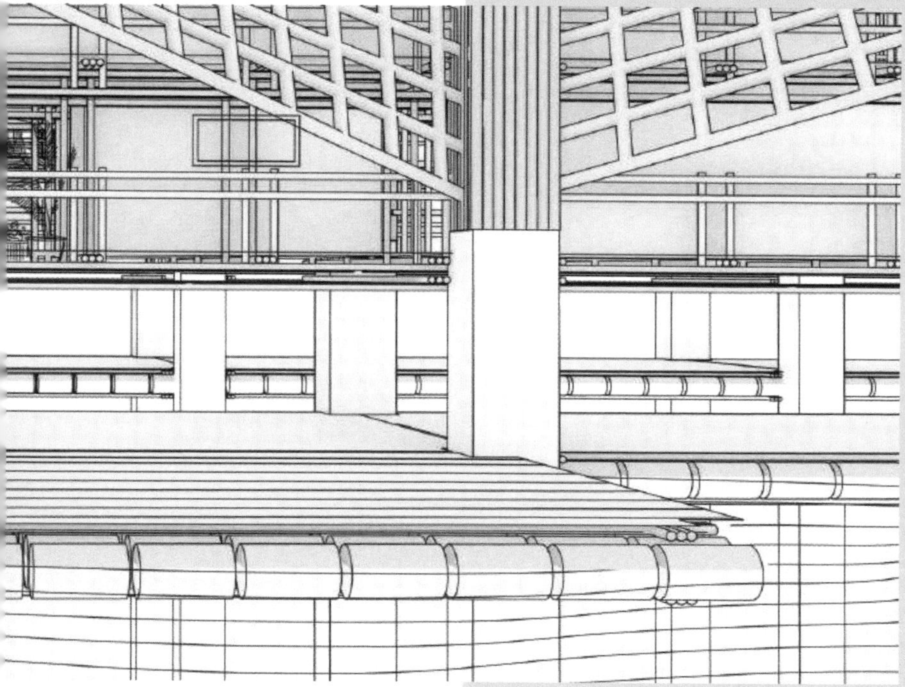

Underwater view, with empty oil containers for buoyancy

FINALIST 5957058PV

WHERE THE BOUNDARiES FADE

Victoria Fedorova
Sofia Ogarkova
Russia

We focused on the growing problem of the lack of the living area for people who move to a big city. At the same time our proposal can be employed by the digital nomads, who desire to be independent from any location. So we decided to speculate on what is the next step in the evolution of individual housing. We designed 4 modes for a basic but transformative 28 sqm apartment with the different levels of mutual components involved that make the tiny living space unrestricted. With VR and AR the boundaries of space fade. More ever comes on the technology opens the way into more democratized society as everyone will have the excess to the luxury and beauty.

TRANSFORMATIVE FURNITURE
PROJECTED RECIPE
TRANSFORMATIVE SINK
AUGMENTED DISPLAY

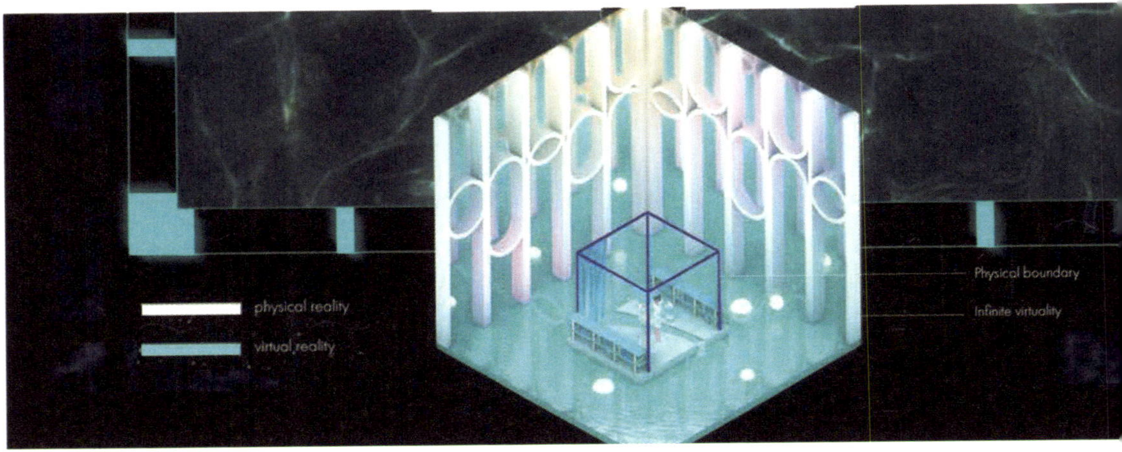

◀ **Household mode**

5957058PV
MIND PALACE: WORKING MODE

FINALIST 6999WXM01

SALUBRiOUS

Jad Moura
Dubai

The Project's program is a space for users to experience virtual spaces through the means of virtual and augmented reality. This becomes the means of income to sustain resources and continue in reactiving spaces through providing electricity to the housing, food to the majlis, and water for the mosque. He shells along the enclosures house certain projectors and speakers that can augment the surrounding site through multimedia design projects. Allowing the built environment to alter the natural environment without harming it. This form of a program aims to activate the site through events, concerts, art hub initiatives, and gallery exhibitions.

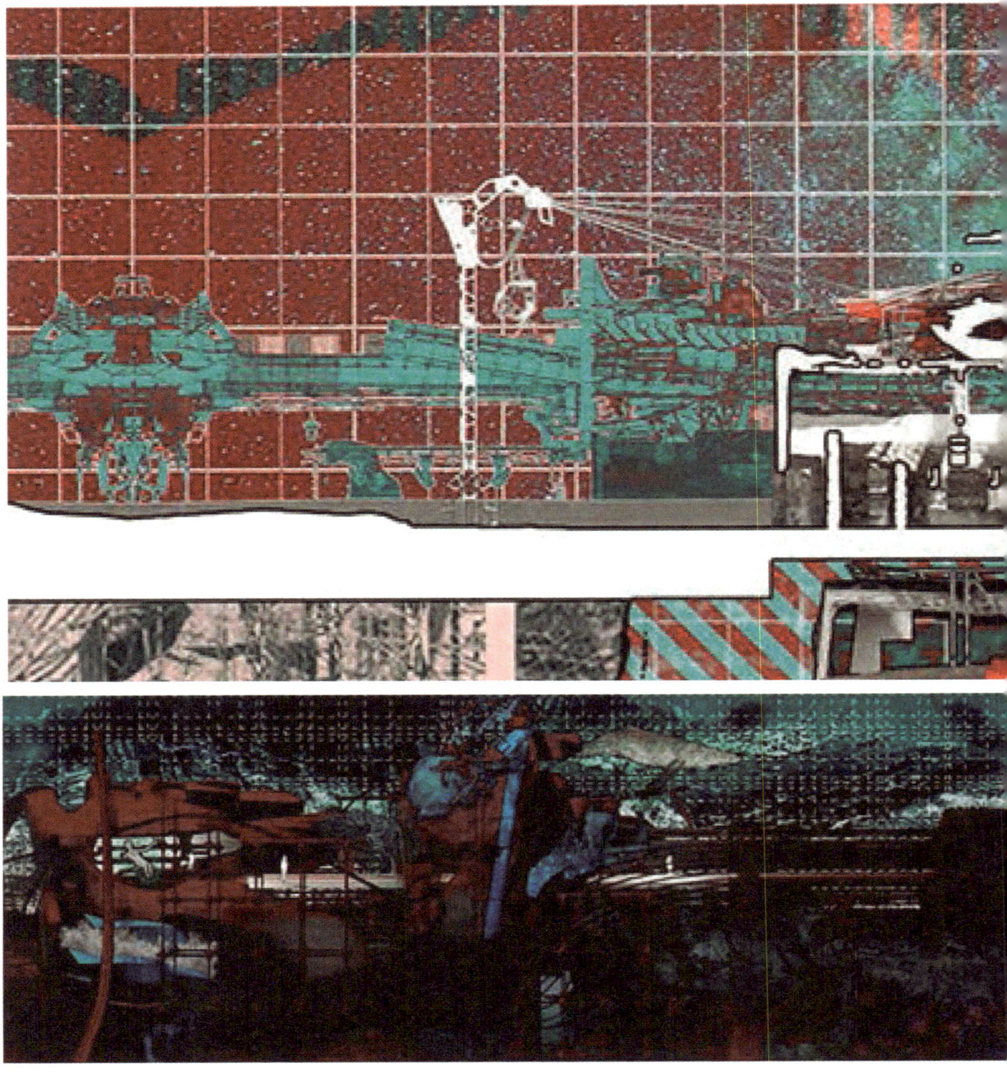

**Salubrious simply designs the tool,
the machine, the infrastructure, the actions
through a period of time**

FINALIST 578K7KLX

HOW TO BUİLD THE SUBURBS

Alícia Pons Díez
Miguel Martín Carballo
Barcelona

Over the years, the suburbs will be urbanized due to the growth of the cities. As opposed to the models of single family residential housing or large suburbs, we propose a chessboard-order-building. Anything is possible, even being confined for three months in our overcrowded homes. The project proposes empty spaces in height. These modules propose uses such as teleworking spaces, meeting rooms, workshops, exhibition areas, a cinema, spaces for neighbours to chat and organise meetings and gossip, interior gardens, spaces for painting and arts, even a dance floor. These spaces are proposed as free will, colonization and appropiation of the neighbors. The building 'ad infinitum' would be proposed as a practically self-sufficient city managed by its own inhabitants.

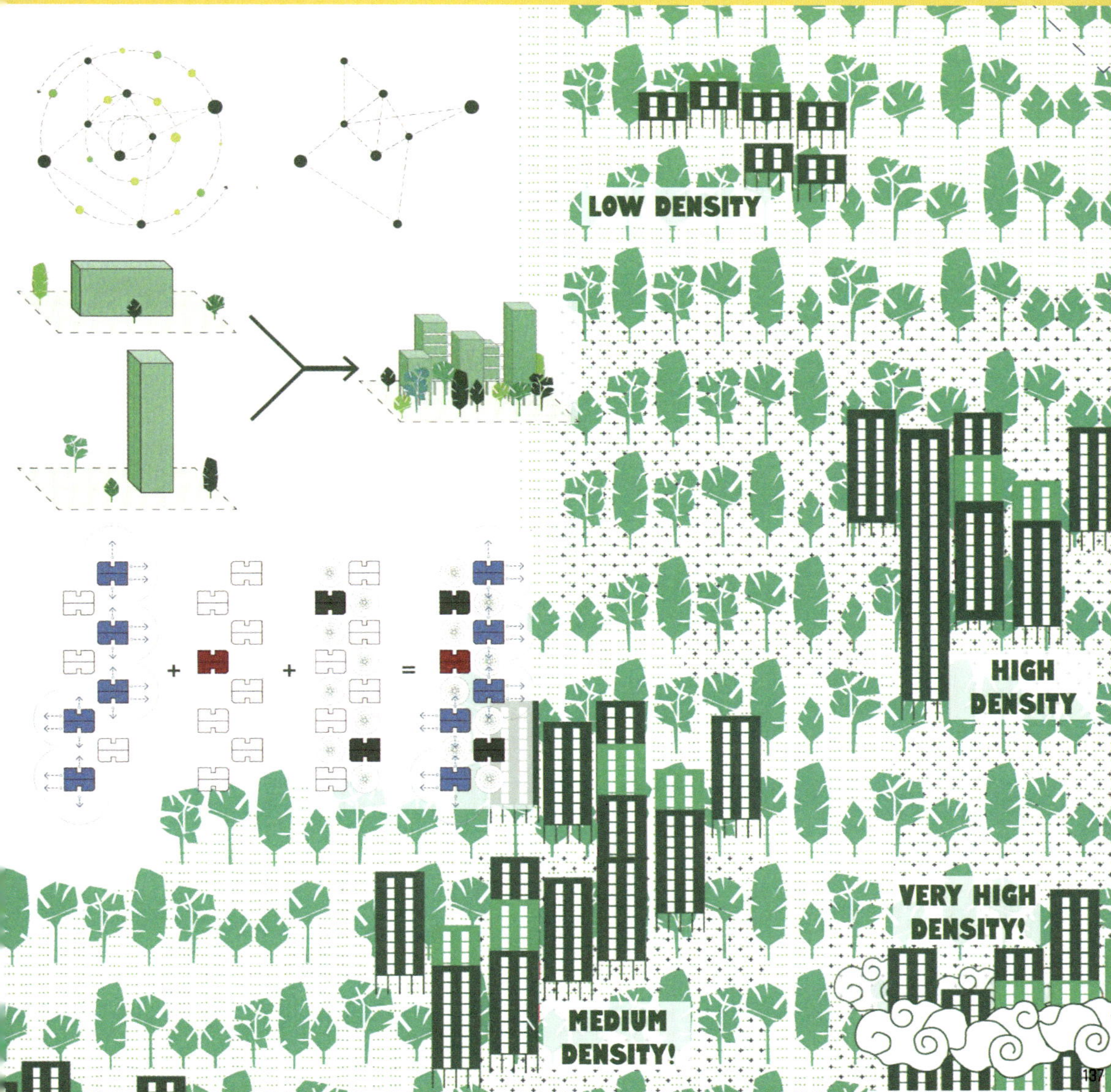
LOW DENSITY
HIGH DENSITY
VERY HIGH DENSITY!
MEDIUM DENSITY!

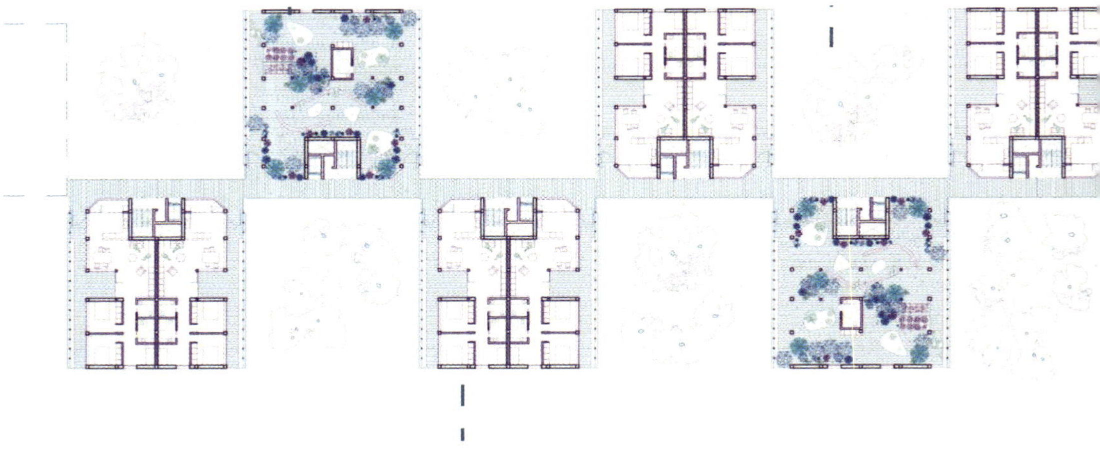

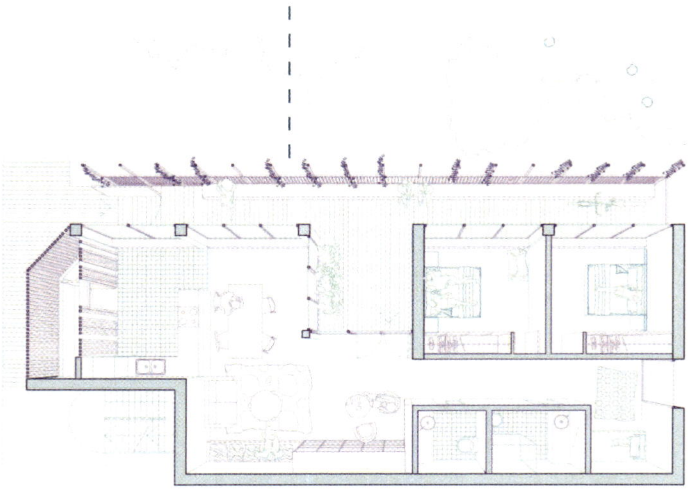

Apartment plan
1/50

The building

578K7KLX

General plan
1/500

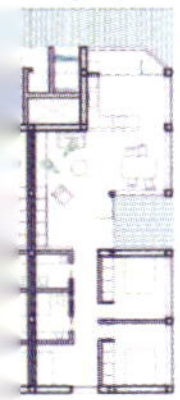

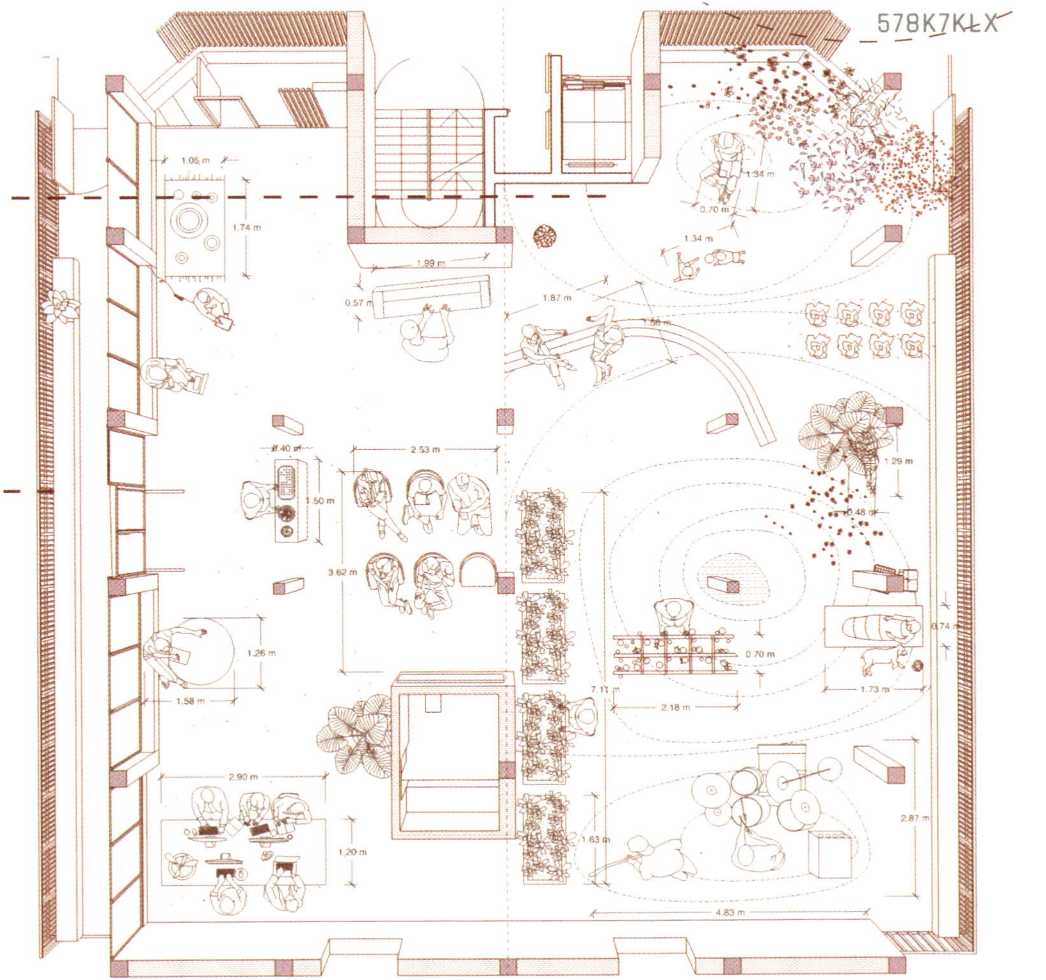

FINALIST 205G97F78

RE-IMAGİNİNG DHARAVİ

Minu Joshi
Ajay Vaidya
India

The purpose of this project is to design the structure that promotes new living system in which beneficial to all living , death and the earth Looking towards the idea of closed loop self-sustainable system (based on cradle-to-cradle templates), instead of considering death as the end of human life cycle, turning it to become aesthetically valuable traces that support daily routine. The design take advantage of fundamental metabolisms process to convert dead body into a temporal renewable energy for dwelling and respectively, provides nourishment for upcoming nature to grow. As a result, death creates life

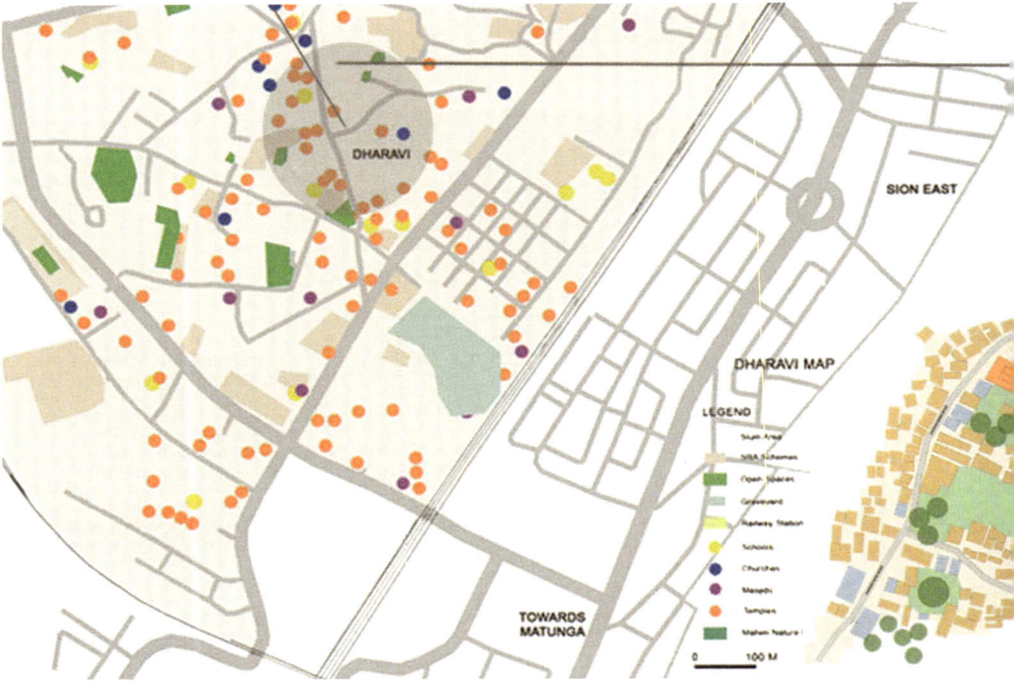
DHARAVI
SION EAST
DHARAVI MAP
LEGEND
TOWARDS MATUNGA
0
100 M

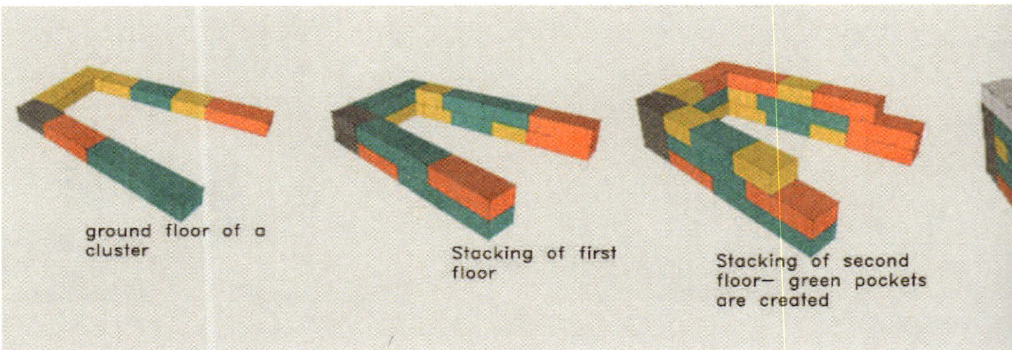
ground floor of a cluster
Stacking of first floor
Stacking of second floor— green pockets are created

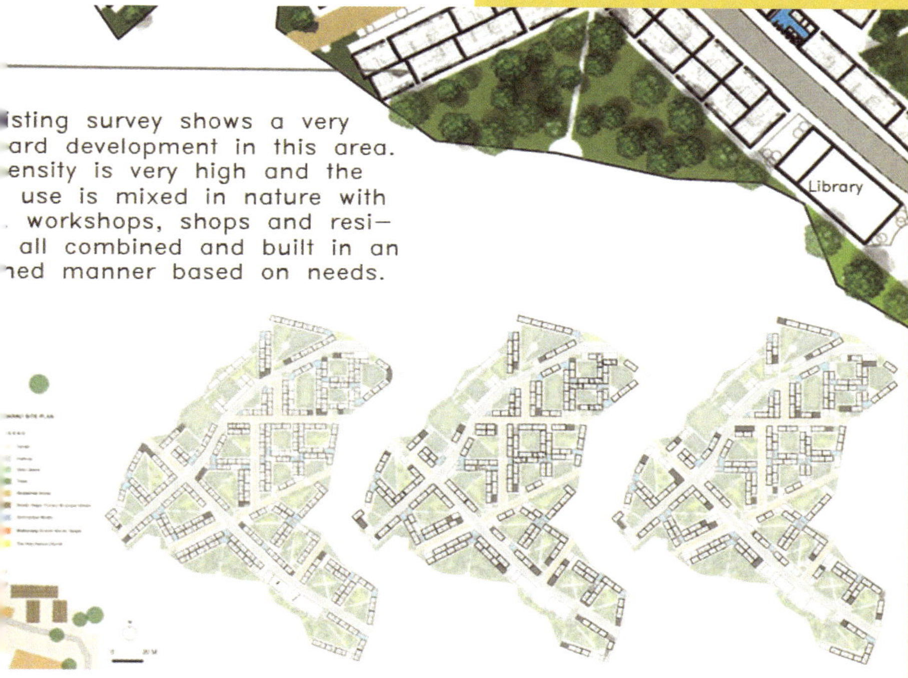

Plan showing extent of Dharavi and the site location

FINALIST 245X2R9A6

LIVING IN TWO

Julia Nogueira da Silva
Brasil

The house played a key role in the recent global crisis. Forced to adapt as an office, school, gym, vegetable garden and even a restaurant, the house was subjected to the height of hybridism. In a 2m distance grid between units, the proposal embraces the hybrid program from different apartment layouts that would be connected in a newly created "plug-in type" connection system. In this way, the residents guarantee an adequate work, leisure and decompression space, free from domestic interference, but, nevertheless, directly connected to the home.

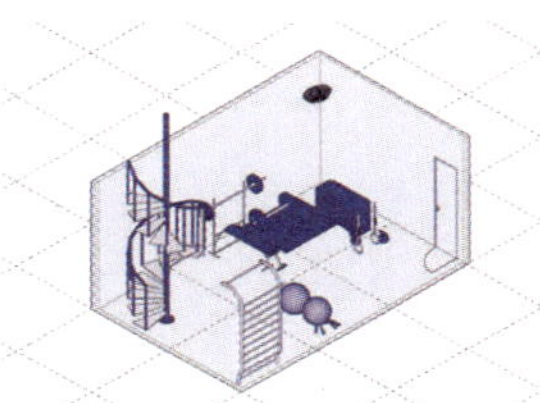

gym

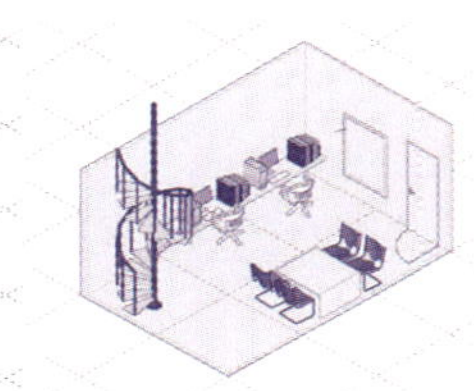

office

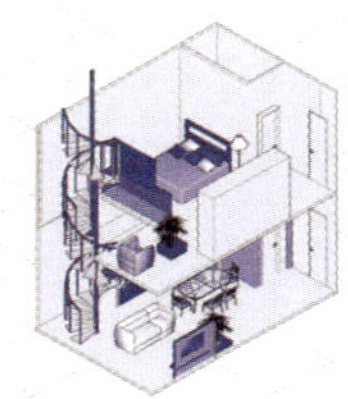

sleep and cook

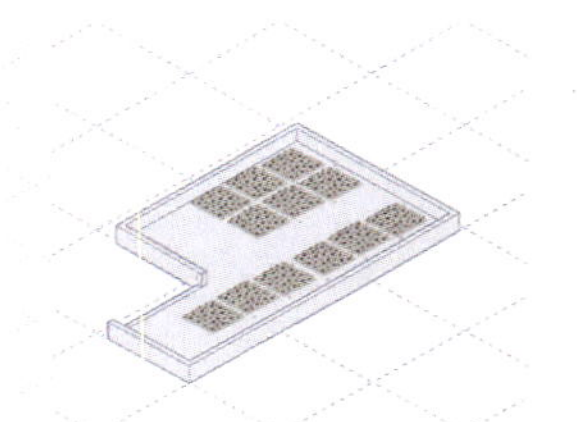

grow

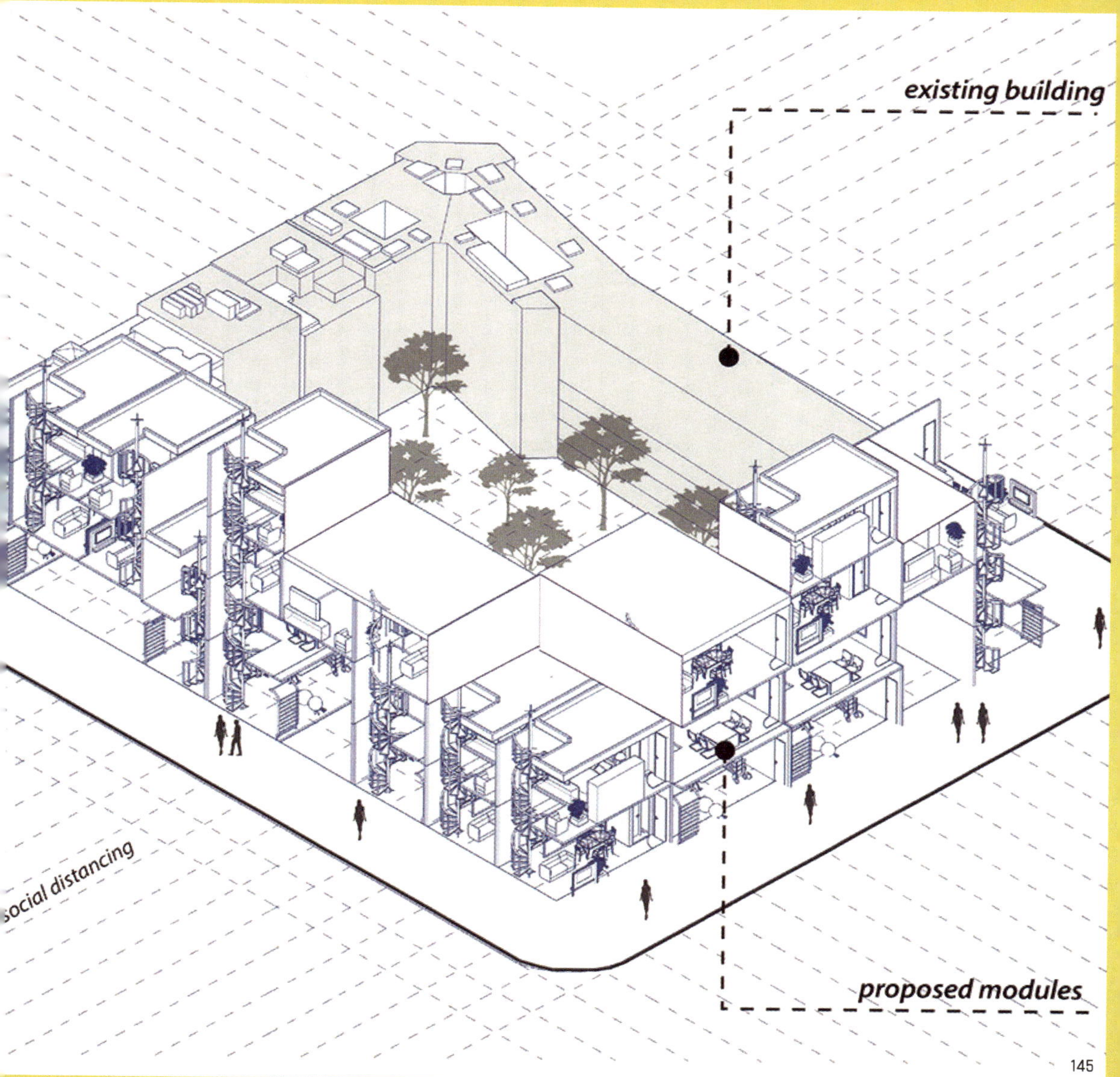
existing building
social distancing
proposed modules

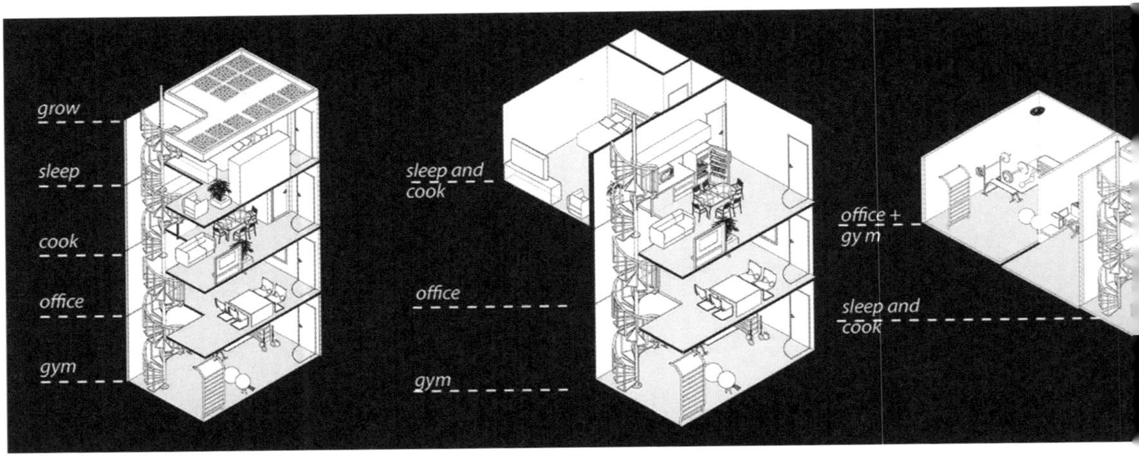

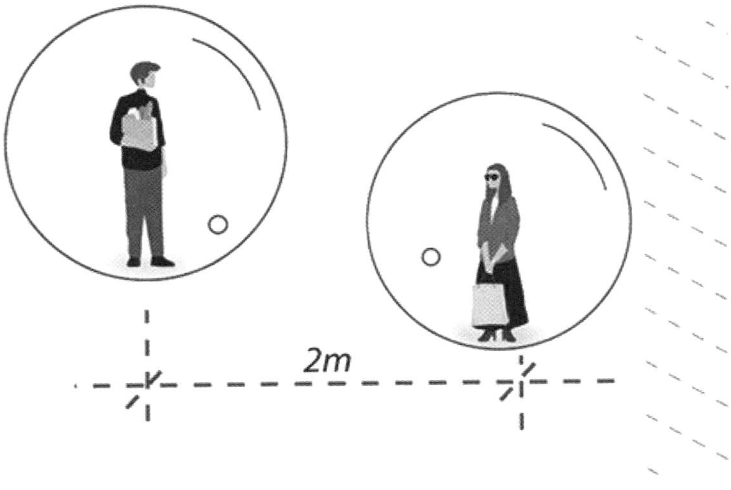

Allowing people to maintain a strong dialogue with each other in this new approach to living.

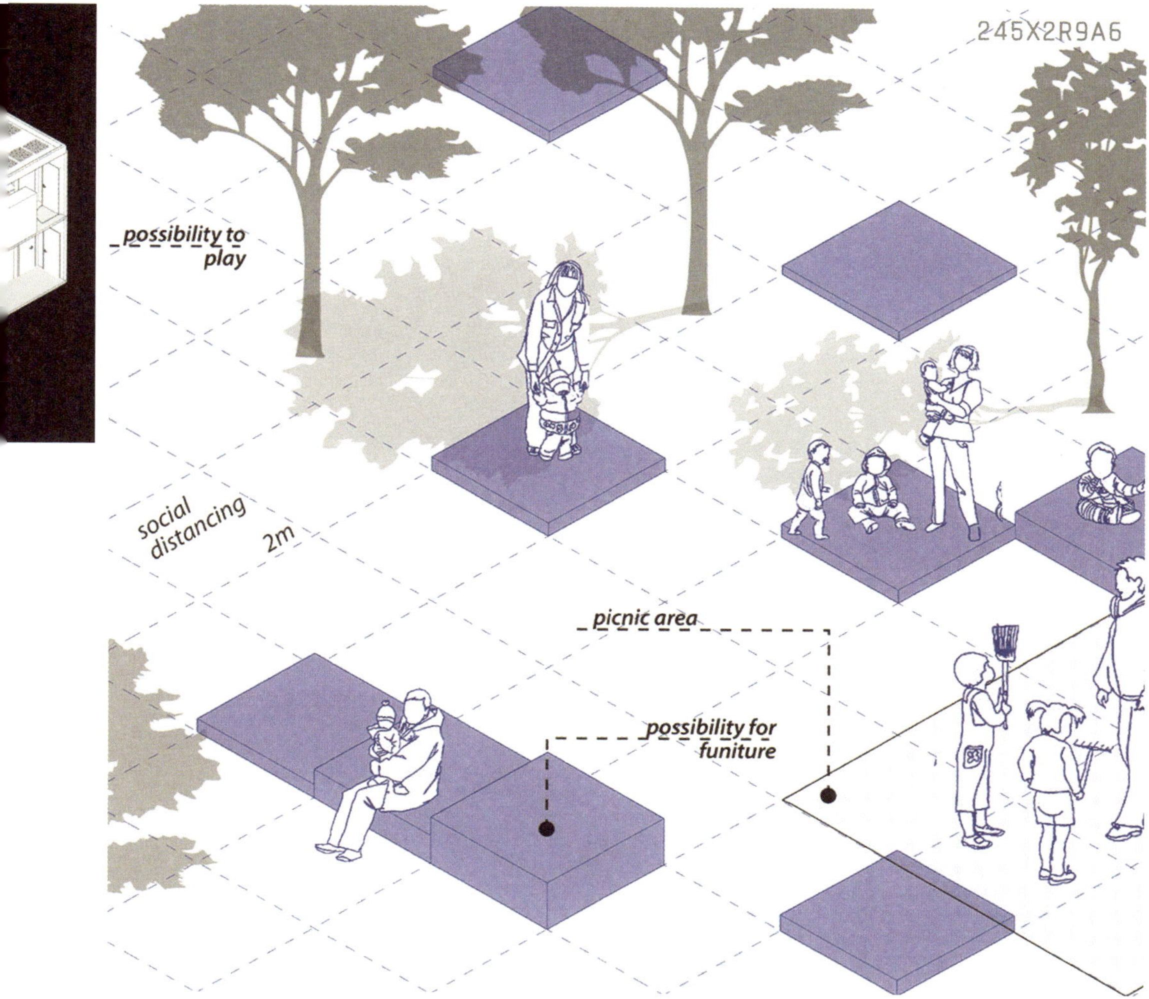
245X2R9A6
_possibility to play
social distancing
2m
_picnic area
possibility for funiture

FINALIST 468ASK9BF

PARENTHESİS

Lissette Del Busto Pacios
Marien Reyes Puebla
Cuba

The current sanitary crisis will generate changes in all fields, especially in architecture and urban design. Homes have become the scenery of our daily activities, incorporating uses they were not prepared for. The challenge is to rethink the housing scheme to reduce the isolation feeling, while also adding a closed-loop of renewable resources like rain water collection and solar energy. This proposal adds three new spaces to our homes: "Transition" for disinfection before entering, "Multiple Activities" to accommodate the activities that were carried out in other buildings, and "Outside-In" to reconnect with the natural outdoor environment.

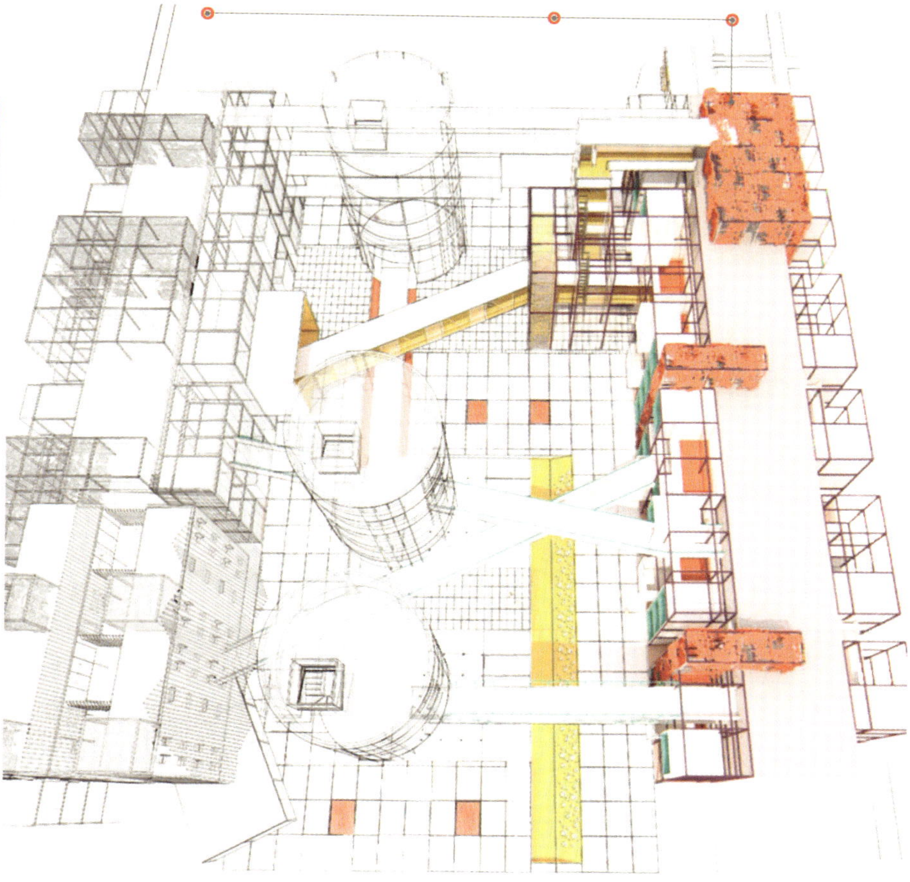

Home activities paths and scenes

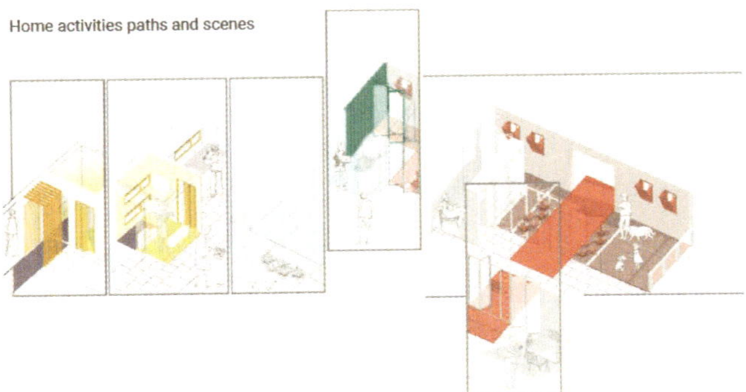

Home activities paths and scenes

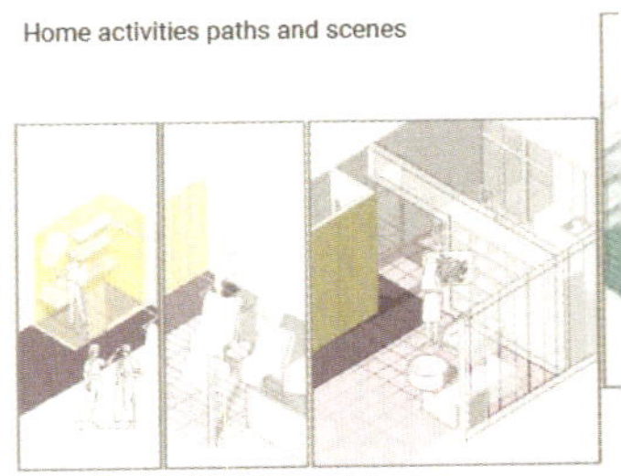

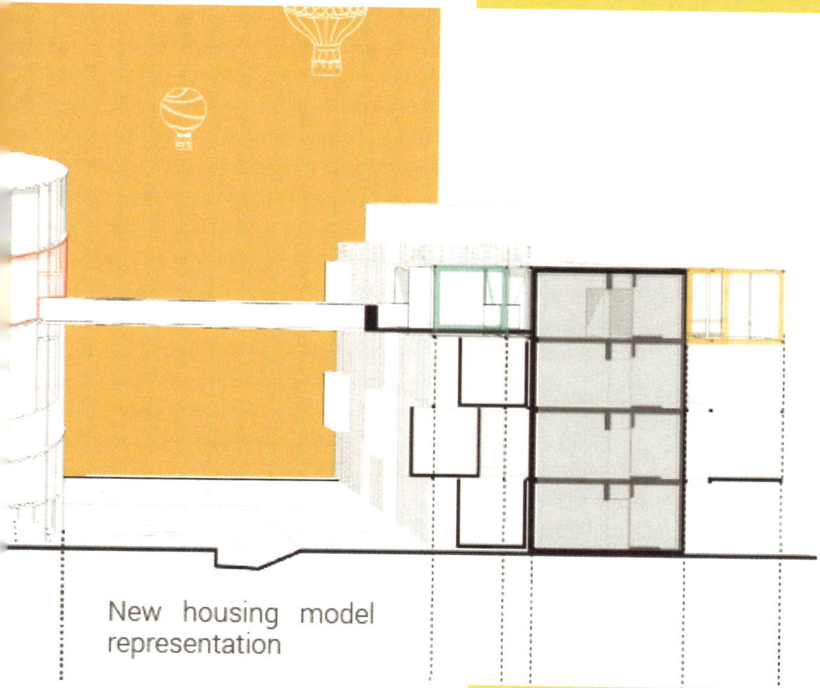

New housing model representation

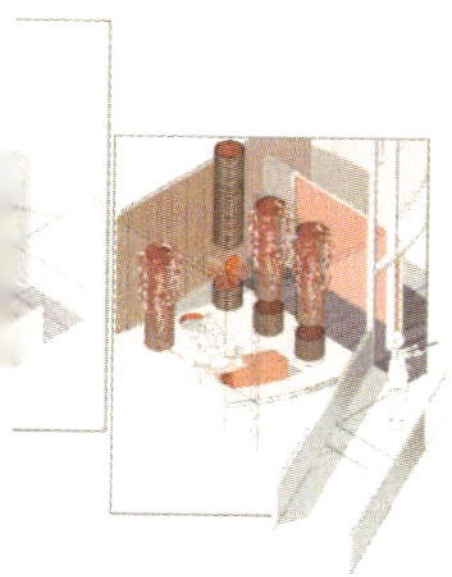

"...everything looks so different. Have I changed, or has the city changed(...) What if everything began right now?..."
Gutiérrez, T.(director).(1968).Memorias del subdesarrollo [Film].Cuba

FINALIST 317VN4EB5

BRANCH RESiDENTiAL COMMUNiTY

WangYue Zhao
China

In the context of the COVID-19 global epidemic, we began to rethink residential areas, because of the need for isolation, each family should have a safe social distance. Secondly, according to the government's home isolation policy, how can we meet the self sufficient food supply at home, how to contact nature as much as possible, how to exercise at home and keep healthy. These requirements change the form of residential buildings and adjust the functions of the community. In a community, the public environment should not only be open and shared, but also provide comfortable and safe venues for activities in special periods. The three-dimensional transportation includes ground walking and two-story corridor, which gives people more choices to reach public space. The interior of the building can also provide a small range of open-air gardens to meet a certain number of people's communication activities, which are to disperse the flow of people, reduce the pressure on the square, and avoid overload accumulation of people.

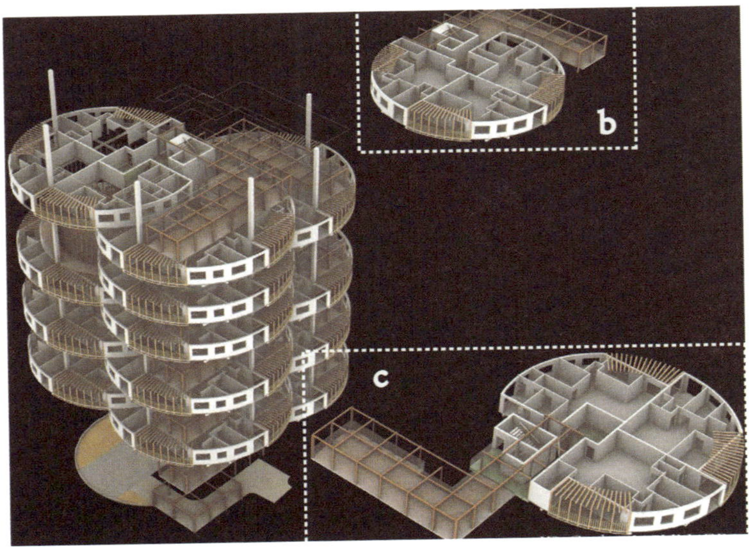

Branch residencial community

317VN4EB5

FINALIST 289XAGPWZ

PRO PODS

Allison Aber
United States of America

The Eiffel Tower in Paris and The Vessel Heatherwick in Manhattan are two such monumental structures which have been closed to visitors since the outbreak of COVID-19 began. These two structures, like many architectural tourist attractions around the globe, are able to handle enormous amounts of foot traffic everyday, and therefore have the potential to become essential in times of a pandemic.
With PRO, they can adapt more necessary functions and even accommodate future urbanization. PRO is a system of pods which can be used as medical clinics or emergency shelters. As consequences of urbanization, space will become more valuable and the homeless population will inevitably increase.

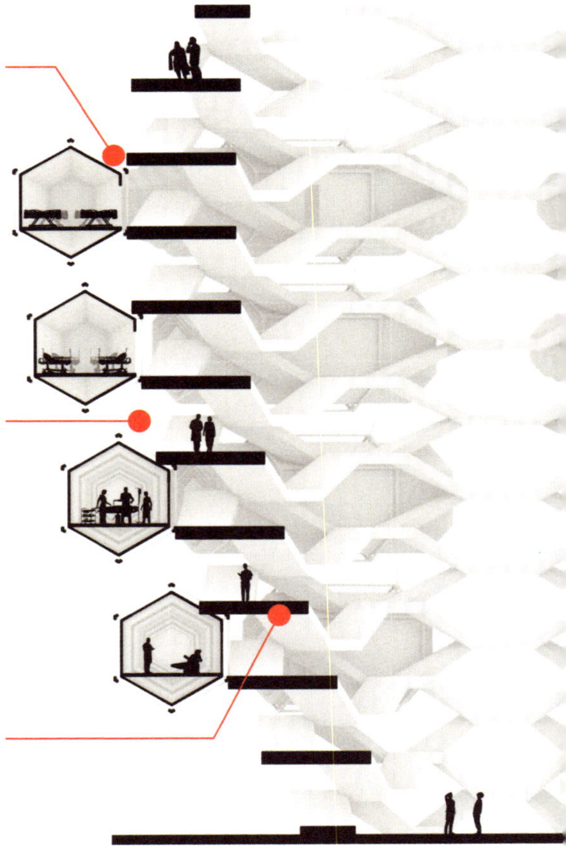

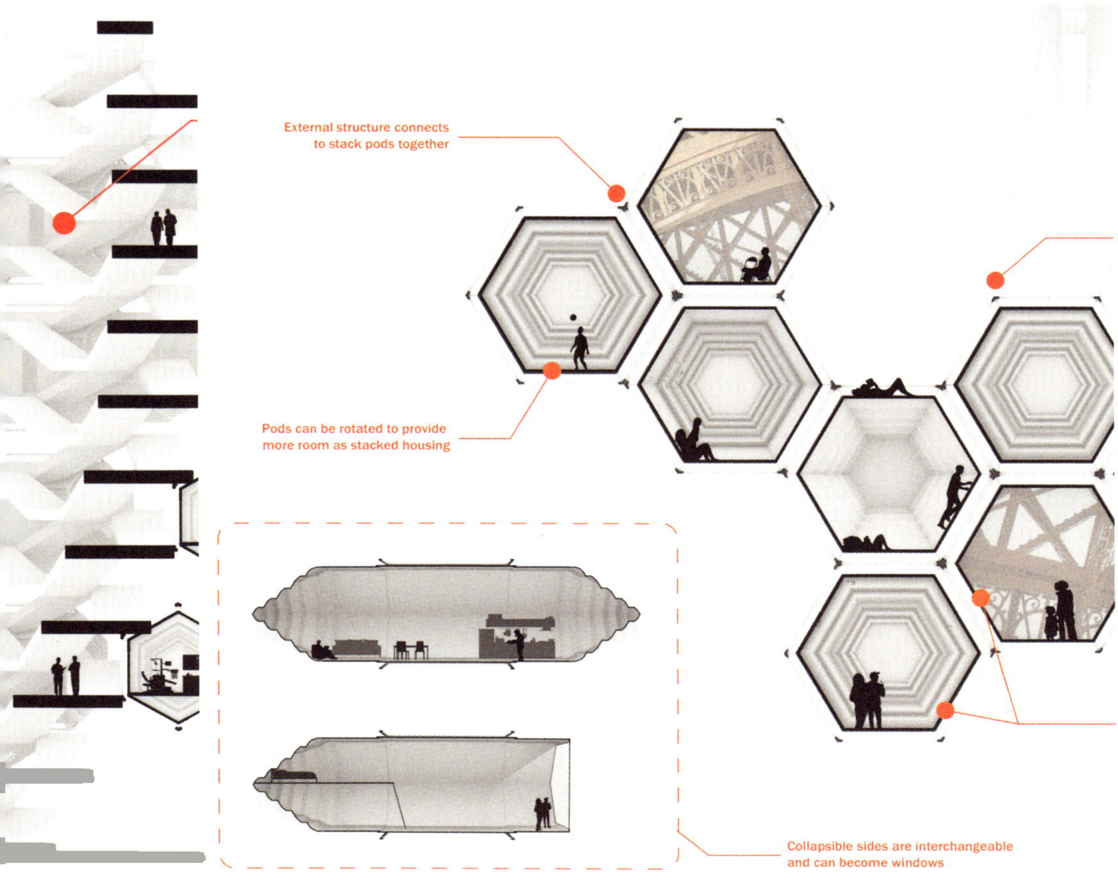
External structure connects
to stack pods together
Pods can be rotated to provide
more room as stacked housing
Collapsible sides are interchangeable
and can become windows

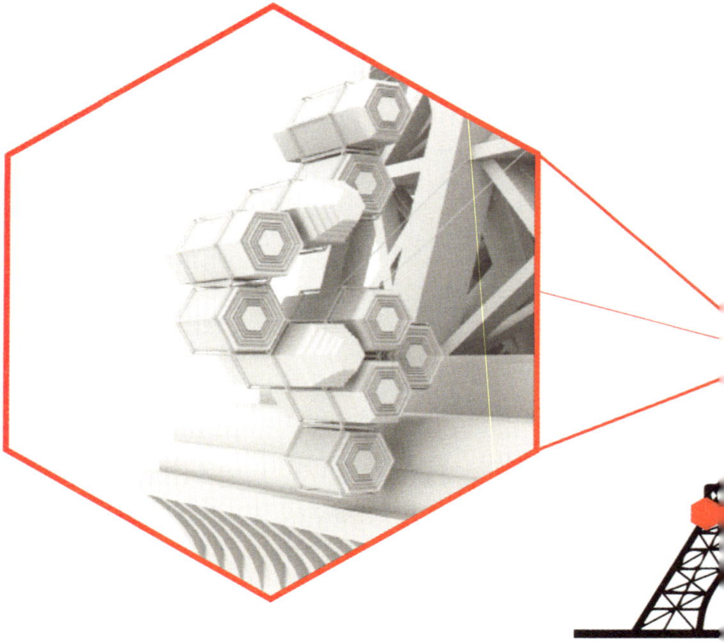

By 2050 more than 2/3 of the world population will live in major cities

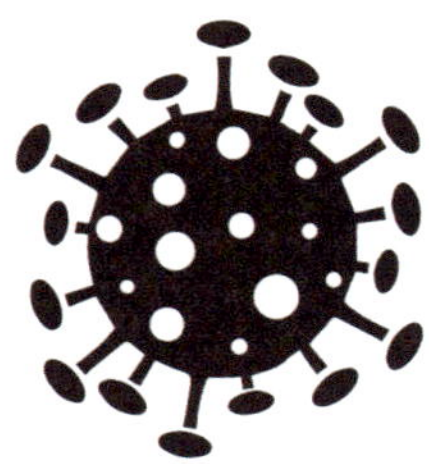

Pandemics are going to become more frequent

Urba
to a

vill lead
nerable
ns

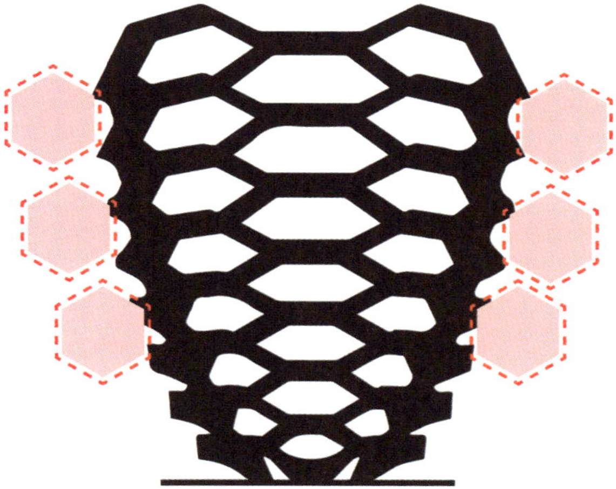

PRO utilizes the existing structures of monuments to react.

FINALIST 27006PZAI

REACTIVATE OUR PERIPHERIES

THE ENDLESS CITIES

Gabriel Madrigal
Mexico

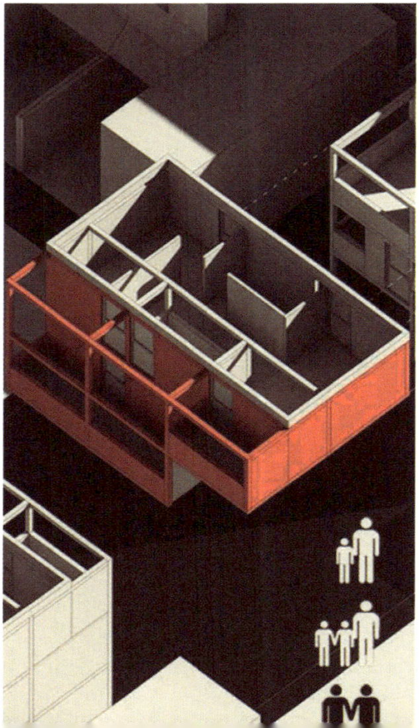

Our home is the place where we define our way of living, it's the space where we grow, learn, share and experience; it defines us as individuals and therefore it defines us a community.
In order to rethink our habitat and our communities, it's fundamental to rethink the least privileged households. With millions of abandoned houses in a state of neglect and deterioration, it's necessary to reconfigure our cities from them. Reactivate marginalized areas is possible through the diversity of land uses, it's versatility and capability of creating a community; complexes that regardless of their size are capable to serve the basic necessities of their inhabitants. It's necessary to offer simple solutions that are capable of adapting to the current contexts. And, somehow, benefit from the resources already invested in innumerable development in the same conditions.

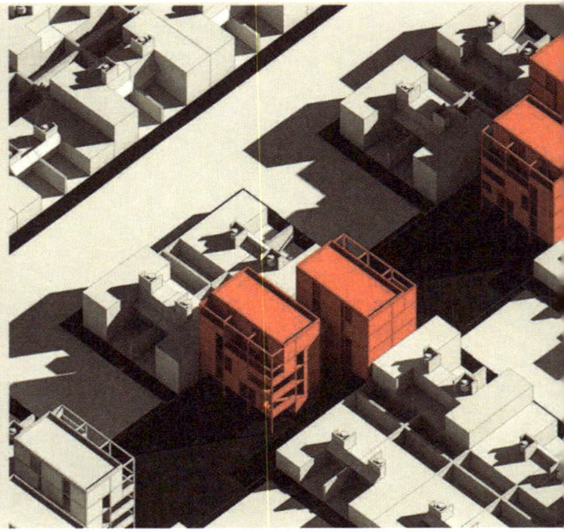

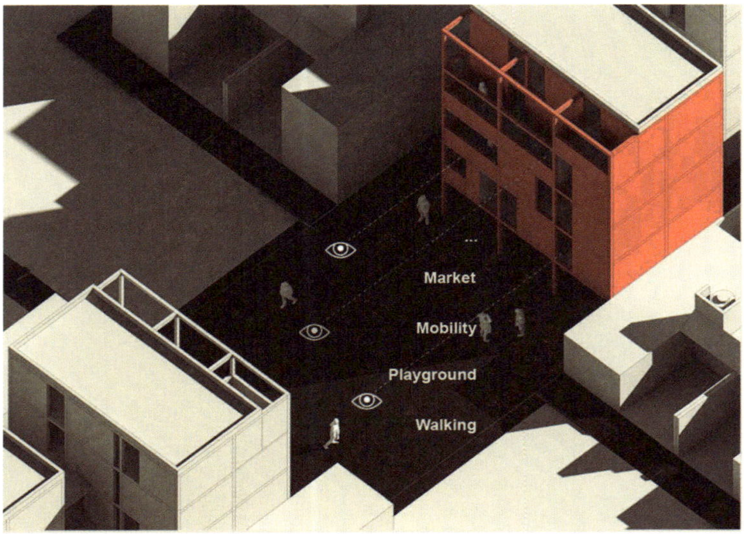

This, more than a building design, can be the key to successfully transform our habitats

27006PZAI
TACOS
SUADERO
CABEZA
TRIPA
$10

Permanent Quarantine
Ching-Wen Huang

SELECTED WORKS
2020

SELECTED PROJECTS 248MOY1UG

TREE RESİDENSE COMPLEX

Ganesh Meena
India

The design incorporate innovative method to increase the energy efficiency which make the residence complex net positive building. In order to make that, the building called eco-trees, they behave as vertical gardens – generating solar power, acting as exhaust air towers for nearby recreational dome, and collecting rainwater.

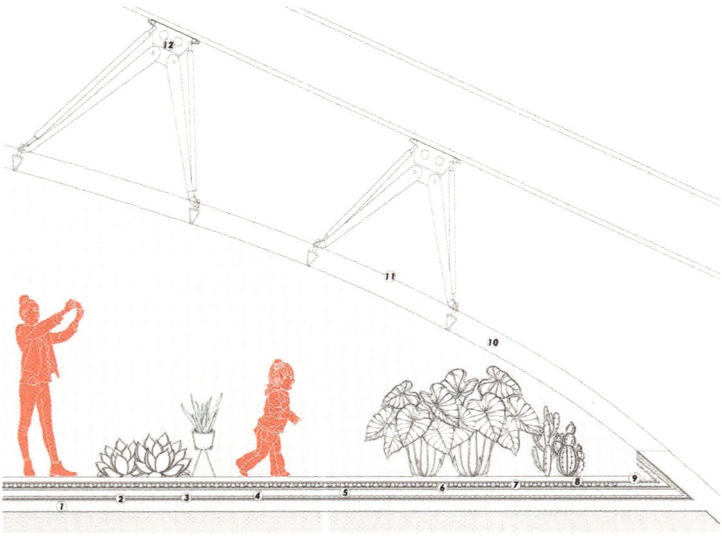

Construction details

248M0Y1UG

SELECTED PROJECTS

5001WE9FB

HOME FOR THE HOMELESS

Brother Hu Rui Hu,
Cui Siqi
Guo Hao
China

The design “dwelling narrowness” - aims to provide a temporary shelter for urban “vagrants” in the event of epidemic or disaster. In the context of the global epidemic. Cities have taken measures to seal off cities. Resulting in a number of temporary “homeless” stranded people. The design is aimed at these “vagrants”. Providing them with a simple living place.

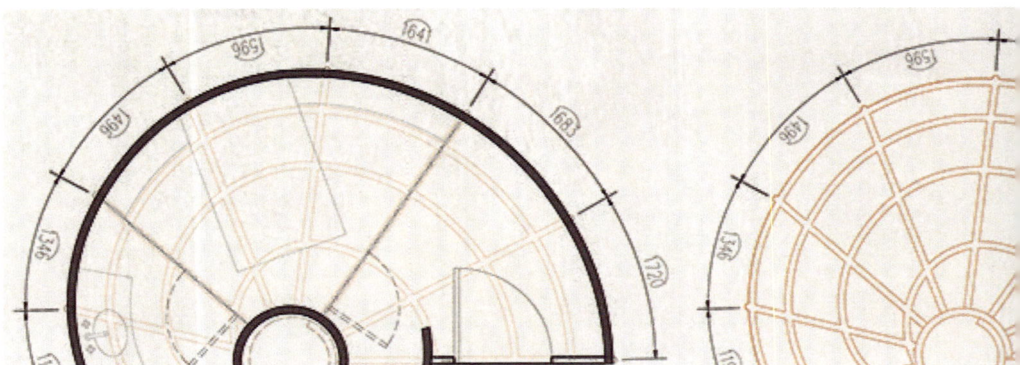
1596
1641
1496
1683
1346
1720
1596
1496
1346

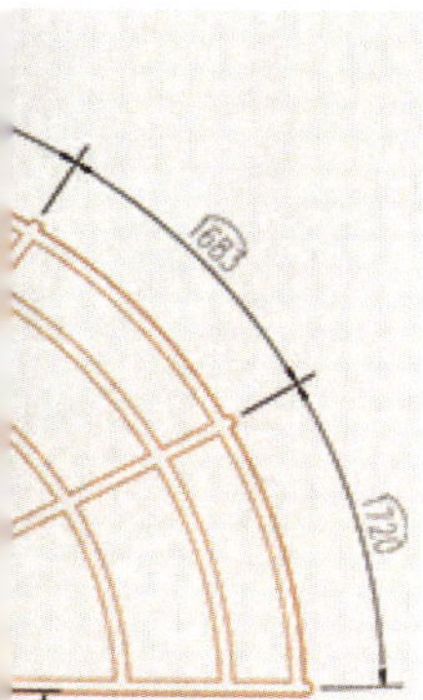

In principle, the design can be placed anywhere in chinese cities: Beside buildings and by rivers

SELECTED PROJECTS

1338I20TK

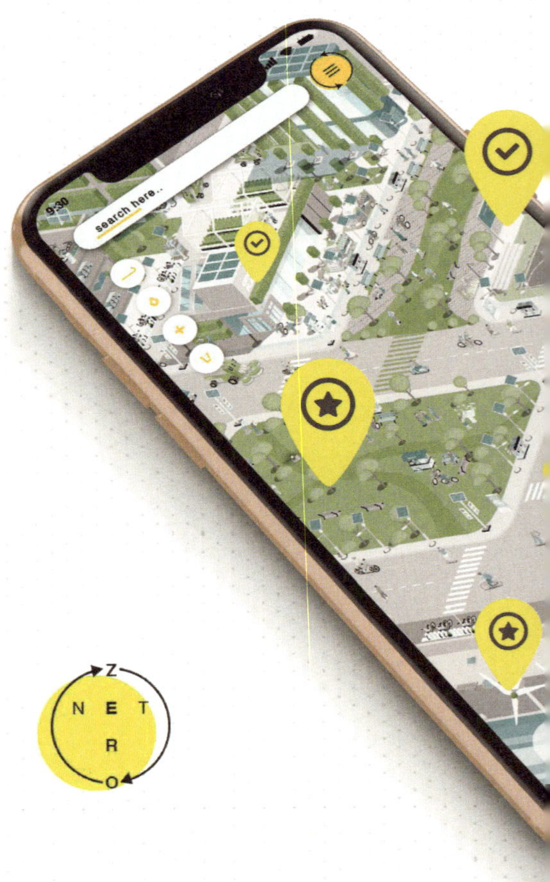

NET ZERO

Aangi Shah
Mansi Palak
India

Net Zero is a systemic platform that incorporates institutions, companies and city governments to induce a sense of responsability and conciousness towards the very resources that affect our well-being. We pair our in-depth understanding of the following elemental resources with the power of data science to incentivise all citizens to make a positive contribution to each other and the planet. Net Zero users are eventually rewarded for all positive actions taken towards resilience and sustainability.

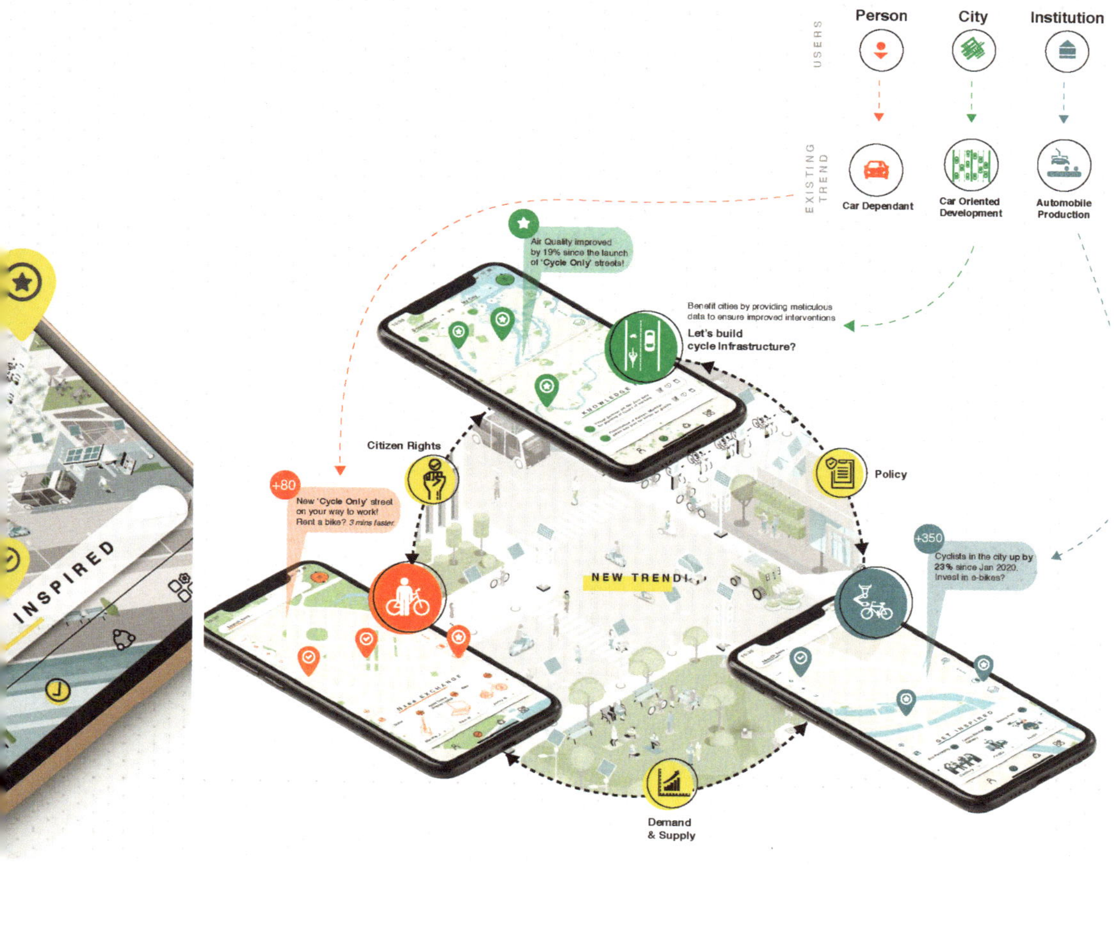
USERS
Person
City
Institution
EXISTING TREND
Car Dependant
Car Oriented Development
Automobile Production
Air Quality improved by 19% since the launch of 'Cycle Only' streets!
Benefit cities by providing meticulous data to ensure improved interventions
Let's build cycle infrastructure?
Citizen Rights
Policy
+80
New 'Cycle Only' street on your way to work! Rent a bike? 3 mins faster.
+350
Cyclists in the city up by 23% since Jan 2020. Invest in e-bikes?
NEW TREND
INSPIRED
KNOWLEDGE
BIKE EXCHANGE
GET INSPIRED
Demand & Supply

How we work...

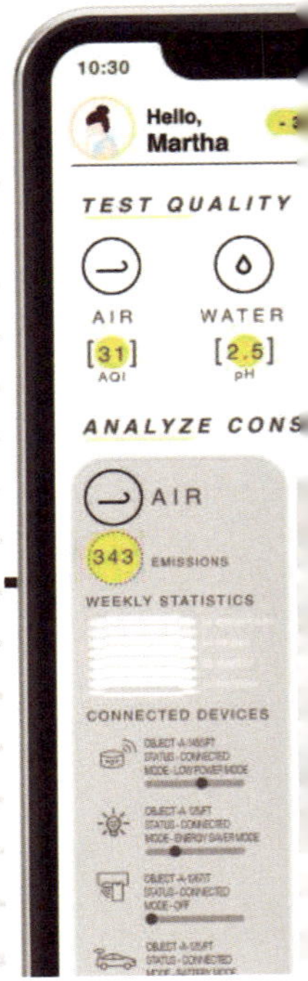

User Login

Person

Institution

City

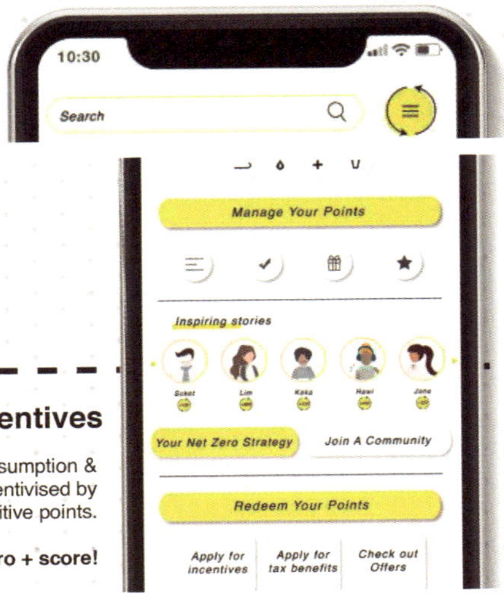

4. Points & Incentives

Negative points are given for consumption & pollution. All positive action is incentivised by way of positive points.

We hope you hit Net Zero + score!

Heal
Peo

1. Test & Measure

We monitor the quality and consumption of the 4 elements from the devices as permissed by you.

We further analyse data via IoT & machine learning from the vicinity for accurate and refined recommendations.

tainable
itutions

Resilient
Cities

Team Net Zero works with city governments to incentivise all citizens who maintain a zero+ score in the form of tax benefits, public facilities benefits and more.

SELECTED PROJECTS

6681643SA

LEiSURE CAPSULE

Alberto Browne
Chile

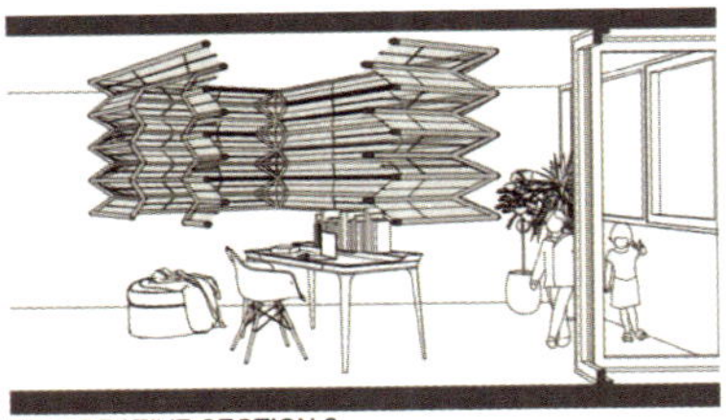

PERSPECTIVE SECTION 2
CAPSULE IN PROCESS OF UNFOLDED

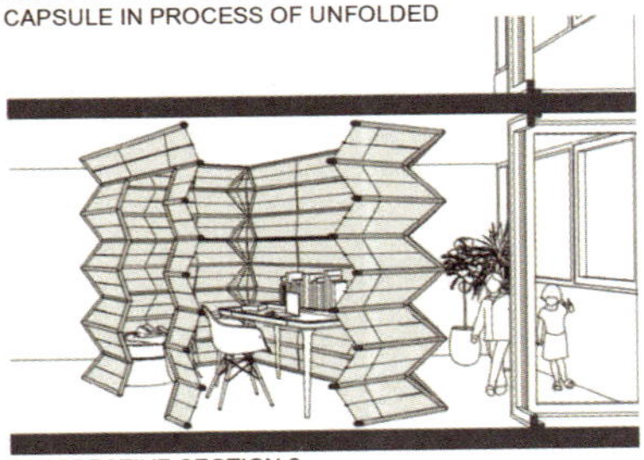

PERSPECTIVE SECTION 3
CAPSULE INSTALLED

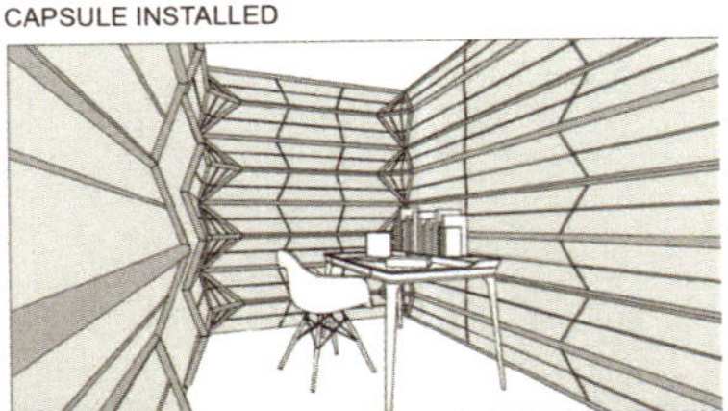

Originally in latin, the word leisure (otium), implied withdrawing from certain matters to participate in activities considered artistically valuable or enlightened. cicero also worked on the concept by coining the expression 'otium cum dignitate', translated as 'worthwhile leisure', in the sense of activities that deliver peace. In other words, the concept of leisure had something virtuous, something good and necessary for the spirit. furthermore, technological efficiencies should respond to this ancient problem, where the management of time can reconcile the production and cultivation of the soul with the development of our interests. the flexibility in mobility, work and uses of different space should be synchronized to obtain improvements that allow the development of new activities that complement work and hobbies. To conclude, this project seeks to emphasize the development of the "otium" concept through the design a capsule that allows space and privacy necessary for personal development.

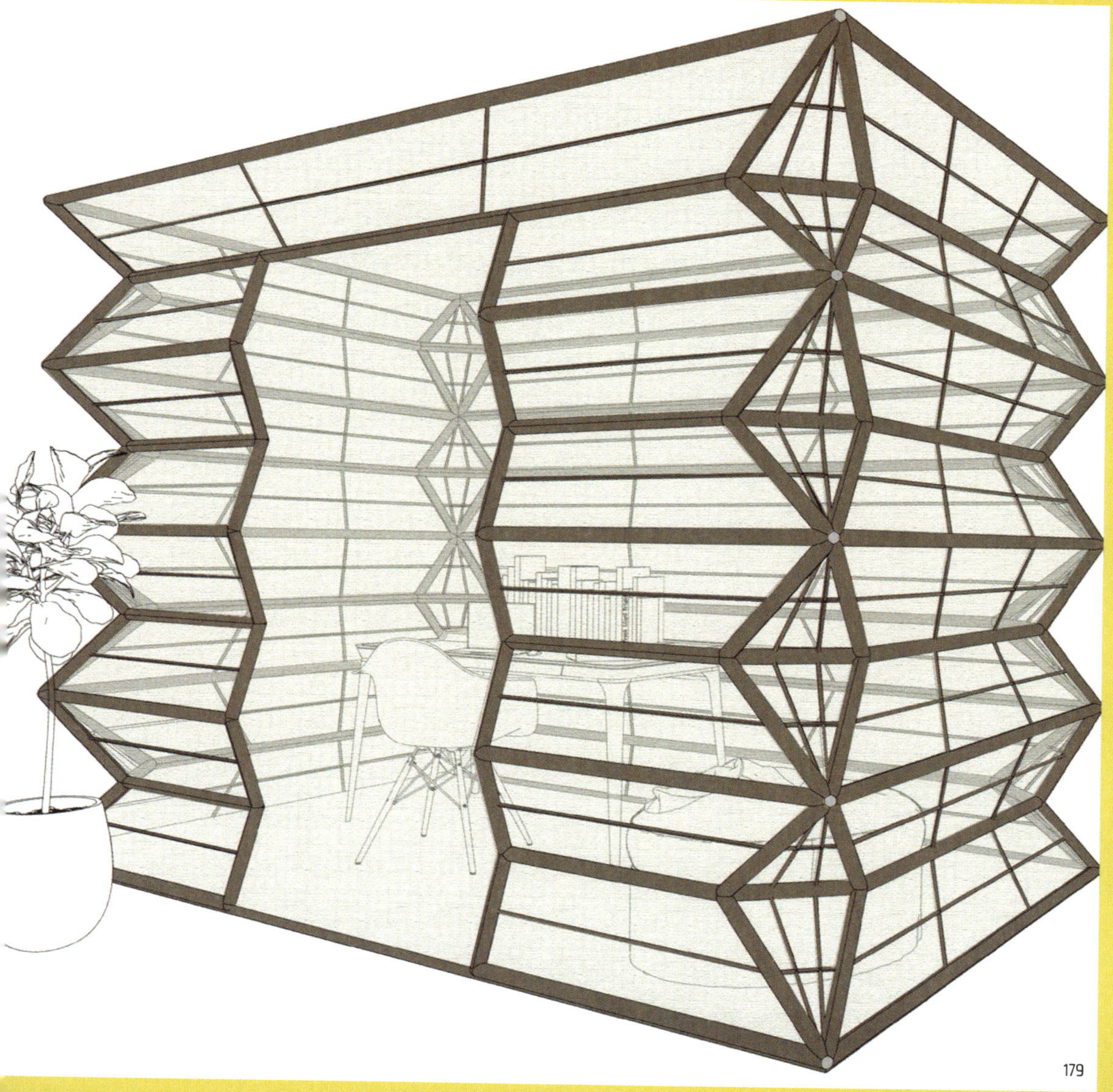

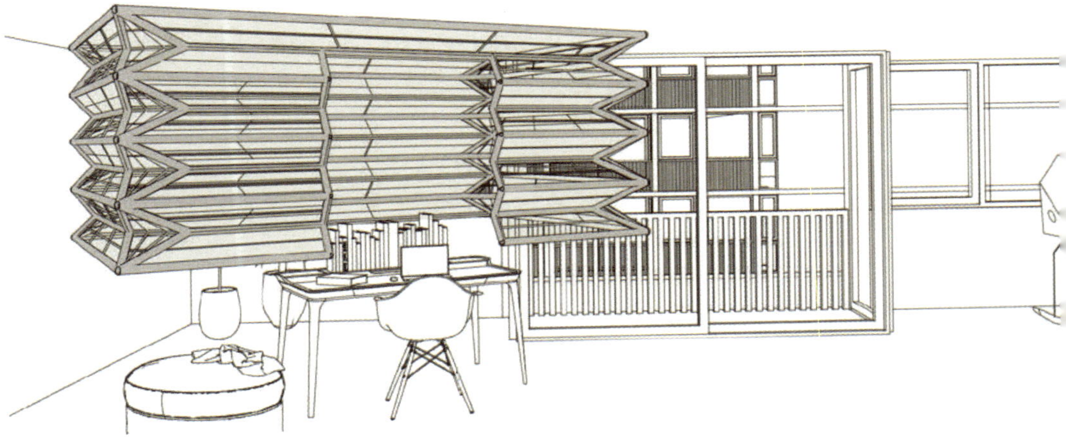

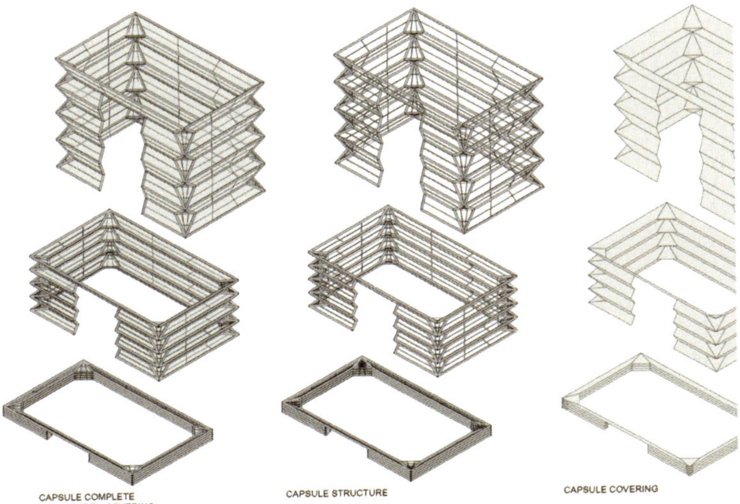

Capsule's fragmentation

6681643SA

SELECTED PROJECTS

577UJ9RQN

HOUSİNG FOR SOCİAL COHESİON

Andres Montoya
Colombia

Much of the homes in the world have been developed in the lively informality "every day you put an adobe". High final cost, low dignity, great risk. It is time for Technology and the Power of the Simple to come together and Power of the Simple to come together and allow less favored communities to have the opportunity to self-manage their new homes, guaranteeing accessibility to remain in their surroundings, providing a safe home for their families and forming easy to manage micro communities that enhance collaborative work.

POKER
TIENDA DE PEDRO

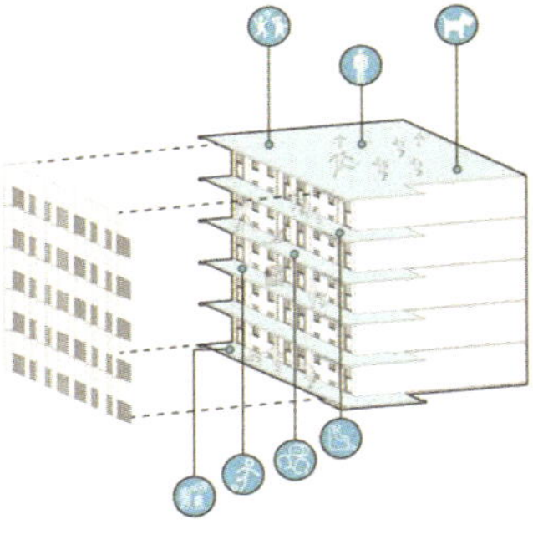

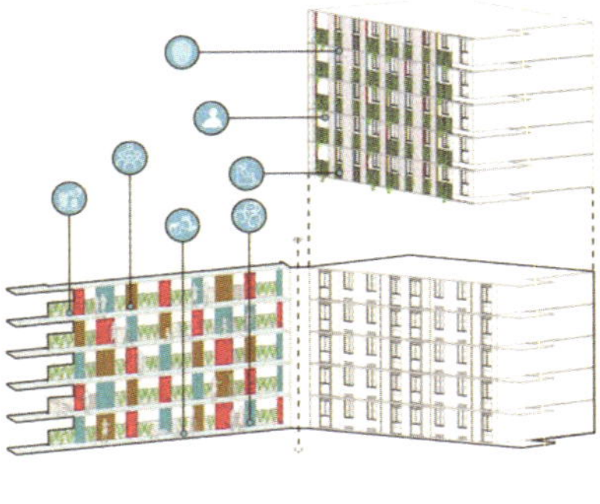

VCS is an urban project in contexts of human settlements understood as a collective space that goes beyond a solely technical scope

SELECTED PROJECTS

6810HSFKO

UP HOUSİNG

Ana Carolina Silva Mariano
Brasil

Our project is based on the creation of a community in the middle of Sorocaba's city center, a city in the state of São Paulo, Brazil. This region is surrounded by a railway line, the main city avenue, next to the historical heritage - a Power Plant used by the city industries, which today has the use of a Cultural Center. Besides, the area has a limit the Sorocaba River. The goal is to create a housing complex. Besides, Sorocaba River, together with a park next to the area, adds air humidification, benefiting thermal comfort, wich also helps agricultural productivity for food consumption.

SELECTED PROJECTS

703A6G2LS

A LETTER FROM BORNEO

Andrew Kurniawan
Ariel Bintang
Australia

We chose to rebuild the wasteland of Borneo, the land of palm oil and quarries. We no longer want to damage forests, so we heal the damaged ones. We are building cities that coexist with the forest, an elevated one so that we no longer disturb the animals in their own land. However, we prefer to call it our villages because we feel closer together. They are scattered as they are democratic agents of reforestation, greening each vicinity until it meets and the whole land becomes green again. It is a composition of primaries placed intentionally.

SELECTED PROJECTS

340STIA4R

THE 15 MİNUTE NEİGHBORHOOD

Antigoni Kolokytha
Greece

One of the basic commercial uses we need to find within a walking distance of 5 to 10 minutes is a supermarket. The majority of our produced goods are manufactured miles far from a city's centers, while countless trucks are racing on a daily basis to deliver fresh products. An important quantity of those goods though could be produced much more close to our homes without losing any quality. Our market areas could be as well micro manusfacturing areas.

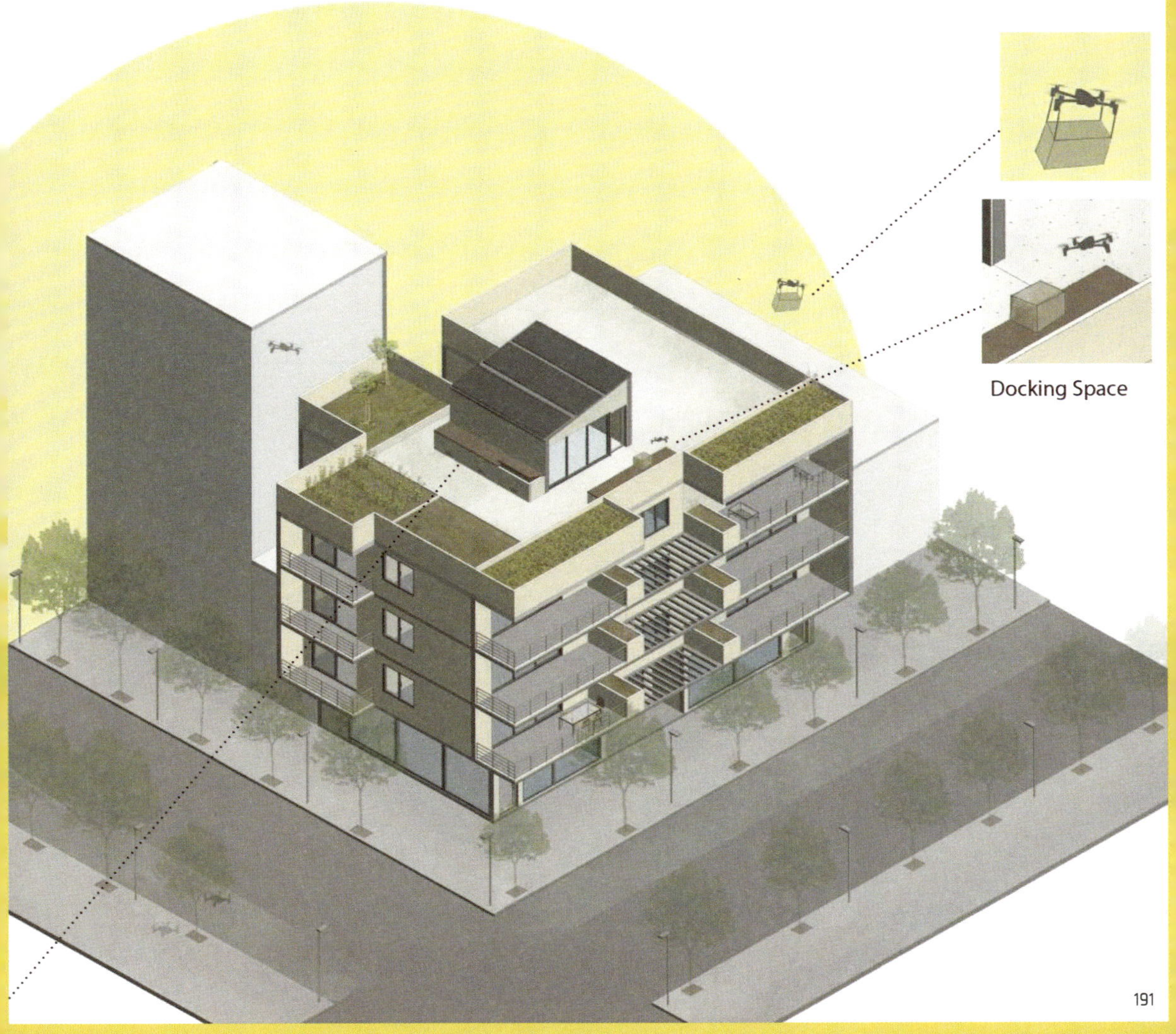
Docking Space

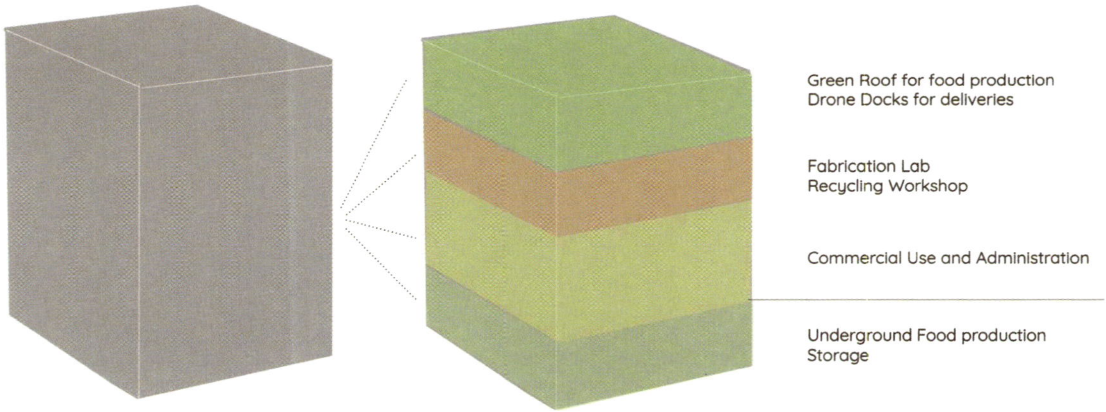

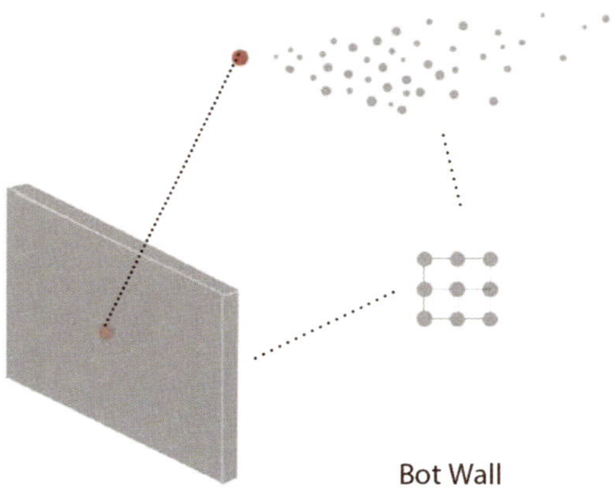

Each 15 minute neighborhood has a center that has enough space for a park and buildings that can serve for social or health services. When these neighborhoods collide they create bigger open spaces for parks and other services for larger audiences.

248M0Y1UG

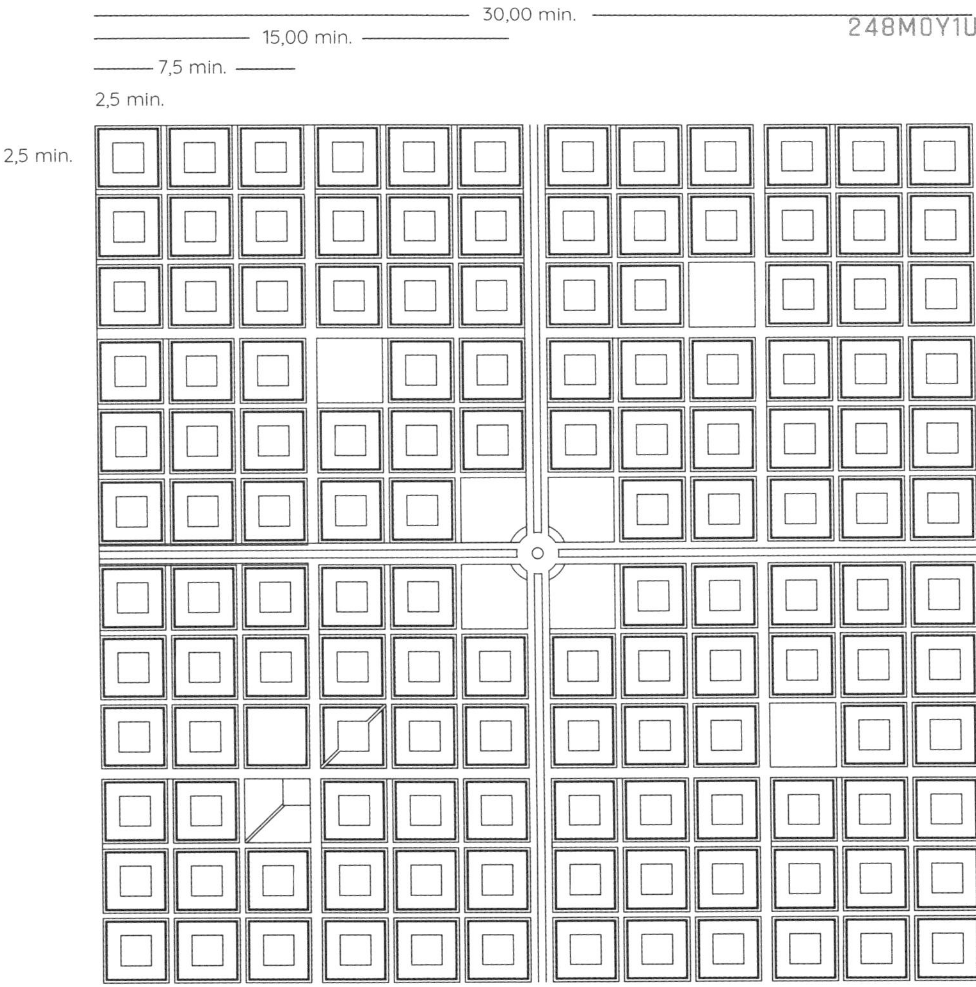

SELECTED PROJECTS

3057870SR

THE REİNCAR-NATİON

GROW A HOME

Noriel Estipular
Philippines

The Reincarnation Project investigates the possibilities of 30%-90% Kerto LVL in "Grow a home strategy" a time based ownership customization model. The project proposed time frame of the current year, 2050 and 2100 to forecast physical and non physical environmental issues using wood as main materials. The designer considers typologies indoor and outside environment to build and instant modular house based on your needs either new house, expansion or a shared housing unit. It exercises the community to practice participatory design, coordination, customization and in relation to adapt time for designing.

ZONING DIAGRAM

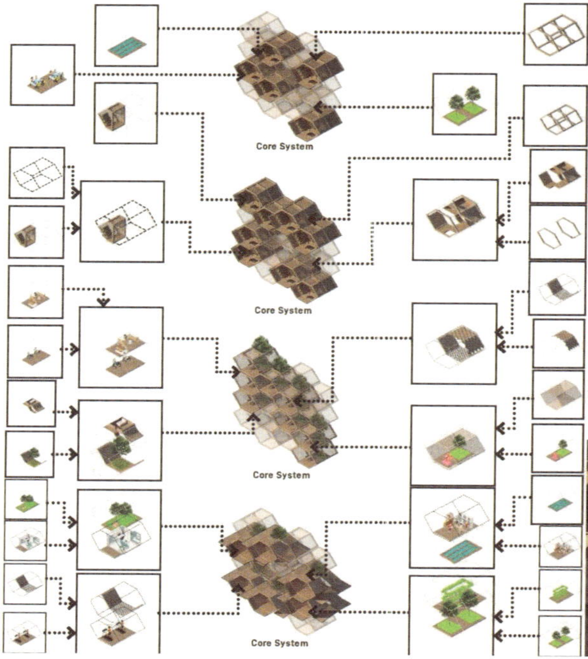

SCHEMATIC SECTION PERSPECTIVE / EXPLODED FACADE DESIGN

Deficiency to Efficiency: Biophilic Design and Time Based Ownership as Future Habitation

SELECTED PROJECTS

3547K2993

ELECTRIC FILIGREE OF REAL TIME DATA FLUX

Luis Ariel Zuñiga Guerrero
Santos Giovanny
Martínez Alvarado
Mexico

Brain City is a net of stimuli, data, digital representations and interactions among a series of interconnected buildings via IOT, AI and AR interfaces that create a more democratic and informed society. Placed un Aguascalientes in the year 2050 on it's historical downtown, this reinventions of human habitat proposes real time streaming to detect phenomena of political, economic and social nature of utmost importance. User data coming from gadget and buildings is used to communicate cases of corruption, abuse of power, racial and gender violence, environmental hazards, even the emergence of unknown deseases into a screen-membrane that coats buildings.

CORONAVIRUS PANDEMIC
"I CAN'T BREATHE"
FLOYD'S FAMILY & MINNEAPOLIS MAYOR CALL FOR 4 FIRED OFFICERS TO BE CHARGED WITH MURDER
CNN
CNN Center
CORONAVIRUS PANDEMIC
SURGEON GENERAL: U.S. MOVING FROM "CONTAINMENT" TO "MITIGATION"
Dr. Sanjay Gupta
RIGHT NOW
EL CHAPO SENTENCED TO LIFE

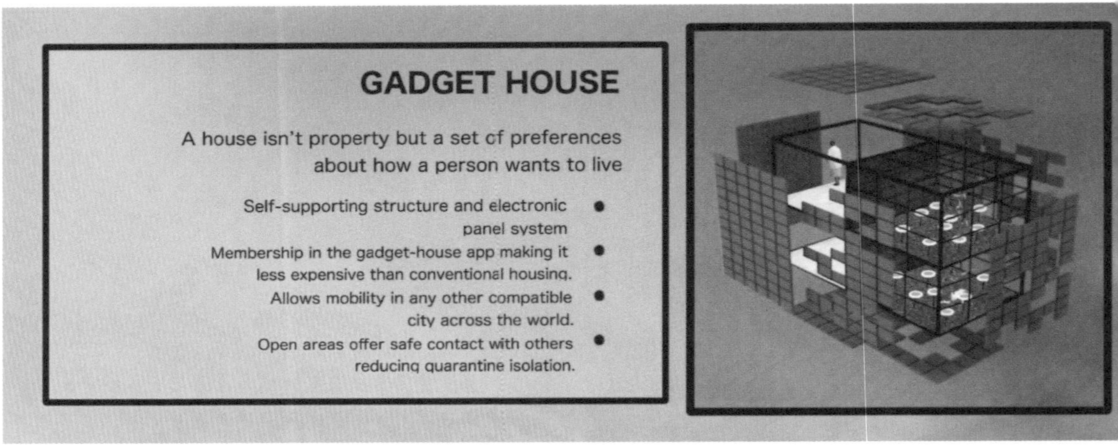

Each new tower offers a new housing system that integrates affordable materials and a user-friendly interface: "a house is a gadget for living it"

HISTORICAL DOWNTOWN
Housing for rest, streets to live. New buildings reactivate and redensify the historical downtown, as they've not a real estate business.
• Historical layer remains untouched.
• Towers are built in void areas and hace underground access.
• It promotes a compact city model and pedestrian downtown model. Intensive use of public space in contingency-free seasons.

SELECTED PROJECTS

32WG8TIX

FOREST FOR LiViNG

Juan Camilo Ramírez Ortiz
Colombia

The proposal would then focus on rethinking a project of this type, a real estate development located downtown of the city of Medellín, Colombia, which due to its particular conditions becomes a unique phenomenon, due to the reduced space of the houses, the lack of common spaces and the overpopulation that lives in marginal conditions, that makes it pertinent for a study of strategies that can rehabilitate its conditions of natural hostility towards its inhabitants and makes us think of an architectural project from the point of view of a new 'Machine for living' or better called, a new 'Forest for living' that must be synchronized with the real cultural poetics and the historical moment we are facing.

he project turns the building
nto a new FOREST, into a
erformative device that not
nly brings new ways of living
nside the apartments, but also
ecomes an ecological catalyst
or the city, providing food,
nergy and, thanks to its green
açade, contributing to the
apture of co2, giving the city
ew solutions to the problems
terms of air quality . A
roblem that has become
creasingly dangerous due to
s geographical
onditions(Medellin is a Valley),
nd the pollution produced by
urrent living and mobility
onditions.
The elevator corridor
and stairwell create
small squares where
community meetings
are encouraged
MERCADO
COMUNITARIO
SAN SEBASTIAN
FARMACIA
The Commercial block becomes a
community market where the
products that are produced on the
openwork facades of the building
can be sold

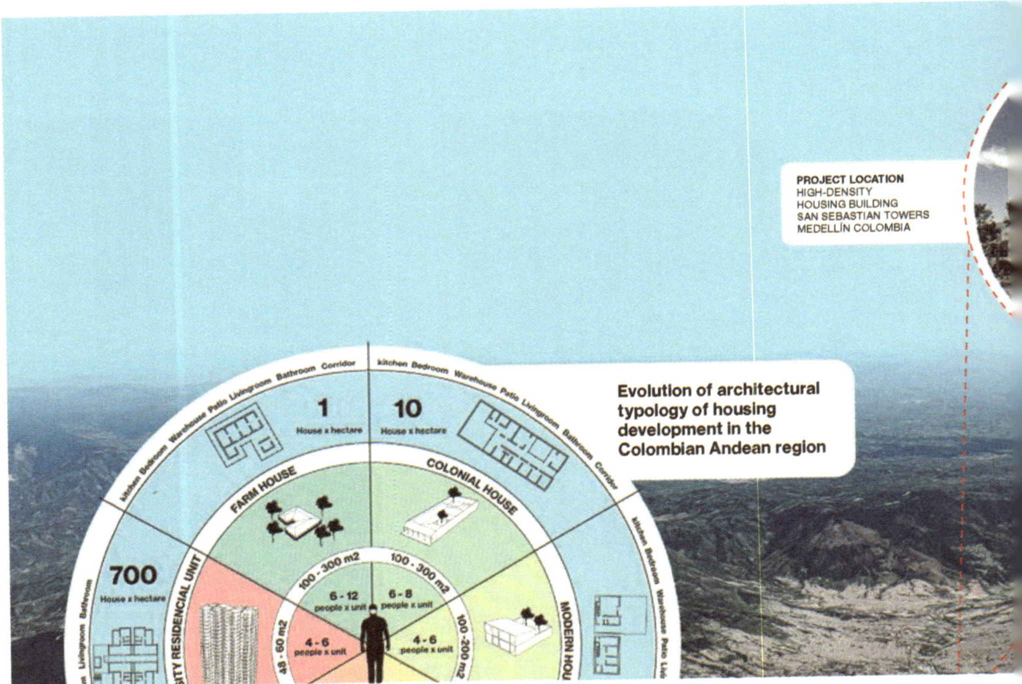

PROJECT LOCATION
HIGH-DENSITY
HOUSING BUILDING
SAN SEBASTIAN TOWERS
MEDELLÍN COLOMBIA
Evolution of architectural typology of housing development in the Colombian Andean region
kitchen Bedroom Warehouse Patio Livingroom Bathroom Corridor
1
House x hectare
10
House x hectare
700
House x hectare
FARM HOUSE
COLONIAL HOUSE
100 - 300 m2
100 - 300 m2
100 -200 m2
48 - 60 m2
6 - 12
people x unit
6 - 8
people x unit
4 - 6
people x unit
4 - 6
people x unit

The project was originally conceived as a bedroom dwelling. It was made for the kind of inhabitants that would only spend the night at home, while the rest of the day the´ll be outside working in different activities, most of them informal jobs. Under this premise the project does not offer common spaces or recreation areas.
The elevator corridor and stairwell create small squares where community meetings are encouraged
The Commercial block becomes a community market where the products that are produced on the openwork facades of the building can be sold

1 THE CORRIDOR

The corridor is the space that connects the interior with the exterior, a space that expands the shelter and the feeling of protection allowing **you to enjoy the different atmospheres that the outside offers. Being outside in the rain without** getting wet, or enjoying sunlight without having to be exposed to its rays.

To inhabit the corridor is to inhabit the interstice, the between, the horizon line where heaven and earth or heaven and sea meet each other, is to have the ability to enjoy both bodies without necessarily being either, in the dynamics of the house, the corridor is the one that allows transformation, inspiration and the place of stay, where the meeting is promoted.

The inhabiting implications and the needs to connect with the ecological issues and the challenges that are evident to us in our coexistence with the phenomenon of the covid 19 pandemic and our life in a post-pandemic future.

SELECTED PROJECTS

505KNLFK1

HAB BETWEEN

Ashi Jain
India

Hab-between utilises the barren land, the between spaces of the agriculture land or ploughland. The barren land is a waste land, no agriculture can be done, therefore, the project utilises the space and creates shelter for the farmers and their family between the farms. Isolated sanitised dome home is constructed which helps in maintaining social distancing. All the preventative measures to avoid covid-19 pandemic are taken. The project responds to health, energy, food, production, and environment.

H
A
B ETWEEN
BARREN LAND
NO CULTIVATION
BUILDING FOR BODY

INCORPORATION OF FARMER DOME SHAPED HOUSE ON THE BARREN WASTE LAND.

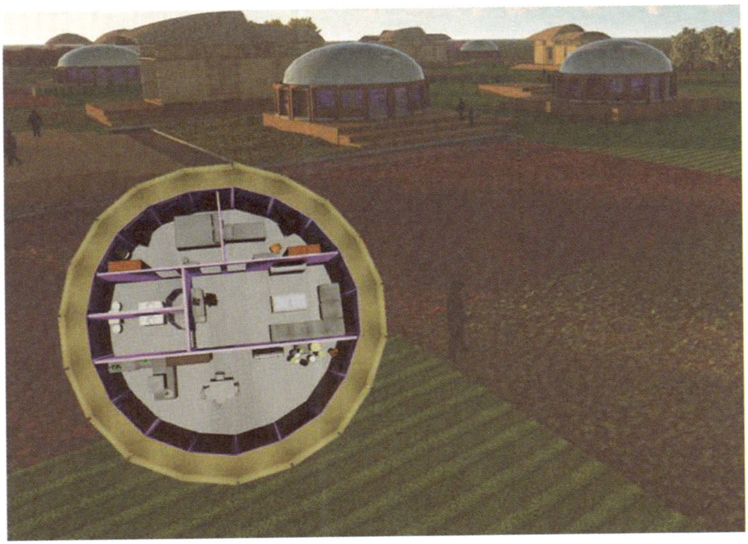

Hab between means habitat between. It refers to the designing of the habitat for the farmers between the Ploughland

505KNLFK1

SELECTED PROJECTS

70000BGCS

WATER CİTE

Brian Lv
China

In the future, people can live in the city on the water. The ball-like city can use the area efficiently and the distance from a point on the ball to another point is shortest. This will promote the communication among people.

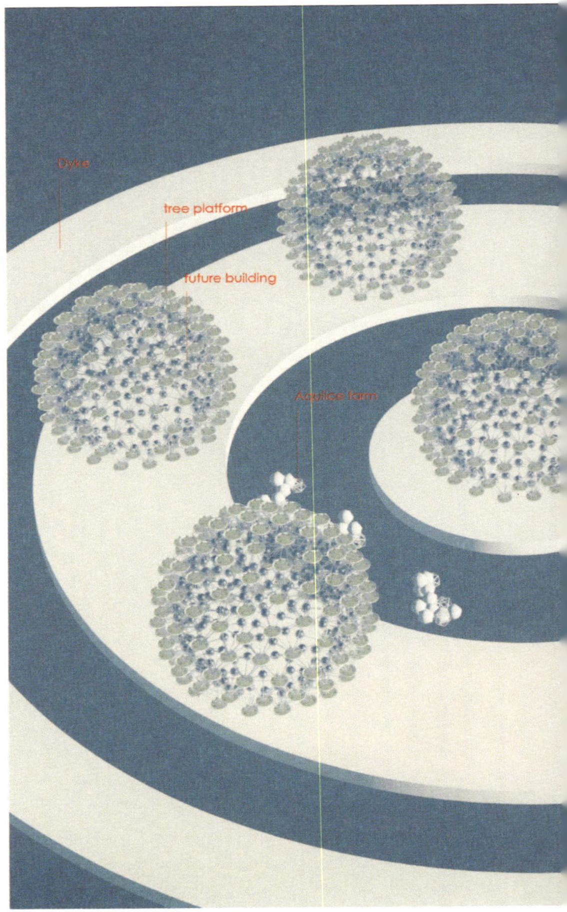

70000

Water city is city of the future

SELECTED PROJECTS

609GD3BTA

SUMMER SHELTER

Seyedeh Ayeh Mirrezaei
Iran

Summer shelter is a wooden structure with opening on the roof due to posit the green roof and solar panels. It includes cooling system and sitting area for people in public spaces of the city. Solar panels generate energy of cooling system, internet and lighting. Indeed, people enjoy sunny days in outdoor spaces even in hot temperature. In addition, Algae shaped sculpture is placed around the site due to act as lighting sources for night time. The glassy bubbles of water which filled with algae plants is the basement of the design. The system is comprised of a network of translucent bubbles which micro-algae flow. Indeed, algae colony consumes carbon dioxide, emits pure oxygen and effectively clean air. In addition, It acts as an energy-generating furniture due to transform CO_2 into light.

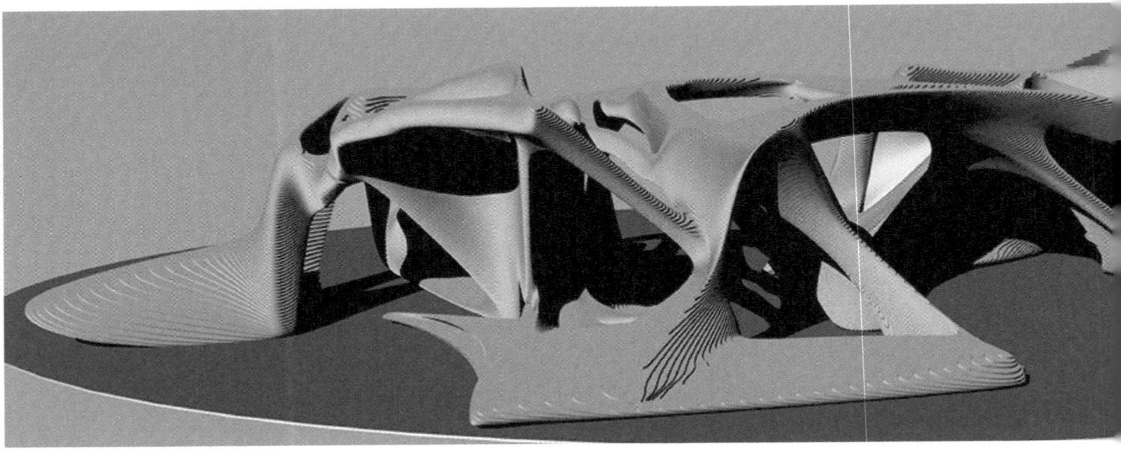

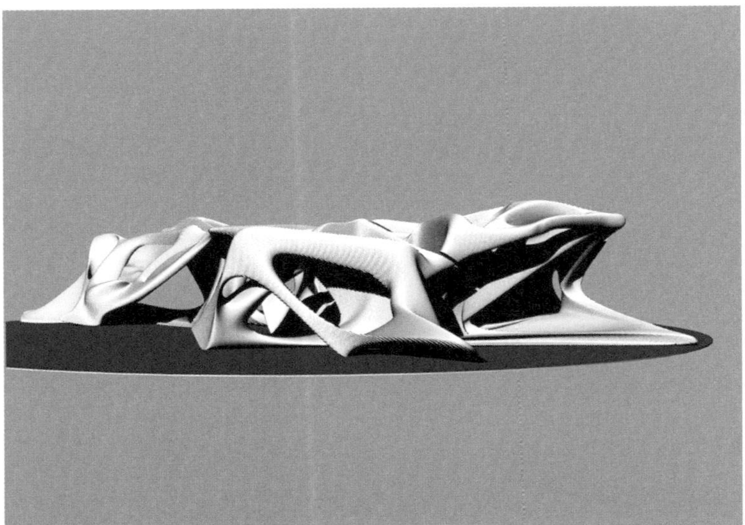

Summer shelter
is a shading concept
for providing a relax
spaces for people

SELECTED PROJECTS 603TJHSLX

NATURALLY HOME

POST COVİD HOME SPACE

Ameni Ayoub
Tunisia

After confinement, many suffered from stress boredom… Many wanted to leave their house, breath, feeling imprisoned suffocating in their own house.Naturally home combines built and natural materials, letting nature in by using indoor and outdoor vegetation, light, sun rays, but also water as water surfaces, ponds below glazing to walk above water and in walls as un water walls. Same thing applies for vegetation by using boxes and compose with them as to become a wall. And in order to overcome boredom many spaces are through to vary the activities such as playing, simulations, do sports, relaxing, reading, studying, working.

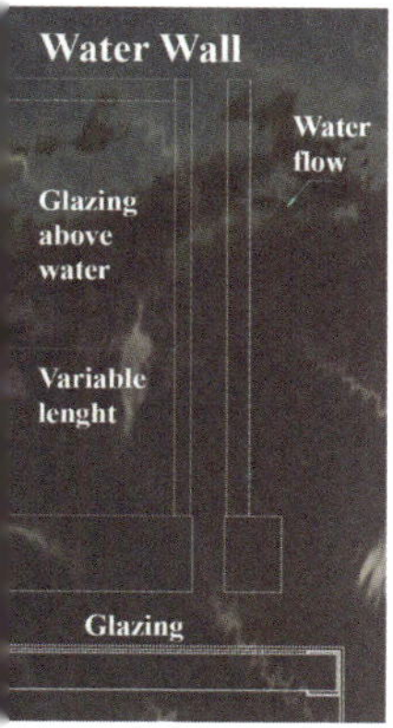

Voids are also used to let the reading, working area and the play and sport area communicaate with the living space participating in creating continous natural ambiance

SELECTED PROJECTS

406LIZM

BREEDİNG EDİBLE SHELTER

Nontawat Jittrong
Thailand

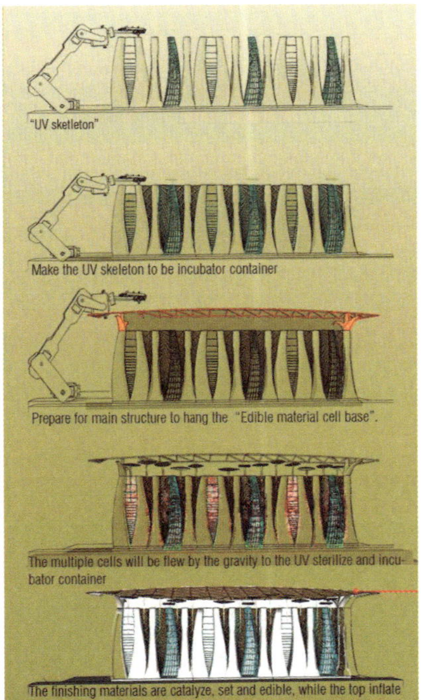

This project proposes the fabrications system that use 3D printing hybrid technology with bioreactor for vitro cell base meat and plant to produce or build the shelter that is stable and edible. There could be an edible-shelter type as a kiosk in a small plot of land or a step wall of staircase in an apartment in urban area. The variable of edible shelter might be connected as an edible shelter remoting community to exchange or share goods. Furthermore, this project could even be developed for breeding edible shelter on Mars.

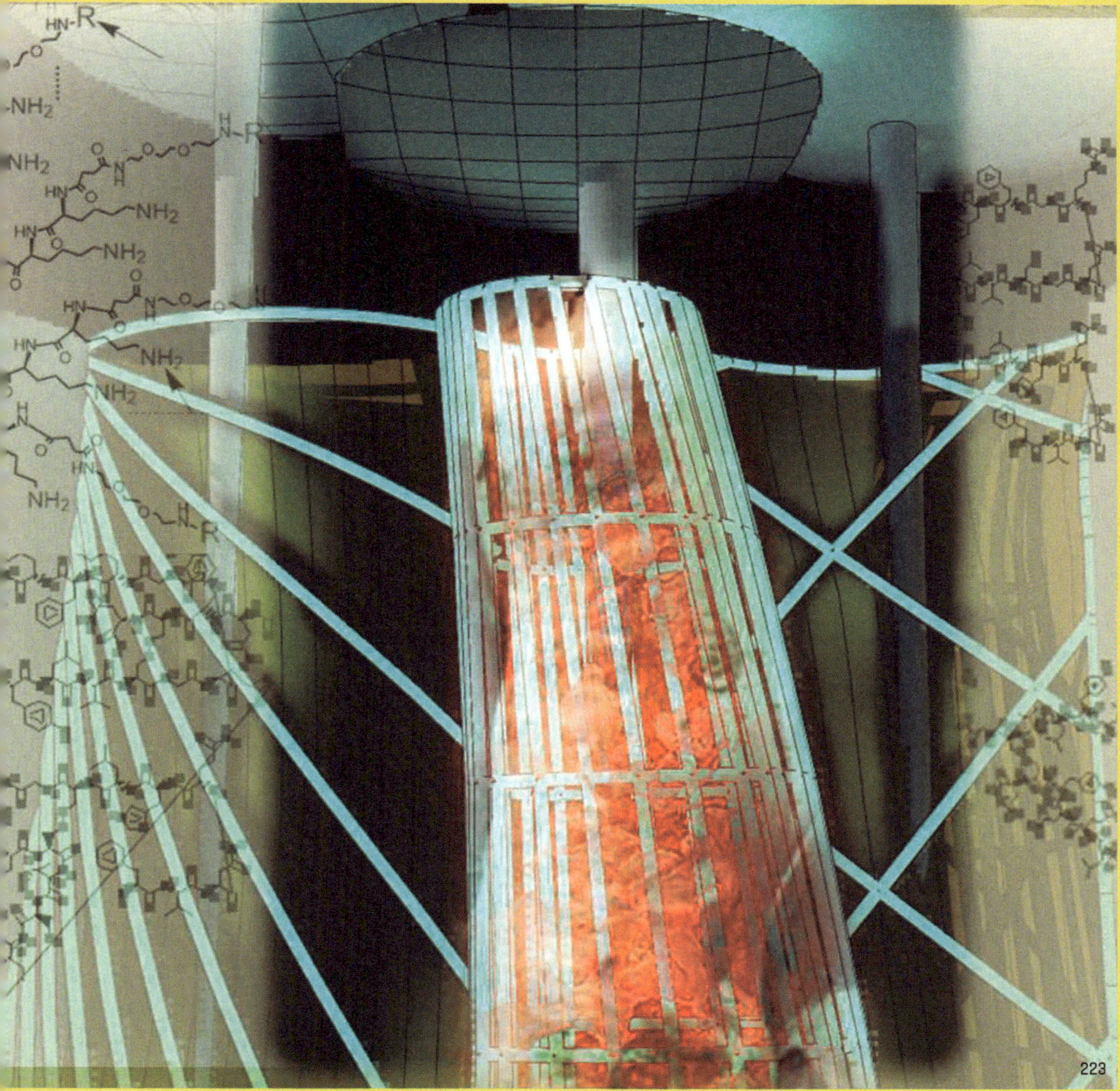

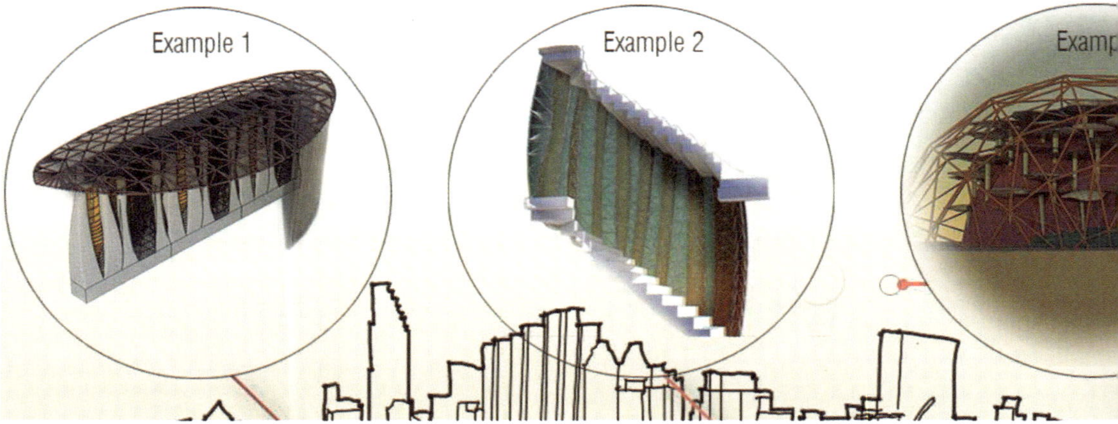

We are not only "construct" the building but also harvest the shelter

405LIZM

SELECTED PROJECTS

6082A6G8P

TRANSiTiONAL SPACES

Broby Leeds
United States of America

My concept was to create an open structure capable of housing transportable residences. Incorporating smaller private spaces, these container-like dwellings best suit the densly populated urban cities. When vacant, the building serves alternative functions and can easily be repurposed on remodeled if necessary. Acting as a traditional home base for recharging, users can relocate their dwellings in response to ever changing demands and desires whether that be climate concerns, disease or other requirements. Each dwelling could be capable of living off the grid for extended periods of time without bearing as permanent of an impact to nature.

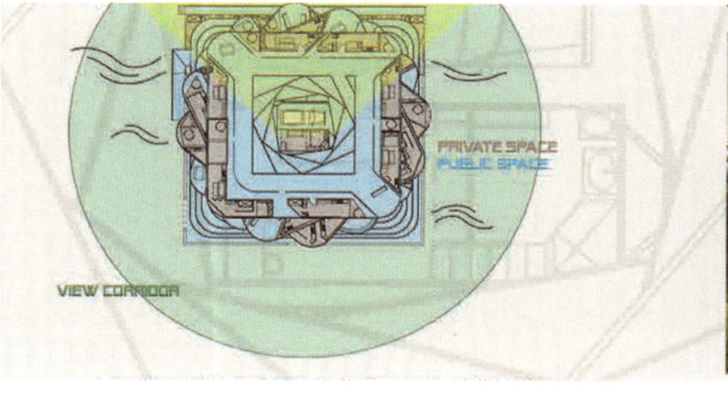
PRIVATE SPACE
PUBLIC SPACE
VIEW CORRIDOR

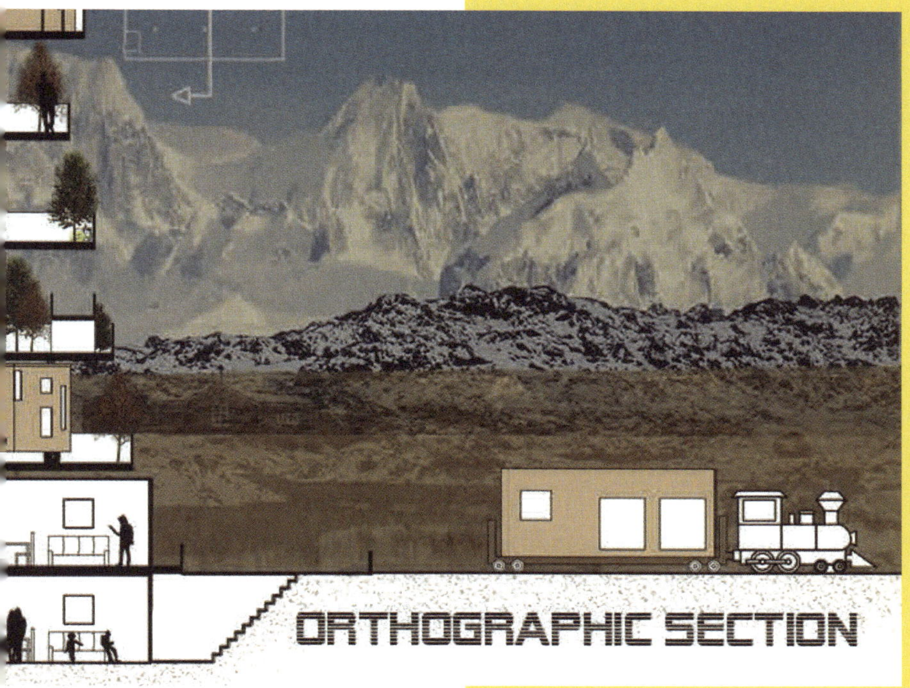

Impermanence is an immediate strategy which will best establish a gateway to any future habitats

SELECTED PROJECTS

611G8BYH3

HEART WALL

Camila de Oliveira
Bernardo Yono
Bruno Aricó
Guto Requena
Isabella Previti
Brazil

Heart Wall is a hybrid of art sculpture, interactive installation and wall light. The elegant wooden shape was modeled with the use of parametric design tools in order to create modern cocoons. Into these concavities, micro LEDs are installed to provide a soft and cozy light effect. Each one of the cocoons will light up and pulse at the rhythm of one person's heart frequency, forming a constellation of heartbeats. And how does it work? A heart rate sensor, installed inside the piece, will collect the person's heartbeat and send it to an app, specially developed for this project. The app will then record this heartbeat and allow you to choose in which of the cocoons you would like to see this person's heart to light up and pulse.

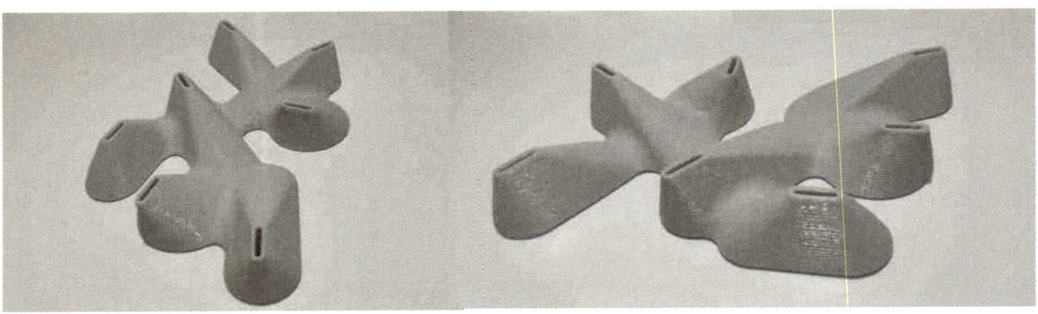

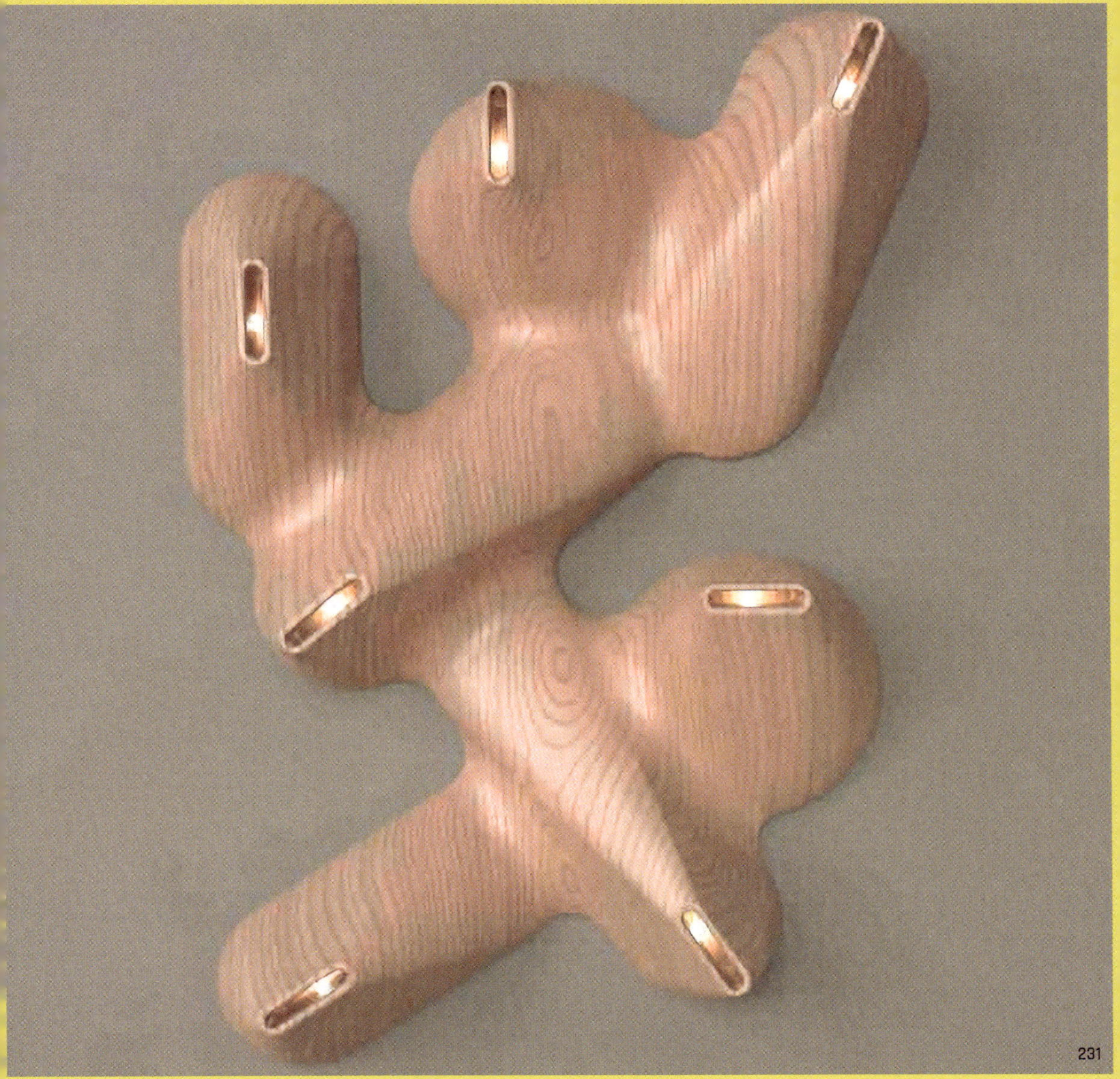

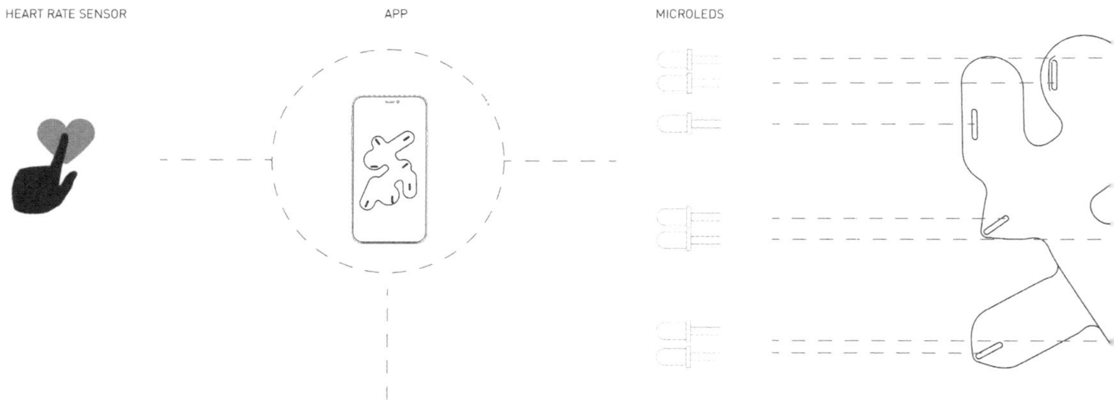

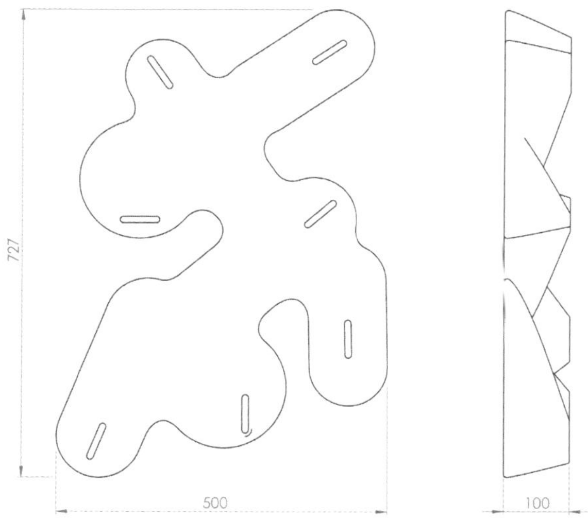

An offshoot of the Estudio Guto Requena's research that seeks to unite affections and technologies in projects investigating the impact of digital culture through design.

611G8BYH3

SELECTED PROJECTS

511MVU4I0

FROM ONE TO COMMUNİTY

Carolina Gualdron
Colombia

The proposal aims a change on the way we live as human beings and as a part of a community, it involves the entire building as a society the person can be related to in case of isolation. it all starts with the house of one person, making a changeable house, a space that can be adapt to your changeable needs, that happens thanks to the foldable multidirectional walls strategically situated inside the house, every unique module also has an exterior place which gives the chance to have an orchard for the human food self-sufficiency. The reproduction of that module plus multipurpose rooms, services, commercial properties and offices wives us the result of the community, a community that can close itself, be connected and be sustainable in a quarantine.

Rainwater collector

Variations

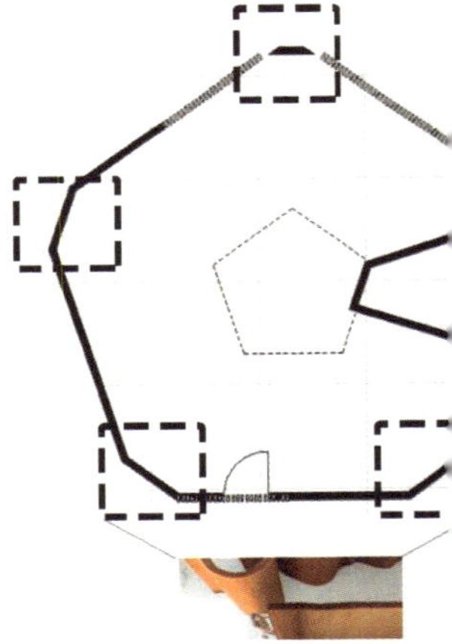

Module

Floor
1 / 3 / 15

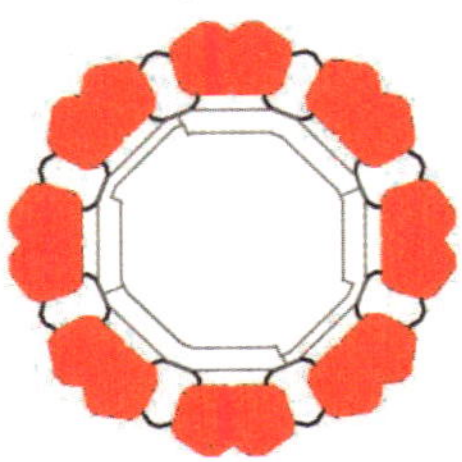

Floor
4 / 12

Floor
2 / 6 / 8 / 10 / 14

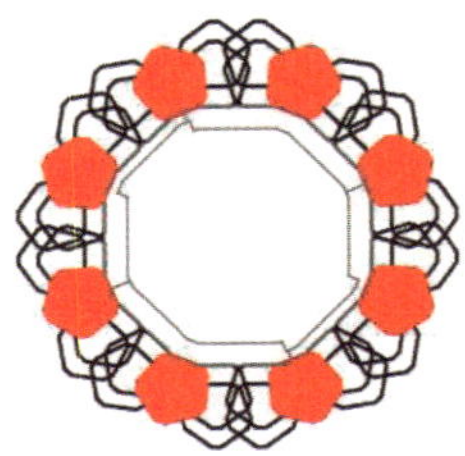

or
/13/15

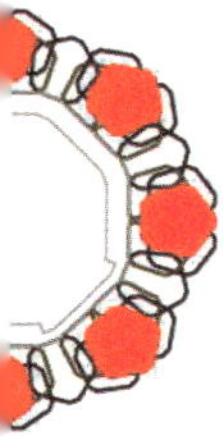

There is another module which it's the result of an union of to modules, this one works for bigger homes and for community spaces

SELECTED PROJECTS

669VUX3DG

PERMANENT QUARANTİNE

Ching-Wen Huang
Taiwan

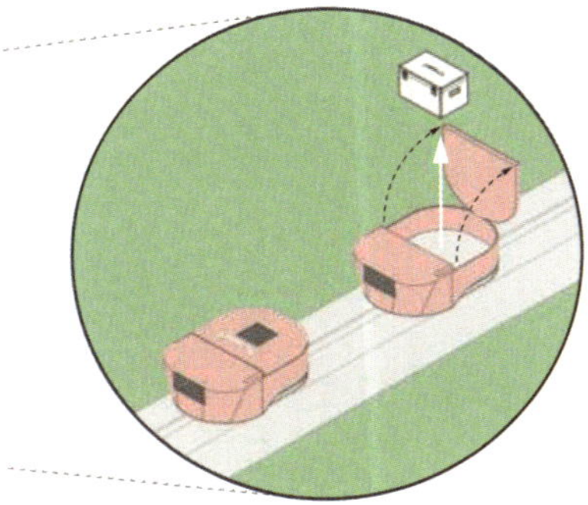

The relationship between the human body and architecture is like architecture to the city. Habitations have become the place where we live, work and, connected to the world, then habitations must practice social distancing as people. Despite being isolated, we still need to engage in social activities that are not through the information networks. Hexagonal grids system, with a side length of 25 meters, can ensure that a single person could link 6 other inhabitants. Based on 6 Degrees of Separation, any two people can connect to each other in a maximum of six intermediaries. Face-to-face interaction plus geographically localized communities, then we have neighborhood relations.

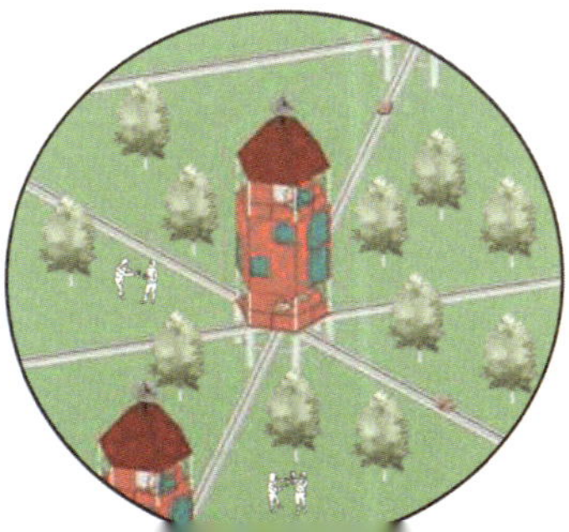

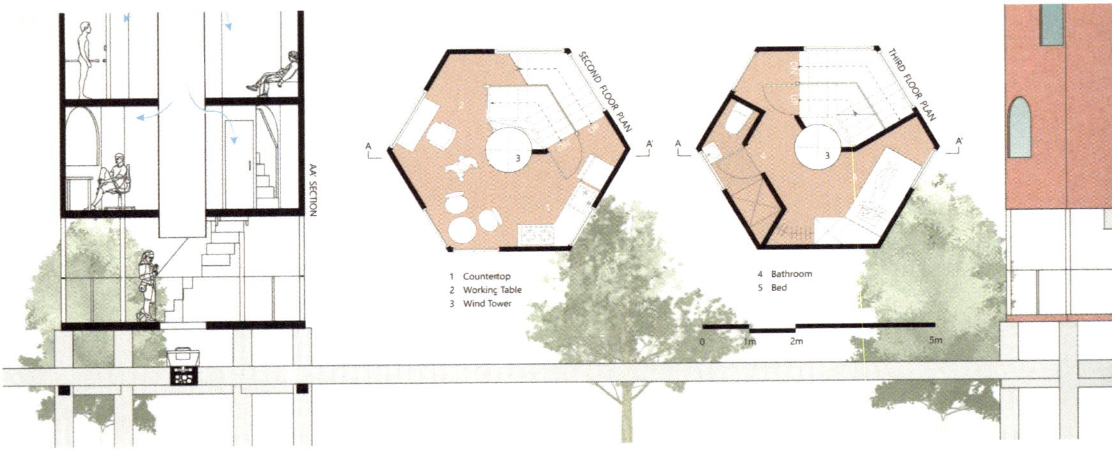

Social Distancing, hexagonal grids and neighborhood

669VUX3DG

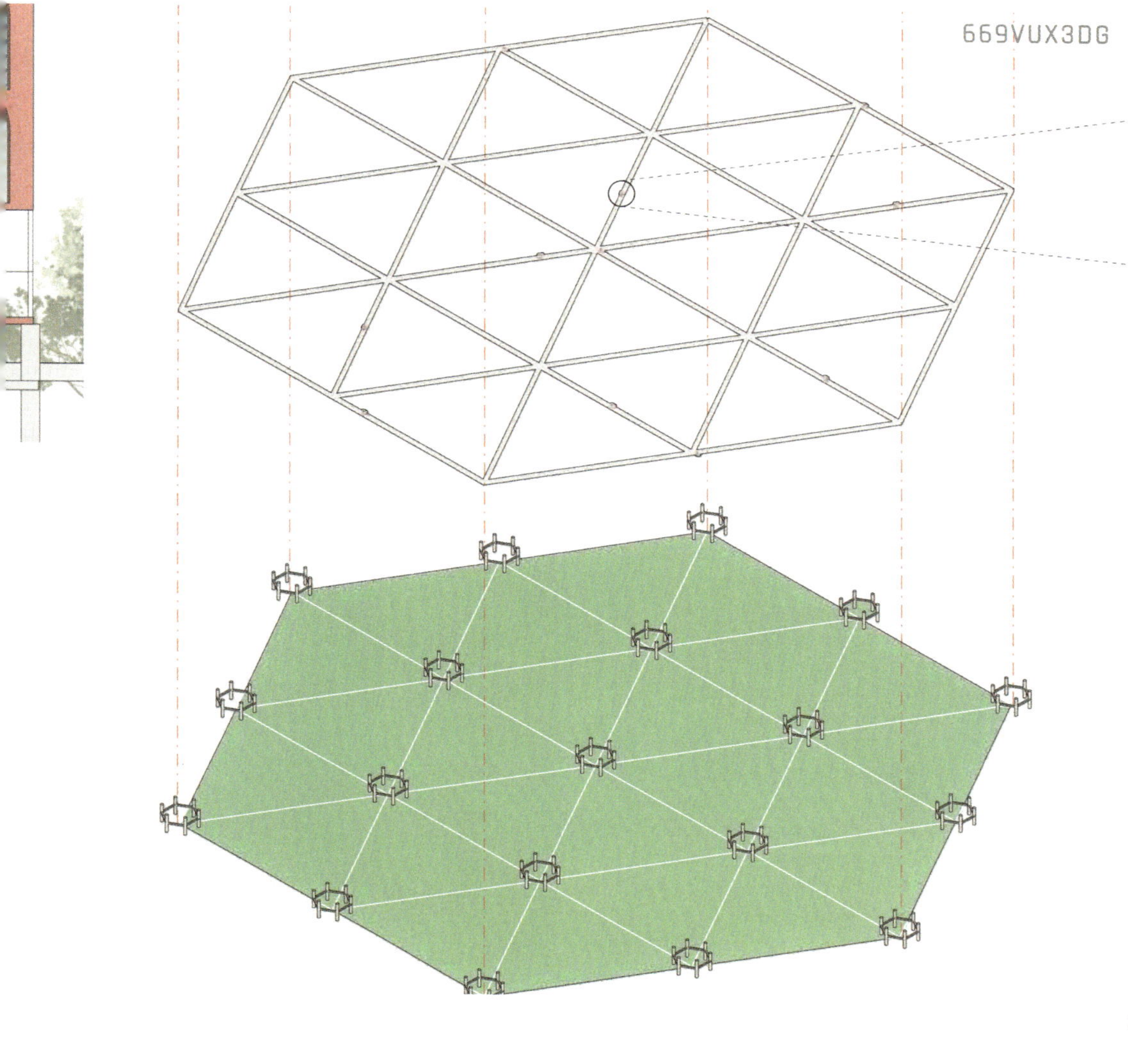

SELECTED PROJECTS

1037LFPN5

NEİGHBOR HOME

SAFELY CONNECTED COMMUNİTY

Ahmed Yassine Choubani
Morocco

The intention is to create micro-communities inside a community unit that could be multiplied to create a city. Located in the heart of the unit, the public and shared services provide a social link to all the inhabitants and encourages the social interaction. The nature infiltration is meant to resolve the growing fracture between the rural and urban spaces and to reduce stress. The three controlled entrances in each unit make it possible to generate an immunity against any unwanted biological invasion. As well as being energetically self-sufficient, there zero waste units provides an eco-responsible community with bio-engineered and innovative ecological means.

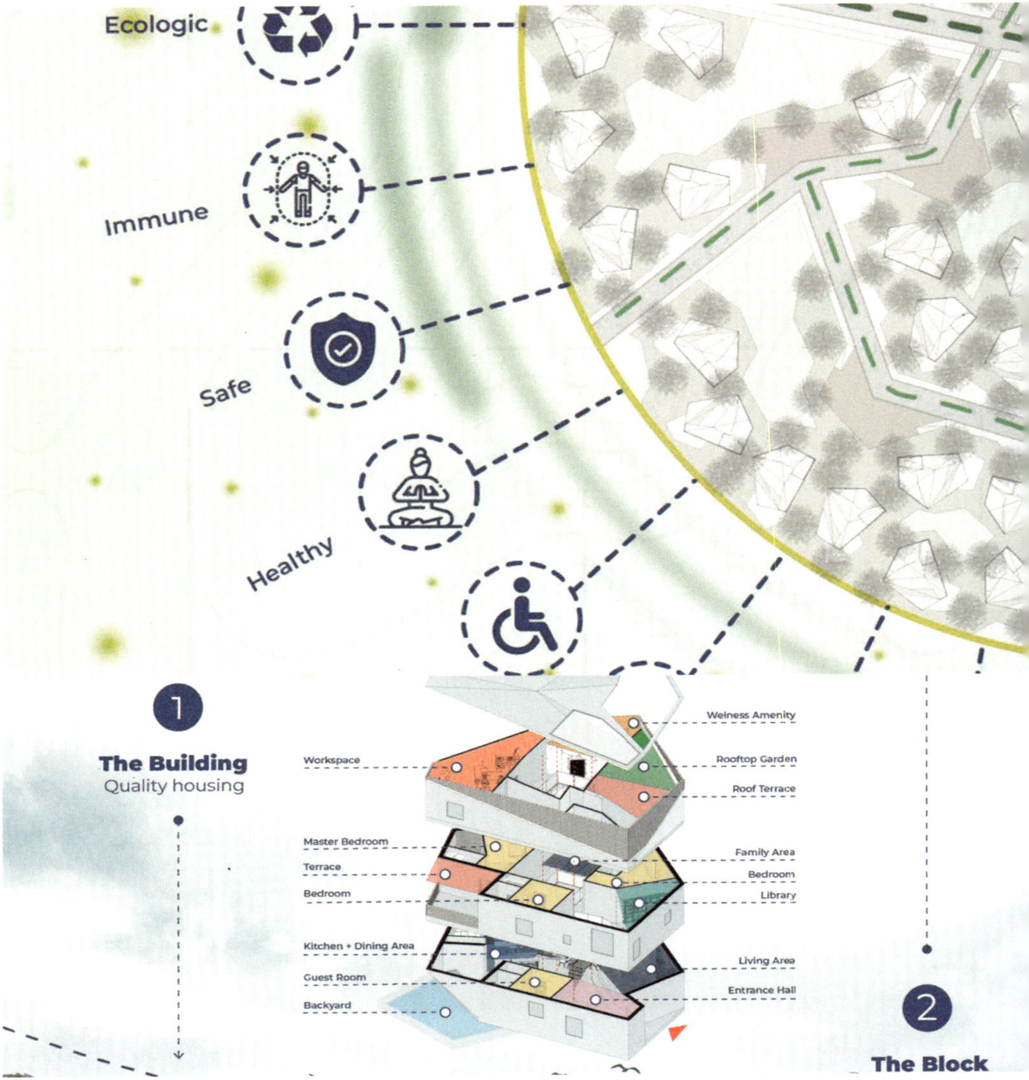

Ecologic
Immune
Safe
Healthy
1
The Building
Quality housing
Welness Amenity
Workspace
Rooftop Garden
Roof Terrace
Master Bedroom
Family Area
Terrace
Bedroom
Bedroom
Library
Kitchen + Dining Area
Living Area
Guest Room
Entrance Hall
Backyard
2
The Block

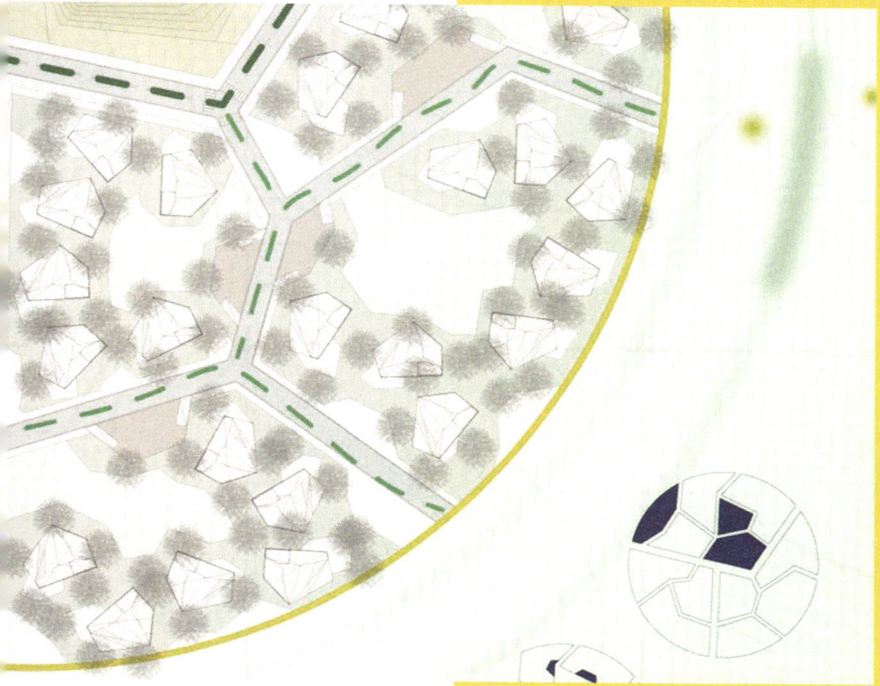

Micro-communities inside a community unit that could be multiplied to create a city

SELECTED PROJECTS

696BUU811

LİVİNG RECYCLED

OCEAN RESTURATİON PROJECT

Cole Brockhoff
United States of America

Before humans started to escelate the amounts of trash and toxic gases, the ocean was the biggest natural cleansing resource we had. Many different kinds of underwater ecosystems were able to break down chemicals and gases that were then produced into clean oxygen and food. With growing populations leading to more waste, the ocean can't naturally keep up. My proposal of recycling the discarted plastic in the ocean to create floating communities will help clean what the ocean can't while creating more underwater ecosystems to help cleanse the water even further.

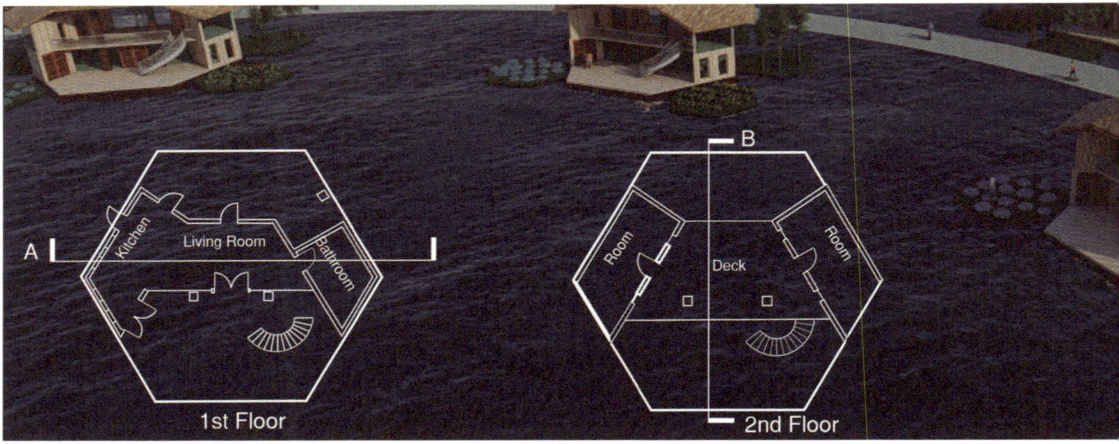

The houses in the community are constructed of recycled plastic bricks which are strong enough to hold two story homes. The bamboo adds easthetic and structural support

696BUU811

SELECTED PROJECTS

160DY9W58

ADAPTATİVE SPİDER WEB

WATER-ENERGY HARVESTİNG SYSTEM

Danny Vallejo
Alejandra Loaiza
Ecuador

In the year 2050 at Ecuador's capital city, with high levels of accumulated emissions of greenhouse gases in the atmosphere, the greatest threat is intensive periods of drought and when it rains it tends to be more extreme causing flooding as a consequence of global warming.

In the equatorial region there is a greater intensity of radiation which will have an increase ue to two determining factors of the city, such as the city's height of near 3,000 AMSL. The consequence is an increase in the incidence of cancer of skin. The economic crisis will be accentuated by continuous due to the already political crisis.

SELECTED PROJECTS

34410LFME

EQUALLiWELL

Nicholai Go
Philippines

Due to the ever changing demands and needs of healthcare, EMU's are designed to aggregate in many forms including on EMU District Hospital. This is especially needed during the interim time between immediate response and recovery during a natural disaster. The EMU's can start as an emergency pop up and slowly grow to become an EMU District Hospital depending on the demand. The EqualliWell Healthcare system has the unique ability to connect all health assets using the Equaliwell Mobile units (EMUs) as conduits. This is possible due to the equaliwell Docking system which simply attaches to any existing healthcare facility.

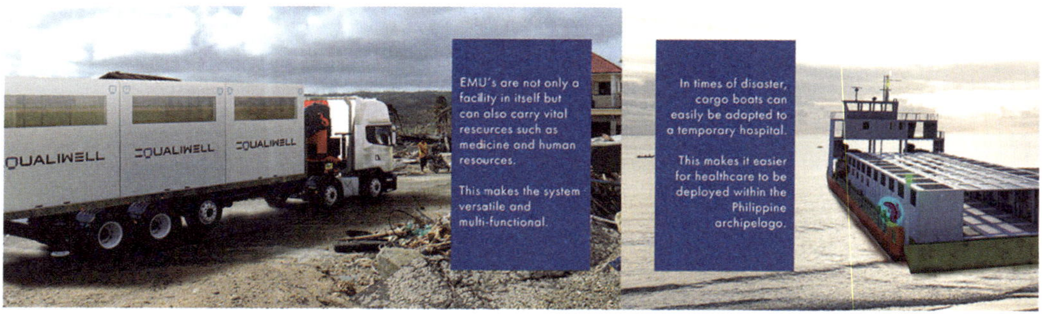

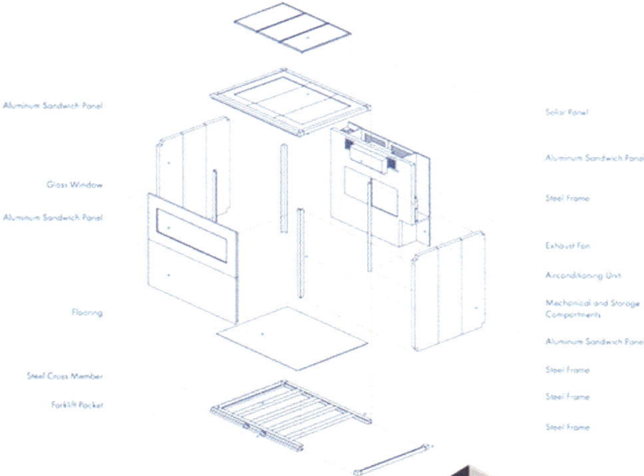

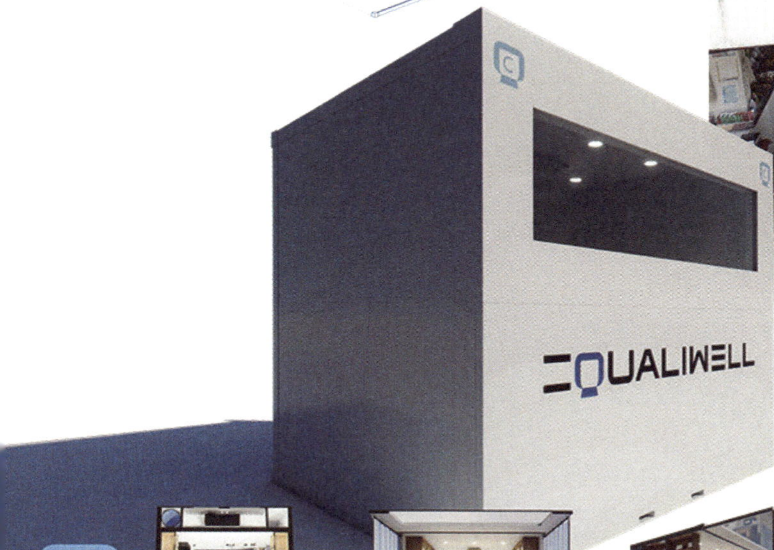

Clincal Room Module

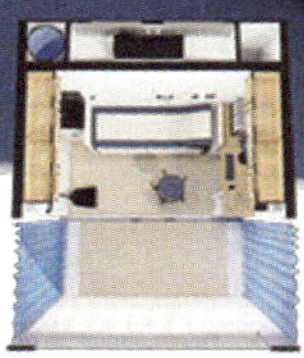

Floorplan

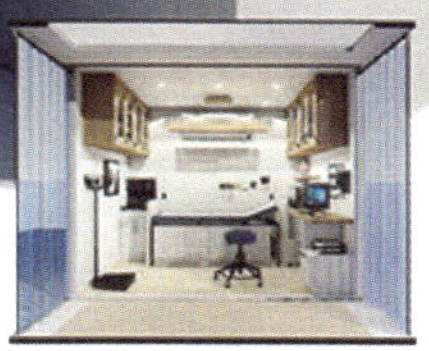

Elevation

Section Perspective

Radiology Module

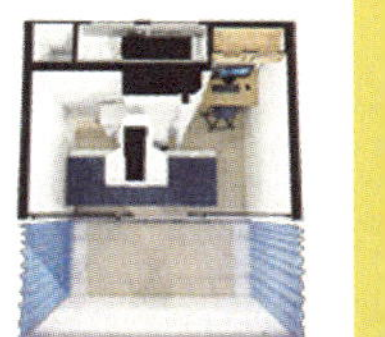

Floorplan

EQUALIWELL SYSTEM

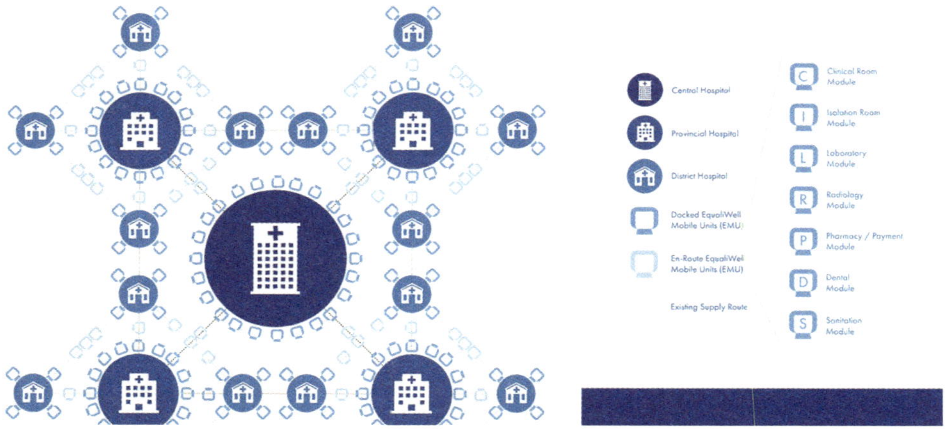

SCENARIO: NATURAL DISASTER

SCENARIO: DISEASE OUTBREAK

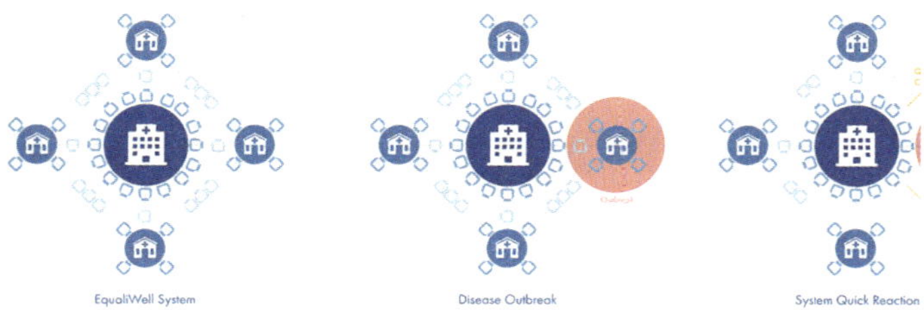

Our revolutionary healthcare system. Equitable quality wellness for all

34410LFME

EMU AGGREGATION TYPE 2:

EMERGENCY POP UP

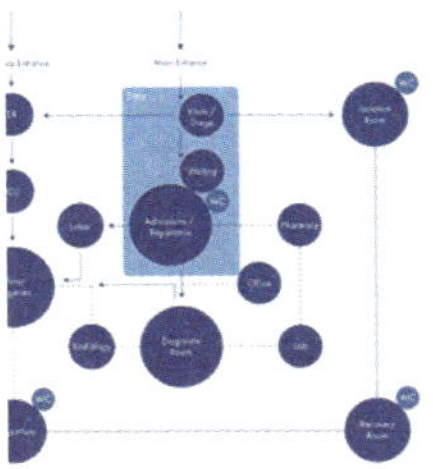

Due to the ever changing demands and needs of healthcare, EMU's are designed to aggregate in many forms including an EMU District Hospital. This is especially needed during the interim time between immediate response and recovery during a natural disaster. The EMU's can start of as an Emergency Pop Up and slowly grow to become an EMU District Hospital depending on the demand.

SELECTED PROJECTS

639BRTLN3

BREATHİNG TOWER

Diana Mingazova
Russian Federation

Shanghai is a big city in China, which faces huge problems with air and water quality. The huangpu is Shanghai's Mother River, connecting the East China Sea and the Taihu Lake. Unfortunately, this River is polluted. So it can't be used by citizens neither like a source of water, North like a place for swimming/rest. And damages heavily the taihu lake. Purification of Huangpu can help the whole region with getting water with better quality. The second huge problem is the Asian dust annual Meteorological phenomena. It comes from the northwest. During this period Citizens have to wear masks or to not to go outside.

Aeroponics and hydroponics installations

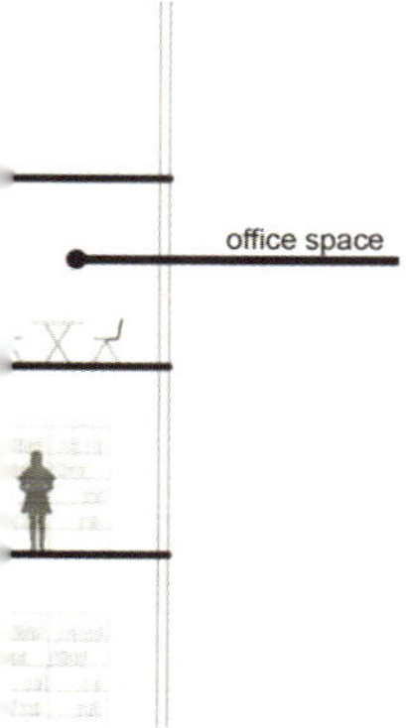

This proporsal allows us to decrease environmental impact and to improve worker's life

SELECTED PROJECTS

53220YEZO

CYBERMEDİNAL URBANİSM

Abderrahmane El Kendi
Denmark

This project aims to answer the two major questions in the world of architecture at the moment: COVID19 and climate change. The project investigates the potential of creating a dual layer city: the upper one, a cybermedinal city, made for heat requiring acitivities like agriculture, generating energy and transportation. And the lower one, an oasis in the desert, where greenery grows thanks to the shade provided by the upper city, hence creating a cool and warm dual city, with each one of them having an independent role, while interacting with each other for transport of goods and people through gigantic urban columns.

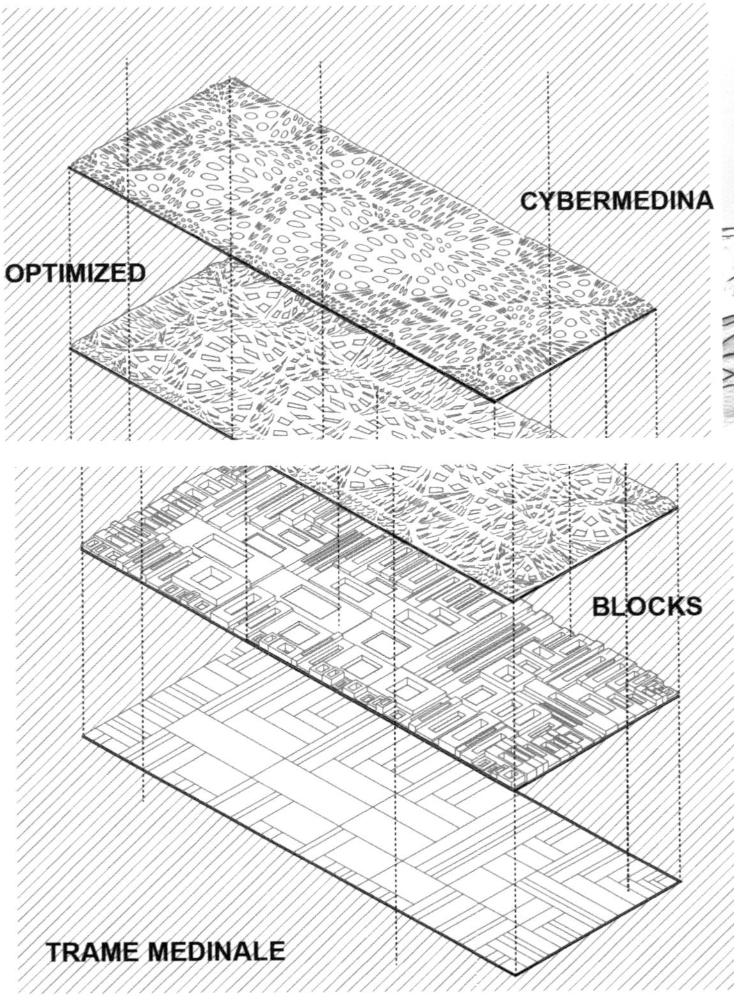

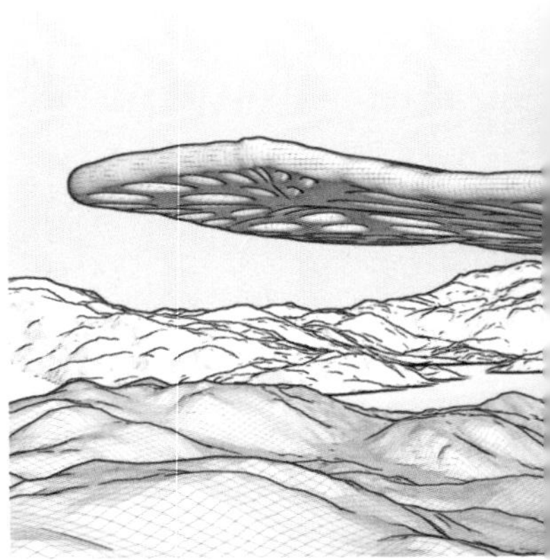

Temperature simulations ▶

53220YEZO

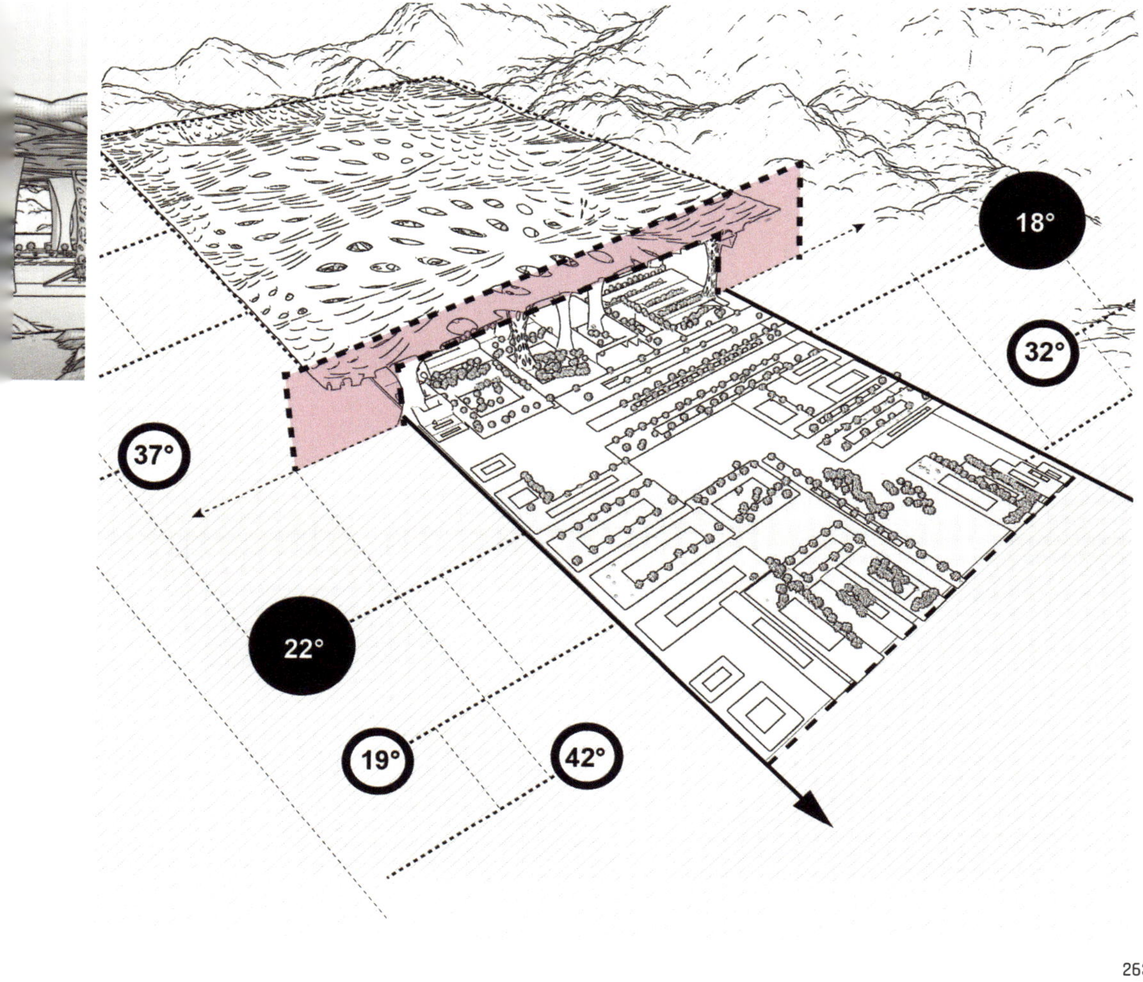

SELECTED PROJECTS

67310PC02

THE ALLOY

Fady Thoma
Ahmed Mohammed
Egypt

Stuttgart is becoming more international, especially in the past decade. The site lacked the connection between the neighbourhood and the city, as well as the people, together This is done by continuing a path that starts from the Hauptbahnhof, to the StadtBibliothek being the first destination, and then onto our building, being the second destination, by using the same morphology of the library and experiencing a different function, which is inspired by the idea of Urban Acupuncture. The main concept of this proposal is Living + Culture, where people from different religions, nationalities and races come together. There they can connect to various cultural music, arts & backgrounds. In our building, we vertically transform the public into the private, and the private into the public, where we have the idea of the public decreasing as we go up, thus transparency to opacity.

FORM
CIRCULATION
TRANSPARENCY
FINAL MASS

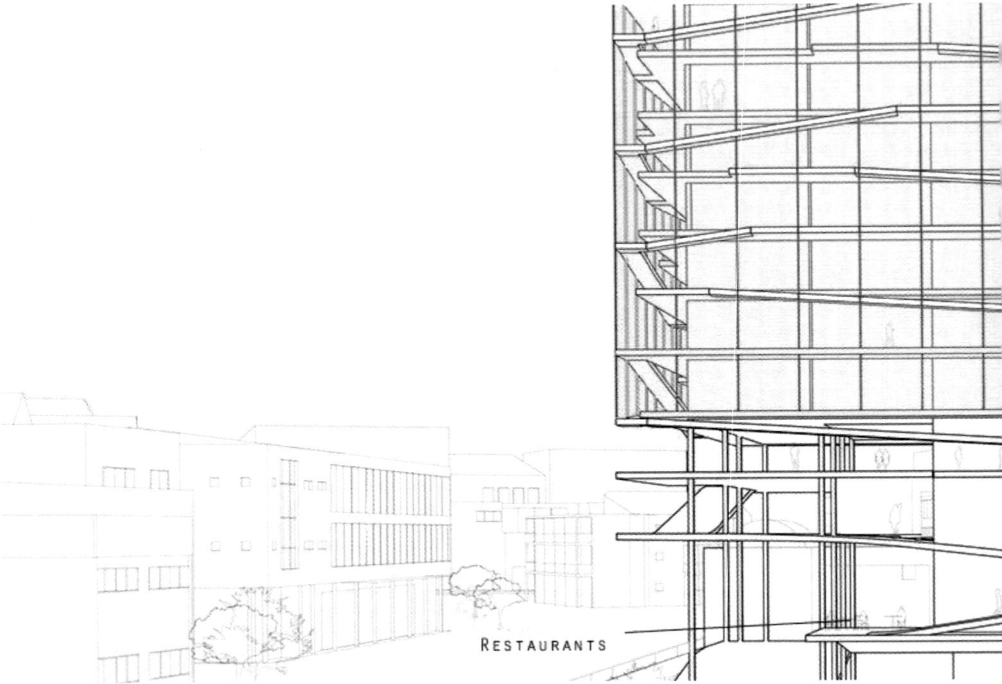
RESTAURANTS

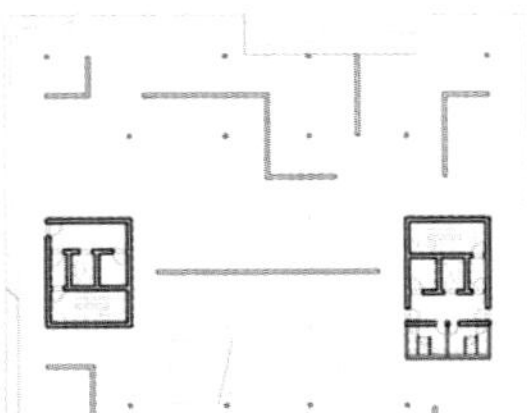

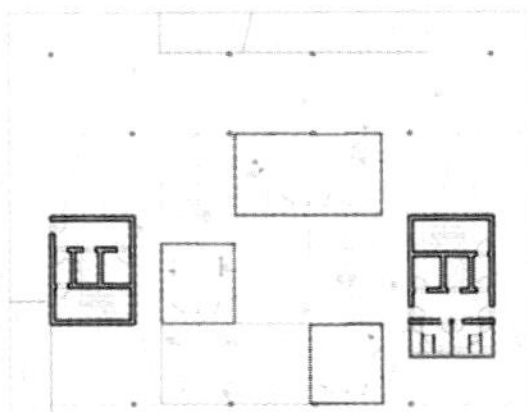
FIRST FP / MUSIC ROOMS

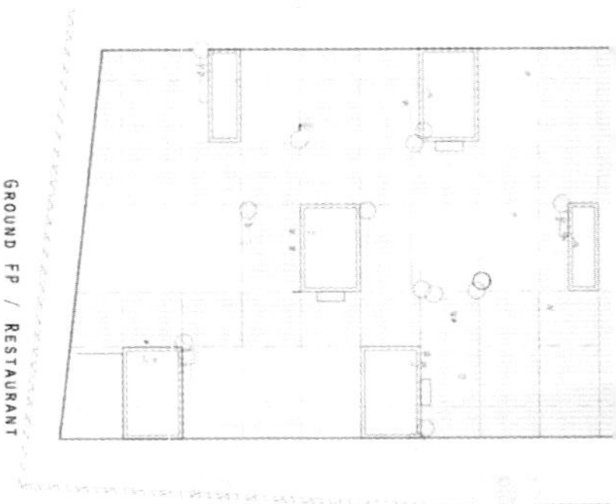
GROUND FP / RESTAURANT

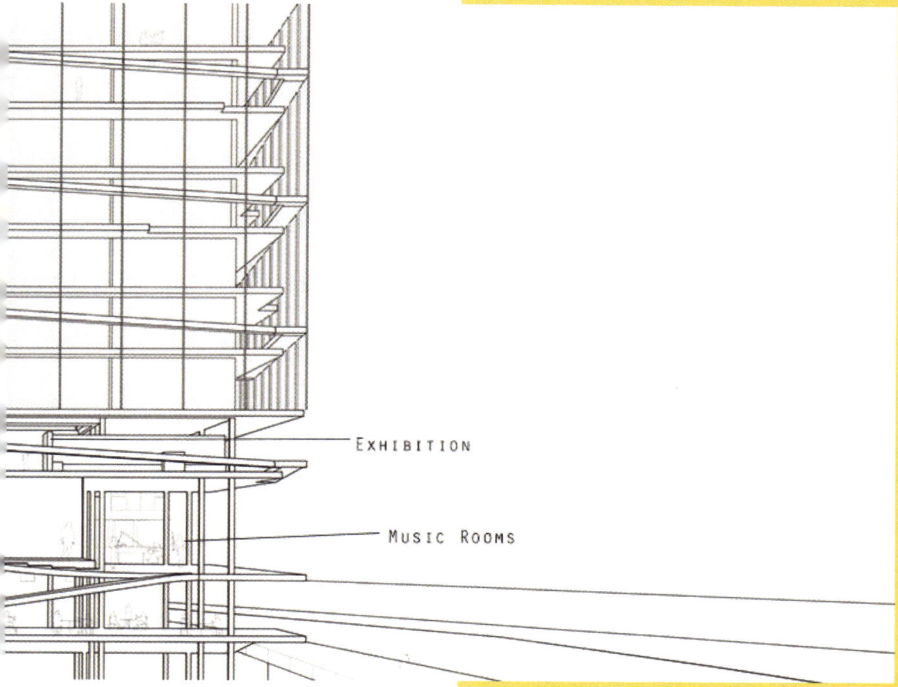

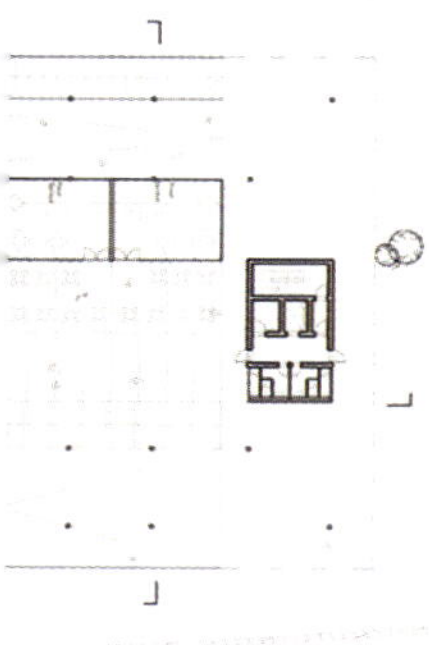

The residential units increase in size as we go up and the public communal spaces decrease in size. All the residential units have intermiate zones that interacts with the public communal spaces

SELECTED PROJECTS

395RGBCOR

BALANCED ERA

Egit Fandikson
Indonesia

Learn from the Dayak tribal life system human habitat must live in peace with nature and make it part of technological developments in the coming decades. Living in peace with nature = returning to an ancient life. Where the condition of the earth is much better at that time. Then the peace of society is very dependent on the mind and the mind is very dependent on what is felt and inhaled and seen. Based on that, the main emphasis on design is to create an atmosphere that indulges the census making the tech technology system as a new human eye and seeing invisible objects. Changing the system of routine activities (education and economics) and new clothing standards on humans.

PONTIANAK CITY
2020
male : 277.971 (50.1%)
female : 276.793 (49.9%)

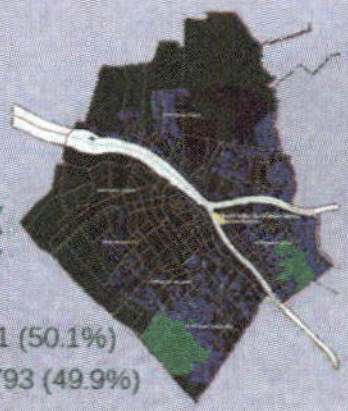

DE SIGN PRIN- CIPLE

CULTURAL	HEALTH-SENSE	SYNERGY-TECH	NATURE
make new routine additions	health protocol development.	with government and society	marry naturally and artificially

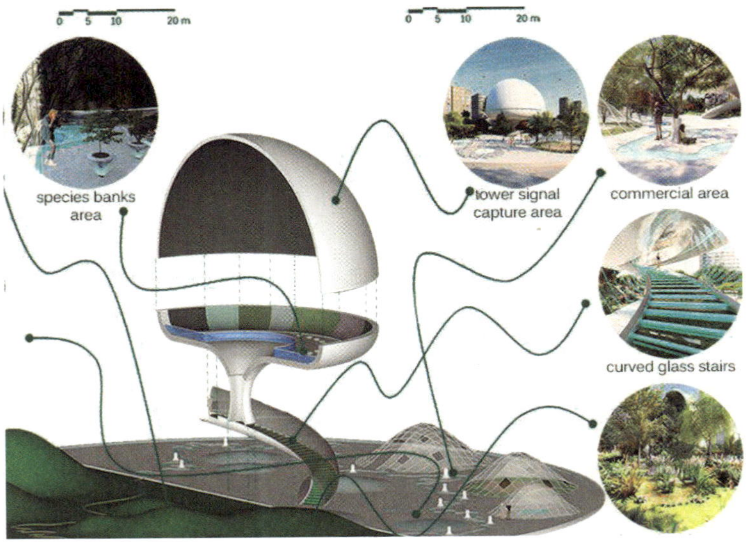

Design guidelines ▶

NEW NORMAL CITY FACILITIES
THE NEW NORMAL HUMAN LOOK
THE NEW NORMAL GOVERNANCE SYSTEM
395RGBCOR
Species Banks + Virus Detection
Slim Ambulance
Nose Mask
New Normal Activity Routine System - Lastual
New Normal Transaction System - Self savings
CULTURAL
not eliminate cultural expression
study the environment of the Dayaks
new culture by utilizing technology
HEALTH
become a standard attribute in humans.
improve the new health facility system
protection by a healthy environment
SYNERGY - TECHNOLOGY
create a new government constitution
orientation on smart - info and interaction
technology integrated with nature
NATURE
protect and develop human habitat
become a world leader before technology
nature integrated with technology

SELECTED PROJECTS

348MVRVXS

PROJECT BARRIO ARRIBA

Jose Francisco Flores
Mexico
Today, we must regenerate, re-think, re-use and re-do the way we live, work, move, eat and Connect using an ecosystem of innovation wear Concepts like technological democratization, collaboration and networking, design thinking, distributed design and systems that makes systems are applied on an urban locally-produced and globally connected a structure to promote circular, creative, human, healthy and ethical cities. The Barrio Arriba project its proposed to build in the city of Leon Mexico in the old industrial area known as Barrio Arriba and to face current challenges of poverty, violence and abundant territory with a functional Urban structure that provides tools, living and working spaces, educational resources, data, food and technology in a 101^{m2}.

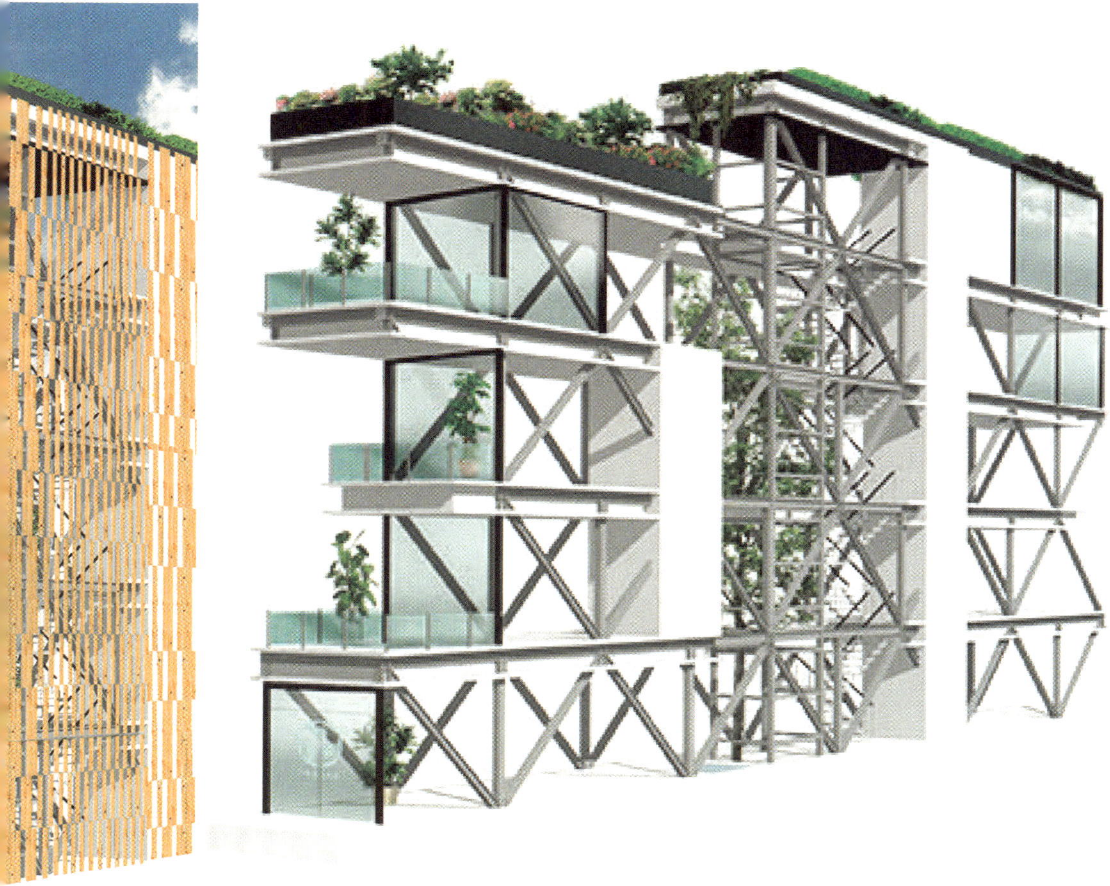

RE-THINK

Optimizing abandoned or challenging spaces is a way to avoid **unnecessary extraction and save (economical and material) resources** using creativity and considering all possibilities to improve every single m2. This is also an invitation to re think our consumption habits and re create our living spaces.

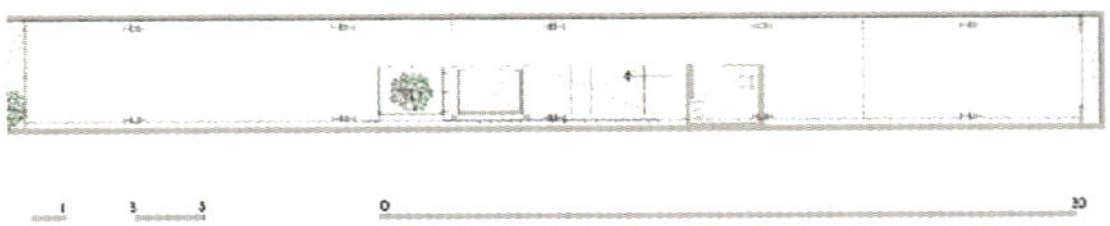

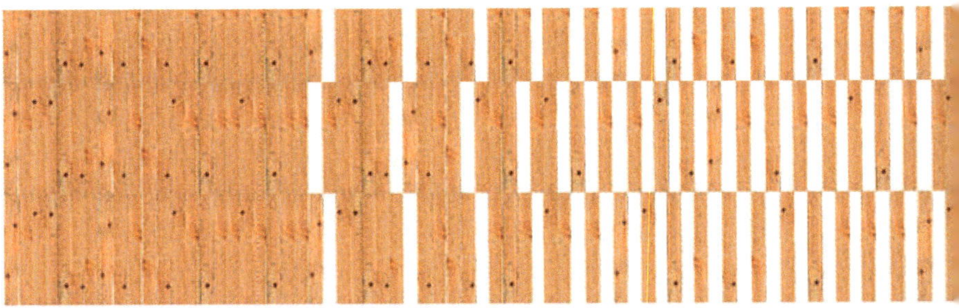

← Breathable Pallet Texture

Breathable Pallet Texture

RE-DO

On the ground floor it is proposed to set a **Fab Lab**, which is an important piece in the ecosystem of innovation because of the material transformation, idea prototyping and to be use by the people to obtain knowledge about fabrication through the "learn by doing" process.

This can help us to become a more circular society by giving the opportunity to everyone to test their ideas, therefore innovate our (linear / centered) fabrication systems.

We all have many questions and fears about the future, and there is one simple and poethic truth, also an invitation to awareness that motivates me: you build your future today

SELECTED PROJECTS

6634A7XMC

BUTTERFLY SAVE LİVES

Ferlein Molina Aley
Colombia

The concept of housing for future cities is metamorphosis, adaptable and versatile spaces capable of analyzing the environment and changing shape, responding to emergencies caused by environmental catastrophes or diseases. The prototype has spaces for agriculture, and drinking water reserves in case of drought, likewise the dimensions can vary according to the needs of its inhabitants, it can have a maximum of 3 floors.

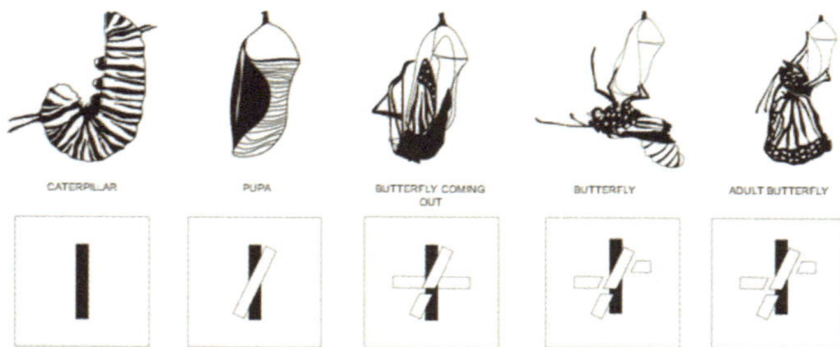

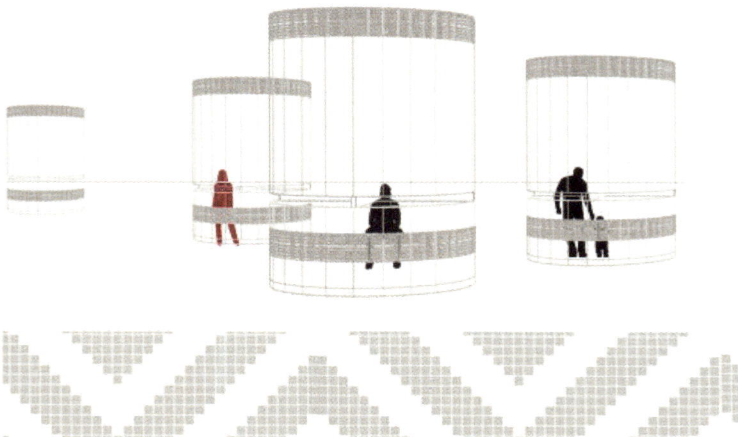

◀ **Home suitable for insulation**

PROTOTYPE EMERGENCY

HOUSING IN THE COVID 19 PANDEMIC

One of the biggest problems for Colombia has been social distancing and maintaining quarantine, but this has not been met since people must go out to work in order to buy their food.

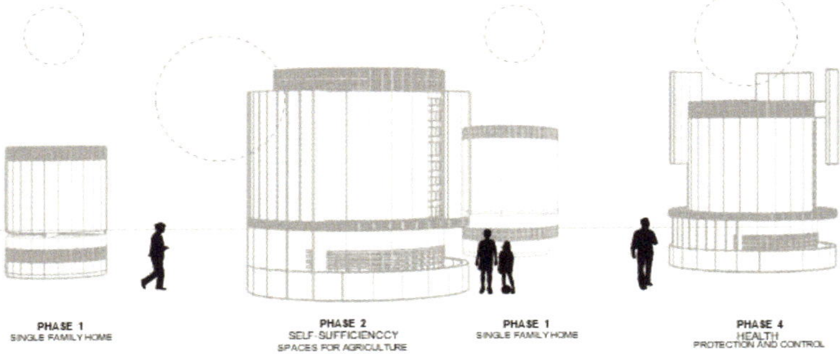

SELECTED PROJECTS

710H6M3RU

MANSORY FLOWER

Graziela Nivoloni
OcupaLAB
Brazil

The brasilian city São Paulo has a lot of cooperative buildings unoccupied at the same time people who work on the streets with informal or manual labor such as garis, popcorn vending car man and many other people who live in the suburbs, spend from 3 to 6 hours going to work in the city center close to where these skeleton cooperative buildings are located. the coronavirus pandemic made most corporatives companies adapt themselves to home office and they are motivated to keep this format or migrate to an hybrid model, making the vacancy rate of these huge buildings raise.

Mauá

The attacheble cardboard space dividers allows people to do choose what to do with the space

SELECTED PROJECTS

2933GD5P3

GREEN MOVEMENT

Gabriel Soto Farfa
Peru

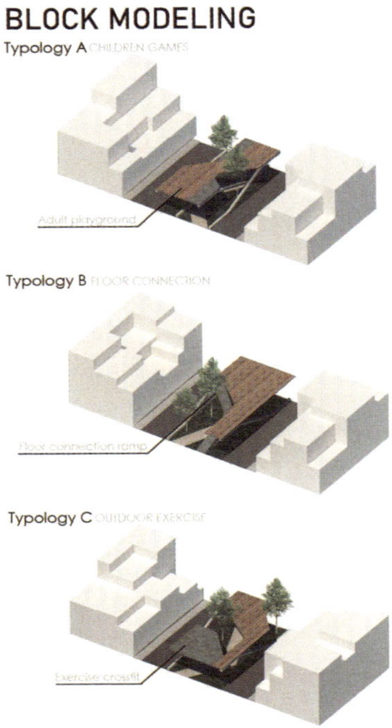

These days we saw how the planet earth stopped being polluted for 4 months. The planet Earth gave a great break but now that everything's back to normal the planets will be polluted again mainly by all the Co2 that a human being produces. In the city of Lima, despite its extensive Solid Waste Management, there are still places where all this accumulates, generating a negative impact. The World Health Organization recommends that DCR does social distance daily in the activities that people generate and one of the best ways to content discs challenge is to increase the green areas in large and small cities.

◀ **Lima, Peru**

SELECTED PROJECTS

3723KW5QS

RE-MOD

Giovanni Caci
Italy

How many times walking through our cities we see an empty facade of a building, or a facade hundreds of meters long with small and narrow windows, how many times we happen to stop in front of a wall and think "This place could really use some nice mural, because it is really ugly!" It's time to say STOP, enough of this thought, it's time for RE-MOD, a module, a basic structure that still fits into the existing building and that resurfaces it. A very simple structure that can take on an infinite number of forms and functions: those investigated in this project are a small part of the infinite world that can be investigated and the great potential that this simple object has.This is just an IDEA, not a project, but like many other great ideas can change the world.

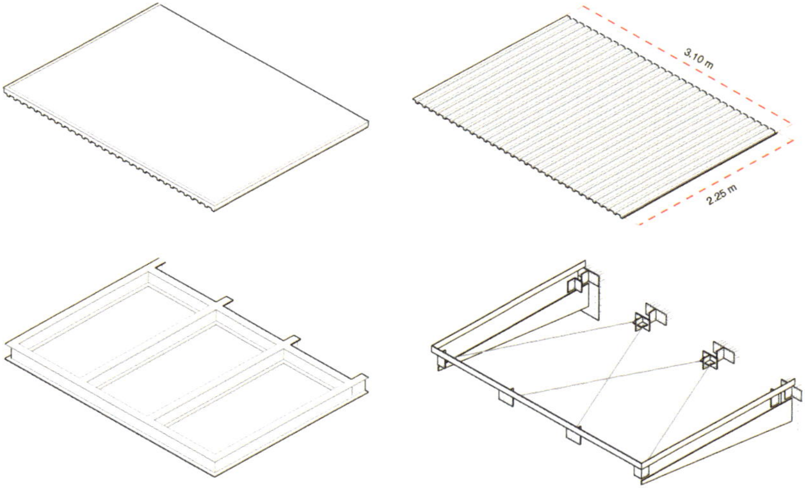
3,10 m
2,25 m

Section AA'

SELECTED PROJECTS 476VAWGRK

REVEIL

Hanaan Llewellyn
United States of America

ADDRESSING RIGHTS OF MINORITY CULTURES AND RELIGIOUS COMMUNITIES IN AMERICAN HIGHRISE APARTMENTS

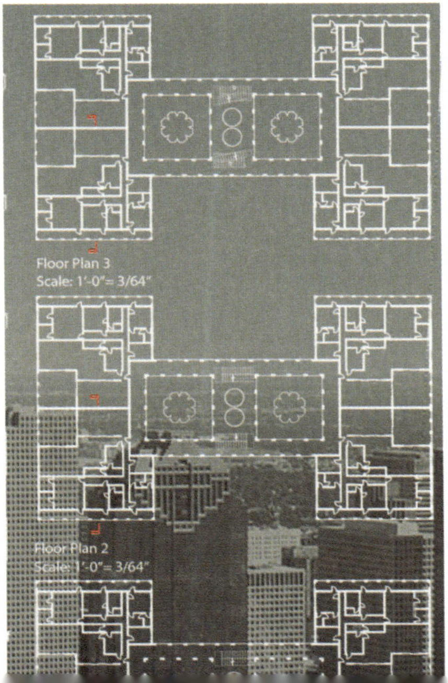

This trending apartment design unintentionally gentrified cultural and religious values off Menorah tree communities in the US, and global communities around the world. It's ingrains in the minds of non-western folk set the arrivals in relation to design are inferior do the volumes of the modern West. Despite the recent pandemic, creating dense urban living spaces is still the preferred mode for the future. The challenge is to make these spaces more lively, culturally appropriate and natural.

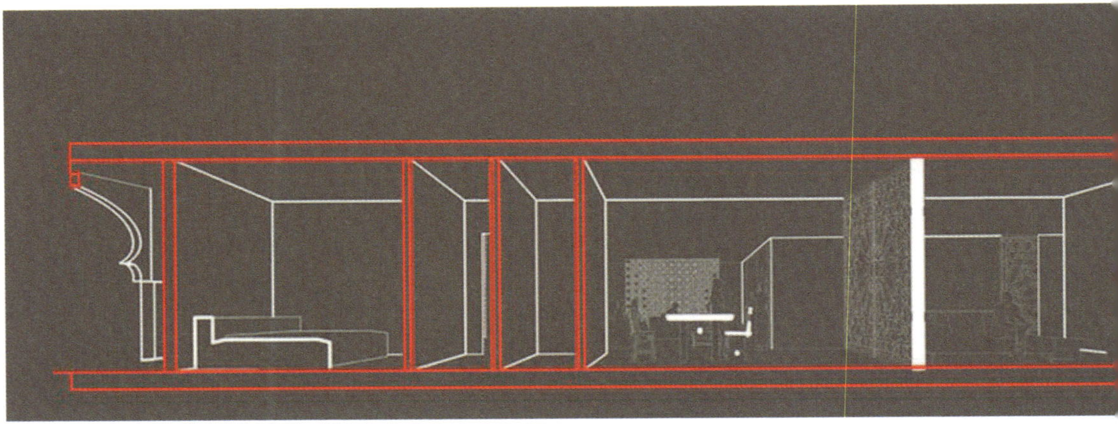

Isolated section cut of and apartment

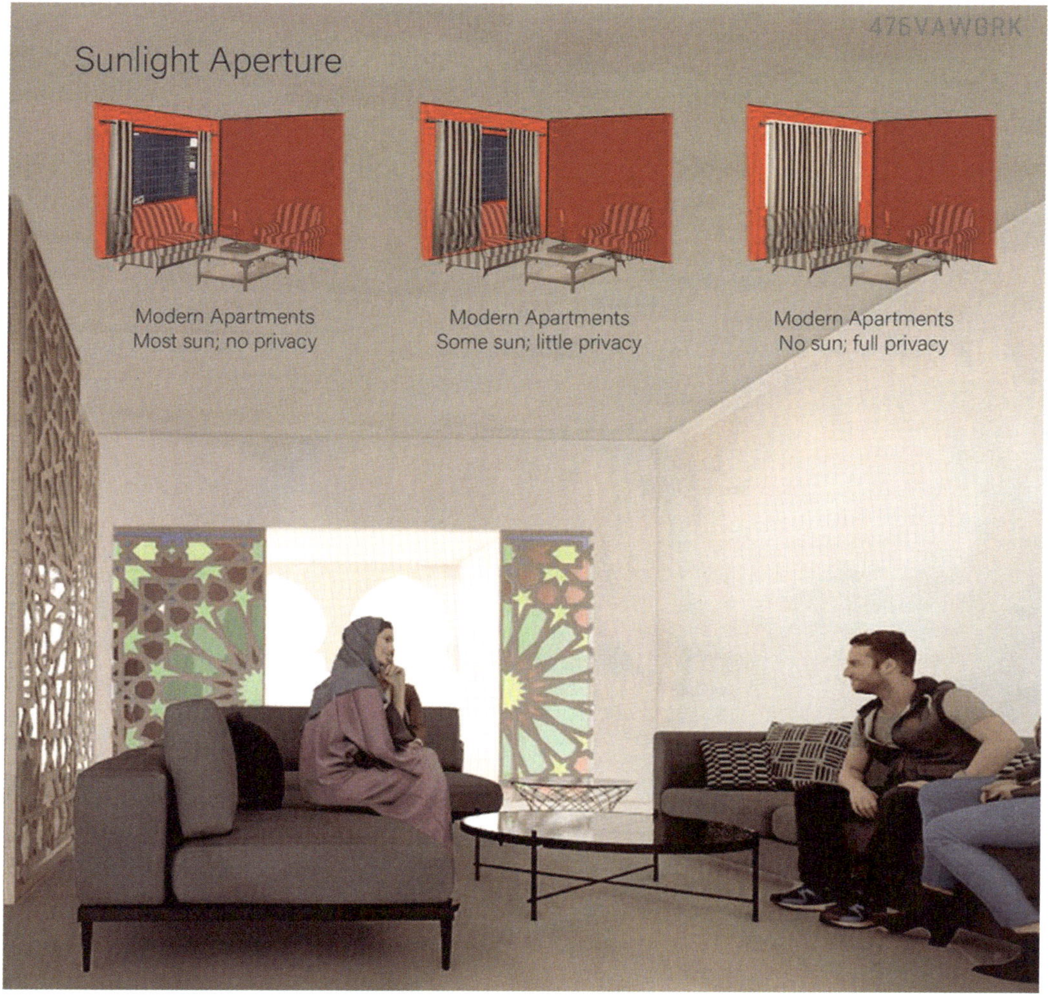
476VAWGRK
Sunlight Aperture
Modern Apartments
Most sun; no privacy
Modern Apartments
Some sun; little privacy
Modern Apartments
No sun; full privacy

SELECTED PROJECTS

430XUS5P8

THE ACTİVATOR

SPACE YOU ACTİVATE. SPACE THAT ACTİVATES YOU

Dóra Hegyi
Hungary

The Activator project understands the community as a socio-spatial unit organized both virtually and physically around a data driven public space. In this alternative Budapest, the square takes on the mission to make our life feel more local while enhancing our physical and social activity. It functions as a dynamic system, where your behaviour, your movement pattern defines the space and its features. A space you activate and a space that activates you.

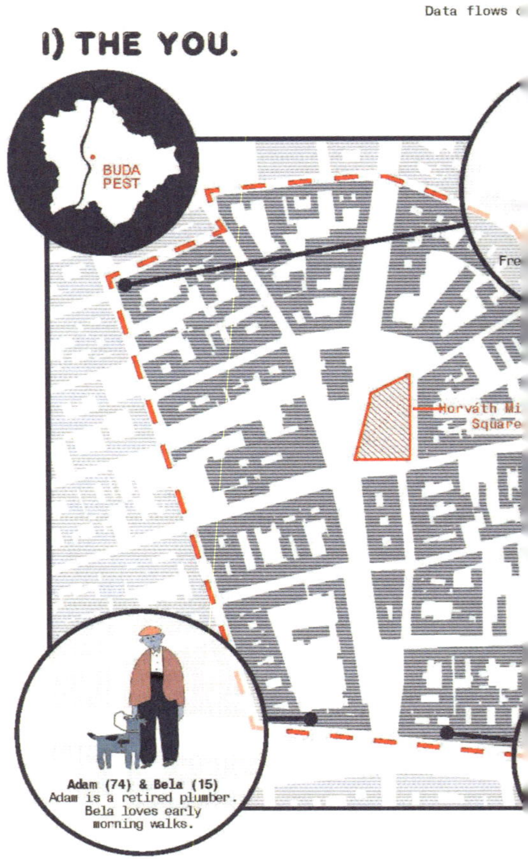

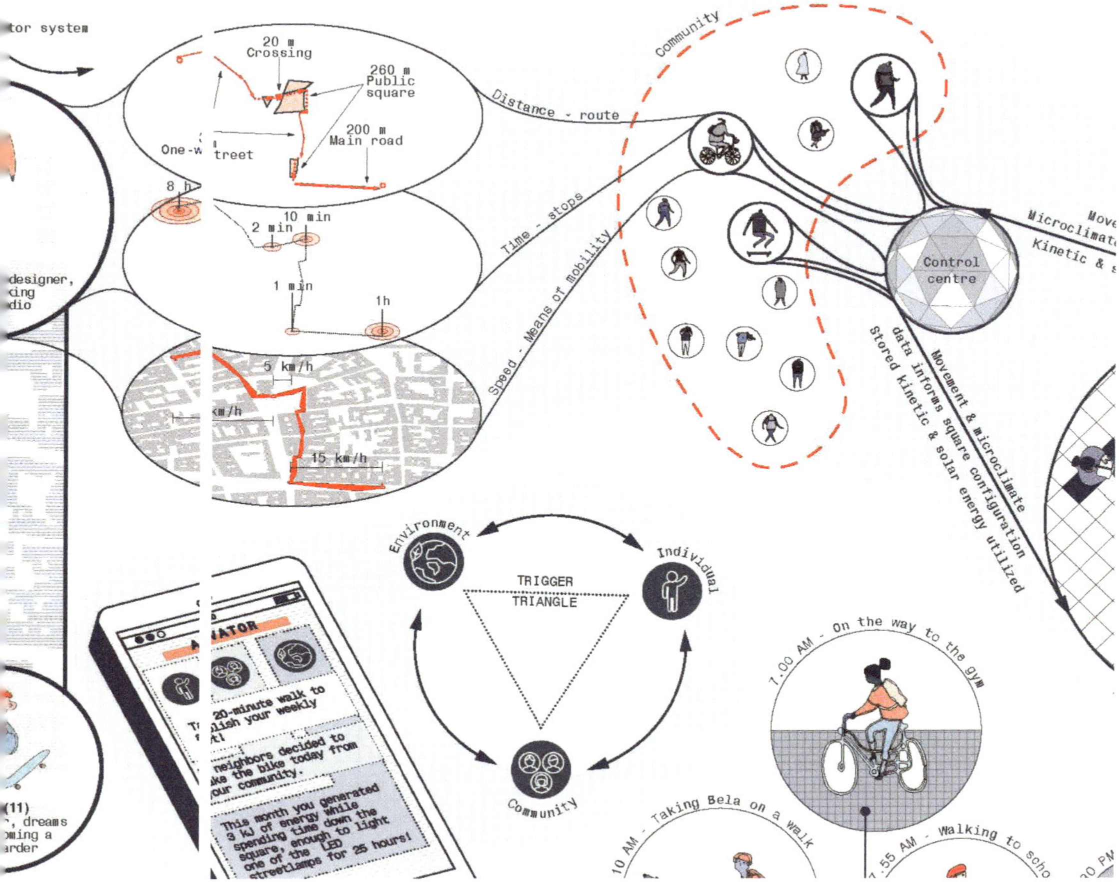
20 m
Crossing
260 m
Public
square
200 m
Main road
8 h
10 min
2 min
1 min
1h
5 km/h
15 km/h
Distance - route
Time - stops
Speed - Means of mobility
Community
Control
centre
Kinetic
Movement & microclimate
data informs square configuration
Stored kinetic & solar energy utilized
Environment
Individual
Community
TRIGGER
TRIANGLE
7.00 AM - On the way to the gym
Taking Bela on a walk
This month you generated
3 kJ of energy while
spending time down the
square, enough to light
one of the LED
streetlamps for 25 hours!

With the spread of Activator communities, new possibilities could open up to activate the people of Budapest. Communities could compete with each other to win the most active neighborhood title and further strenghten a sense of belonging. Seeing how the actions of one person or one community add up to city level impacts could also teach us to see the bigger picture and show us the power of bottom up changes.

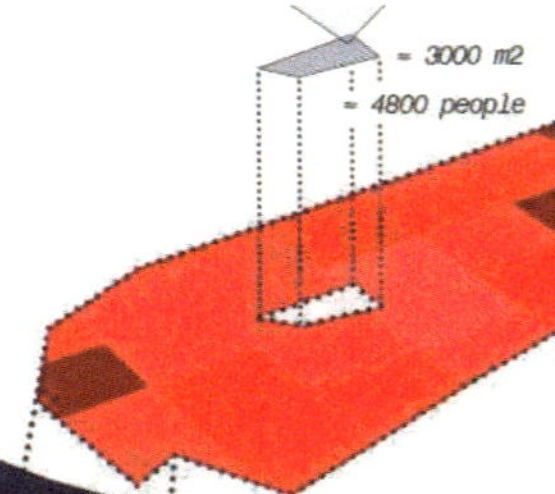

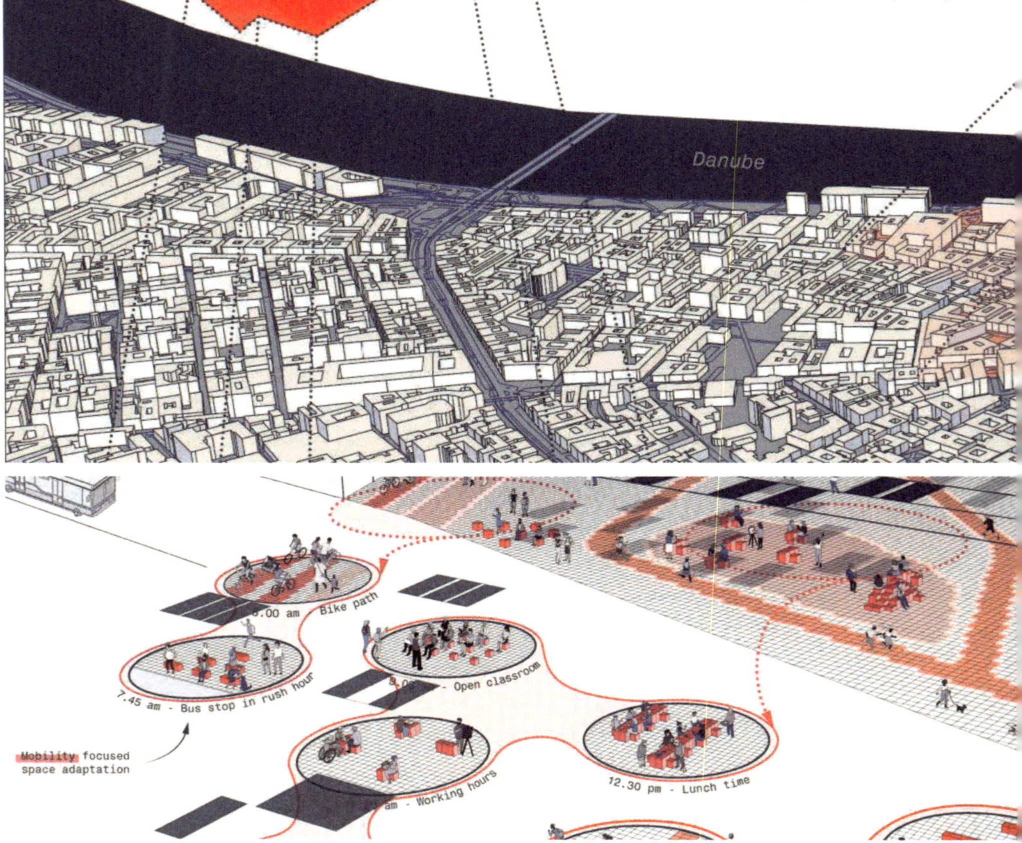

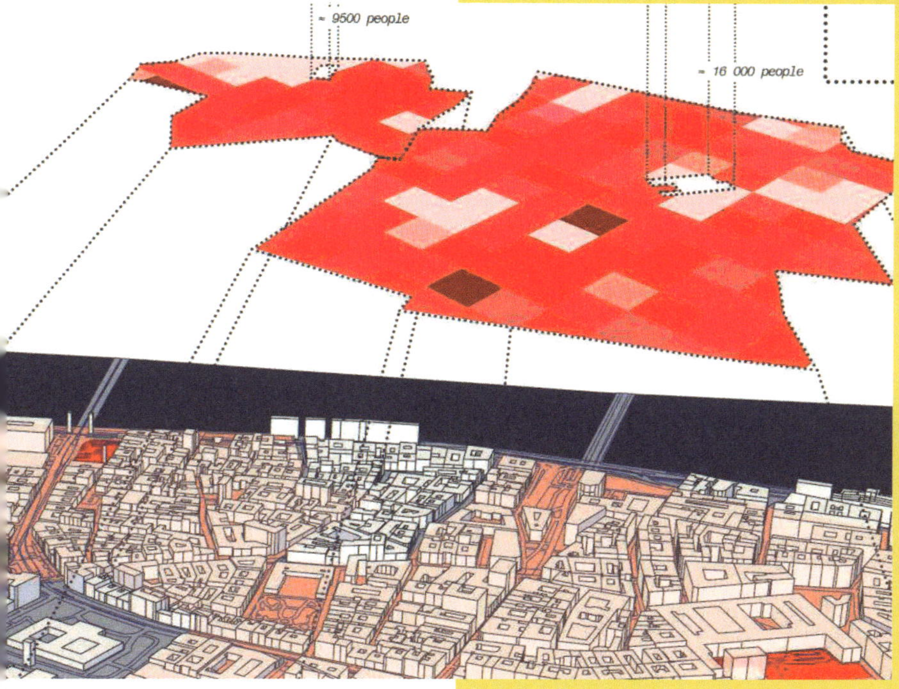

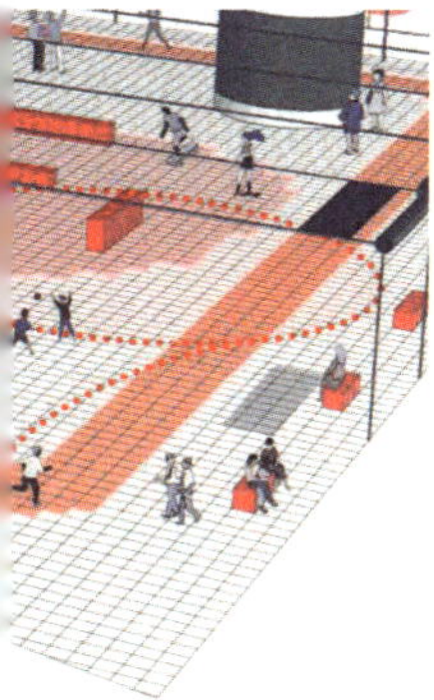

The age of social disconnect challenges us to - once again - renegotiate the individual-collective relationship and the notion of community

SELECTED PROJECTS

6829WFG50

THE ELEMENT

Denis Kireev
Russian Federation

We see the building as a new species. It is necessary to change the perception of the role and functionality of the building. We don't see it as a static unit. The 'new' building is not a completed facility, but is a constantly transforming structure of a life cycle. Every single ELEMENT is combined with the others in an integrated network, which allows to regulate energy resources consumption. The human acts as a partner to the structure, allotting new qualities and properties of a living organism to the ELEMENT.

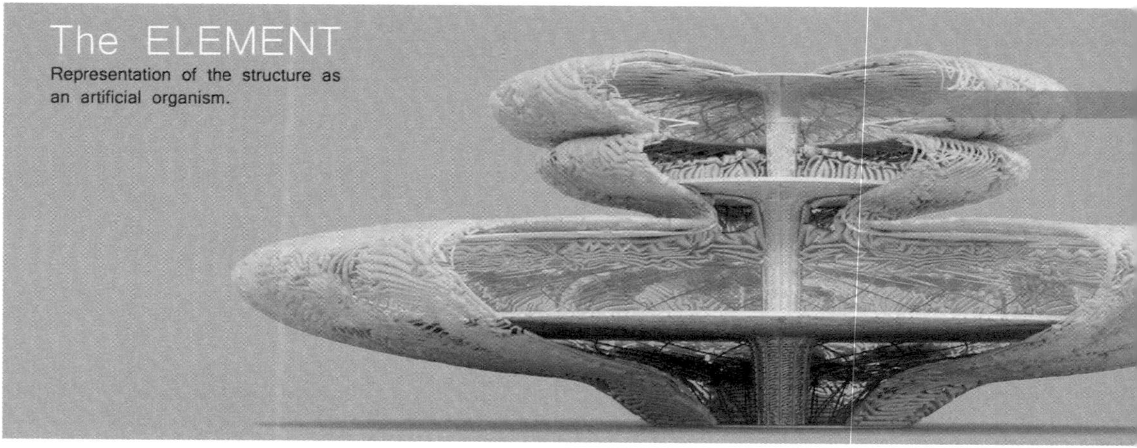

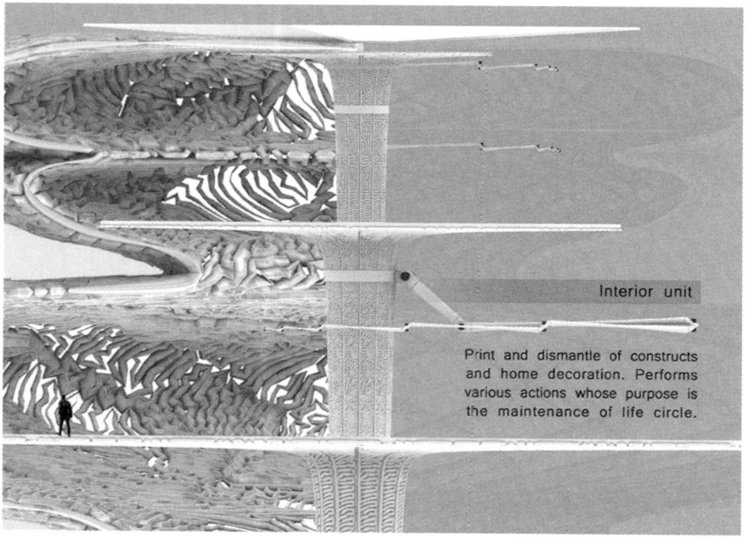

The parts (facade, roof e.g) are not static or decorative, they are combined into a structure capable of choosing an algorithm of action and change the configuration and chemical composition of particular components

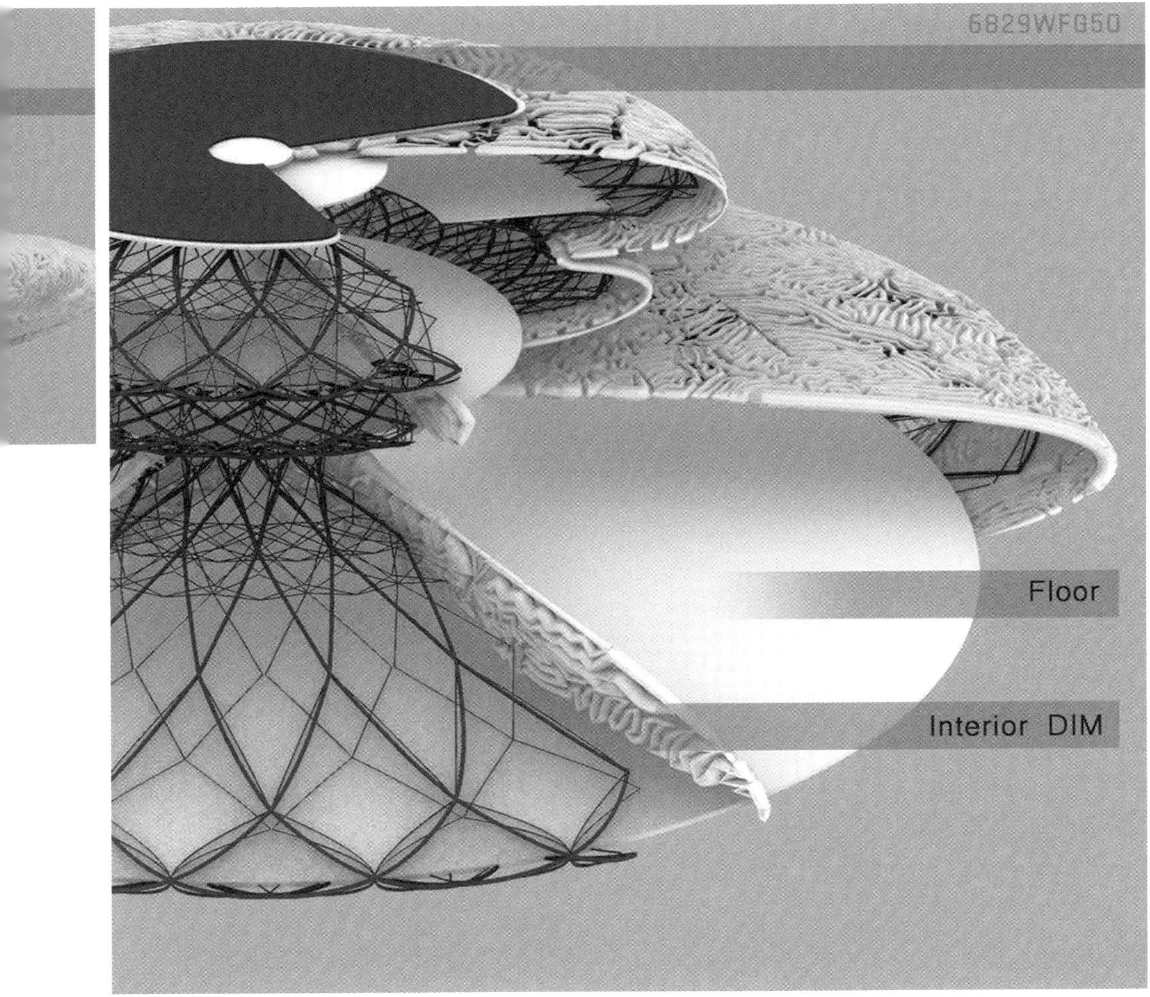
6829WFG50
Floor
Interior DIM

SELECTED PROJECTS

731ATT589

NEW URBAN LAYER

THE ELEVATER CHECKER BOARD

Inés Burdiles
Juan Eduardo Ojeda
Chile

After global lockdown, ONG and Climate Organizations around the world began promoting reduction of face-to-face encounters, reducing mobility and displacement within great cities for work and study purposes. The level of mass production and economic growth never came back to the state it was by the end of year 2019. In turn this new lifestyle brought the rise of new micro economies within neighborhoods and local exchange long lost by the frenetic urban lifestyle of the early XXI century.

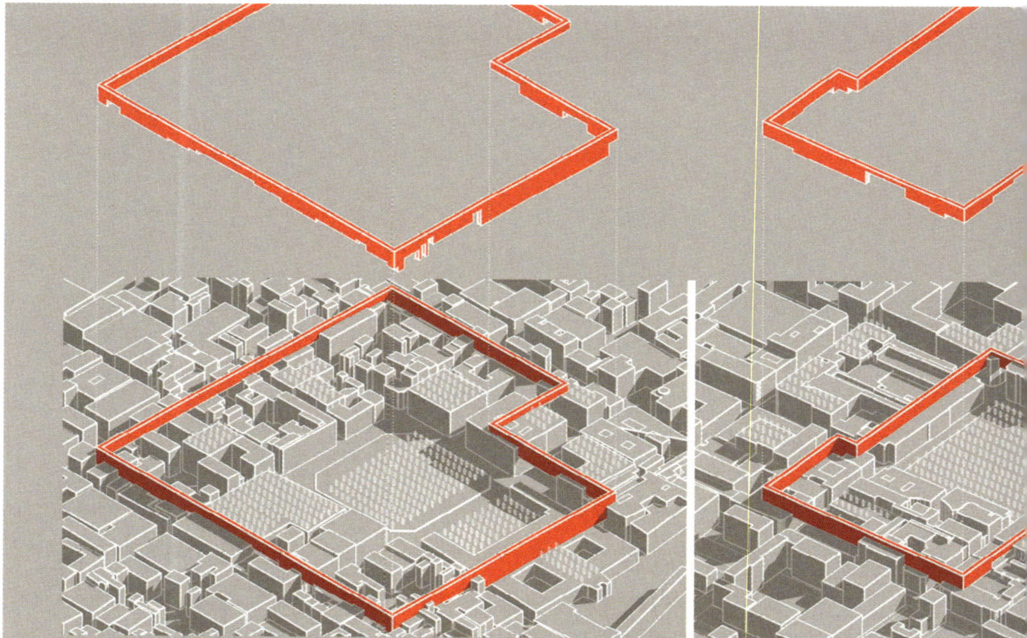

REFOUNDATION OF THE HISTORIC CENTER OF LIMA | PERÚ

REFOUNDATION OF THE HISTORIC CEN

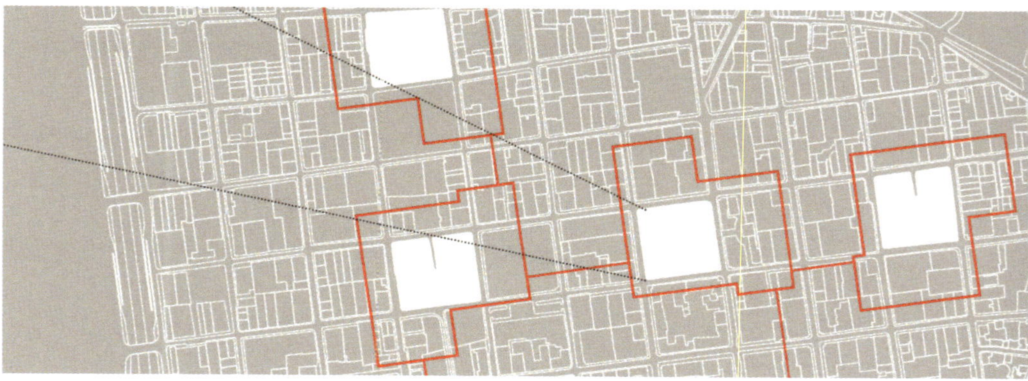

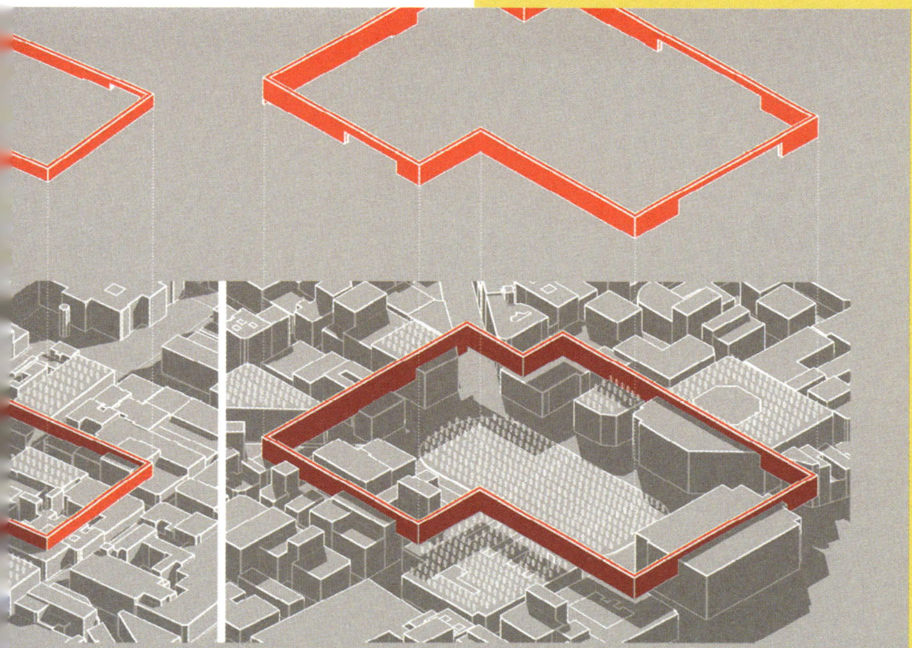

ANTIAGO | CHILE

REFOUNDATION OF THE HISTORIC CENTER OF BS AIRES | ARGENTINA

Within confined communities, people built bridges from one building to another, to collect the goods and share their crops, creating a new movility network, far from the "normal" city but still being in the city.

SELECTED PROJECTS

516V8ZNAN

FALLİNGNESS - VERFALLEN

Ren Yang
Yuan Menghao
Gong Kuiyu
He Weili
Yang Zeming
Yue Wanqing
Liu Wei
China

We reply with an elastic monument-like proposal. Building, due to the Old High German world buan, is the form we mortal beings dependent on to stand-in-the-world. It's also duration, whose essence itself has already provided the deepest view throughout historicity-of monumental valuse. Underlying those logics, this building will guarantee a greener and wiser dwelling for mobile population in post-pandemic era, and maker all of us deal with care to every minimal facet of thing called living.

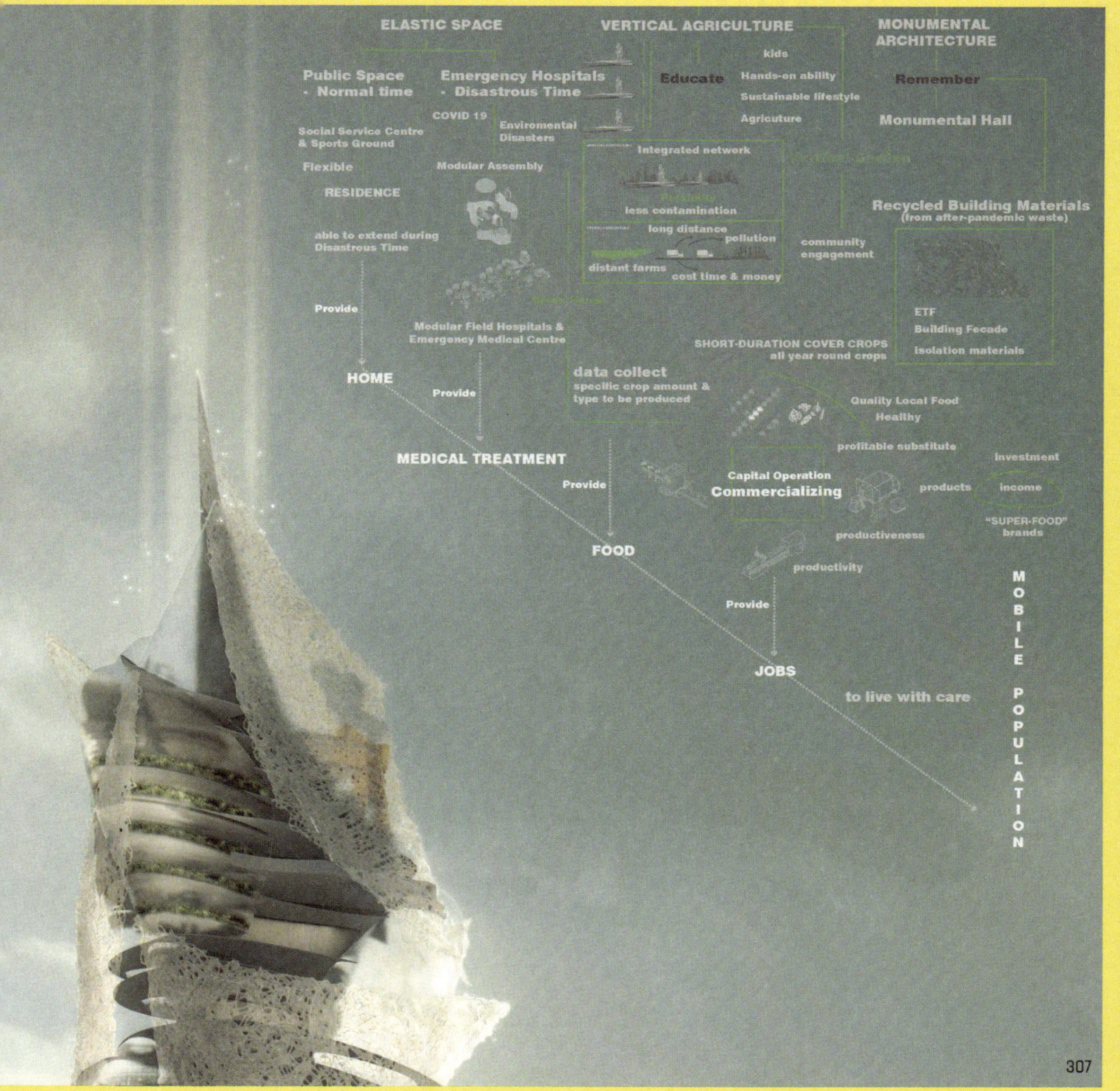
ELASTIC SPACE
VERTICAL AGRICULTURE
MONUMENTAL ARCHITECTURE
Public Space
- Normal time
Emergency Hospitals
- Disastrous Time
Educate
kids
Hands-on ability
Sustainable lifestyle
Agricuture
Remember
Monumental Hall
COVID 19
Enviromental Disasters
Social Service Centre & Sports Ground
Flexible
Modular Assembly
Integrated network
less contamination
long distance
pollution
distant farms
cost time & money
community engagement
Recycled Building Materials
(from after-pandemic waste)
RESIDENCE
able to extend during Disastrous Time
Provide
Modular Field Hospitals & Emergency Medical Centre
SHORT-DURATION COVER CROPS
all year round crops
ETF
Building Fecade
Isolation materials
HOME
Provide
data collect
specific crop amount & type to be produced
Quality Local Food
Healthy
profitable substitute
investment
MEDICAL TREATMENT
Provide
Capital Operation
Commercializing
products
income
"SUPER-FOOD" brands
productiveness
FOOD
productivity
Provide
JOBS
to live with care
MOBILE POPULATION

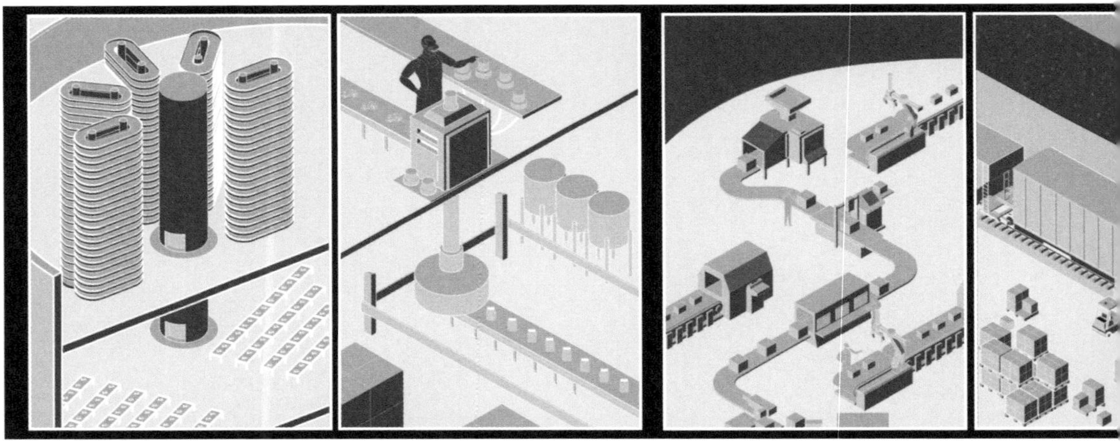

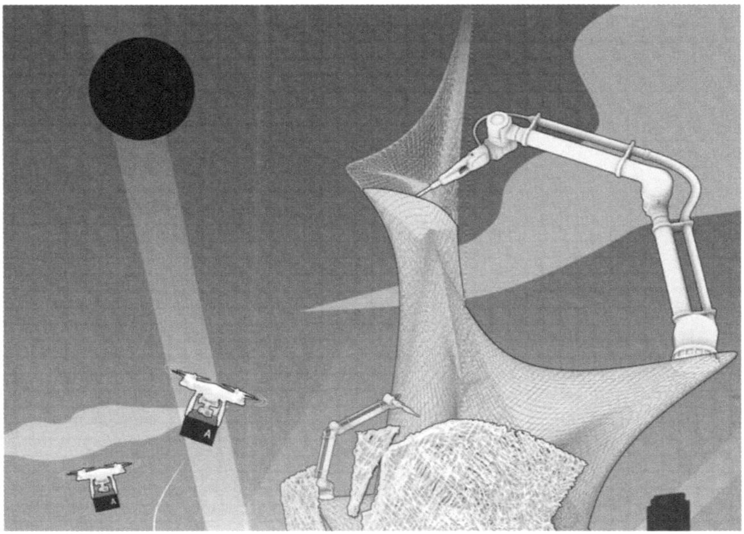

This proposal try to achieve a similar value to Totems, a silent being of condensation which keep warning and engaging us to gaze and hearken the history that it bears

Ground Floor
516V8ZNAN
Plan 2
Plan 3
Reservoir
3D Print Robot
Irrigation & Drinking
Vertical Farm
Sunlight
Sunlight
Rain
Water Storage
Water Collection
Electricity Generate
Vertical Farm
Air Condensate
Siphon Intake
water condensation
Quarantines
Hospital
Memorial Hall
Food Factory
biomass power generation
Clean Air
Domestic Waste
Biological power station
Waste Gas
City Terrance

SELECTED PROJECTS

3125SBH8I

GROUP OF BUiLDiNGS

Inmaculada Melo
Spain

The proposal belongs to a group of buildings, located on the edge of a ravine. They represent a process of transition from city to ravine, generating a progression so that they begin by adjusting to the strict rules of the city to end up by letting go and drinking from the diversity of tensions that nature has. This is materialized in 5 buildings each one more complex than the previous one reflecting its complexity and lack of internal conventionality in its external geometry.

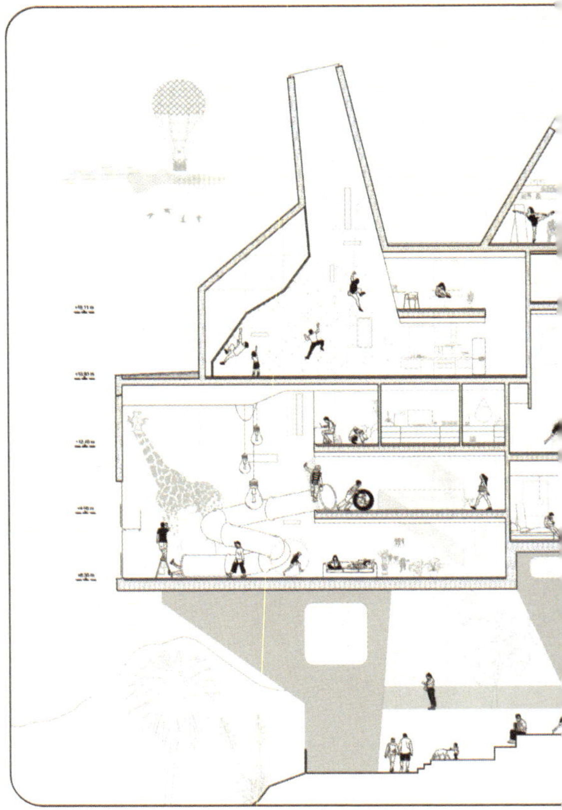

Longitudinal section | E 1:150

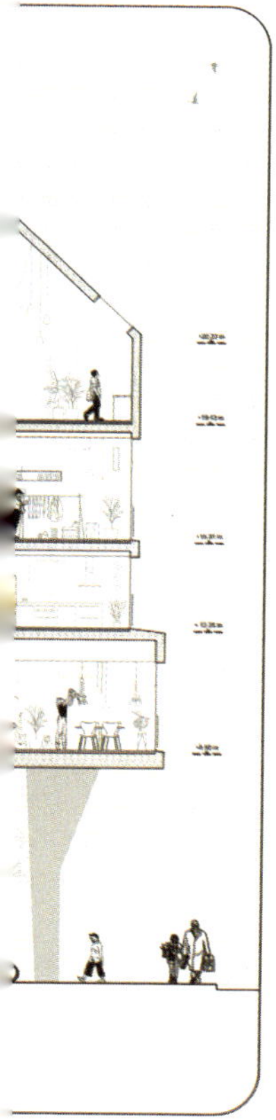

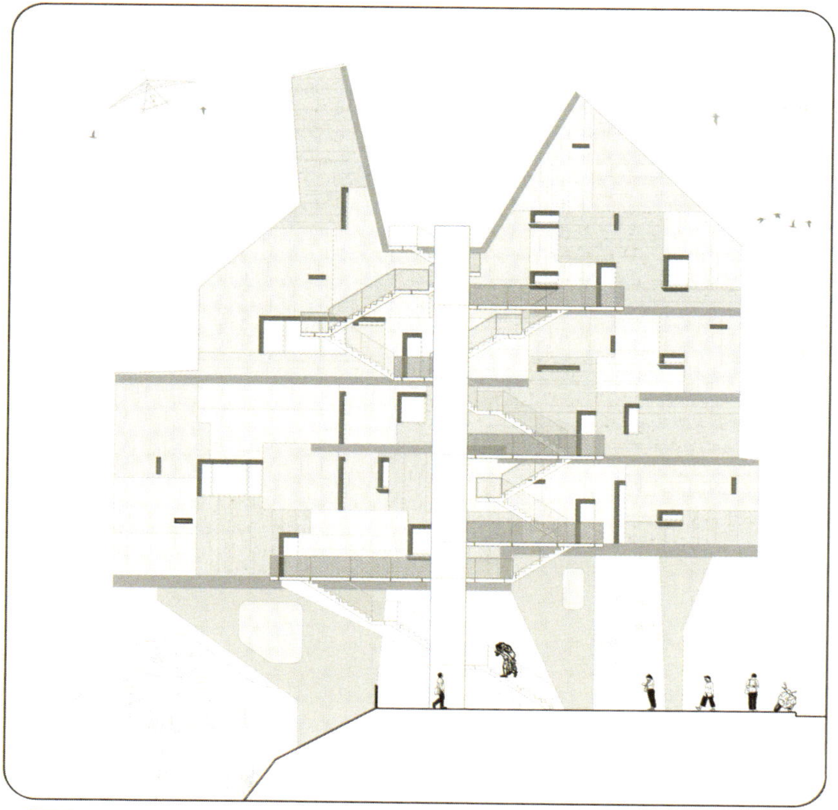

Principal front | E 1:200

Group of buildings

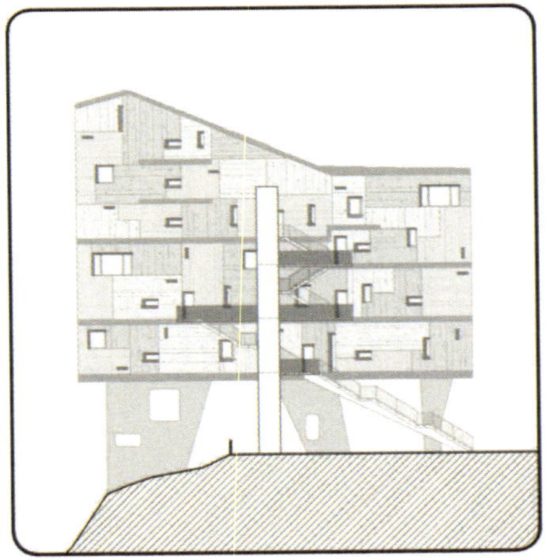

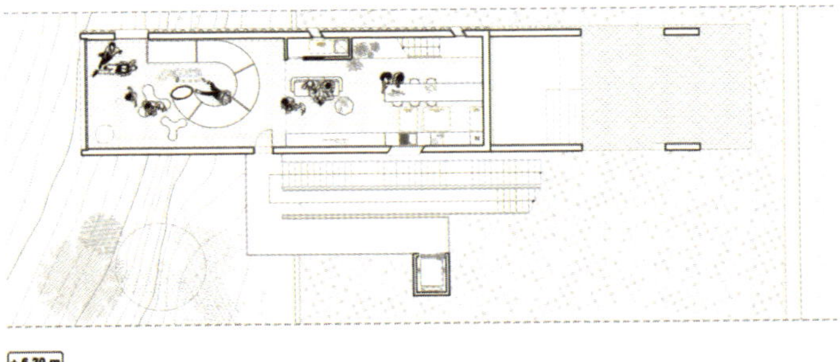

+ 6.30 m

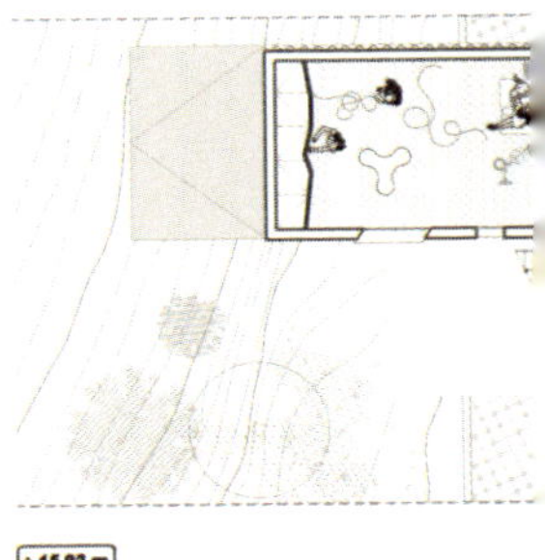

+ 15.93 m

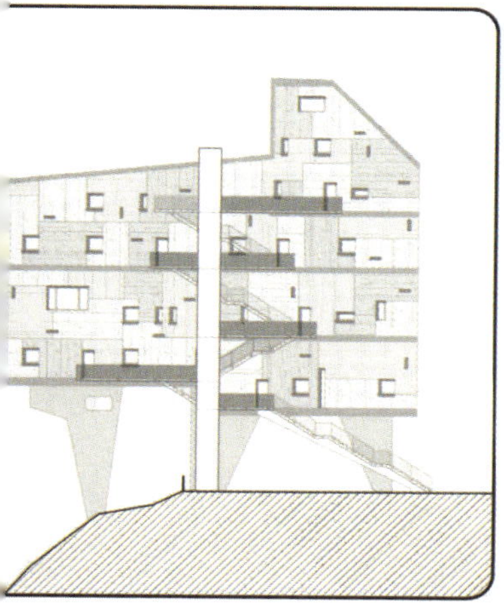

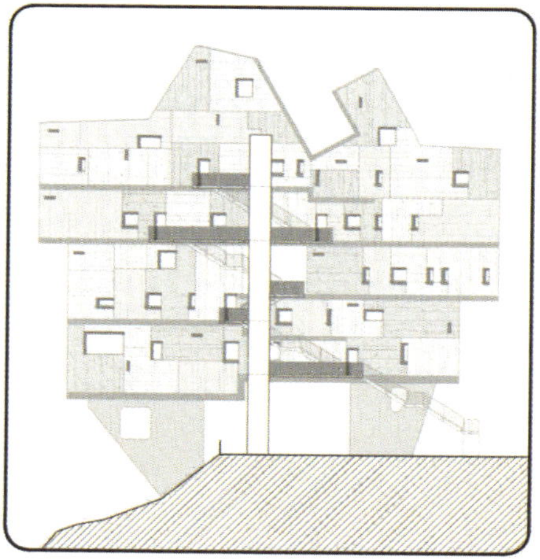

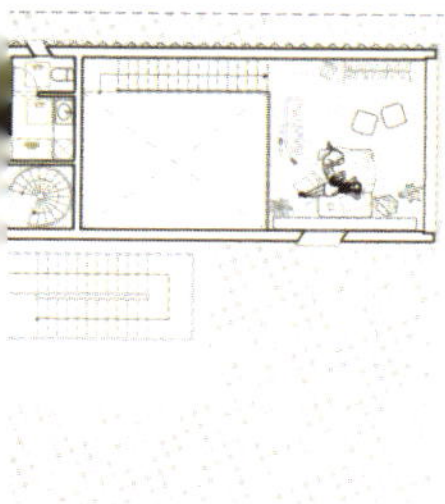

The house is the place where the memory is deposited, therefore, it must have corners and complexity

SELECTED PROJECTS

7255LH02H

LN. 57,HUAXİ ST.: NAMELESS BATHHOUSE

YiWen Wang
Taiwan

Wandering for a day or lifetime. They are all wanderers. Everyone might desire to abandon identity and the reality of their own. Going to Bathhouse might be a way to get freedom.

Duality of Circulatory System
Water Change System & Thermal Cycling
Studied typology and the system of energy circulation for the purpose of clean or luxury, to rewrite experience of people from different world.

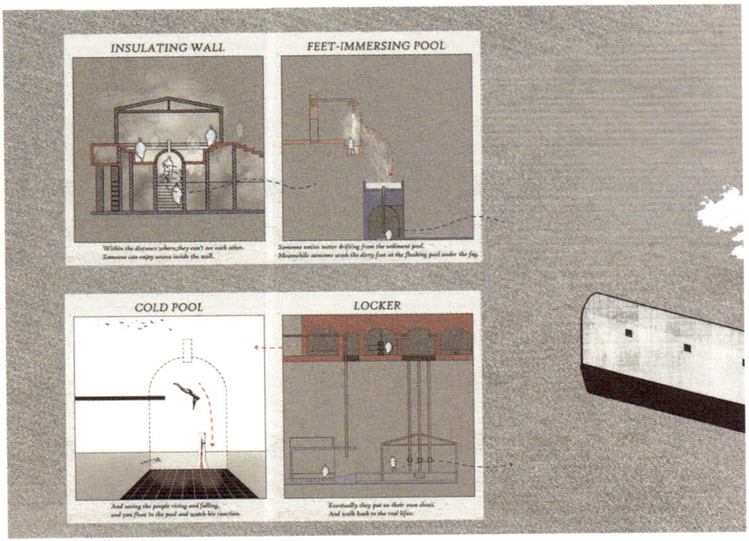

Use the remain energy from entertaining consumption provide free space in the energy circulation system

EXCHANGE AND CIRCULATE
TWO ENTRANCE

SELECTED PROJECTS

288SN9K3G

MİCROHABİTAT

Ivan Reyes
Miguel Angel Tinoco
Mexico

This module gets into actual buildings and embeds into the city in order to make complex programs that allow users to adapt, learn, socialize, work, produce their own resources and reuse their wastes. Likewise in the city, this module adapts according to the necessities of the site in order to complement human habitat, preparing the actual city for a growing population without the need for new land and giving comfort to users. The materialization of these modules adjust to the user and climate being built-in site with local biomaterials that provide organic living skin which works together with the module to self-sustain.

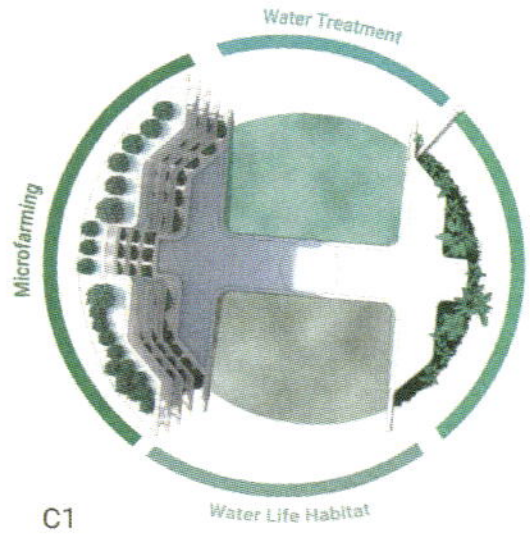

C1

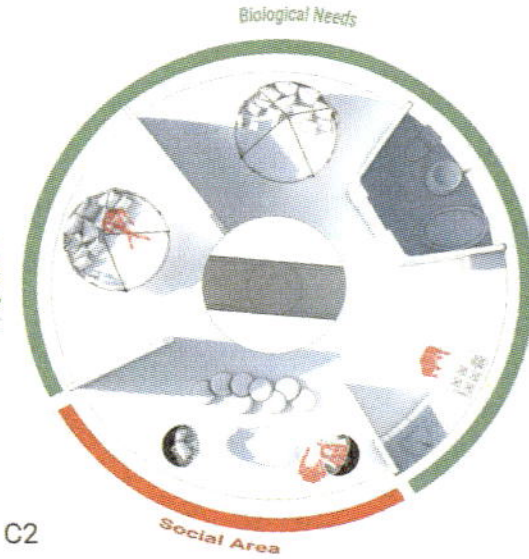

C2

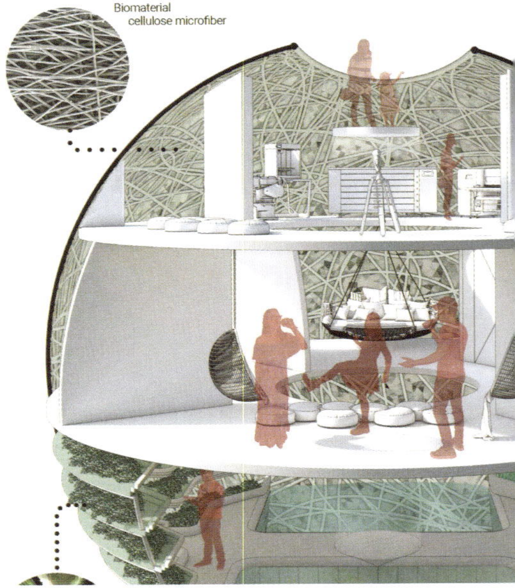

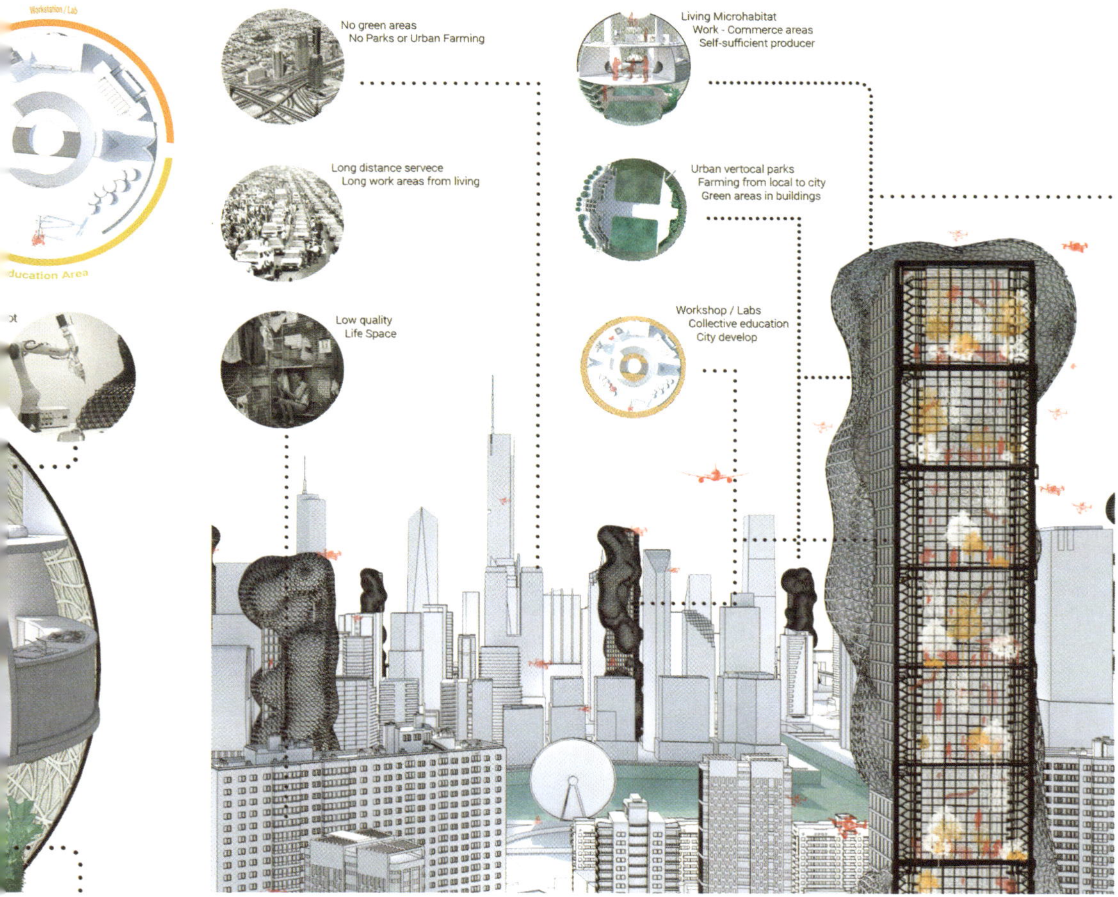
Workstation / Lab
No green areas
No Parks or Urban Farming
Long distance servece
Long work areas from living
Low quality
Life Space
Living Microhabitat
Work - Commerce areas
Self-sufficient producer
Urban vertocal parks
Farming from local to city
Green areas in buildings
Workshop / Labs
Collective education
City develop

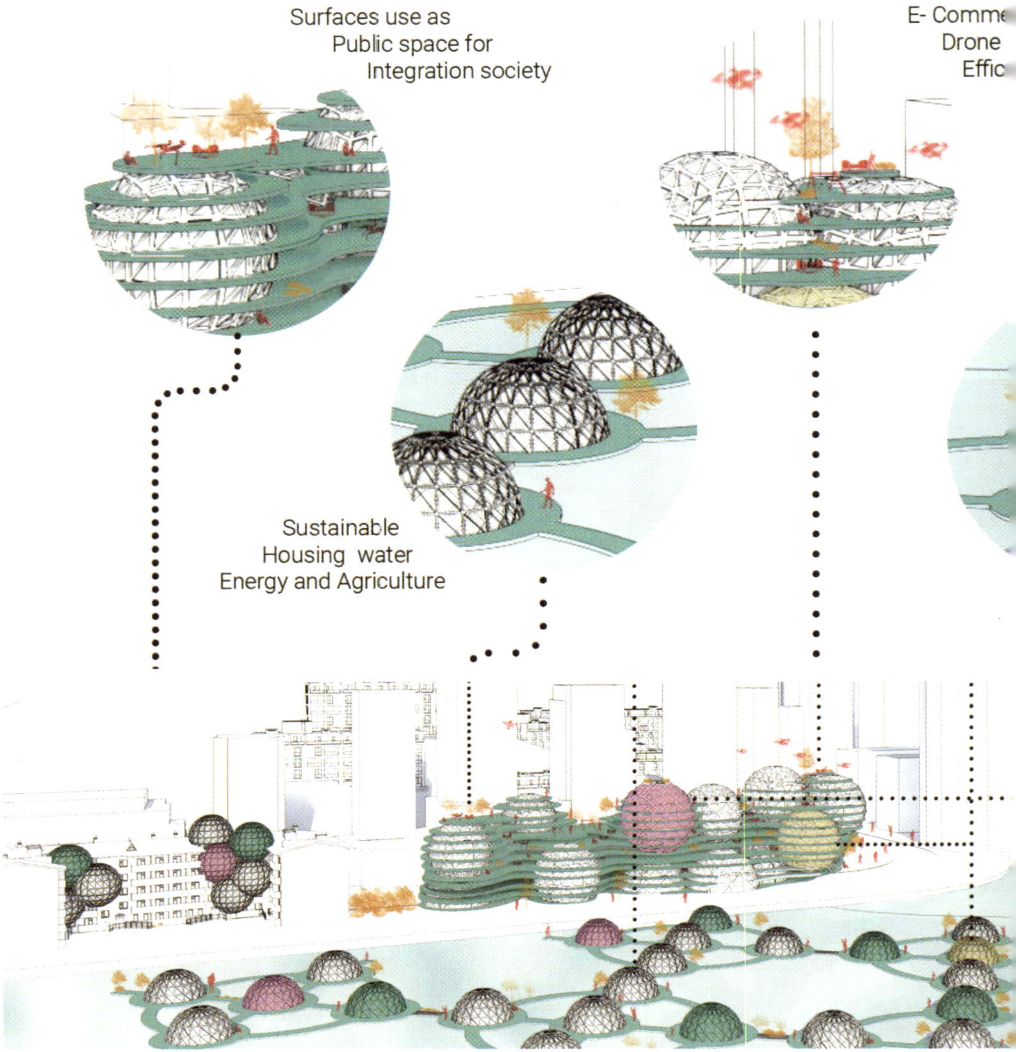
Surfaces use as
Public space for
Integration society
E- Comm
Drone
Effic
Sustainable
Housing water
Energy and Agriculture

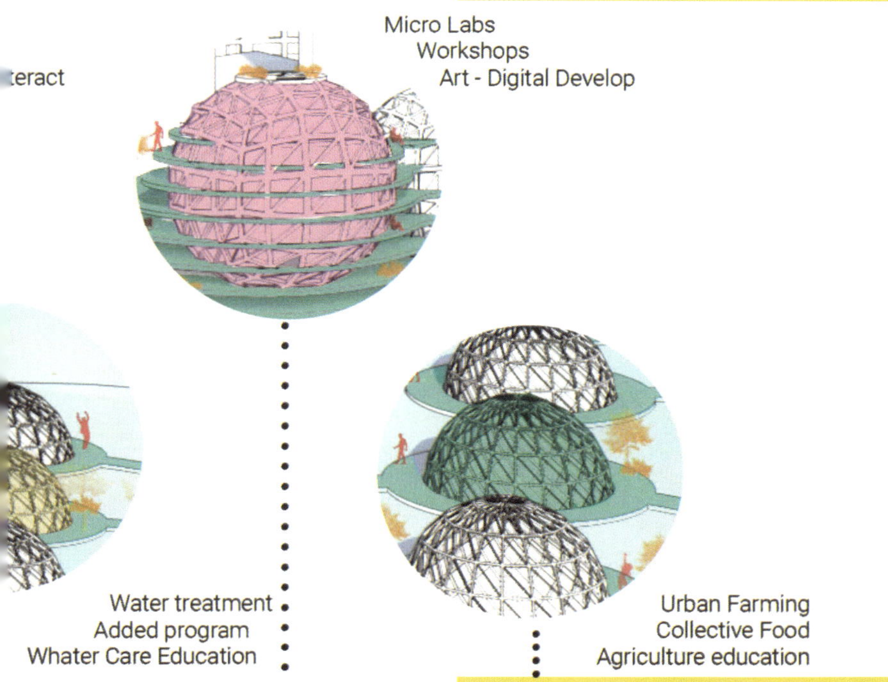

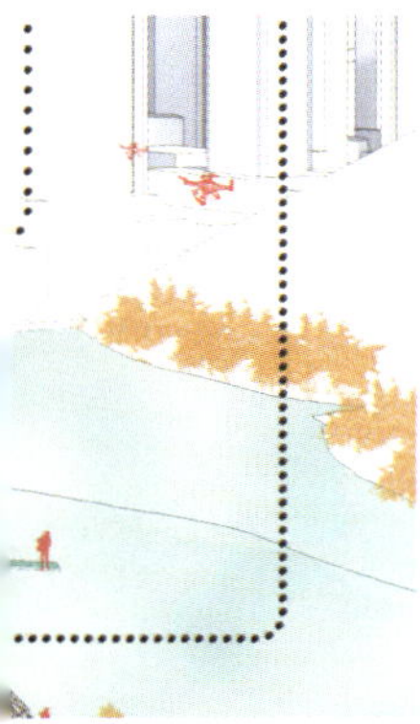

The module uses the vertical space in cities with a deficit of usable land and gets into land and sea in other cases as a way to make these spaces habitable and to give multi-social activities spaces like public spaces, urban gardens, recollection and waste digesters

SELECTED PROJECTS

5802015WU

PULL
EMERGENCY SHELTER

Jonathan Balderrama
Bolivia

Pull is a folding modular system that allows lifting refugee camps in minutes, managing to improve the quality of life of people left homeless by natural disasters or wars, restoring the sense of security and companionship without loss of privacy, linking the concept of community through form and function. PULL consists of a trailer and a folding fabric module, of uniting these two components, the result is a powerful system mobile home and temporary shelter, flexible and modular. PULL is a simple structure, lightweight, easy to carry and deploy quickly, as it requires no tools for assembly, because you just have to pull on one side and adjust to the base of the trailer. PULL provides shelter for a family of 5 members, but thanks to its modularity this can be expanded and group the modules in different ways depending on the location and context.

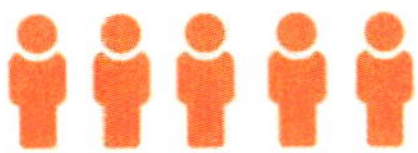

people

PULL has the capacity of sheltering a family of 5 members, but being a flexible space this capacity can be expanded

The modular versatility of PULL can be adapted to multiple contexts and modules can be grouped in linear or circular manner, according to the climate of site (sun, wind, dust, rainfall, etc) and where this linked with the concept of community and spiritual gathering

5802015WU

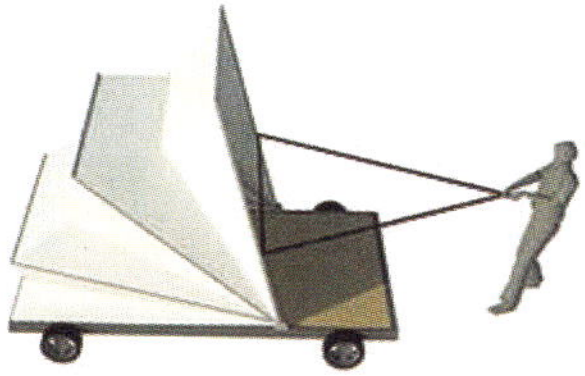

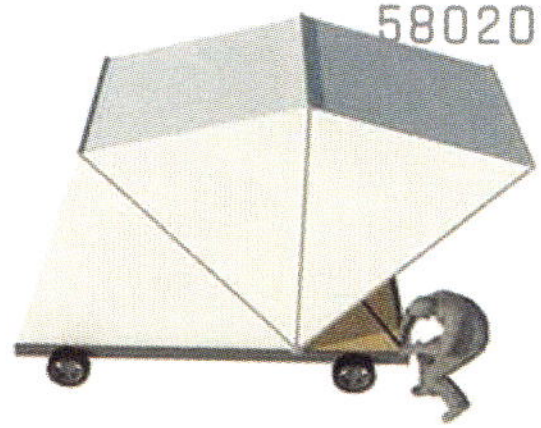

SELECTED PROJECTS

736FY84M0

CONTROVERSY OF INDUSTRIAL MINING

Jan Kovářïček
Czech Republic

The Eutopian Factory outlines an alternative to the current model of industrial manufacturing and preconceived notions of living standards for blue collar workers. Leaving behind an excessive production and environmental exploitation of the last 150 years, it embraces key concepts of pre–industrial labour updated for the 21st Century. It offers a robust vision for short term and long term future of localised work and the phenomenon of digital craftsmanship.

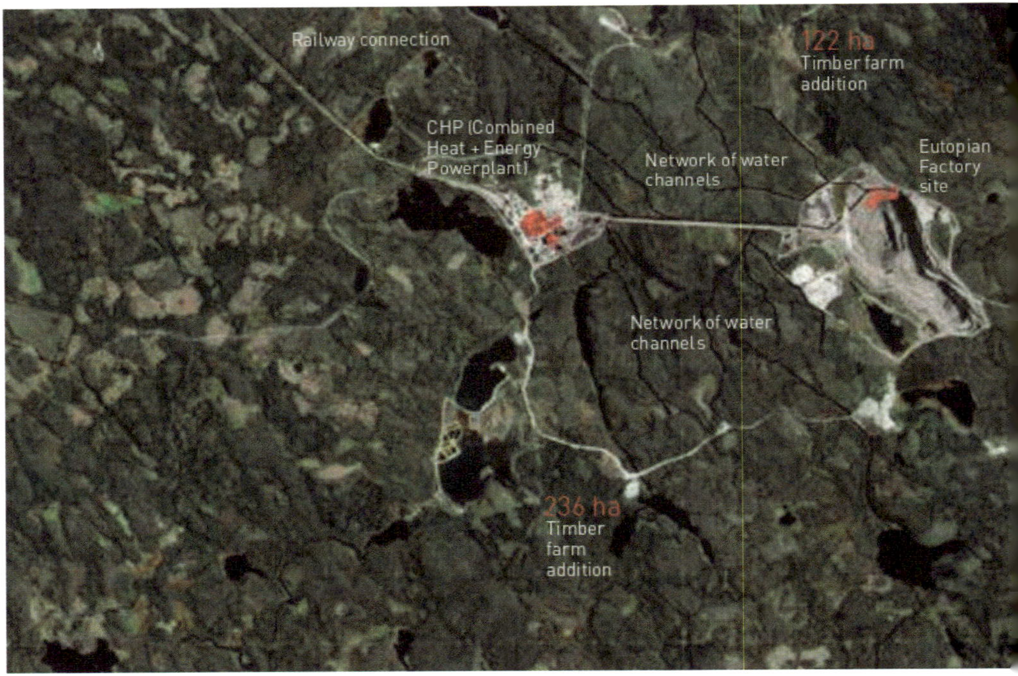
Railway connection
122 ha
Timber farm addition
CHP (Combined Heat + Energy Powerplant)
Network of water channels
Eutopian Factory site
Network of water channels
236 ha
Timber farm addition

400
Employees operating on site daily

TALVIVAARA MINE

236 ha
Primary heap area

122 ha
Secondary heap area

351 ha
Open pit mine

Testing ground for the future of industry work

SELECTED PROJECTS

286SELVVX

MAKER'S SPACE 2.0

Shin-yu Wang
United Kingdom

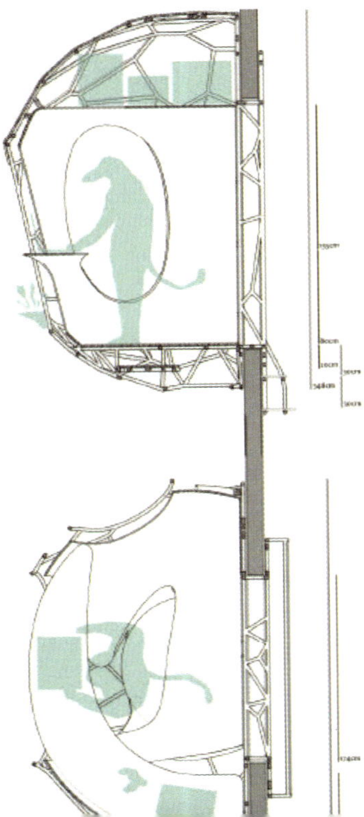

Like all the self-build extension in different countries, the Maker's Space 2.0 reveals the contemporary construction methods and materials. Metal, plastic, wood, and fabric can be easily bought, modified, and used thank to out digitalized world and personal fabrication technology. Maker's Space 2.0 provides a cheap and customized solution for those who need more space. Maker's Space 2.0 can also be removed easily at the end of rental. Maker's Space 2.0 is a solution, in this decentralized era, to solve the space ineffeciency, and helps the new bloods to energise the cities.

MAKE SPACE

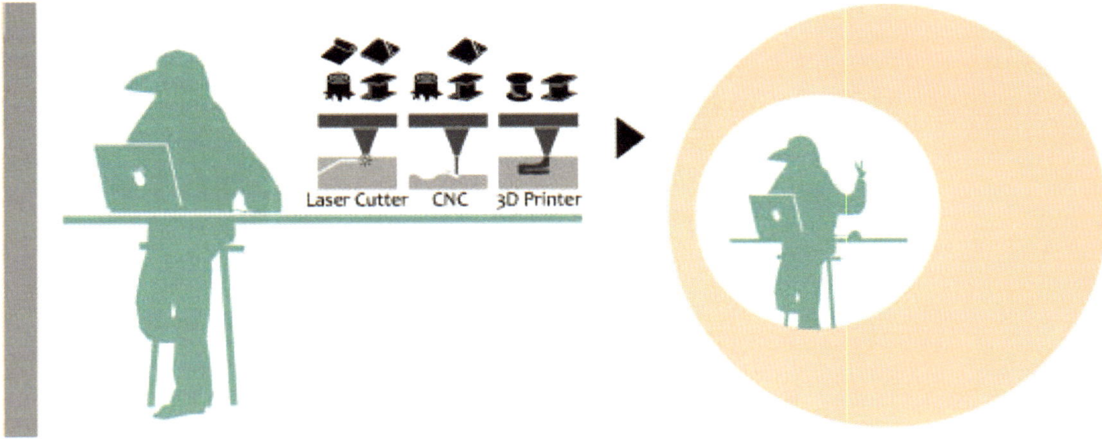

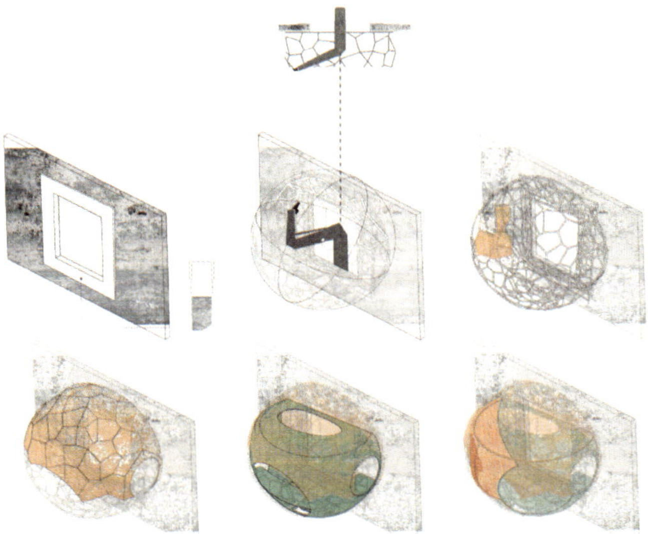

After the 2rd and 4th industrial revolution, production is personalized and customized. Personal digital fabrication is no longer imagination with cheaper and more accessible facilities like 3d printer, laser cutter, and CNC

286SELVVX

SELECTED PROJECTS

59EMR29V

PUBLIC SPACE AMPLIFIER

José Ignacio Rejas Fernández
Spain

This is a proposal for a new field of opportunities for the communities in need. It consists on a network of urban attractors combined with a process of urban public space expansions. The goal is amplifying the space for the citizens. These public space amplifiers provide new possibilities of good quality houses and all the necessities that the community may have. Depending on those needs, the configuration of the spaces will change. It is a completely flexible scheme. The number of levels, their height or the amount of rooms may differ on each neighbourhood.

Vegetation

Rooftops and their vegetation play a key role in the configuration of the social life of the neighbourhood. Plants grow every where in the building, but the roofs are filledd with them. Wide lawns on the surface os the entire level. Bushes and little trees are also located in specific sites of these levels.

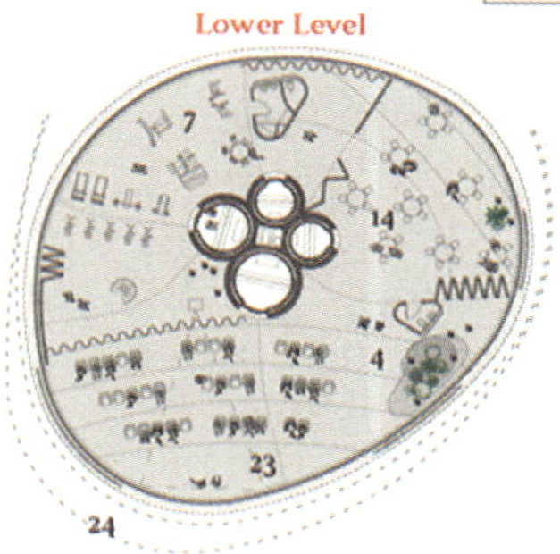

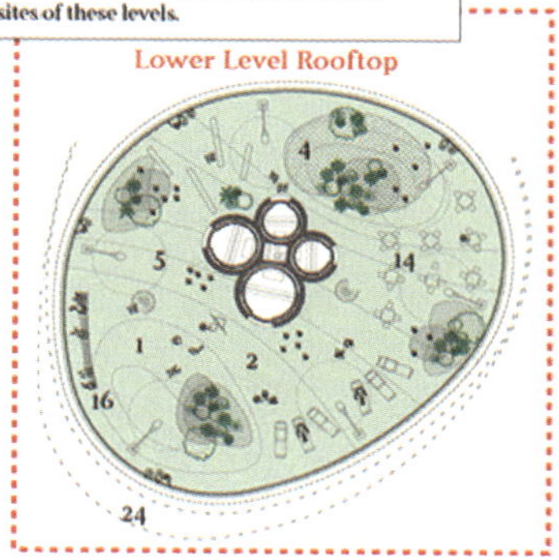

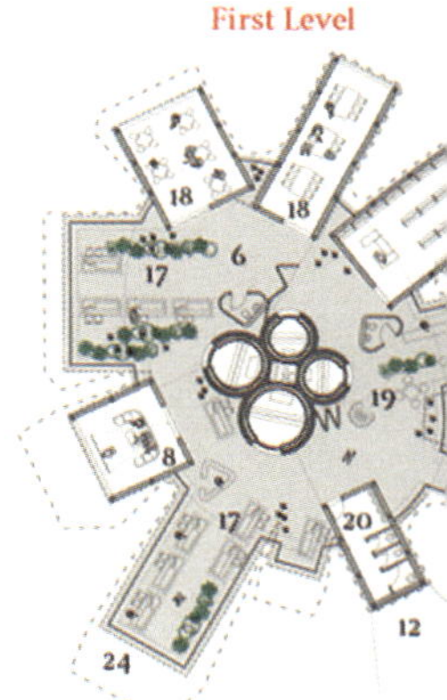

Above every level there is a terrace for outdoors use. The communication through the building is focused in the main column of elevators. There is also a secondary system with spiral stairs along the complex

59EMR29V

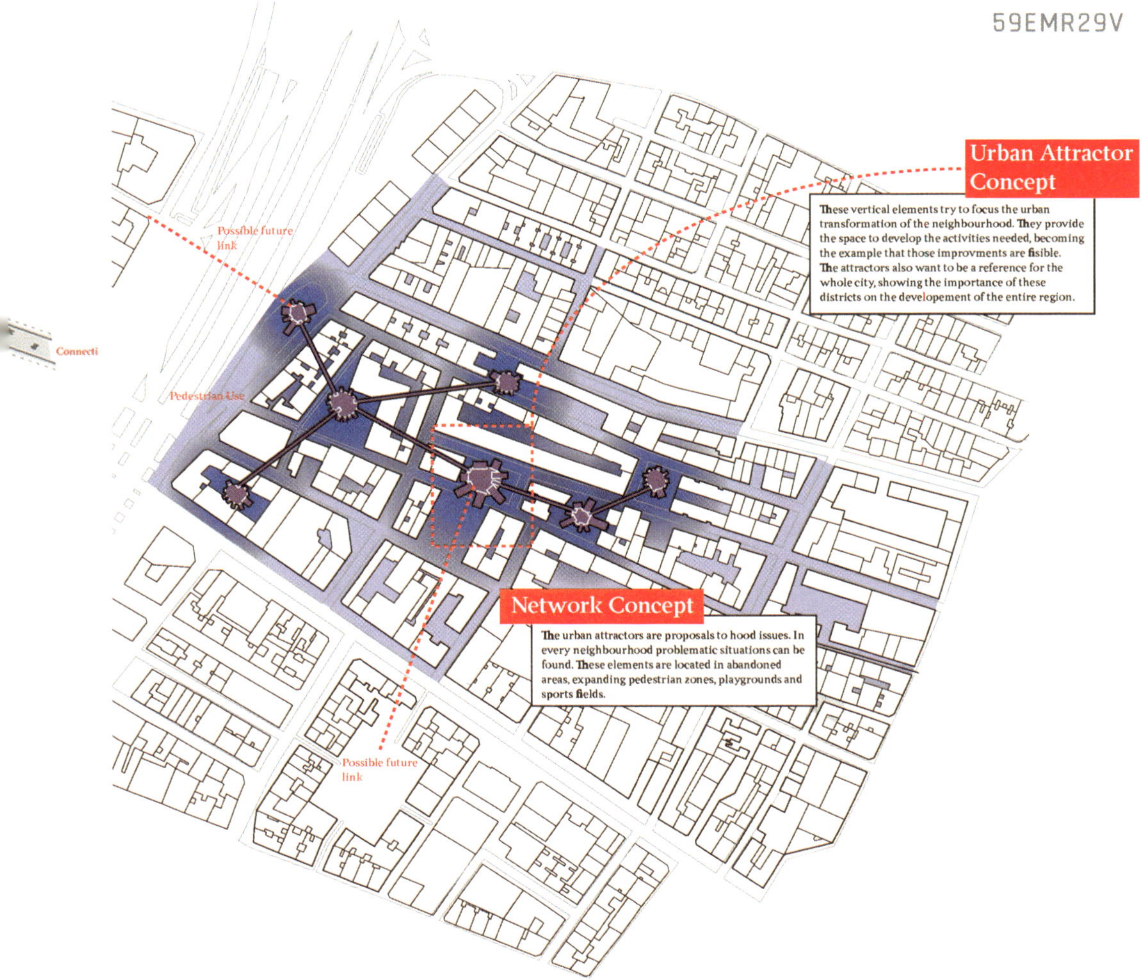
Urban Attractor Concept
These vertical elements try to focus the urban transformation of the neighbourhood. They provide the space to develop the activities needed, becoming the example that those improvments are fisible.
The attractors also want to be a reference for the whole city, showing the importance of these districts on the developement of the entire region.
Possible future link
Connecti
Pedestrian Use
Network Concept
The urban attractors are proposals to hood issues. In every neighbourhood problematic situations can be found. These elements are located in abandoned areas, expanding pedestrian zones, playgrounds and sports fields.
Possible future link

SELECTED PROJECTS

48199G1K8

DWELL

HYDRO-ELECTRİC SELF-SUFFİCİENT COMPACT LİVİNG

Jozef Gach

United States of America

By combining the concept of small scale hydroelectric energy, self-sufficiency, and community living, this project aims to create a single family dwelling that runs off of its own water wheel/generator and produces everything necessary for living. This housing project will ultimately create a system of dwellings that can all run from one or multiple water wheels that will power the home, filter water, grow food, and shelter its inhabitants while allowing dwellers to sell energy to a national grid for a continuous stream of profit. Dwell aims to be the future of living while solving environmental issues, minimizing energy impacts, and increasing healthy living.

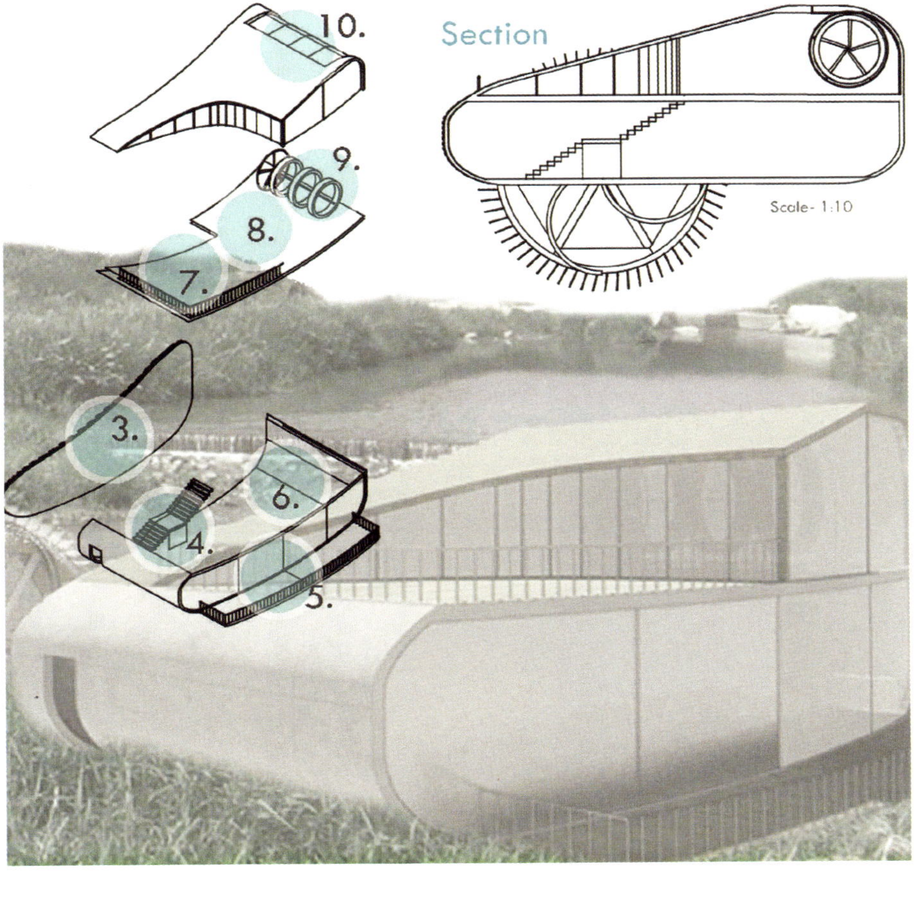
10.
9.
8.
7.
3.
6.
4.
5.
Section
Scale- 1:10

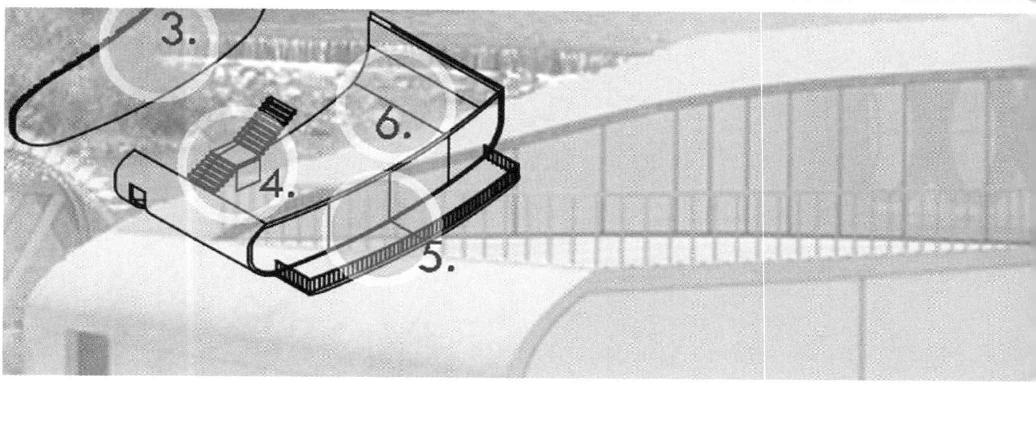
3.
6.
4.
5.

Like most conventional water-wheels, Dwell uses a river's natural current to propel a wheel thus generating electricity. Dwell also utilizes the water itself for use in the interior greenhous and passive moisture cooling in warmer climates

SELECTED PROJECTS 388RM2PXO

RESONANCE

IMAGİNE ALL THE PEOPLE LİVİNG İN HARMONY

Katie Kumro
United States of America

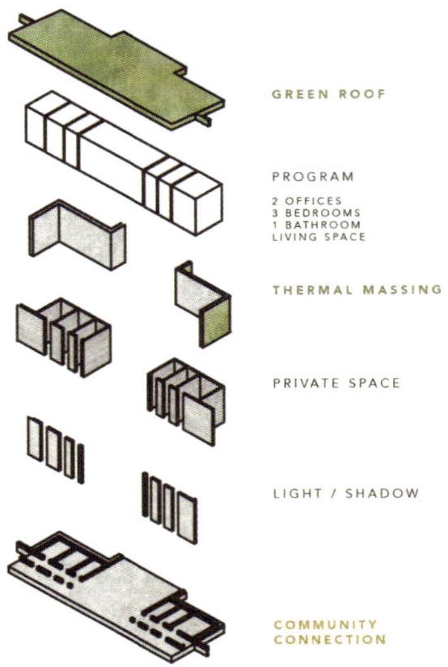

This proposal develops a new typology of empathetic communal living, inspired by coping methods used during quarantine, which demonstrated our deep connection to nature and one another that transcended all else. Through reaching out to our neighbors, spending time in nature, and singing together we were able to endure a dark moment in history. By facilitating these simple, yet mindful actions through architecture, we can allow our lives to become a symphony in resonance with nature and humankind.

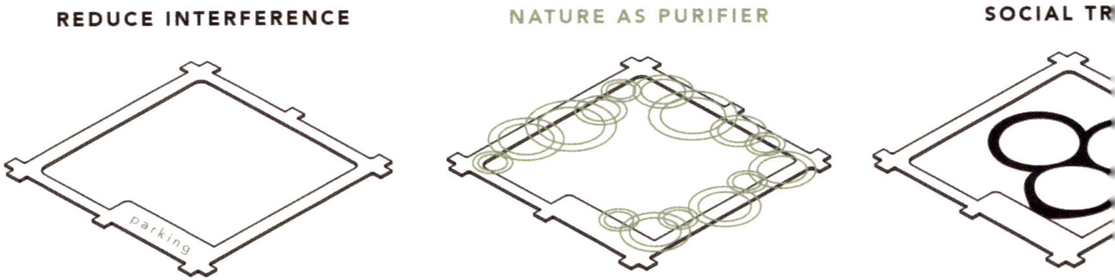

Architecture must amplify our inherent connection to each other allowing the space between our structures to become the symphony in harmony with nature and humankind

388RM2PXO

SELECTED PROJECTS 71ZL3HYB

PLİANT CİTY

Janina Sánchez
Belen Acurio
Kevin Aragón
Ecuador

The proposal for adaptability is founded in the volatility of our setting. Hence to think of resiliency, one must design to adapt. To achieve this, replicable modules are used to create flexibility living quarters. These are independent both in construction and as structure, and can be inserted in the existing buildings to create inclusive communities. This module is built to enable and proliferate networks of green houses and vegetation throughout the city. Moveable panels and built-ins in the living quarters adapt to change. Publicly, the City of Mutuality is designed for change and adaptation, and thus, urban furniture is flexible and allows for the orchestration of bike lanes and streets through rails, according to communal and pedestrian needs.

GREEN HOUSES AS VERTICAL COURTYARDS

FLEXIBLE URBAN FURNITURE ON RAILS TO MOVE AND ADAPT TO SOCIAL DISTANCING

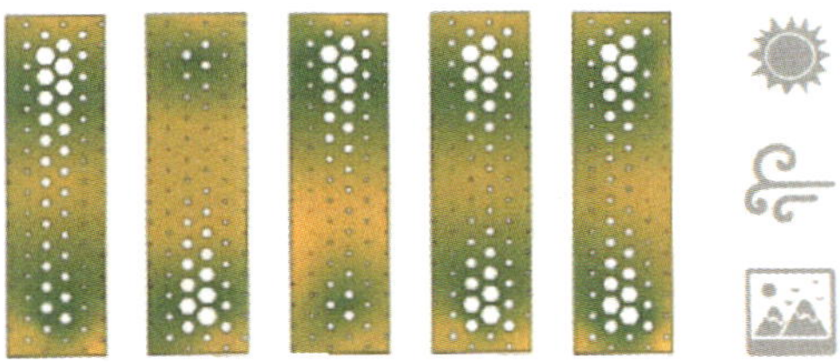

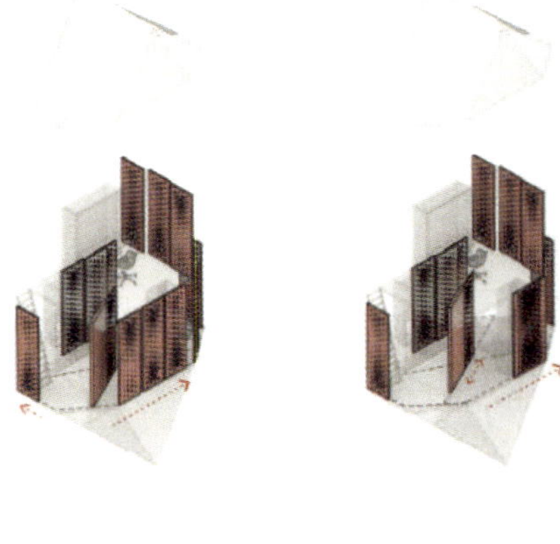

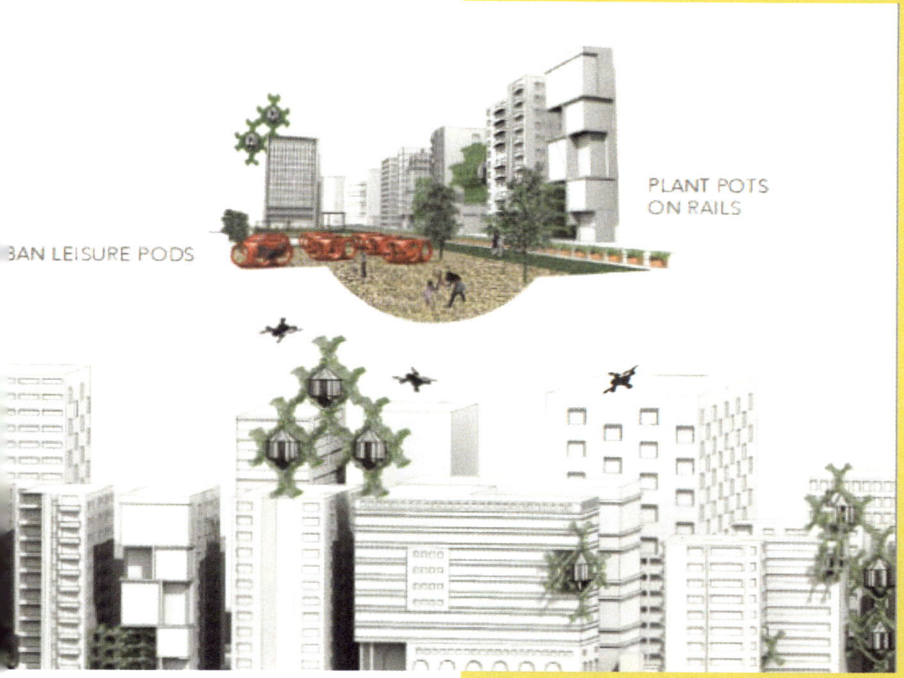

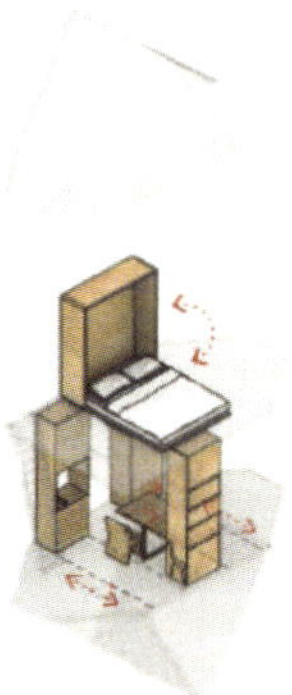

The Pliant City, is not merely an urban environment, but a proposal for a set of strategies that embody the idea of a flexible, adaptable and resilient city

SELECTED PROJECTS

461ZNECZ2

THE STACK

TİNY LİVİNG FOR MİNDFUL DENSİTY

Kylie Bromley
United States of America

The Stack is a multi-unit, modular, tiny-living complex that re-defines how we live on the individual, communal, and city scale. It is inspired by the potential of space found between the infrastructure of typical high-rise buildings. This new living sys-tem features independent modules that allow for more units per square foot as well as having each unit safely spaced apart. Vegetation and open air fill the in-between.

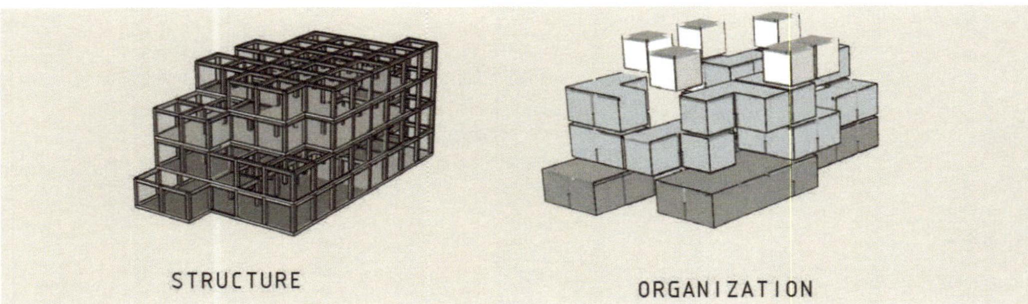

The Stack excels at promoting and protecting human life by expanding the opportunity for housing while exploring new strategies for density

461ZNECZ2

SELECTED PROJECTS

613UOTF5E

HERMETICITY

Luciana Teodózio
Jordi Fernández
Eduardo Gutiérrez
Spain

How can we colonize extreme environments with a reduced footprint? The proposal envisions a new type of habitat that can provide the basic needs for human life to take place in harsh environments. Growing upwards instead of horizontally saves resources and energy. It reduces the impact on the surrounding ecosystem by keeping all the activities concentrated over the same core.

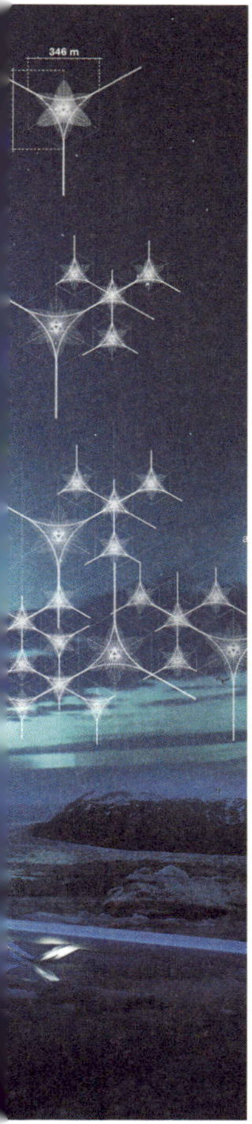
346 m

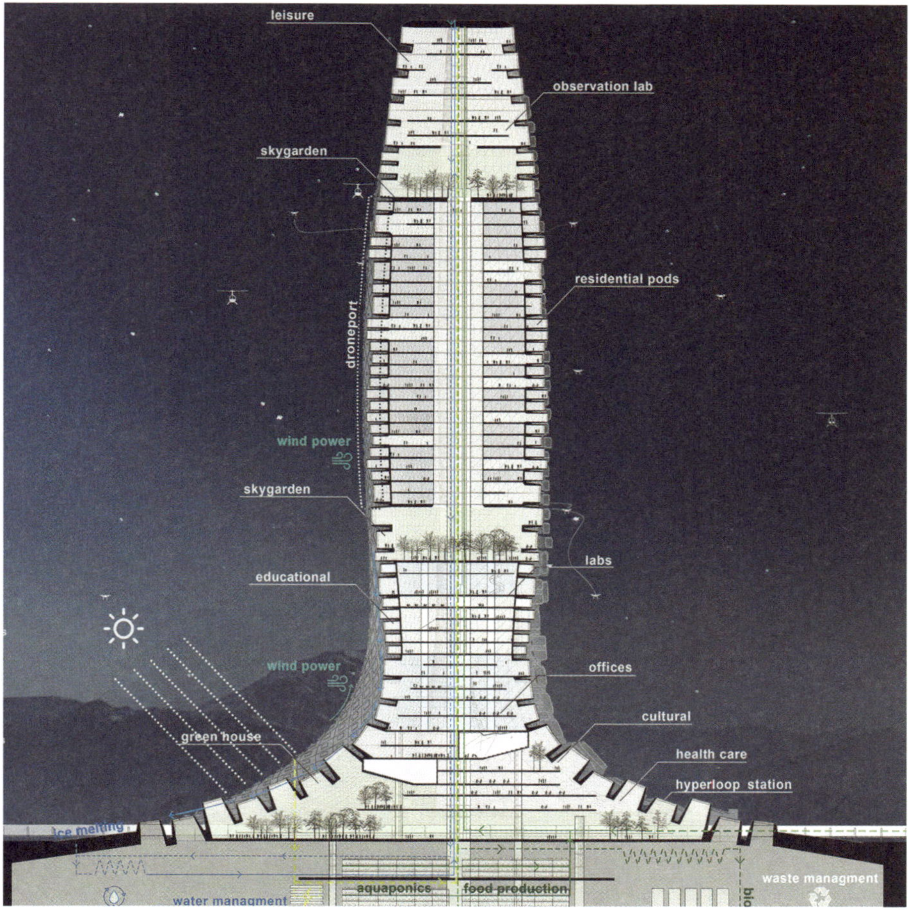
leisure
observation lab
skygarden
residential pods
droneport
wind power
skygarden
labs
educational
wind power
offices
cultural
green house
health care
hyperloop station
ice melting
waste managment
aquaponics
food production
water managment

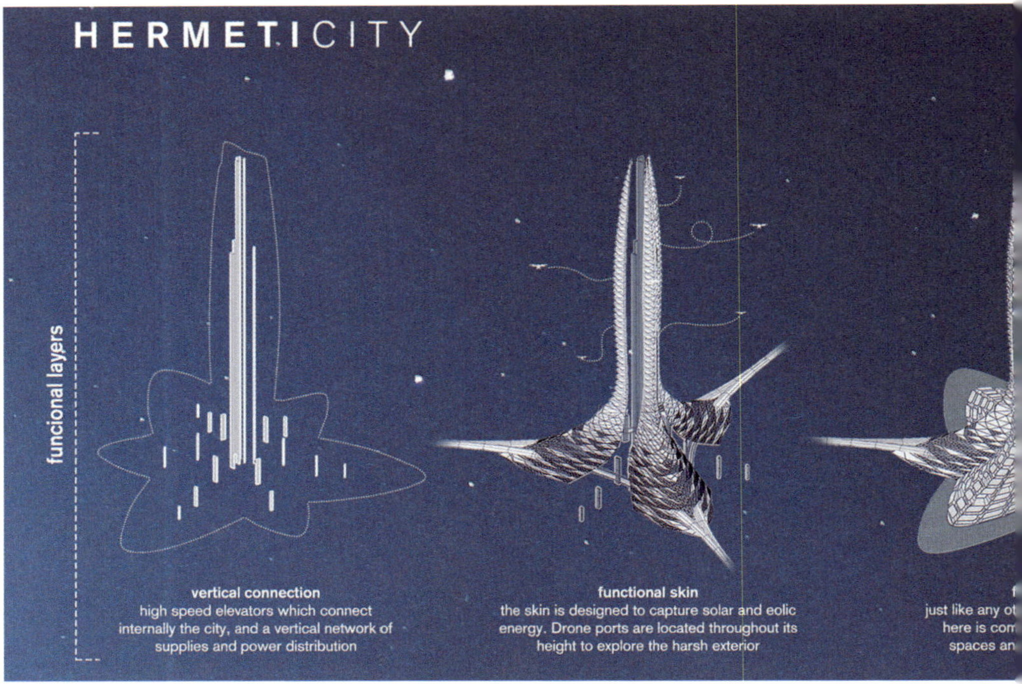
HERMETICITY
funcional layers
vertical connection
high speed elevators which connect internally the city, and a vertical network of supplies and power distribution
functional skin
the skin is designed to capture solar and eolic energy. Drone ports are located throughout its height to explore the harsh exterior
just like any ot
here is com
spaces an

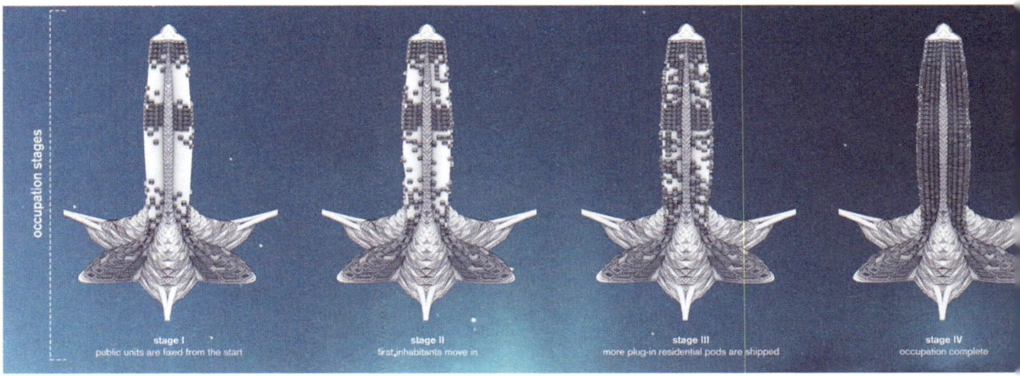
occupation stages
stage I
public units are fixed from the start
stage II
first inhabitants move in
stage III
more plug-in residential pods are shipped
stage IV
occupation complete

This model of urban design could be the key to a sustainable, hyper connected future

SELECTED PROJECTS

225JMNODN

HYGGE

Te Li
Liang An Yee
China

Then we had an aim - to build a community that connects, a place where people can live in harmony and unity - our target is to create a quality and healthy living in the most difficult time. Social distancing between neighbourhood, community autarchy, minimal lifestyle - these became the necessities, and to enhance it even more, studies, exercise and recreations are combined together. Then cubes are stacked on each other, like lego blocks that are scattered on the floor. A green architecture of multiple floors, a place that is comprehended with various flows, connections and spaces, for people to interact in a safe and healthy way. This is the Hygge, a community where contentment and wellness are found.

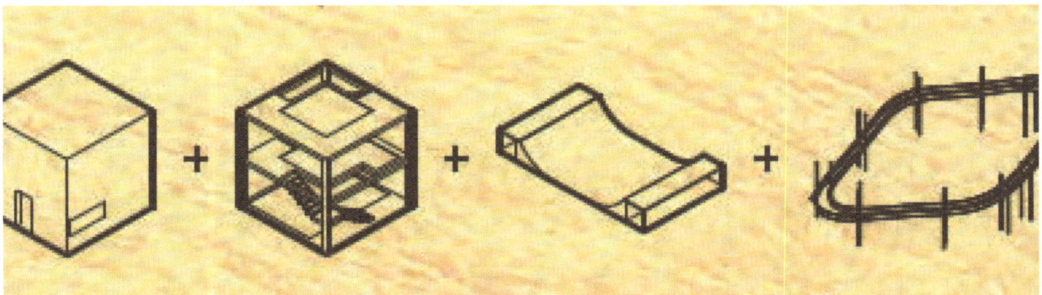

ID Code: 225JMNODN

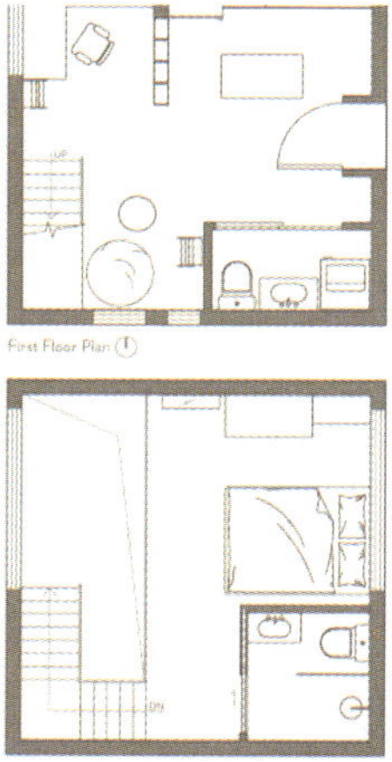

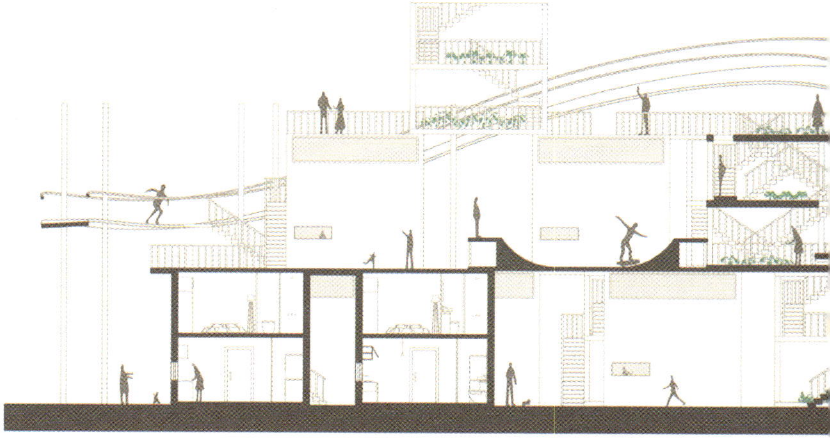

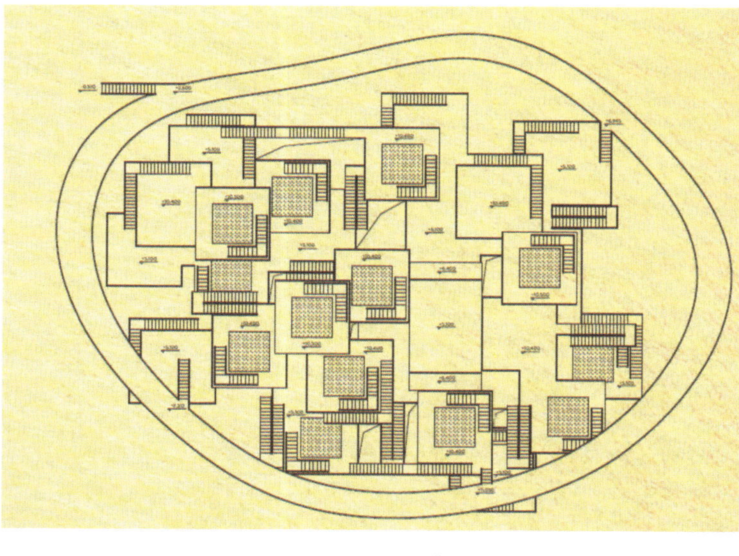

Site plan

225JMNODN

SELECTED PROJECTS

612LYJOGD

FROM İNDİGENOUS TO İNGENİOUS HABİTAT

Marlo Jr. Marana
Cristine Duenas Tebelen
Philippines

The project has developed a theory that in the coming years of the 21st century. Humans will crave for a more organic way of living caused by the fast-phased movement of technology. By analyzing our present events. Humans have developed different breakdowns in any kind: from our bodies to the city. The Project aims to turn the attention of humans to nature in participation of technologically enhanced indigenous communities that can lay the foundation for organic living that greatly defines the future of Environmental revolution.

FORM GIVING DIAGRAM

This Project aims to create the so-called "Heroes of Sustainability for the 21st Century" by creating an innovative Habitat for people of the First World (The Indigenous Human being) as a starting point for what we called "The Environmental Revolution."

SELECTED PROJECTS

6580COZEP

İNDOORSY

Martyna Sykta
Kamil Dąbek
Marcin Niedziałek
Poland

Indoorsy uses virtual reality to create a digital version of the house, which can be shared with other users, rearranged and modified to create a perfect atmosphere for a house party, family meeting or a date. The platform allows to personalise avatars and socialise by arranging virtual get-togethers. Indoorsy enables to spend a perfect time with others through various options, such as streaming movies, listening to the music or playing games in virtual reality. The application responds to the very actual need of keeping in touch with the closest ones and creates an innovative field for entertainment.

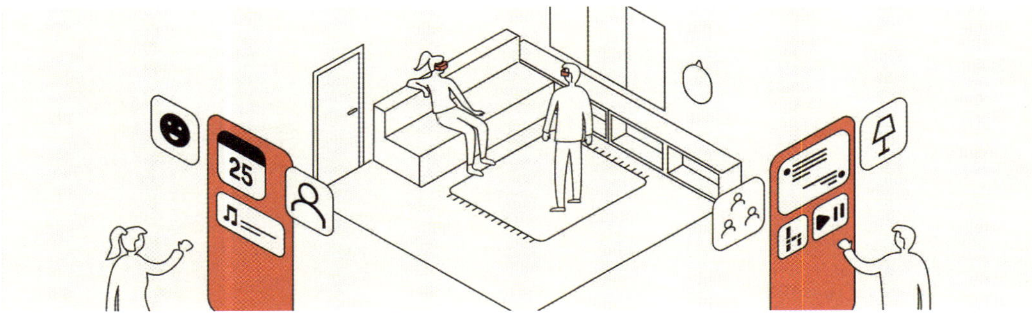

25

12. Adjust the lighting and mood to make a perfect atmosphere

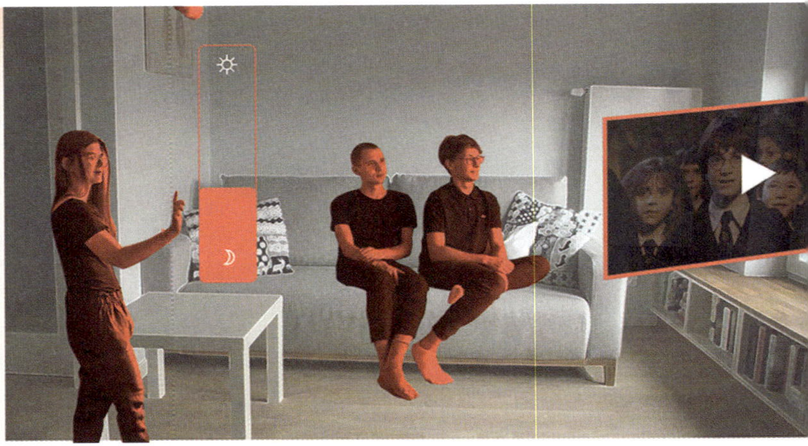

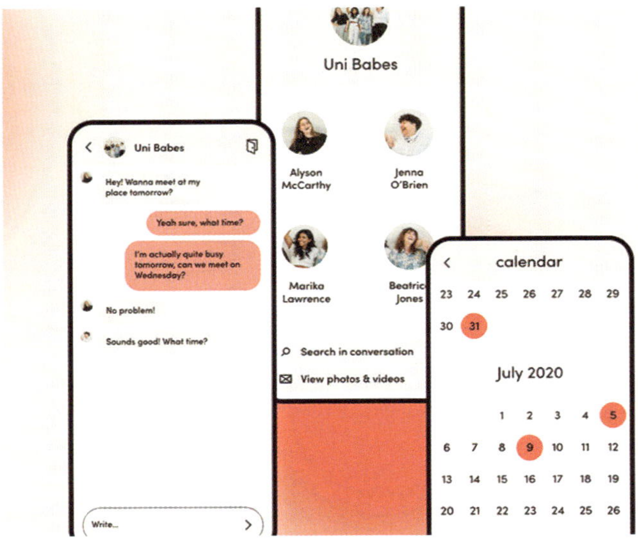

Indoorsy plays with the borders of home by bringing it into virtual reality and opening it to others despite the physical distance

1. Scan your apartment so it can transform into a realistic 3D model

6580C0ZEP

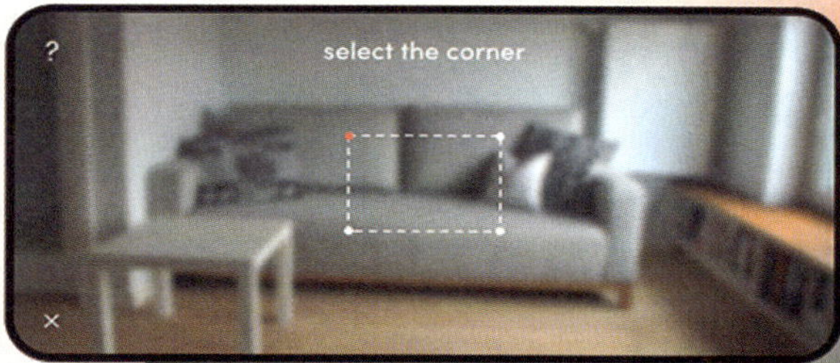

3. Rearrange your virtual home to make a perfect set-up for a get-together

SELECTED PROJECTS

72290YOGA

PUNKTWOW

KOSZE DO SELEKTYWNEJ ZBİÓRKİ ODPADÓW

Ewelina Mężyńska
Poland

My project of the PunktWOW system for the selective collection of municipal waste in public and private spaces.
I designed a small architecture facility that allows for selective waste storage and introduces mobile service.
Additionally, the basket is operated without direct touch contact.
The mobile application is also a benefit system and encourages users to use and maintain statistics. The product design is based on Bauhaus school.

TAXI

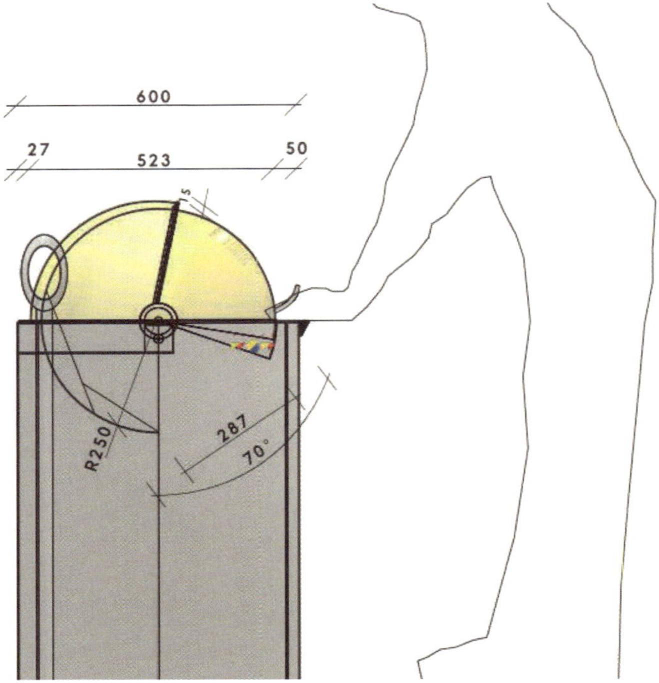
600
27
523
50
R250
287
70°

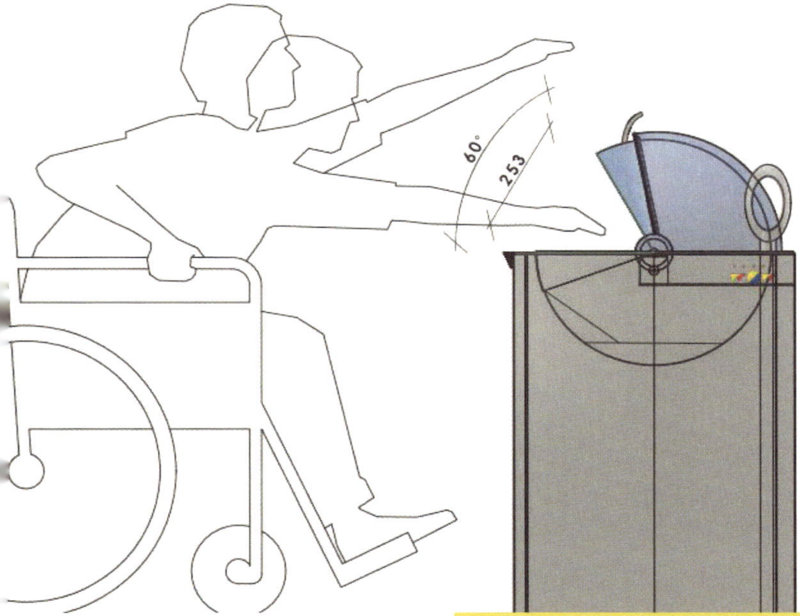

Drawings showing dimentions, ergonomics and accessibility

SELECTED PROJECTS 705UZ9N49

JEANS AT A GLOBAL SCALE

María Fernanda Peña
Colombia

THE LONG SUPPLY CHAİN

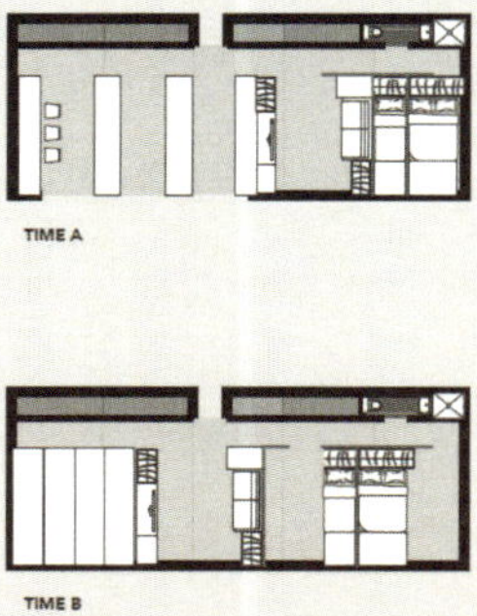

Since the 1980s, there has been a deficit in cotton cultivation in Colombia due to economic opening and drug trafficking, which generated an increase in imports. Raw materials are transported by land from seaports on a journey that can take between 14 and 20 hours to Bogotá, where each transformation process is carried out in different informal and specialized garment workshops, located in different parts of the city. These production and distribution logics have a great impact on the carbon footprint at a global level, especially considering that Bogotá has an area of approximately 17 times the size of Barcelona, where the product is carried from one place to another, until reaching the final consumer.

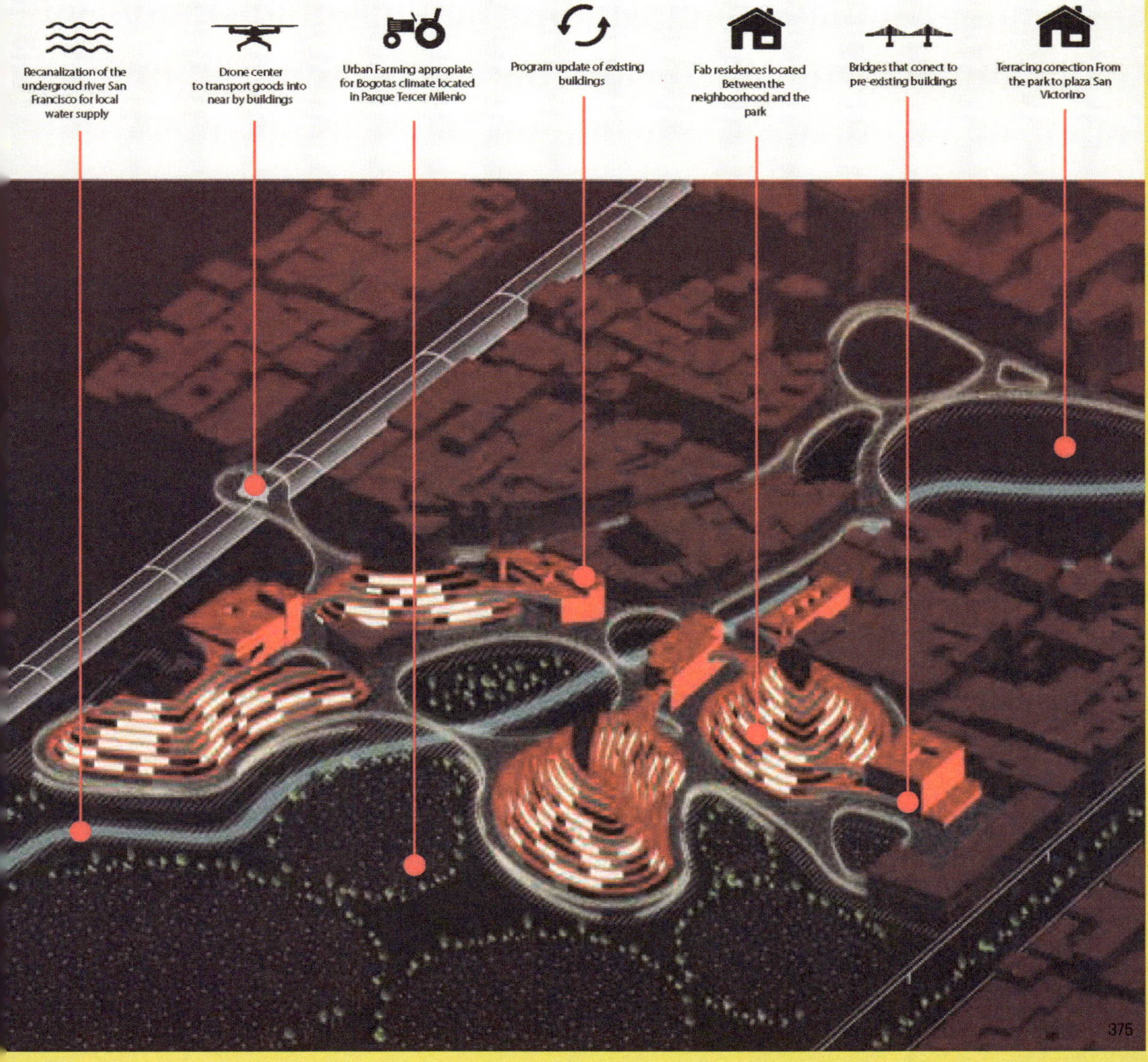

Recanalization of the underground river San Francisco for local water supply
Drone center to transport goods into near by buildings
Urban Farming appropiate for Bogotas climate located in Parque Tercer Milenio
Program update of existing buildings
Fab residences located Between the neighboorhood and the park
Bridges that conect to pre-existing buildings
Terracing conection From the park to plaza San Victorino

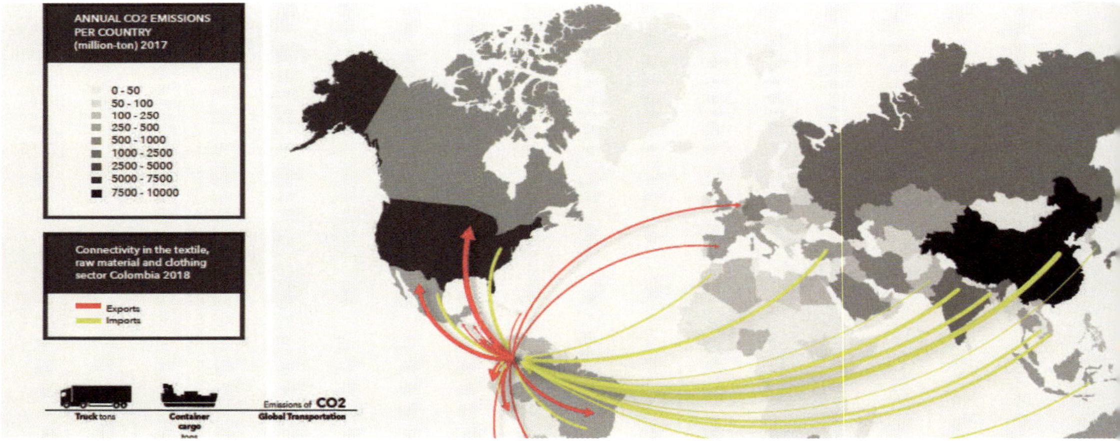

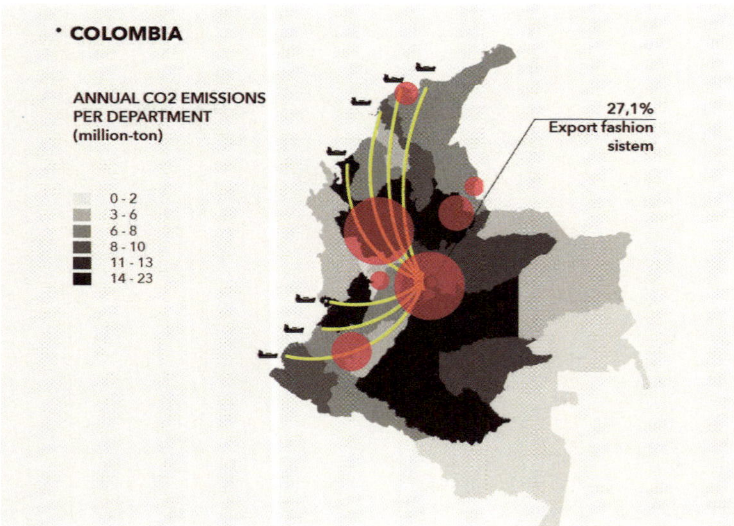

San Victorino is a traditional neighborhood in the center of Bogotá, recognized as an epicenter for wholesale trade.

705UZ9N49

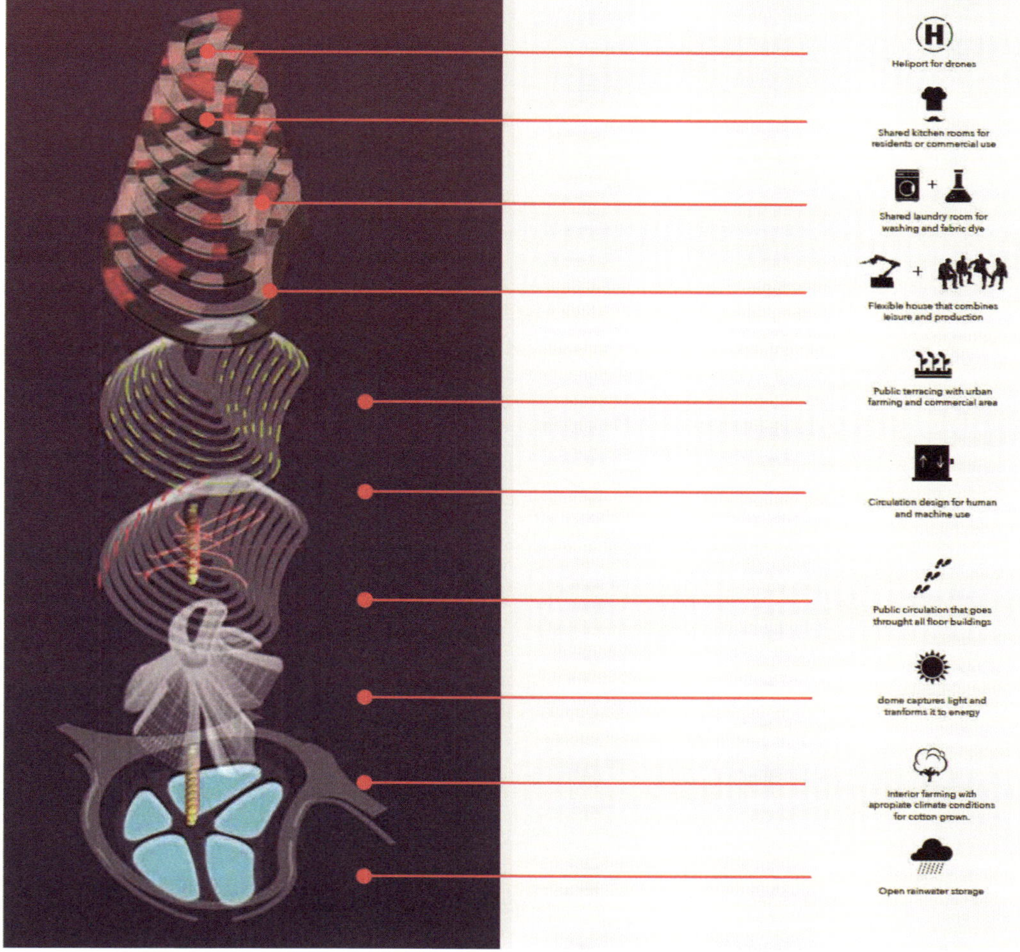
Heliport for drones
Shared kitchen rooms for residents or commercial use
Shared laundry room for washing and fabric dye
Flexible house that combines leisure and production
Public terracing with urban farming and commercial area
Circulation design for human and machine use
Public circulation that goes throught all floor buildings
dome captures light and tranforms it to energy
Interior farming with apropiate climate conditions for cotton grown.
Open rainwater storage

SELECTED PROJECTS

88100ECO

DE-PURPOSED LİVİNG SPACES

LOSİNG PURPOSE TODAY, FOR BETTER LİVİNG TOMORROW

Michael Dicarlo
United States of America

"De-purposing" existing space means removing presupposed notions of what programs are, allowing spontaneous adaptation. In a "de-purposed" paradigm new structures behave like skin accommodating bodily function. There should be a semi-conscious, perpetual dialogue between user and structure. We address climate change by extrapolating the isolationist strategy to Covid at the individual scale, remapped to the scale of civilization. Treating humanity as a singular biome, we can "de-purpose" decades' worth of underutilization to develop a sense of highly efficient living systems.

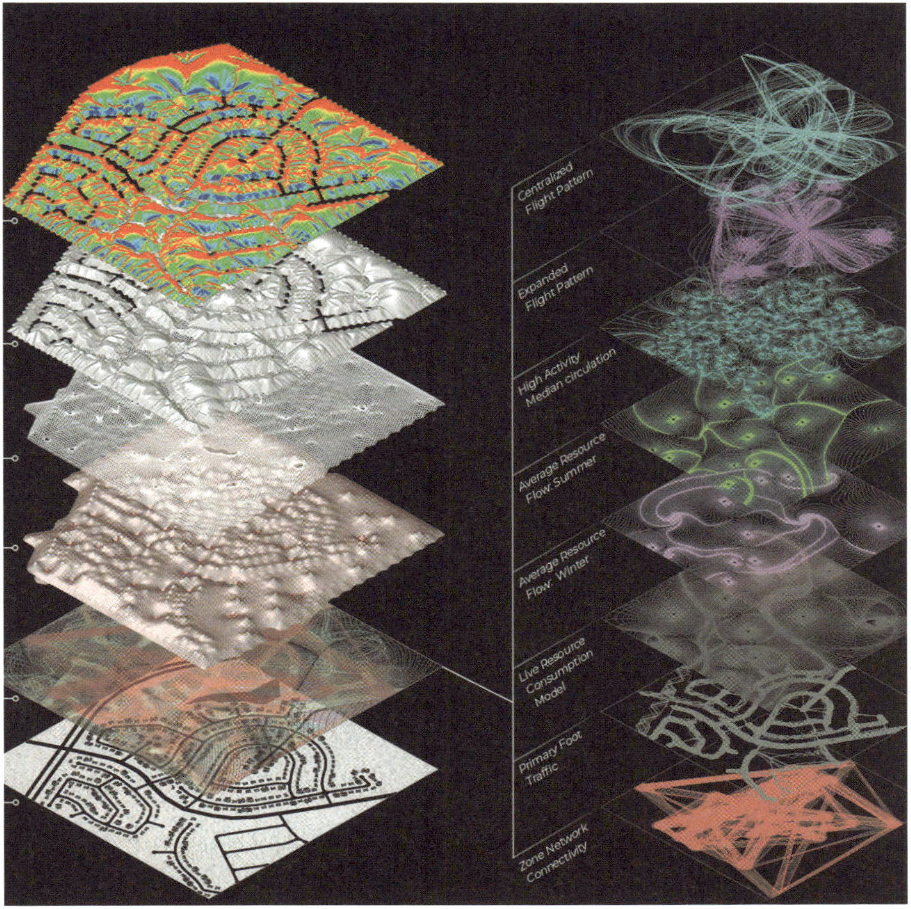

Centralized Flight Pattern
Expanded Flight Pattern
High Activity Median circulation
Average Resource Flow: Summer
Average Resource Flow: Winter
Live Resource Consumption Model
Primary Foot Traffic
Zone Network Connectivity

Manor, Texas, USA sample site for a system which could theoretically be deployed to any suburban sub development, city block, or individual sky scraper

SELECTED PROJECTS 6605AXVI3

KOMOREBİ

REMEDY FOR GENTRİFİED URBANİSATİON

Zhi Xin Hoo
Wong Quin Ee Queenie
Muhammad Haziq Bin Ariffin
Malaysia

Air space among buildings is utilised by KOMOREBI, the [co]llective [mo] bile [re] sponsive [bi]omimicry. It is an automated system of distributed and deployable modular units deployed by big data analytics according to the desires of the citizens. Powered by renewable energy and driven by swarm intelligence, the units self-integrate into tactile surfaces that act as public streets as well as pocket spaces for families and individuals; encouraging urban spontaneity and human interaction. Distribution of the modules evolves and iterates organically according to data collected based on patterns of inhabitations of residents.

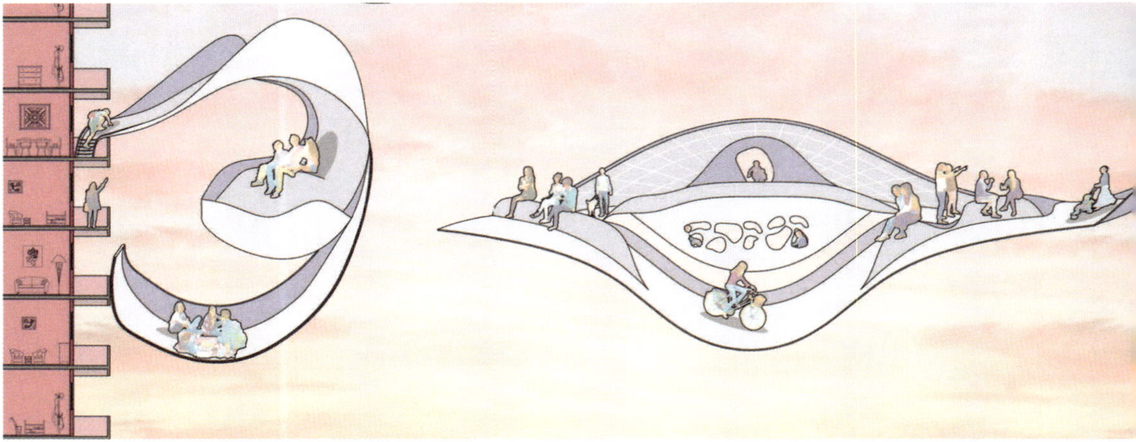

"When ground space is scarce, we look to the sky"

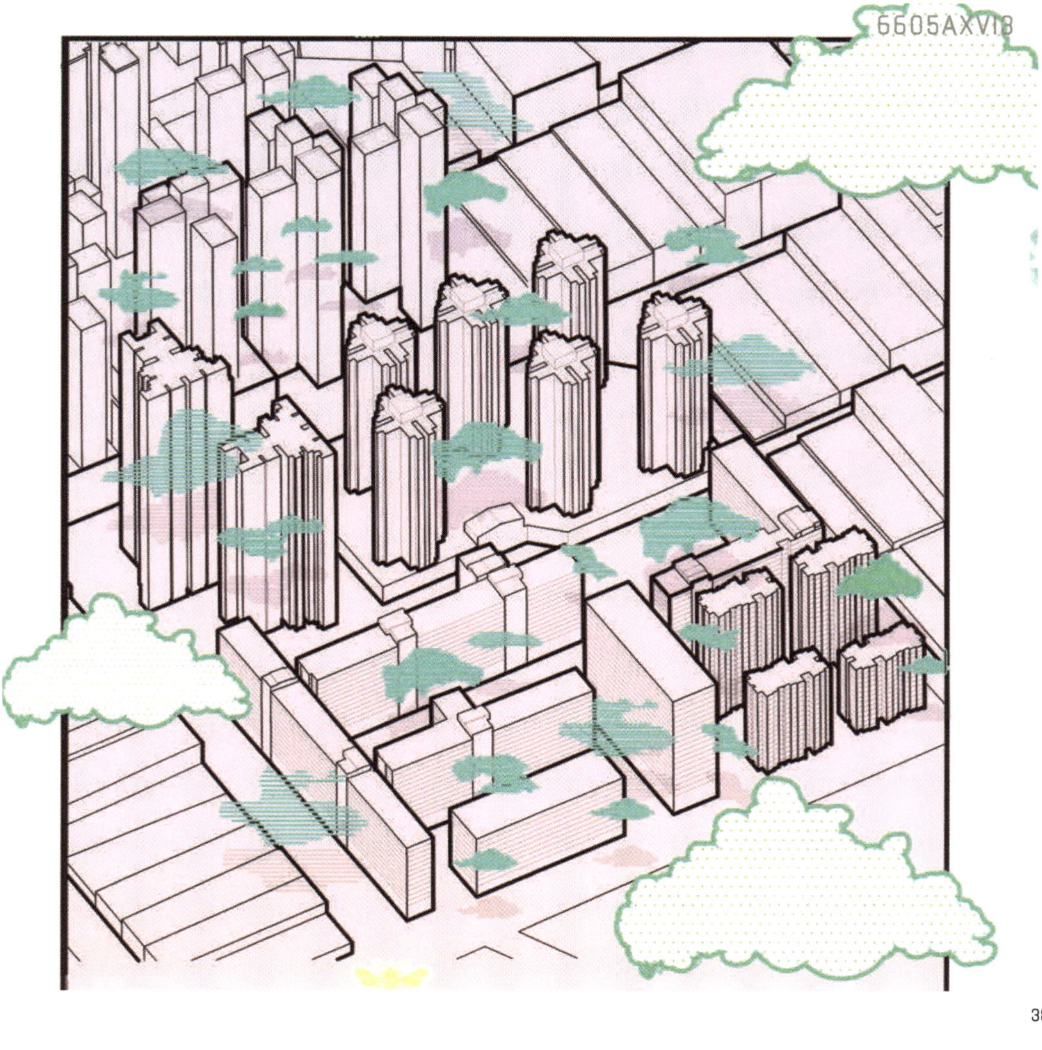
6605AXVI8

SELECTED PROJECTS

480QFQCOJ

RAİLWAY TO HEAVEN

Michael Corvino
United States of America

This proposal re-appropriates existing rail yards and networks freeing thousands of acres of land for new use. These newly freed sites will be developed utilizing components of rail. Abandoned rail cars will be converted into a new nomadic housing typology, mobile businesses, education facilities, medical aid, and more. These moving parts will go throughout the site and the nation connecting people and bring opportunity to larger regions. Abandoned track will be the universal building element of these hubs providing a replicable system hosted in our cities. new life can spring from what was previously devoid and vacant.

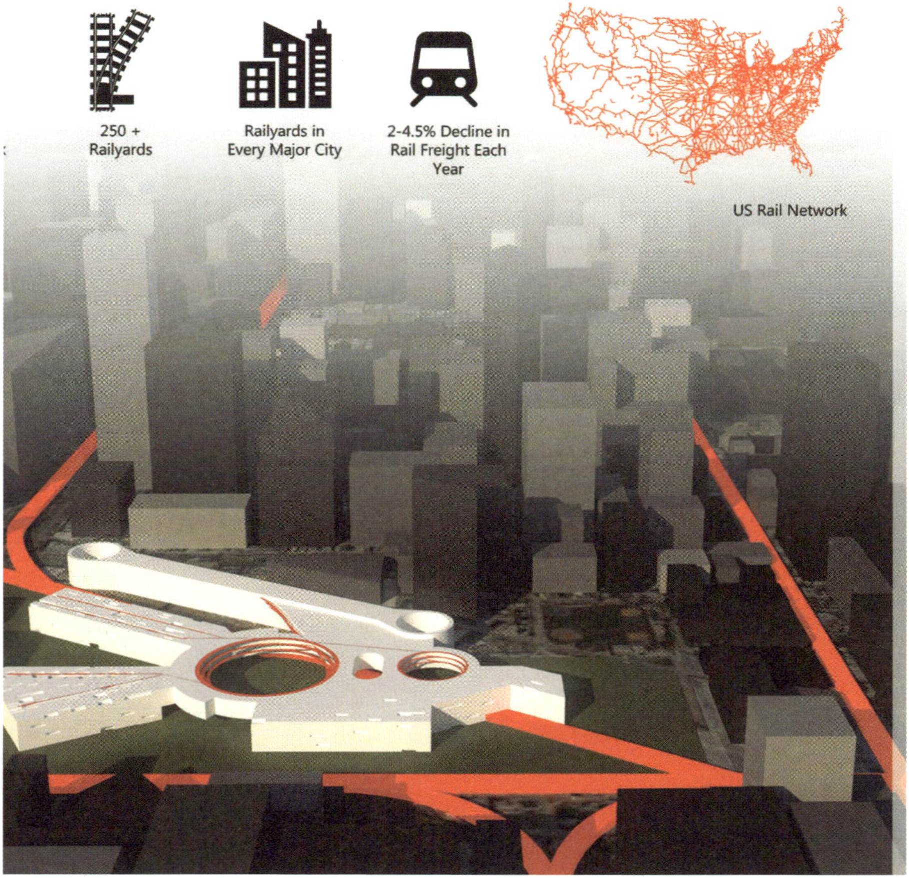
250 +
Railyards
Railyards in
Every Major City
2-4.5% Decline in
Rail Freight Each
Year
US Rail Network

Rail Lines
Interior Parks
East West Orientation
Sun Enters Parks

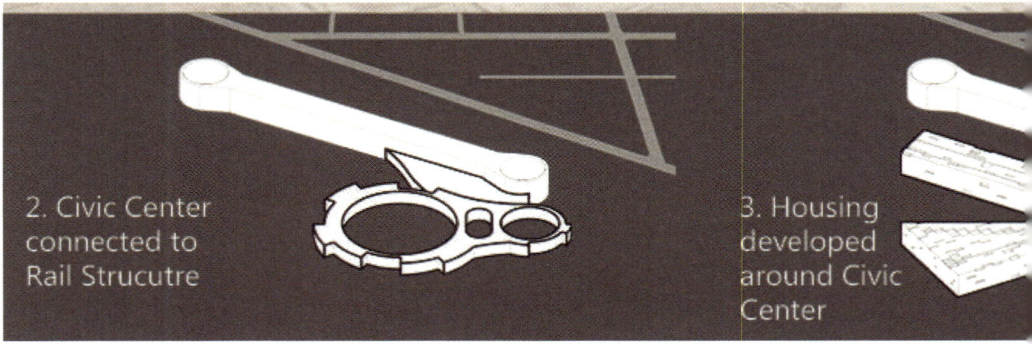
2. Civic Center
connected to
Rail Strucutre
3. Housing
developed
around Civic
Center

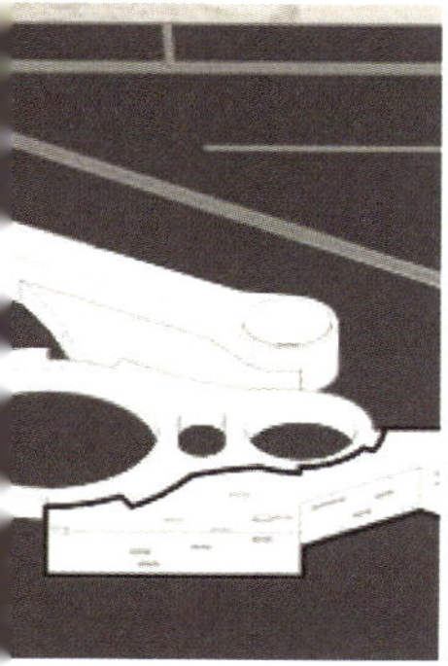

Rail infrastructure is often on the fringe, disconnected from civic life, and associated with blighted areas, diminished opportunities and marginalization

SELECTED PROJECTS

48898DIRM

HİBLA

A VERTİCAL COMMUNİTY

Renzo Patrick Tinambacan
Mac Keley Jones Jucom
Lex Rafael Marquez
Evan Gilbert Basila
Junel Buyagon
Don De Vera
Nela Tapia
Philippines

The proposed community reflects a diverse way of life for its people through use of strategic spatial zoning that integrates principles of sustainable design in addition to health and welfare needs while promoting inclusivity. And through the adoption of new technology, the researchers aimed for a contemporary architecture capable of providing innovative solutions addressing the issues of modern society.

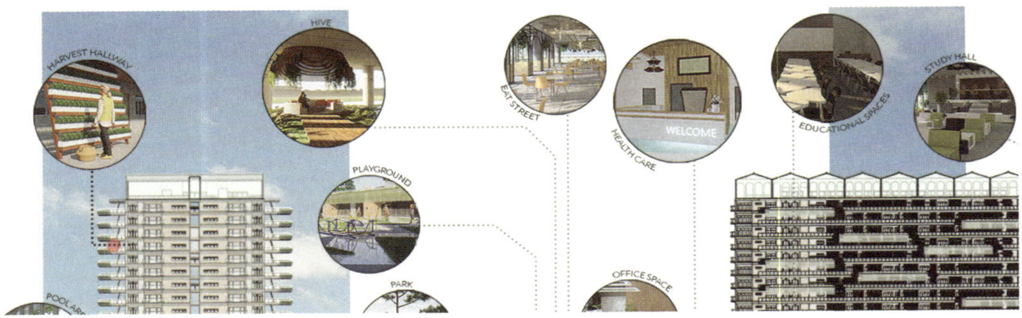

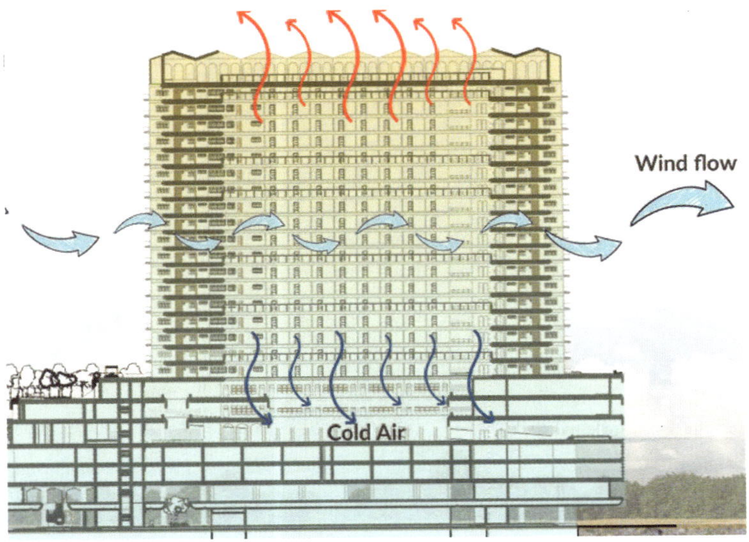

"Hibla" a Filipino term which means "thread" and just like a thread forming a canvas, the researchers believe it to be a great representation of the lives of people bonded within a community

6605AXVI3

ea

Unit

SELECTED PROJECTS

634D0AM1H

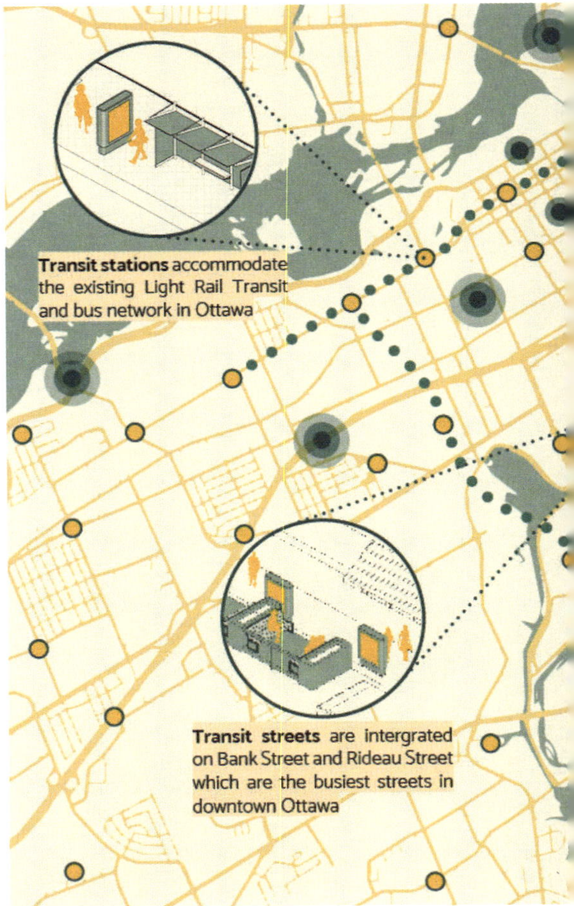

TRANSİT ECOSYSTEM

Huy Pham
Canada
There has been numerous research and development in public transit system and infrastructure to promote the use of public transit.
However, the transit system are often overloaded and unrealiable due to planning, operation, weather and many other factors.
Reports from Statistic Canada have shown very little improvements compared to the amount of efforts and money invested in transit systems. The transit ecosystem approaches transit as a mean of transportation, not just as a mean of commuting. The transit ecosystem deliver public services to people instead of people to the services and use a community based design system.

Rail Transit

information
public service
wifi
restaurants
shopping
courier
outdoor charging
other

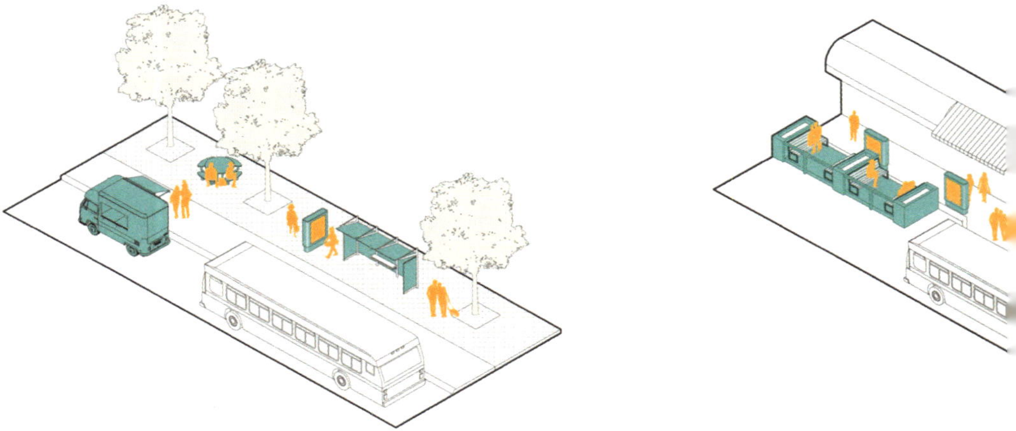

HOME
WORK
SOCIAL
SERVICE
COMMUNITY

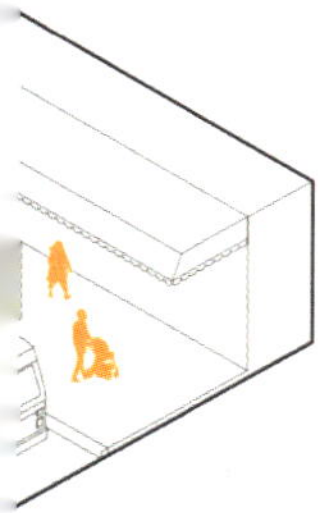

Interactive kiosks allow people to access available services and information from the transit ecosystem. The interactive kiosk is designed to bring the transit ecosystem to every community

SELECTED PROJECTS

460PSOD2E

REJUVENATİON

URBAN JUNGLES TO UNİTE THE DİVİDED

Nicholas Esquibel
United States of America

Endless miles of black asphalt carve their way through towering, lifeless cliffs of concrete and steel. Streets that once fostered community have devolved into rifts as confrontations of speed and impermeability drive the wedge between each of us. It's taken a global pandemic for us to realize our way of living only furthers our isolation. In fact, the decline in commuting has shown our lives depend almost entirely on our immediate surroundings and the people we greet daily. Now, more than ever, is the time to come together, grow as a community, and create a hopeful future for the inheriting generations to come.

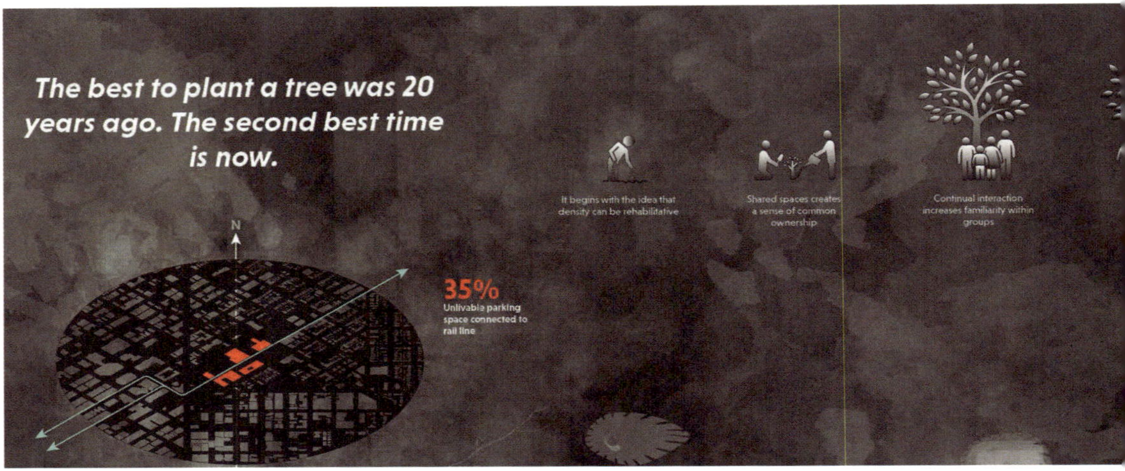

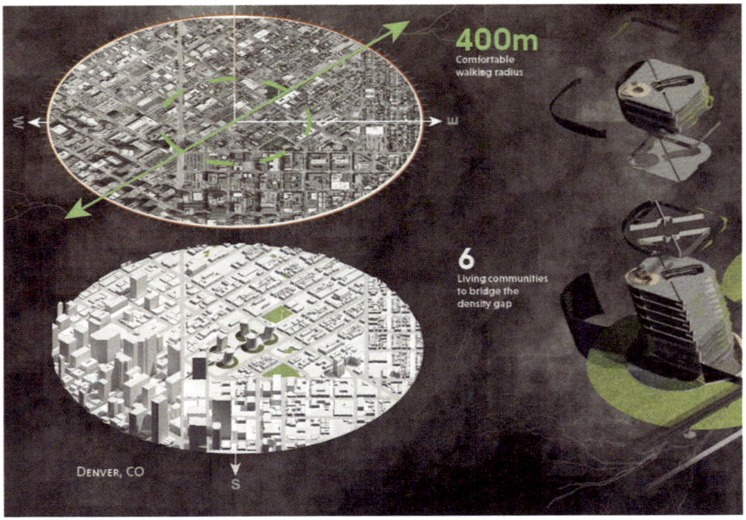

RejuveNATION comes from systematically reimagining the urban corridor with the wellbeing of all life in mind.

mmonality
mmunities

0' 10' 20' 40' 60'
0' 24' 48' 96'

SELECTED PROJECTS

693NOAS8K

UNDERWATER FUTURE

Nina Kaminska
Poland

Humanity is facing a global crisis. Planet Earth is getting hotter and hotter like the current political situation in many countries. Riots, manifestations, aggressive moods. Floods and extreme heats at one time. Social inequalities, racism, and hunger threat. There will not be a better time to rethink human habitats. Inhabitants can grow with their city together at the one time. Completely modular habitat respects everyone's needs. Higher or shorter buildings, bigger or smaller module flats - it is absolutely up to the individual preferences. No need to plan the whole city at once, it grows in every direction in response to future world challenges.

31°55'S 71°31'W
LOS VILOS // CHILE
Avda. Costanera
Los Vilos

CORAL REEF IS THE ANSW

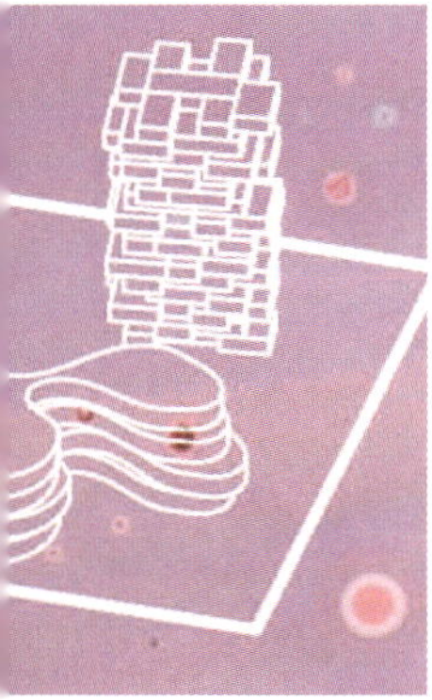

◀ Ecosystems - Selfsufficient quarters

SELECTED PROJECTS

738BHOONL

SYNERGY WiTH THE CONTEXT

Cristian Ovidiu Pavel
Italy

The most important value of an architecture focused on life is synergy, harmony with the surrounding space. An architecture is in synergy with context when it manages to bring the environment around within the project itself, merging with it and preserving itrs identity at the same time.

ging nature into the city

The project is placed in the middle of nature, consequently, to better integrate the buildings into the environment, nature itself has been "helped to climb" the towers.

Welcoming the flora in the city is not always a popular choice, however, an architect must reflect on the impact that his work can also have on the environment

Where today there is a building there was once nature, life, what the house has done is to take away "life", occupying its place.

Today it is necessary to reintroduce that "life" again in the houses because we have all the means to do it, nature can continue to grow alongside the city and improve the characteristics of the architecture itself;

As Gio Ponti said in "Amate l'architettura": "a city with green roofs is a happy city".

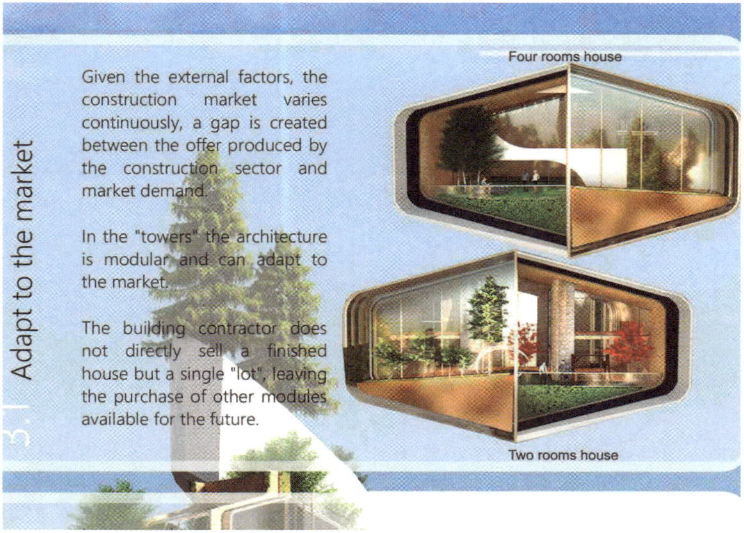

The project is placed in the middle of nature, consequently, to better integrate the buildings into the environment, nature itself has been "helped to climb" the towers

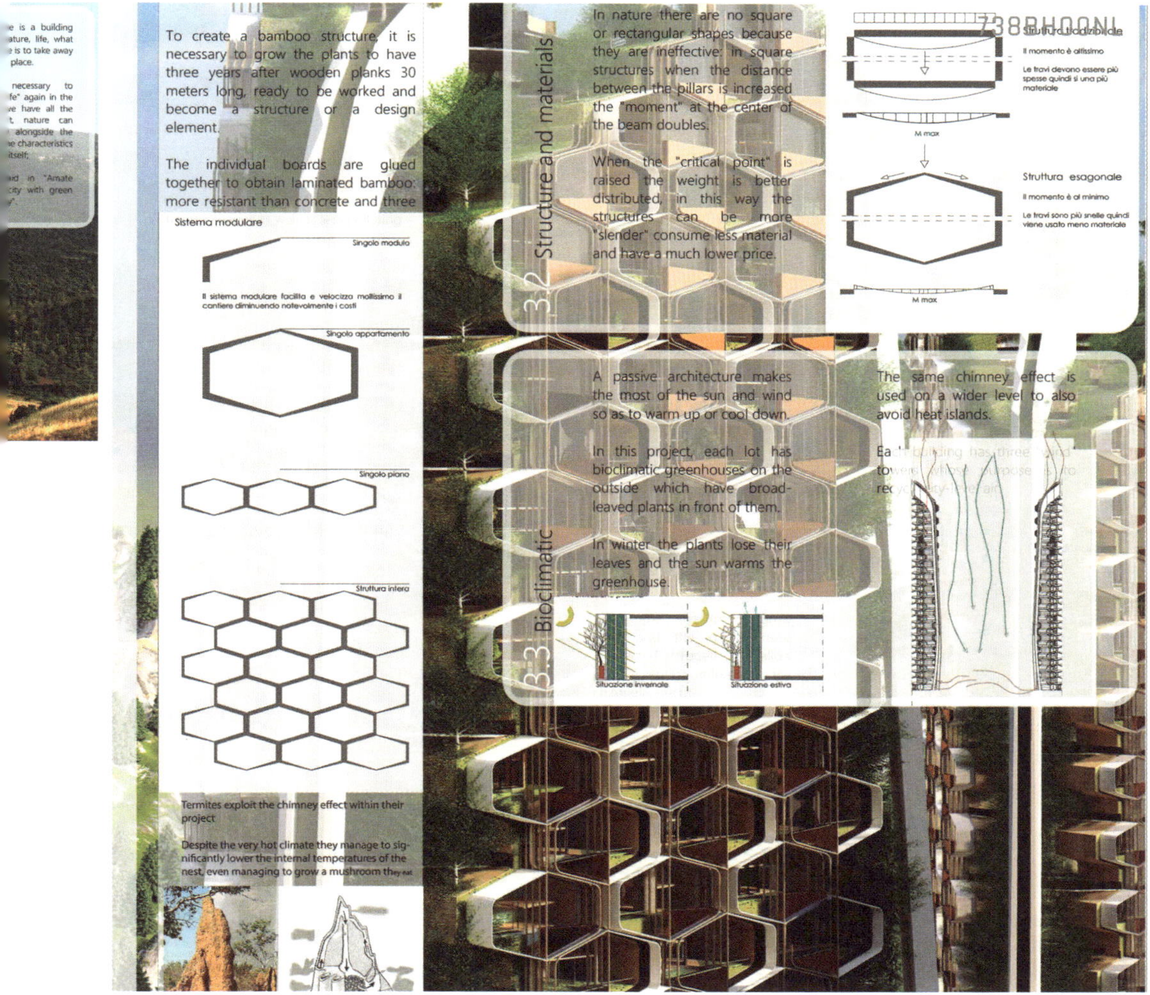

To create a bamboo structure, it is necessary to grow the plants to have three years after wooden planks 30 meters long, ready to be worked and become a structure or a design element.
The individual boards are glued together to obtain laminated bamboo: more resistant than concrete and three
Sistema modulare
Singolo modulo
Il sistema modulare facilita e velocizza moltissimo il cantiere diminuendo notevolmente i costi
Singolo appartamento
Singolo piano
Struttura intera
Termites exploit the chimney effect within their project
Despite the very hot climate they manage to significantly lower the internal temperatures of the nest, even managing to grow a mushroom they eat
3.2 Structure and materials
In nature there are no square or rectangular shapes because they are ineffective: in square structures when the distance between the pillars is increased the "moment" at the center of the beam doubles.
When the "critical point" is raised the weight is better distributed, in this way the structures can be more "slender" consume less material and have a much lower price.
738BHOONI
Struttura tradizionale
Il momento è altissimo
Le travi devono essere più spesse quindi si una più materiale
M max
Struttura esagonale
Il momento è al minimo
Le travi sono più snelle quindi viene usato meno materiale
M max
3.3 Bioclimatic
A passive architecture makes the most of the sun and wind so as to warm up or cool down.
In this project, each lot has bioclimatic greenhouses on the outside which have broad-leaved plants in front of them.
In winter the plants lose their leaves and the sun warms the greenhouse.
Situazione invernale
Situazione estiva
The same chimney effect is used on a wider level to also avoid heat islands.

SELECTED PROJECTS

674YV5BDE

PUBLİC HYGİENE WASHBASİNS

Nikita Ovsyuk
Russian Federation

Hand washing is a routine operation that society needs regularly, for various reasons and several times a day. At the moment, the situation with the ability to wast your hands is simply ridiculous - that can only be done in the toilet. Washing your hands after visiting the restroom is very important, but visiting the toilet is far from the only action before / after there is a need to refresh your hands and face. It is simply amazing what kind of beastliness we live in and what a global pandemic was required for humanity to pay attention to elementary hyfiene procedures. We must prepare our cities for a routine, quick and stylish way to do this.

INSTALLATION PLACES

public transport stop

entrance to the park

entrance to the playground

busy streets

entrance to the sports ground

buzy squares

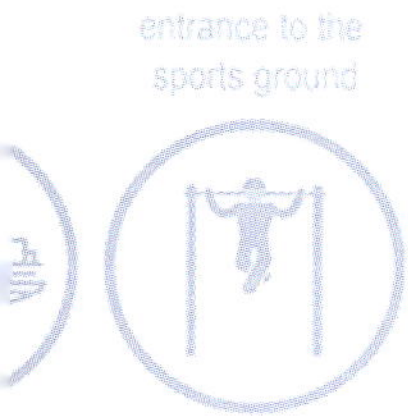

The ability to wash your hands and have lunch that go in the fresh air with less unwanted social contact

SELECTED PROJECTS

683ITDVGP

FOOD AS THE CORE

Patricia Vera Paparoni
Viviana Moreno Troconis
Venezuela

The proposal is to implement the food cycle in residential areas, to give autonomy, accessibility, and sustainability. An urban-rural interface allows reconnecting people, nature, and food production. Gardening and orchard in each apartment and house, a digester in each building, an urban garden in the center of the block, and farms in and around cities are the ways to get back to the root, to recreate an integrated system between urbanization and agriculture, that could rebuilding communities, reconnecting people to nature, and restoring the environment.

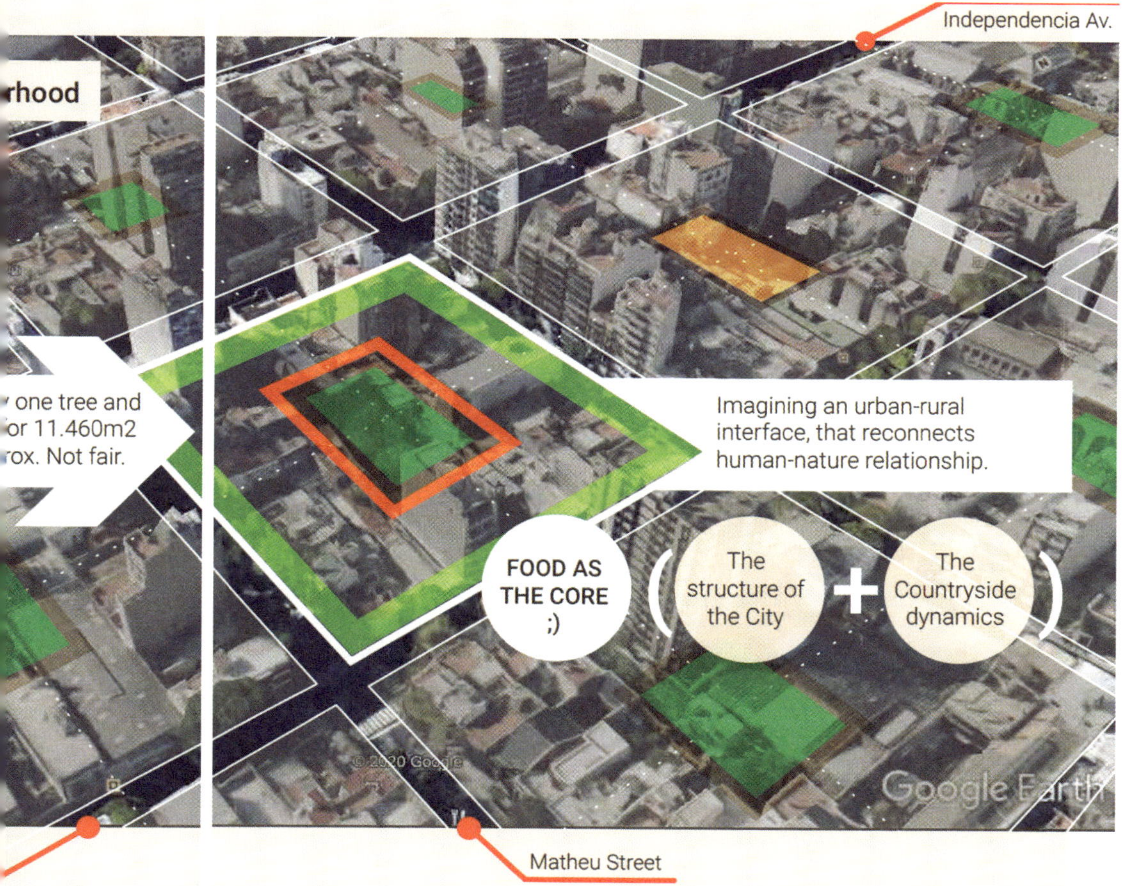
Independencia Av.
rhood
one tree and
or 11.460m2
rox. Not fair.
Imagining an urban-rural interface, that reconnects human-nature relationship.
FOOD AS THE CORE ;)
The structure of the City
+
The Countryside dynamics
© 2020 Google
Google Earth
Matheu Street

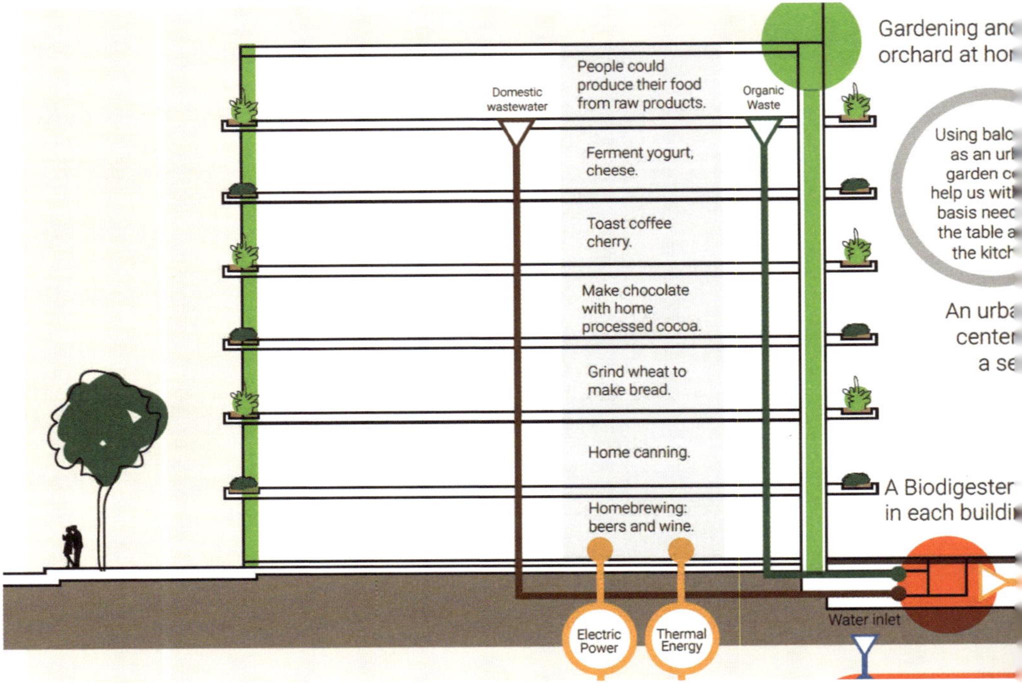

Urbanism + Agriculture

Food Needs
Grains, Fruits, Legumes, Vegetables, Proteins, Dairy, Fats and Sweet, Alcohol, Water

Benefits
Guarantee food
Improving public health.
Rebuild communities.
Reconnecting people to nature.
Revitalizing economies
Restoring degraded environments

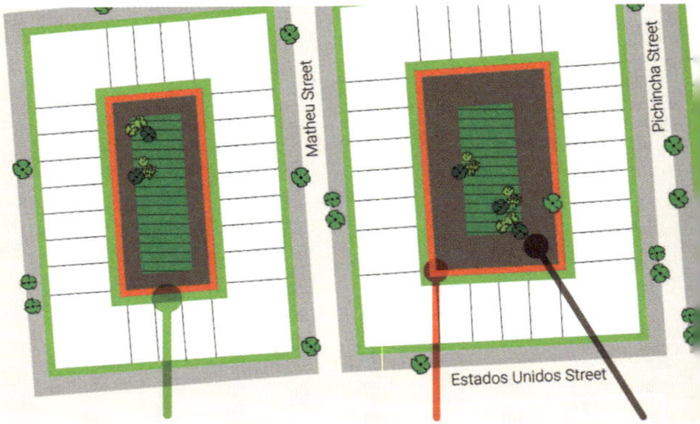

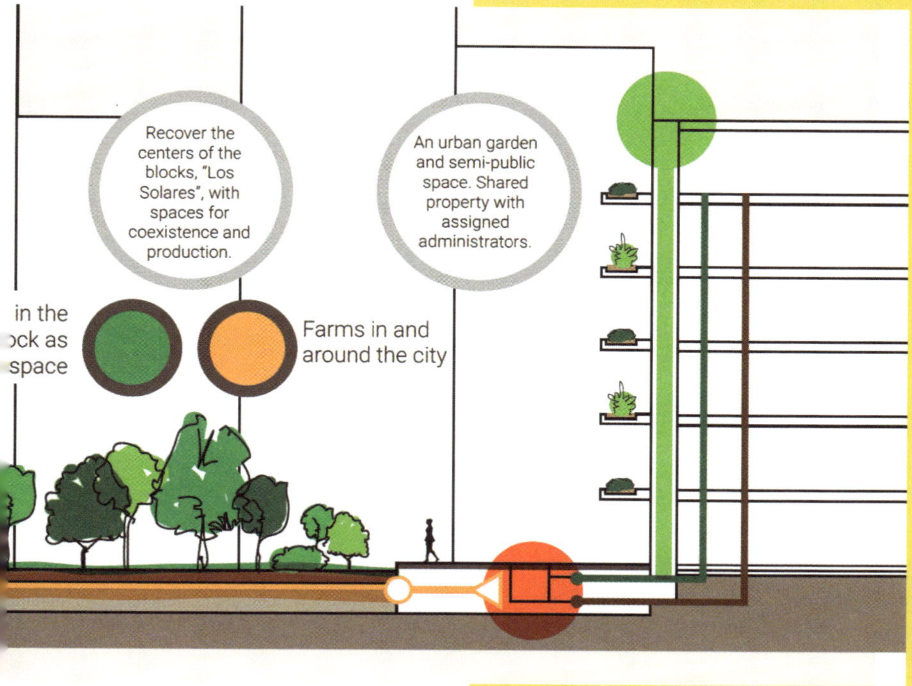

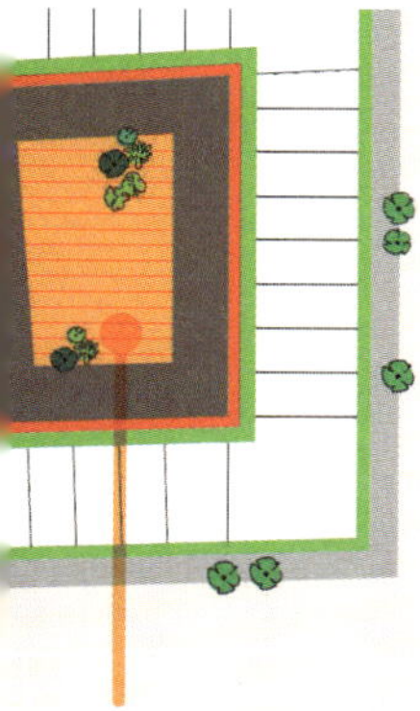

The urban-rural system
Urbanism + Arquitecture

SELECTED PROJECTS

701KI1I7T

ROCK CAST

Rana Salah
Saagarika Dias
United Arab Emirates

The project explores construction through utilizing the 3 elements, rock sand and concrete, available for use in most rural sites. It aims to push towards a more sustainable and less process wastefull methods of construction through eliminating the materials required for formwork use. The method of construction involves the use of the landscape as formwork to hold back a collection of rocks in place until concrete is cast through, binding itself to the rocks and being contained by the surrounding sand. Through manipulating multiple variables such as the addition of an impermeable layer or a flat surface to one side, it is possible to obtain different formal qualities of the cast.
The vertical elements would be cast in place and then surrounding landscape would be excavated out, while horizontal elements would be cast on a flat surface then lifted onto the appropriate placement above the vertical elements.

Through exploring a set of forms the concrete -rock cast could take, it then becomes possible to create a modular housing unit that allows for an adequate living space as well as an open courtyard condition within each unit

SELECTED PROJECTS

571GY9P7X

PATCHCİTY

Bogdan Seredyak
United States of America

PATCH CITY is a proposal for dynamic futures. Using carbon fiber that is rapidly becoming more and more recyclable the project proposes new temporary habitats for multitude of uses. From additional workspaces, shelters, to passageways between buildings. Carbon fibers rigidity yet flexibility allows for almost unlimited freedom of form. With an uncertain, everchanging future, spaces that need to be added for temporary use when required can be installed and dismantled for next use with greater speed and efficiency than traditional building materials. This often times it would mean utilizing the only available spaces in urban dwellings such as rooftops or parking lots.

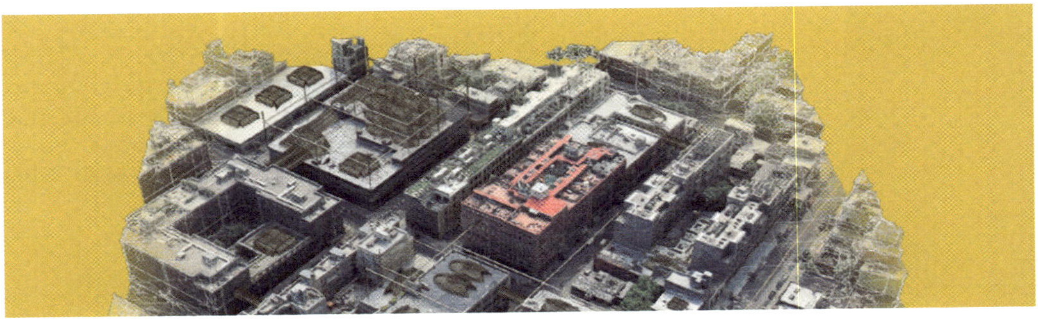

PATCHCITY

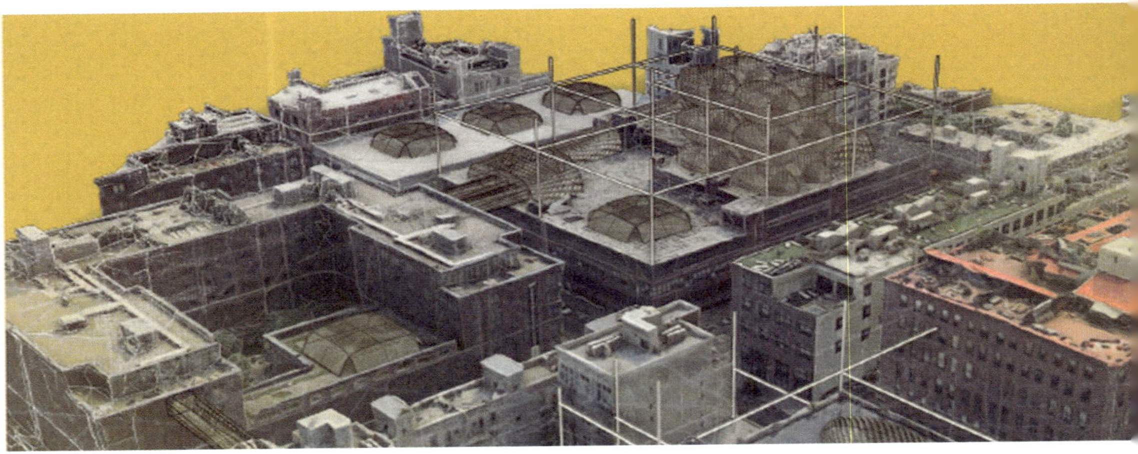

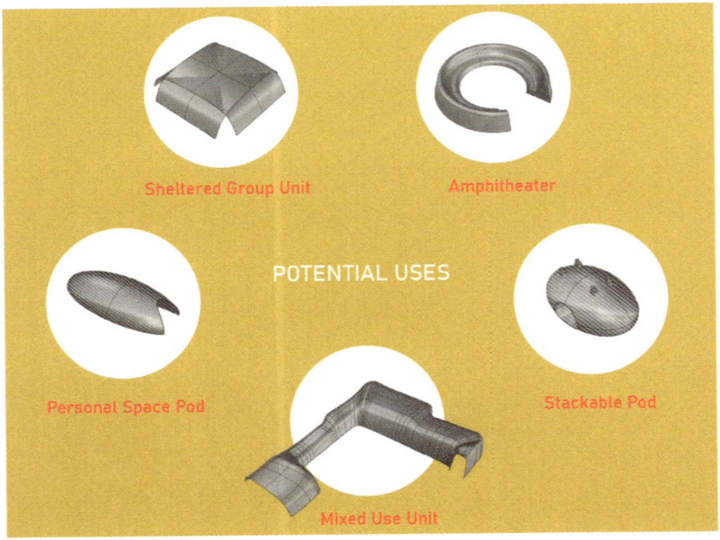

With these patchworks in place, one can imagine a city that is more interweaving, connected and flourishing with the new, social micro-networks, supporting the proliferation of lifestyles.

571GY9P7X

SELECTED PROJECTS

648U2JRDB

ANYWHERE 4X4

Santiago Gómez
Eastern Republic of Uruguay

The 4x4m module, repeated 3 times in horizontal and 3 times in vertical, generates a space of multiple appropriations. Interior and exterior spaces merge into programmatic bands defined by the use and flexibility needed depending on the family structure.
It could be an open or an introverted house, the exterior space articulates public and private areas and incorporates the car in the living experience.
The “4x4 PLUS” space let the inhabitants have an extra space to develop several activities: work, gym, playroom, tvroom, grandparents bedroom. Both, “EXTERIOR” and “4x4 PLUS” are contemporary needs, and the pandemic made it obvious.

FRONT ELEVATION

SECTION

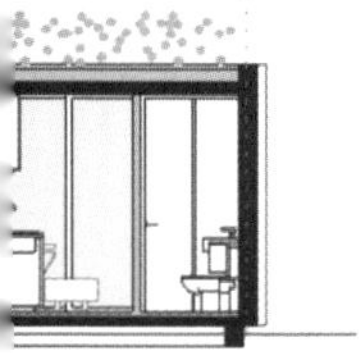

The border is defined by a wood skin translucent, semi-translucent and opaque at the same time, according to the use and the privacy each space need during the day.

SELECTED PROJECTS

502NOYEBO

PLOOP

A UTOPİA FOR GREEN URBANİSM

Shuang He
United States of America

This project reorients an inaccessible public infrastructure- Wastewater Treatment Facility, to establish an interactive public space that utilizes self-sustaining wetland systems, supports urban agriculture and community bonding. The design transforms the current linear treatment flow for a new cyclical paradigm of waste- energy- agriculture. Two Typologies: “Transportation Hub & Urban Agriculture” are layered onto the existing infrastructure creating an engaging landscape, provoking an understanding of our roles as part of a resource regenerative cycle.

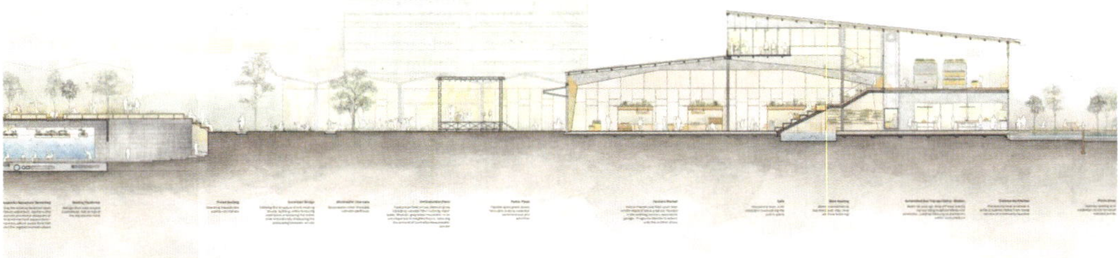

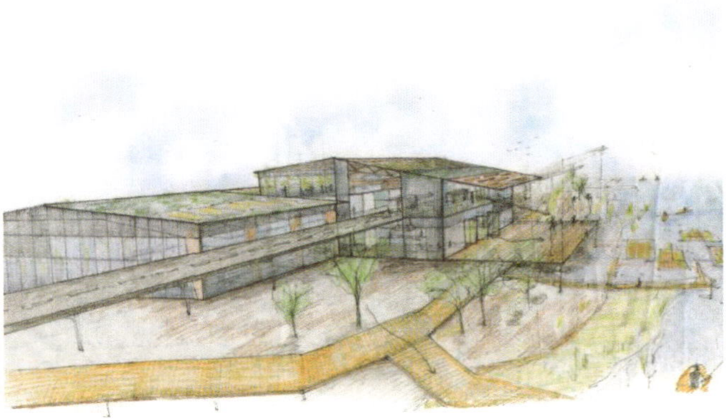

BACK BUILDING EXTERIOR

MARKET PLACE

Transportation & Agriculture are layered onto the existing infrastructure creating an engaging landscape, provoking an understanding of our roles as part of a resource regenerative cycle.

502NOYEBO

SELECTED PROJECTS

5394EVD89

THE H2.64 CANOPY

Shijie Cai
Xiangfan Chen
France

The living pod has combined the living, working and moving functions within one form. Peopel can thus have as much freedom as possible, while being protected by the hazarous environmental conditions in the post Covid times. The living pods are later inserted into the ports of the hubs, wether for living, working, or shopping. The moving unit on top features a self lifting drone for short distance transportation and a cable handle system for long distance travel.

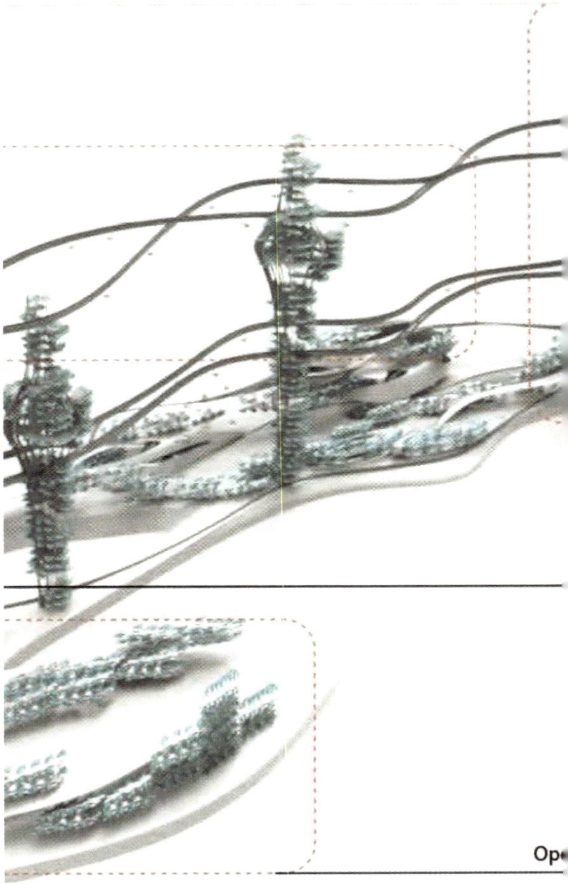

ercial hub

ing space

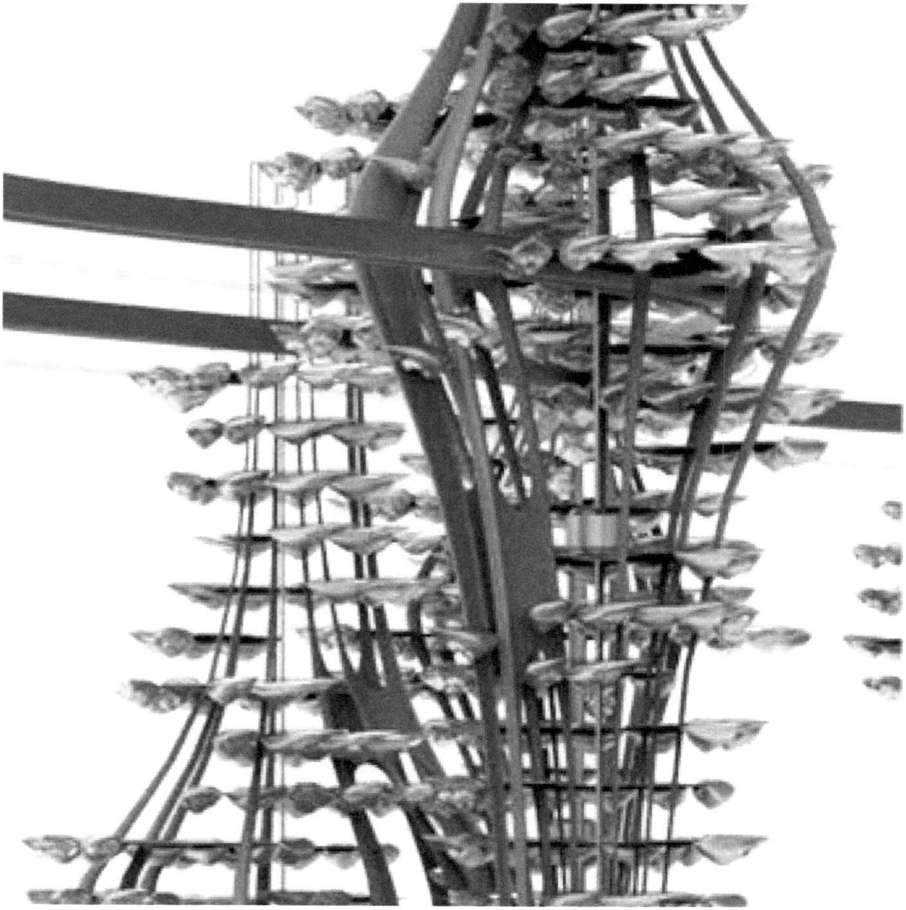

Living hub type 3 with community centers
Living hub type 2 with working studio
Amendities hubs (shopping centre / hospital etc.)

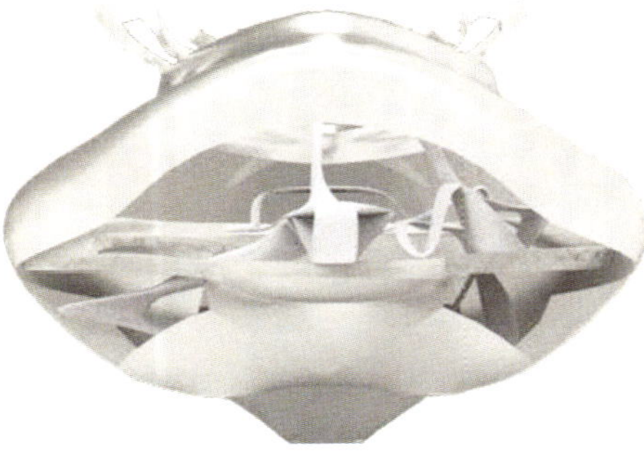

While the culture of working at home is the absolute majority, we offer those working spaces for necessary face to face interactions.

SELECTED PROJECTS

643JDU08N

A POETİC MARTİAN HABİTAT

Mehdi Shirvani
United States of America

Fractal geometry is a highly ordered geometry. I used fractals as a diagram to make my program work. The richness of fractal and of course the different modules and different scales it gave me, helped to understand better how to put different functions and spaces of my program or how to think of spaces like “black boxes” where engineering and mechanical facilities will be put. These 3d diagrams show the steps and process of the whole complex forming. As could be seen, first the poche, and thick walls where be built using the local material from the surface of Mars, Regolith, built by 3d printers. Then the columns and piers will be constructed. Dwelling zone is designed in 2 clusters (6 groups of 6 rooms) to host the 72 first Mars colonists.

Master plan with the help of fractal & chaos diagrams

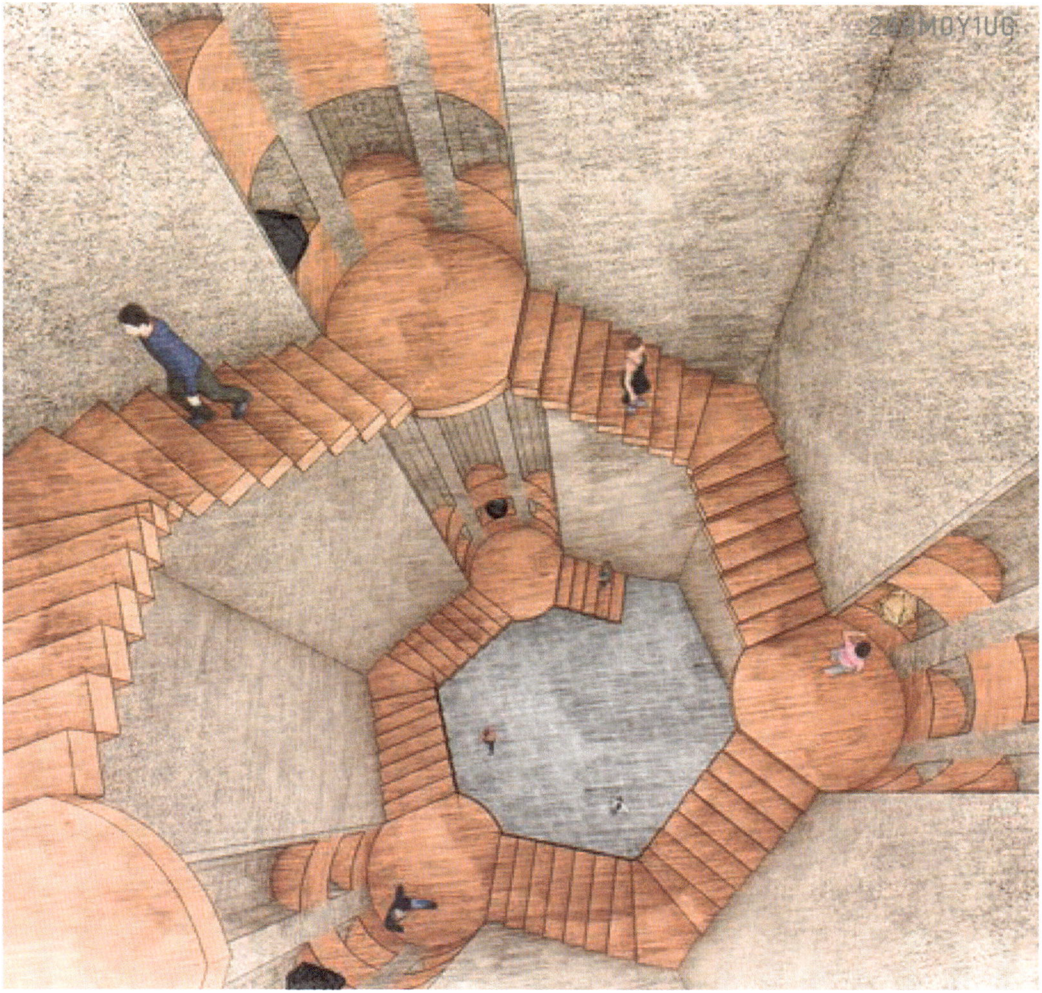

SELECTED PROJECTS

687KQCB36

RECLAIMING AN URBAN DENCITY

Shreya Gupta
India

When analysing on a macro scale, population and density is the origin. It has led to irreversible damage to the environment, pollution, waste generation, and climate change. Urban growth is a driven force that brings people together and makes them productive and simultaneously divides cities into small communities. Hence, Reclaiming the Urban Den-city by bridging the gap between self-made micro-cities which are inside big cities.

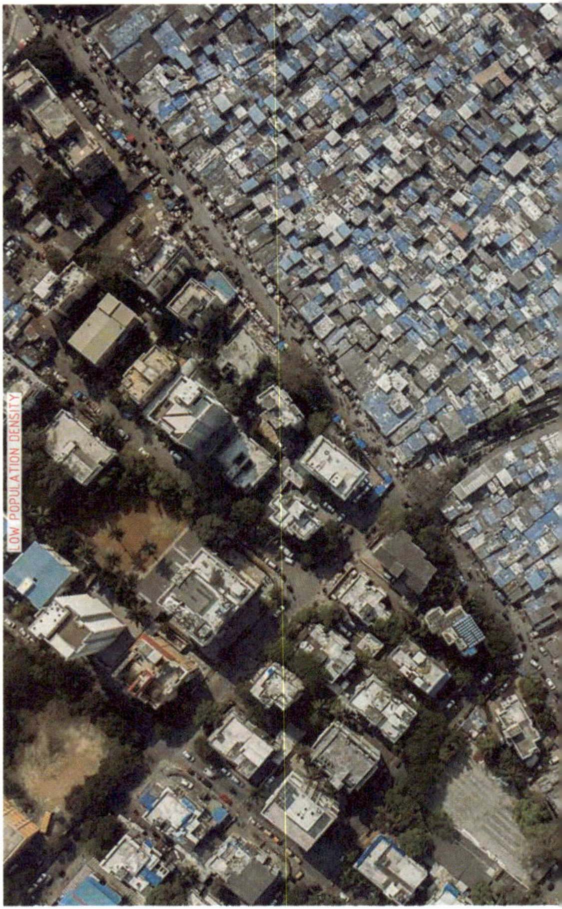

HIGH POPULATION DENSITY

2200hrs
2000hrs
1700hrs
1500hrs
1200hrs

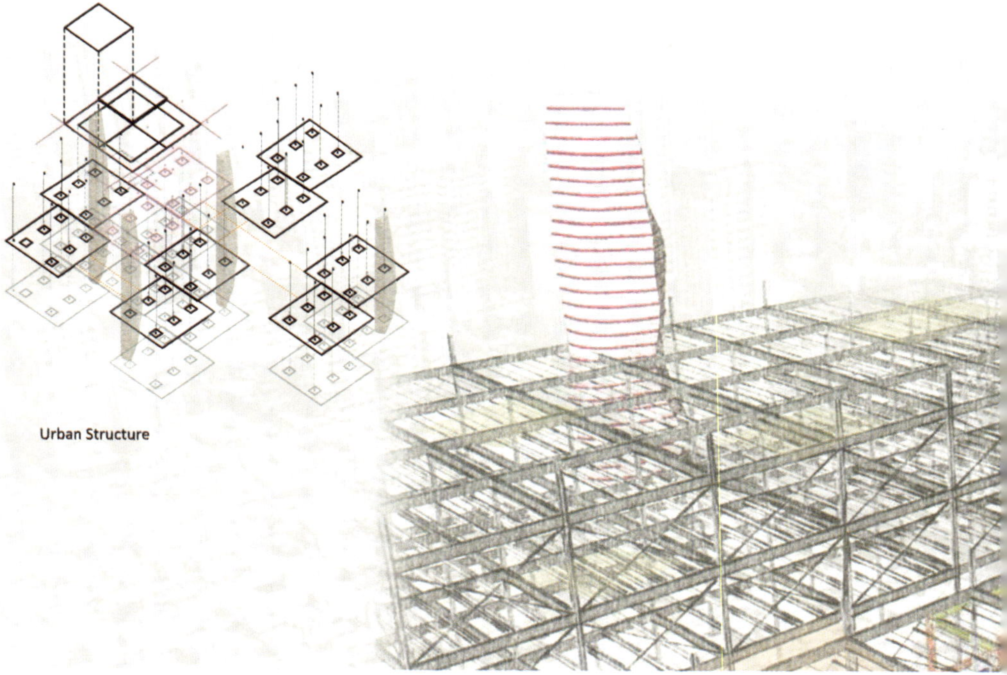

HYBRIDISATION

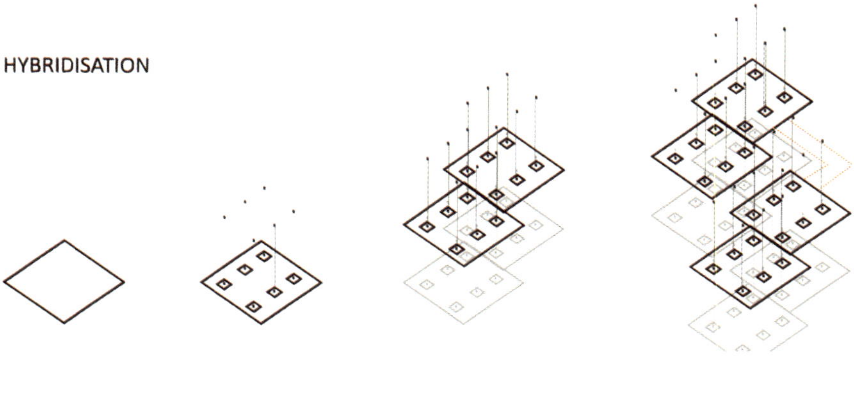

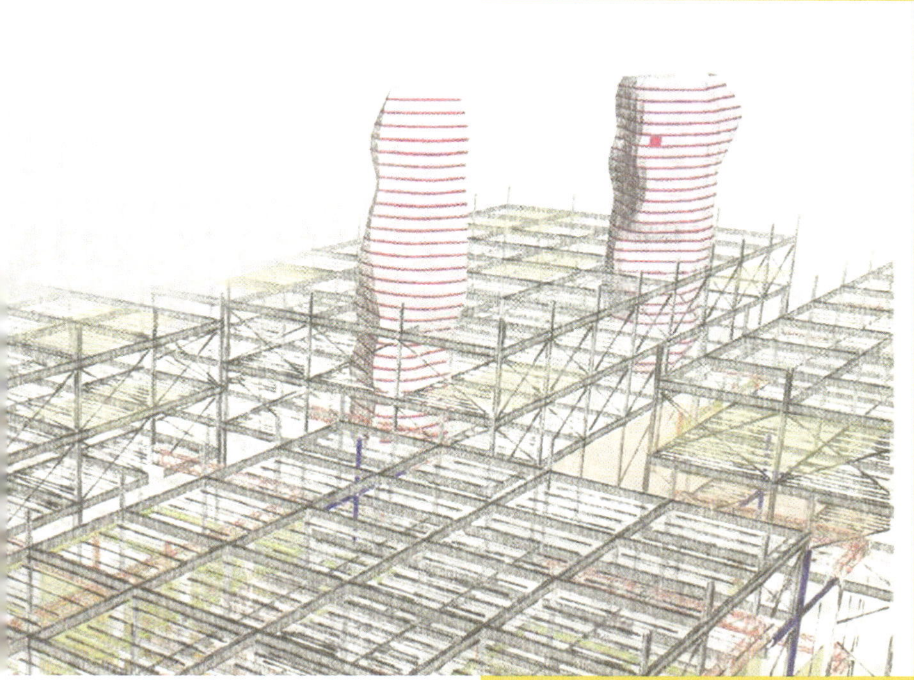

Therefore, envisioning a self-sustaining community – DHARAVI (slum settlement), which can serve as a contemporary intervention for big cities by rebuilding a clean and humane ground with current needs and parts of the old to serve the future environment

SELECTED PROJECTS

560X8J2ZA

UNTİTLED

Suffian Abdussalam
United Kingdom

Here is my concept, the building has 190m long, 45m wide and 6m height. The outdoor park invites you to enter tehe large public space covered on the upper floor, where you can find the restaurant, the offices or open-air festival. Pedestrians can cross the upper floor using a stair that's across the building's upper floor. The upper floor served as the perfect outdoor room for the client's relaxation.

SELECTED PROJECTS

422R7180Q

HOUSE OF BAMBOO

Rustom Tamayo
Philippines

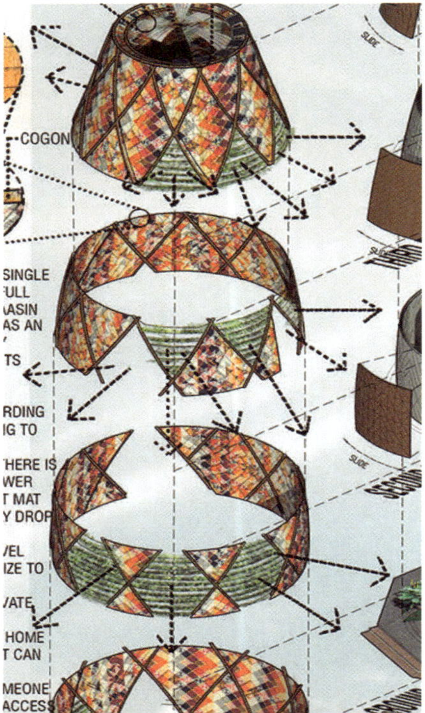

The project aim is to maximize the use of bamboo since in Maasin it is already well taught the traditional filipino bamboo crafts. In this project the main sustainable materials is bamboo. It will be used as a walls, coverings, post and insulation. By reconfiguring and maximizing the use of bamboo through this project we can showcase how we can preserve the traditional filipino bamboo crafts in modern societies and at the metting our human needs.

HOUSE OF BAMBOO
RIGHT-SIDE SECTION
NATURAL VENTILATION
WARM
COLD
WFH OFFICE
LINEN CHUTE
GYM
T&B
MASTERS BEDROOM
LIVING
PLUMBING CHASE
KITCHEN
ENTRY PORCH
CHANGING AREA
LEFT-SIDE SECTION
NATURAL VENTILATION
WARM
COLD
GYM
GARBAGE CHUTE
WFH OFFICE
MASTERS BEDROOM
UTILITY CHASE
T&B
KITCHEN
LIVING
LAUNDRY AREA
HANGING GARDEN

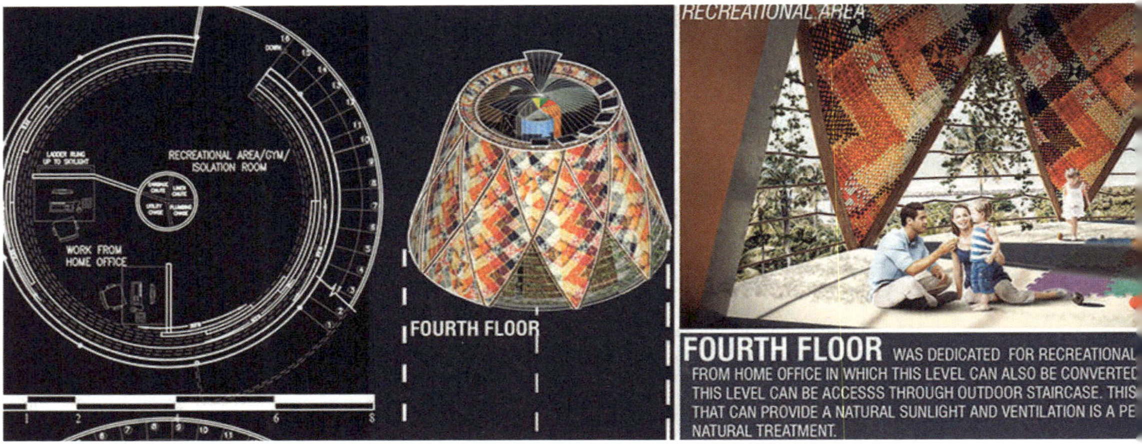

Simplicity of the form from traditional filipino bamboo products meld with contemporary modern architecture

WORK
ION AREA AS
Y ROOM
A SUIT FOR

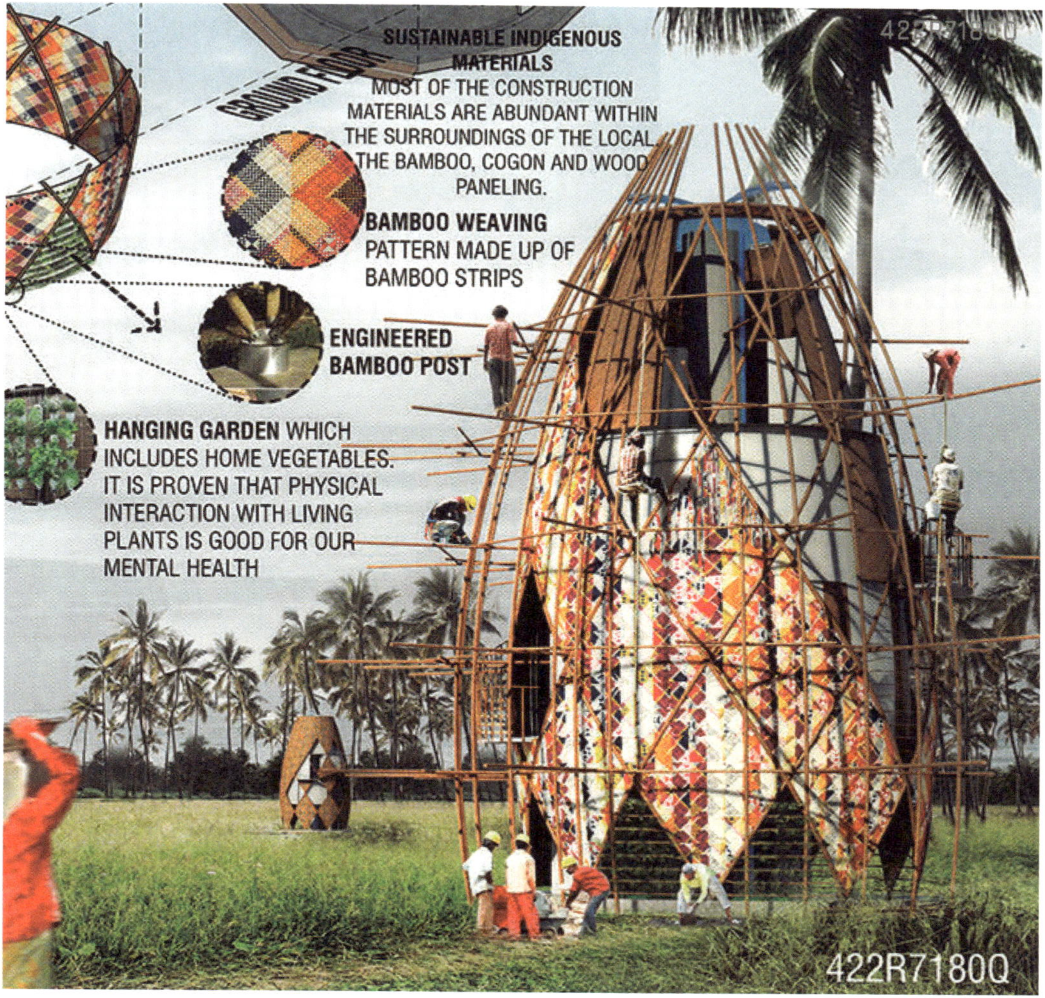
GROUND FLOOR
SUSTAINABLE INDIGENOUS MATERIALS
MOST OF THE CONSTRUCTION MATERIALS ARE ABUNDANT WITHIN THE SURROUNDINGS OF THE LOCAL. THE BAMBOO, COGON AND WOOD PANELING.
BAMBOO WEAVING PATTERN MADE UP OF BAMBOO STRIPS
ENGINEERED BAMBOO POST
HANGING GARDEN WHICH INCLUDES HOME VEGETABLES. IT IS PROVEN THAT PHYSICAL INTERACTION WITH LIVING PLANTS IS GOOD FOR OUR MENTAL HEALTH
422R7180Q

SELECTED PROJECTS

4755N64WF

COASTAL WEAVE

Taylor Evans
United States of America

The COVID pandemic has highlighted global connectedness; it is not simply about the re-evaluation of cities and daily rituals. Rather, the human habitat depends on a greater support of the ecosystem. In order to sustain human life in the future, the scope must broaden to address the health of the planet and thereby all inhabitants. Stead shores, replenished fish stocks, healthy marine life and active coral reefs are central to a thriving human habitat. Coral reefs are the buffer between the ocean and coastal living. These reefs, which absorb 97% of energy before reaching shore, are crumbling by way of fishing, poaching, and human-driven climate change, among other careless human activity.

Proposed Site
1 Mile

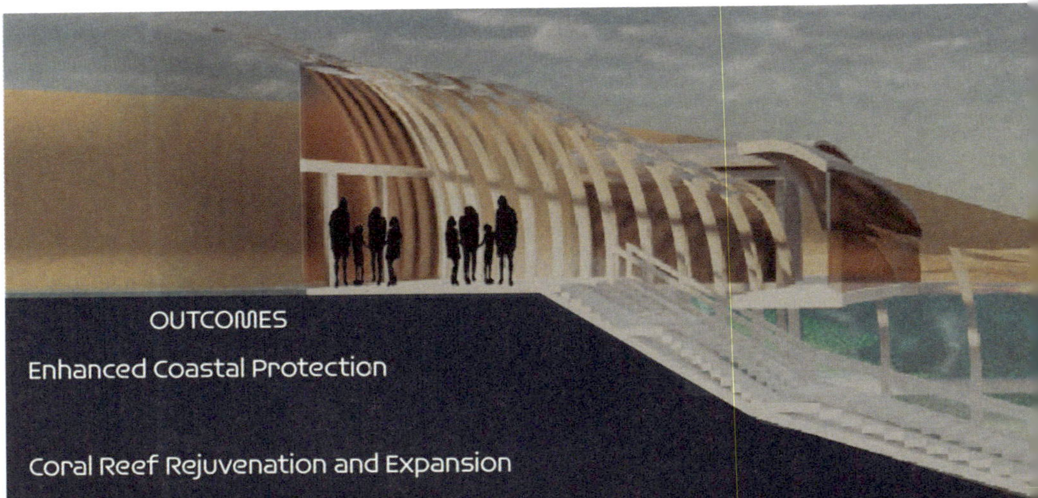

OUTCOMES

Enhanced Coastal Protection

Coral Reef Rejuvenation and Expansion

Increased Fishing, Tourism, and Research Opportunities

A Better understanding of the Connection Between Human and Marine Life

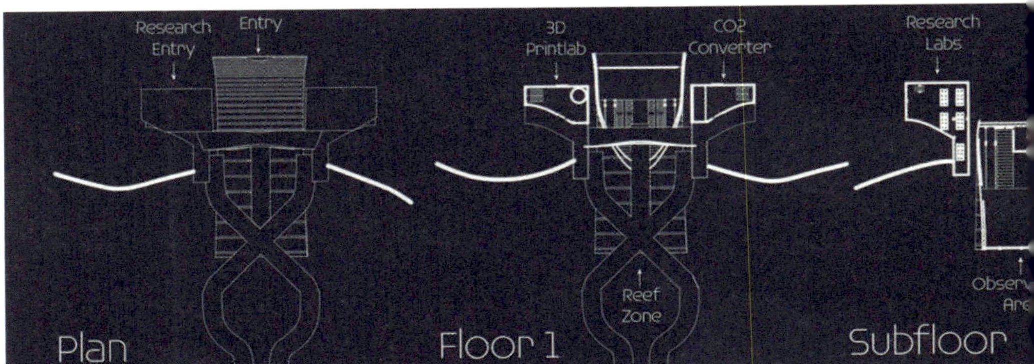

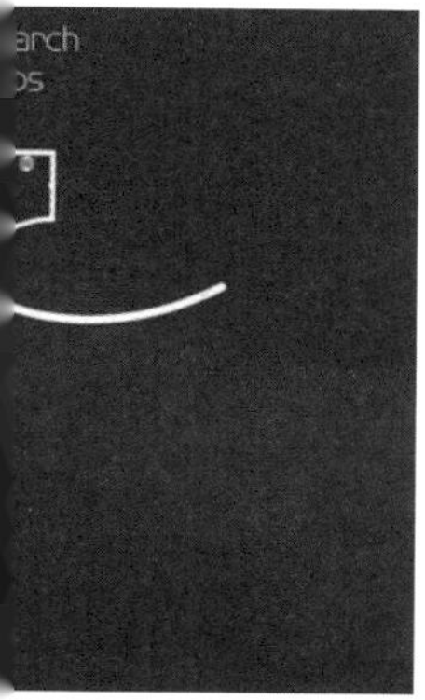

Coastal Weave aims to create an infrastructure that will benefit the corals as much as the humans that depend on them

SELECTED PROJECTS

551IOISUK

NEW PANDEMİC, SAME OLD PROBLEMS

Israel Leandro-Flores
Aarón Condemaita
Nathaly Schwarz
Luis Velasquez
Gabi Vilcas
Peru

This pandemic teaches us that is not only about our bodies. Is about our city. Our nature. We can harness the resources by simply looking at them. This is not about smartness. This is not about high tech. This is about being sincere with what we have. At very low cost, these proposals are based on ingenuity rather than technology. More with less. Our ancestors dealt with the same context: pandemics, natural disasters, even social havoc. But what they did is more important. They appreciated the natural systems. Let's do this together!

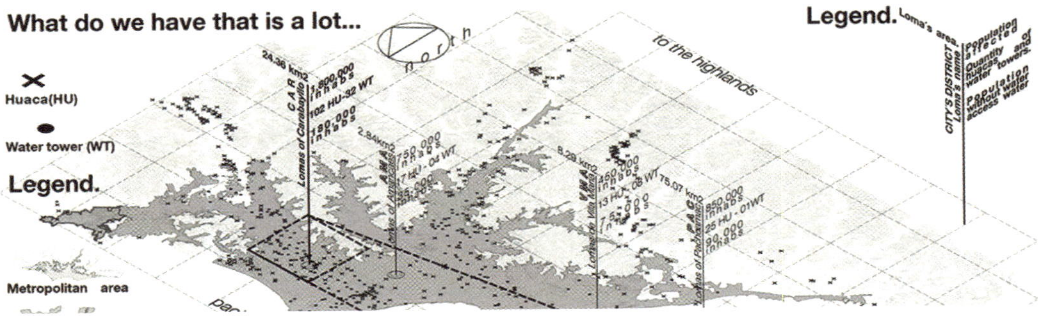

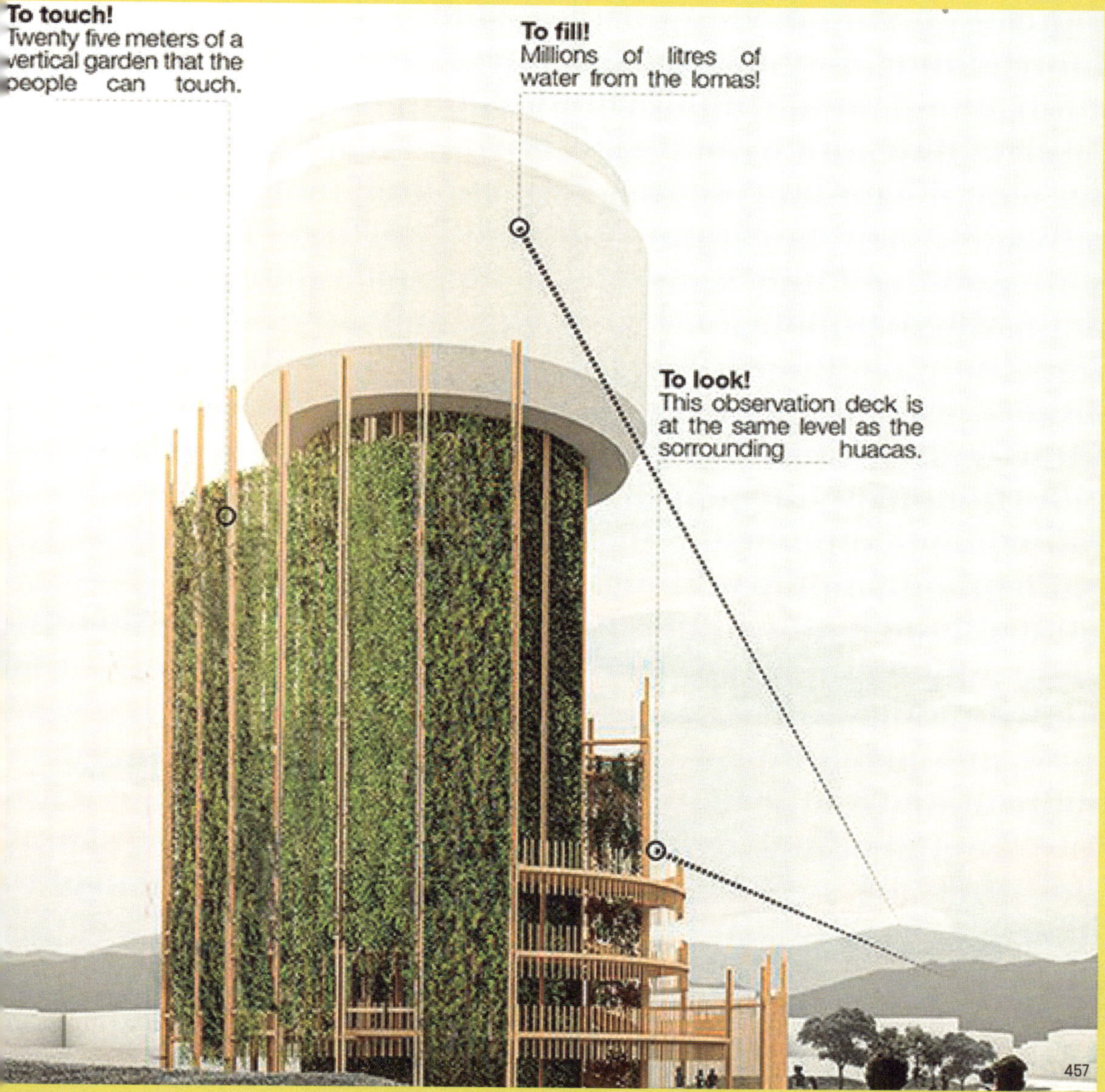
To touch!
Twenty five meters of a vertical garden that the people can touch.
To fill!
Millions of litres of water from the lomas!
To look!
This observation deck is at the same level as the sorrounding huacas.

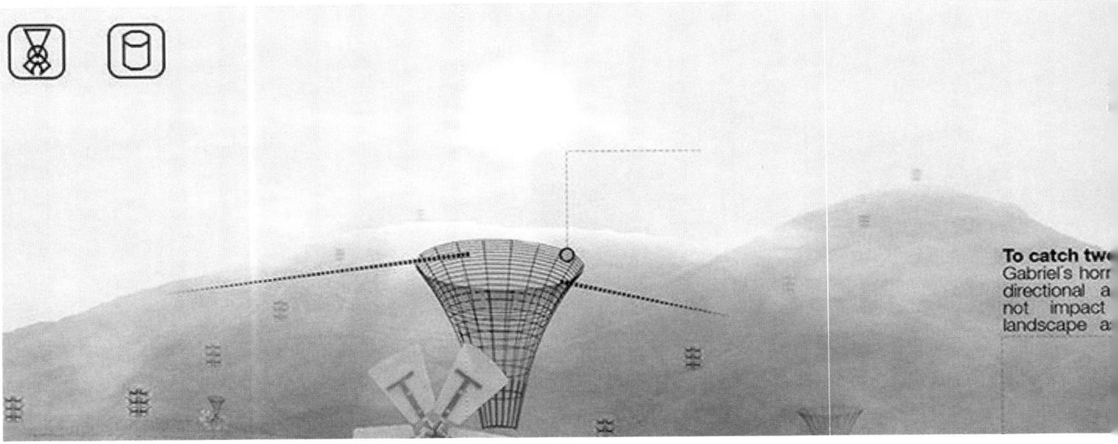

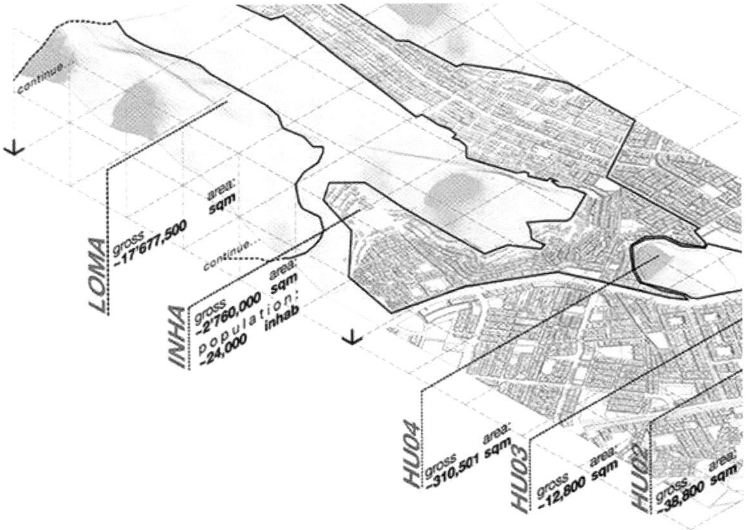

Lima is one of the biggest, driest and densest city capital in the world. More public spaces? There is no room left? More water? There is no source? More access to buy daily products? We can move the markets? We can't move people!

551I0ISUK
To catch two!
Gabriel's horn is multi-directional and does not impact in the landscape as others!
Water to spare one!
More water to irrigate parts of the lomas and huacas even in dryer m o n t h s !
Water to spare two!
And, whenever needed, people can use it!

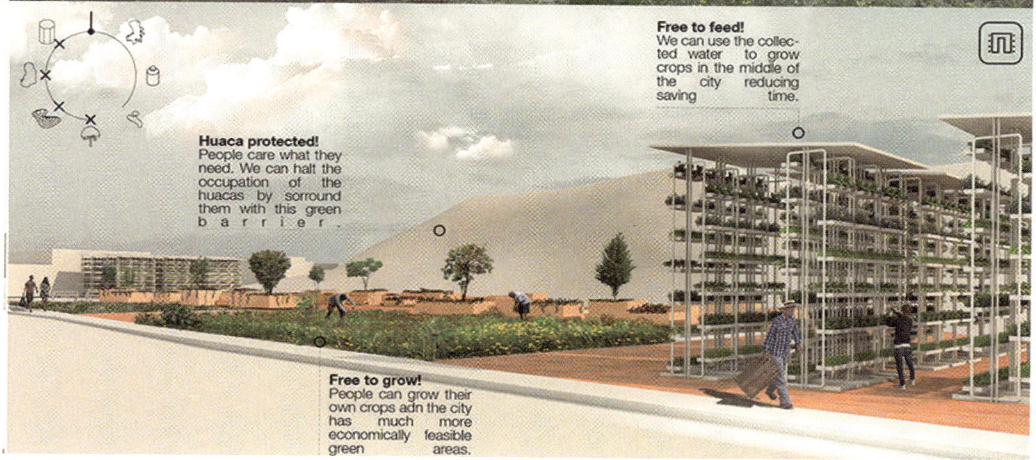
Free to feed!
We can use the collected water to grow crops in the middle of the city reducing saving time.
Huaca protected!
People care what they need. We can halt the occupation of the huacas by sorround them with this green b a r r i e r .
Free to grow!
People can grow their own crops adn the city has much more economically feasible green areas.

SELECTED PROJECTS

368WD3AR5

URBAN MİCROBİOME DESİGN

Ma. Beatrice Villoria
Philippines

This project aims to explore the 'Microbiomes of the Built Environment'. We know these microbiomes affect our health, but to what extent can we manipulate microbiomes to create a healthier BE? To test if architecture can influence microbiomes, experiments were done. Focus was on behavior and levels of bacteria per type of space function. Although in collaboration with a microbiologist, the output of this project is still highly conceptual. With a small experimental scope, this project strives to balance the good and bad of bacteria. More understanding would enable us to manipulate these microbes architecturally.

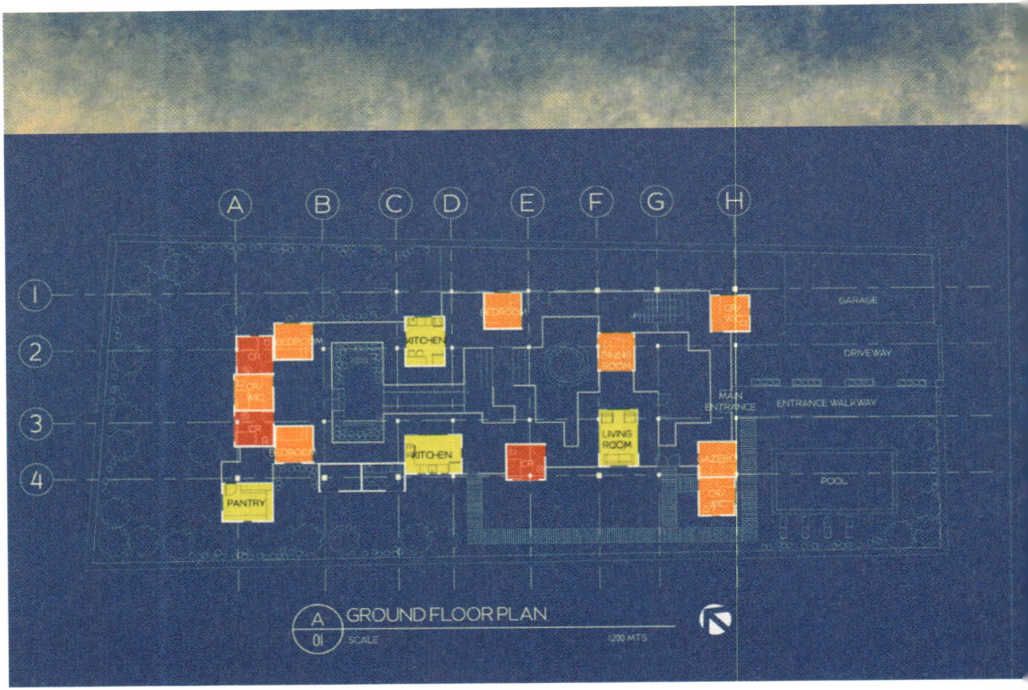
A
B
C
D
E
F
G
H
1
2
3
4
GARAGE
DRIVEWAY
MAIN ENTRANCE
ENTRANCE WALKWAY
POOL
KITCHEN
LIVING ROOM
PANTRY
GAZEBO
GROUND FLOOR PLAN
SCALE
1:200 MTS

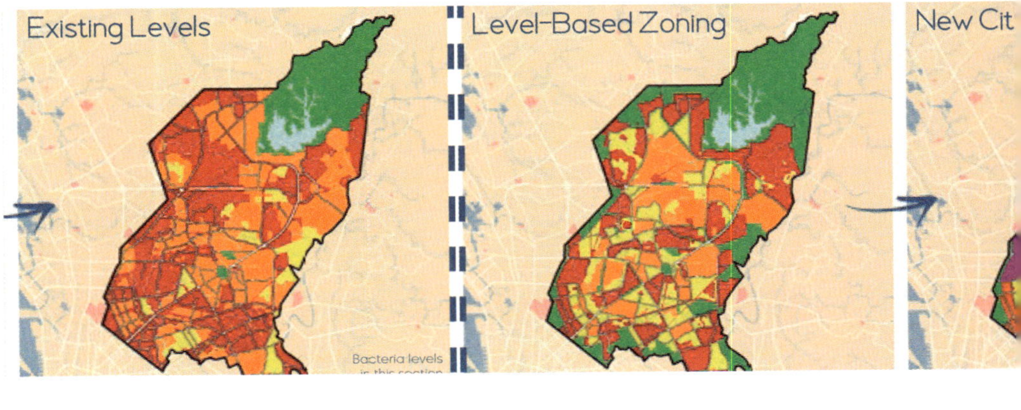
Existing Levels
Level-Based Zoning
New Cit
Bacteria levels

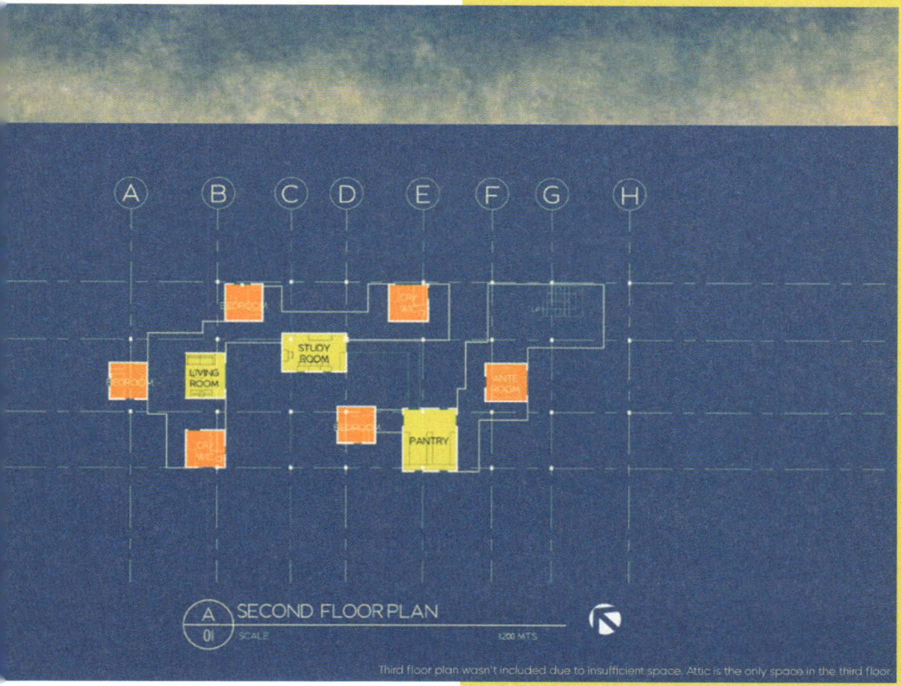

Through this, not only can we design healthier homes, we can also create healthier city zoning

SELECTED PROJECTS

429LF0GK5

NEO-SPOLİA 2060

Thomas Espinos
United States of America

We are in 2060. The Grove's famous Traolley is redisgned with spare parts from other vehicles such as a submarine and a crane. It analyses the different "historical" houses of Los Angeles through different categories: style, appropriated century, appropriated region, year built, number of artifcats and remaining life span.

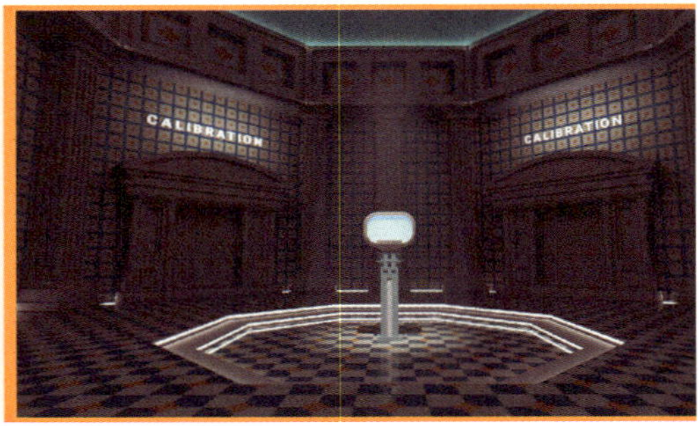

Underground, the masonry debris are compounded into two composites that will be necessary in the construction of the houses

429LFOGK5
COMPOUNDING FACILITY
DEBRIS
MASONRY

SELECTED PROJECTS

517ZUT7LE

PORTABLE BOX

CONCEPTUAL İDEA FOR VULNERABLE POPULATİONS

Andres Torres
Colombia

It will be sought by means of the modular and ephemeral architecture to provide a solution to this problem; Starting with movable housing modules, the aim will be to generate a new design paradigm for vulnerable population groups; This design may be applied equally to different groups of people and situations, for current and future.

ビジネスホテル
24-2156

Growth

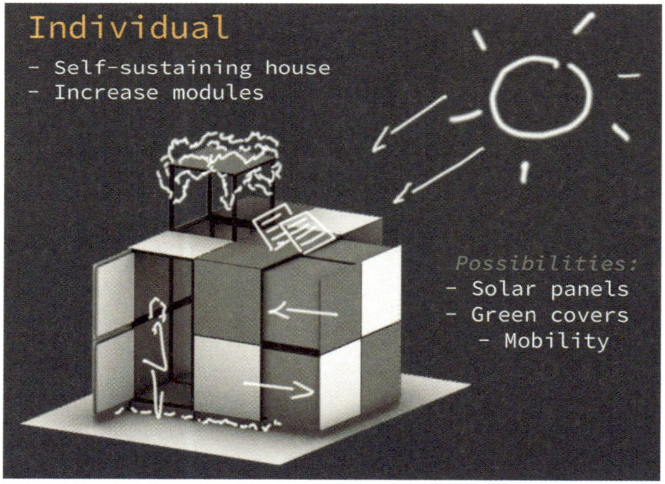
Individual
- Self-sustaining house
- Increase modules
Possibilities:
- Solar panels
- Green covers
- Mobility

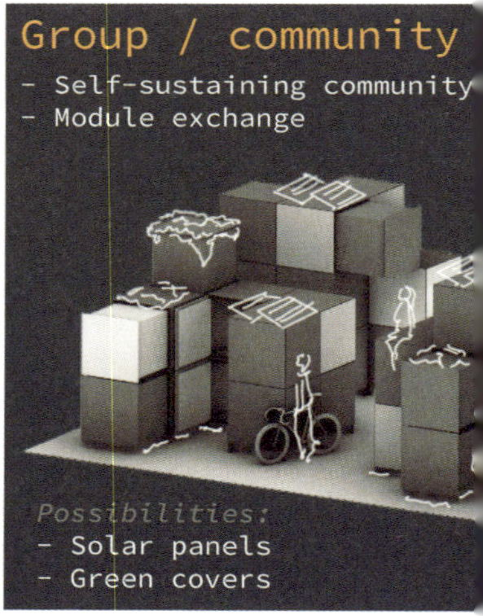
Group / community
- Self-sustaining community
- Module exchange
Possibilities:
- Solar panels
- Green covers

Provide the possibility
Homeless people
from deficiencies
to opportunities
Have

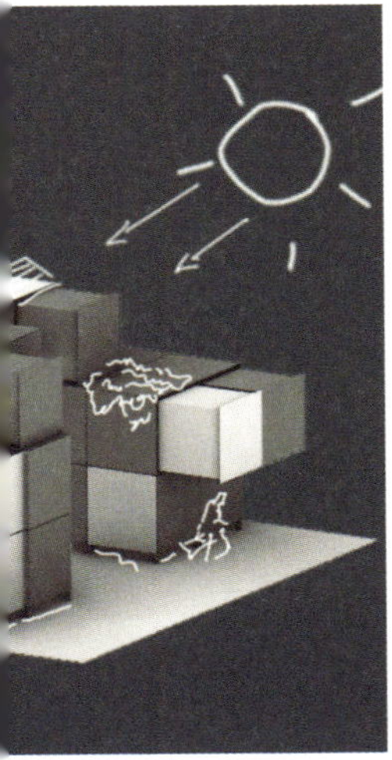

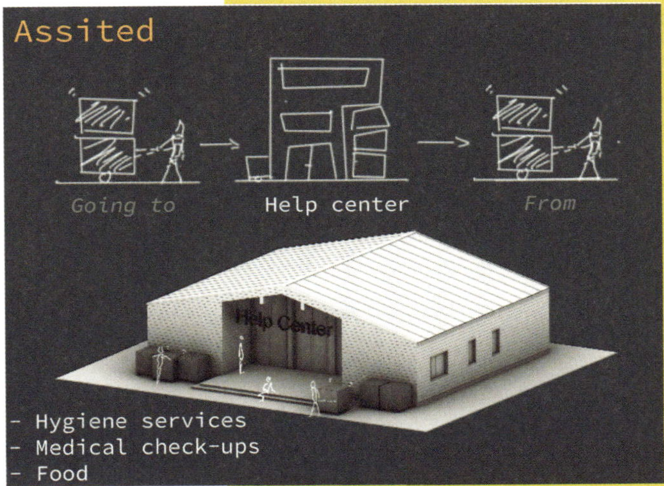

home

This problem will affect more strongly third world countries as well as developing countries

SELECTED PROJECTS 2001RPR4V

OTAKUTECTURE

A NEW VISION OF HUMAN INHABITATION BASED ON THE SPECULATION OF MEGA-INFRASTRUCTURE

Jiawei Liang
China

The "multiple identities" of such people are used to study the cultural alienation hidden beneath the city surface and the tension and distortion of the global infrastructure system on the spatial realization.
As an infinite extension of the Mega-infrastructure and capsule modules as an assembled community, it aims to achieve "terminal architecture," a space wrapped in infrastructure systems, through gamification, virtualization and other escapism.

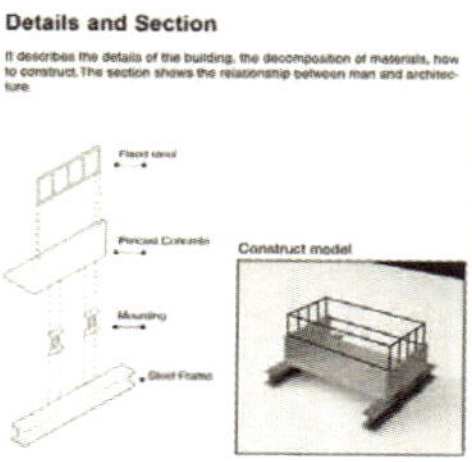

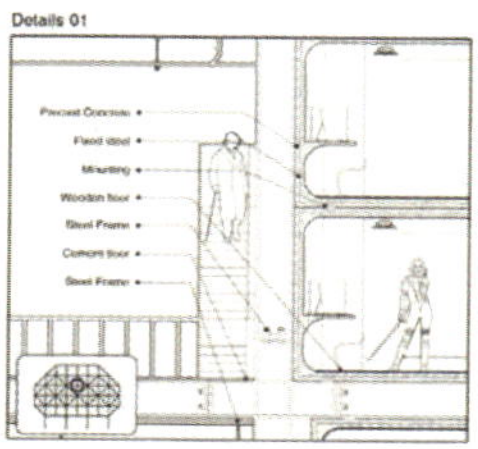

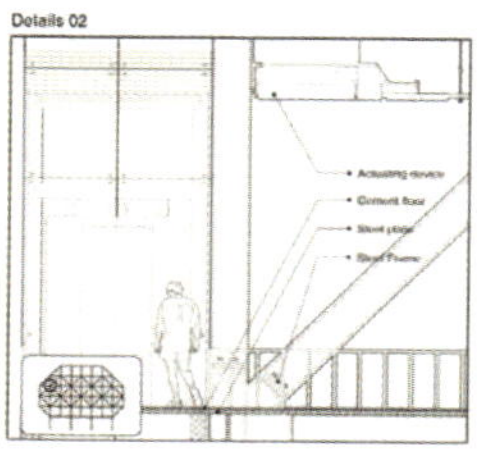

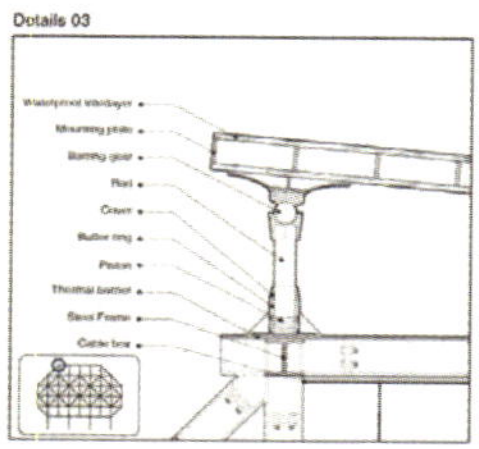

Construction

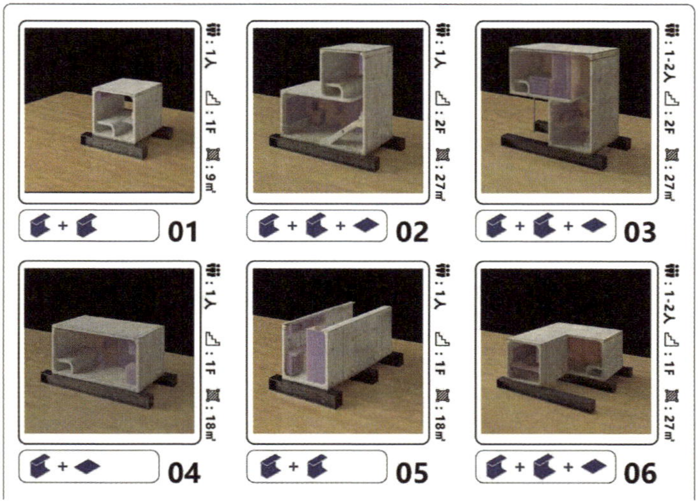

Embracing technology, obsession, tradition, perversion and malfunction, we jumped into the symbolic overload of the modern city and emerged as Otakutects!

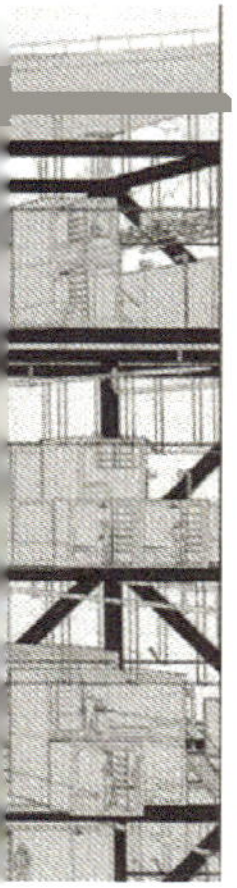

2001RPR4V

SELECTED PROJECTS

723Q55363

İNSİDE-OUTSİDE

QUALİTY OF SPACE

Yasmin Hassan
Yara Zeidan
Egypt

Bringing the outside (people) to the inside (garbage city) and exposing the energetic community that recycles 85% of cairo's garbage and enhancing the living status of the settlers by creating better quality of space and boosting their economy.

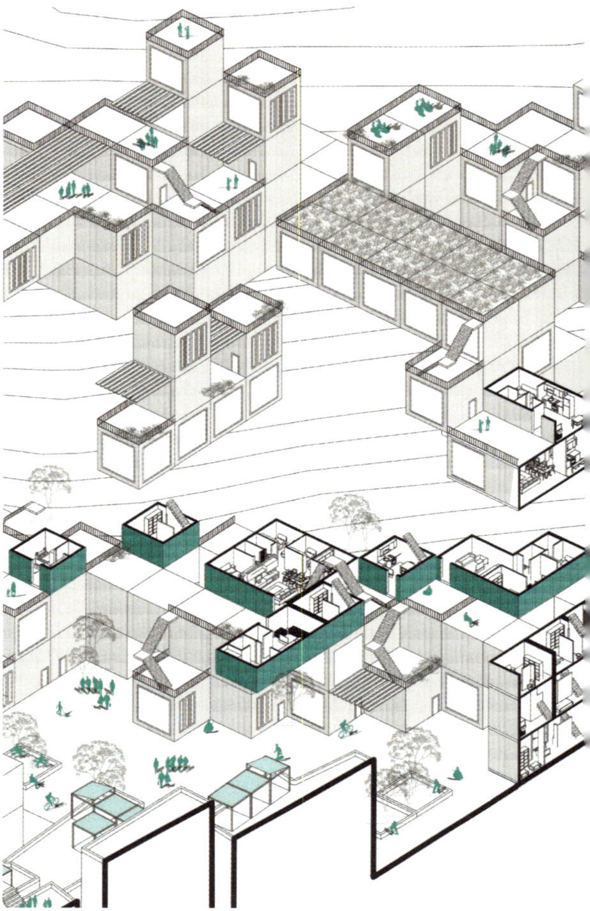

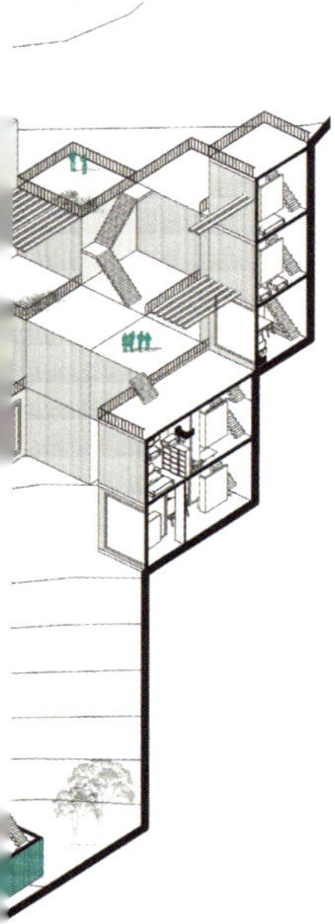

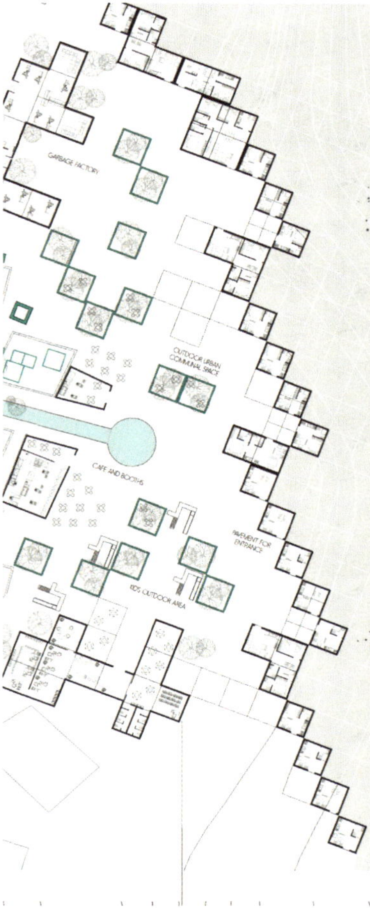

WINDOWS AND DOORS ON PREFERENCE

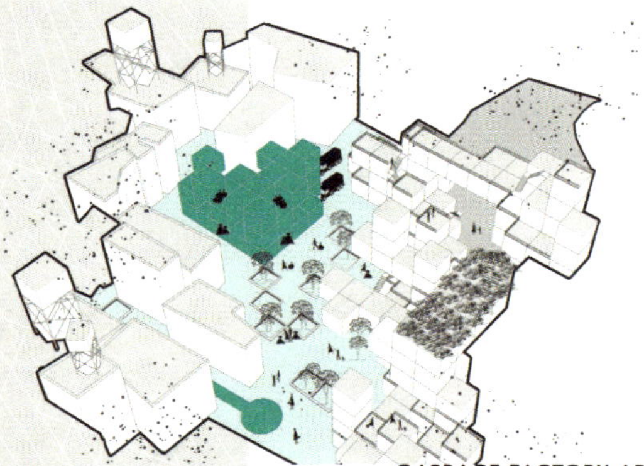

GARBAGE FACTORY AREA

SINCE THE AIM OF THE PROJECT IS TO CREATE A BETTER QUALITY NEIGHBORHOOD FOR THE RESIDENCE TH GOAL OF ADDING JOB OPPORTUNITIES AND SMALL KID EDUCATIONAL SECTOR WILL THRIVE THIS SMALL COMMUNITY AND MAKE IT A PROTOTYPE FOR OTHER INFORMAL SETTLEMENTS

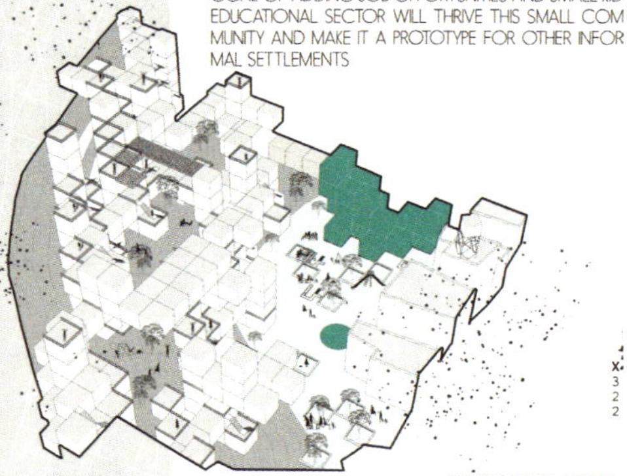

NURSERY AREA

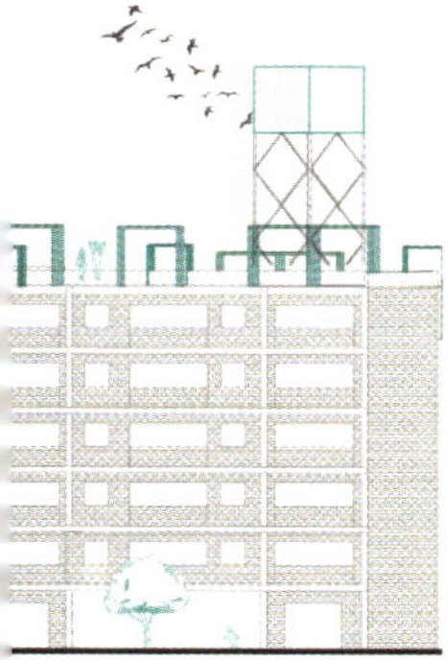

“They are not informal sttlements, they are habitats made by people”
Lorena Zárate, the president of Habitat International Coalition

SELECTED PROJECTS 661LOVGCM

APARTMENT PLUS

Yasmine Adel Farag Khouzam
Rana Mohamed Abdelrahem
Egypt

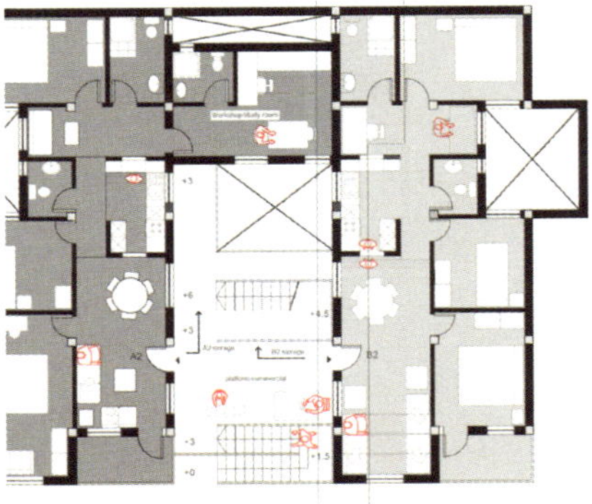

Apartment Plus is an exploration of a housing alternative to the ongoing Peri-Urban expansions and urbanization of Qalyoub Almahattah in Egypt. Qalyoub is characterized by a certain way of living including work-live typologies, the flexibility of expanding homes, changing spatial functions and extending domestic activities into the street. The idea of Apartment Plus is to re-introduce these values while following the building laws of the area and property divisions of the new masterplan. We started by defining a common staircase for each two residential buildings, the way the stairs are shaped expands its function beyond circulation into a multifunctional communal space, providing alternating indoor and outdoor spaces that keeps a visual connection to the street thus becoming an active semi-public space where neighbors can meet.

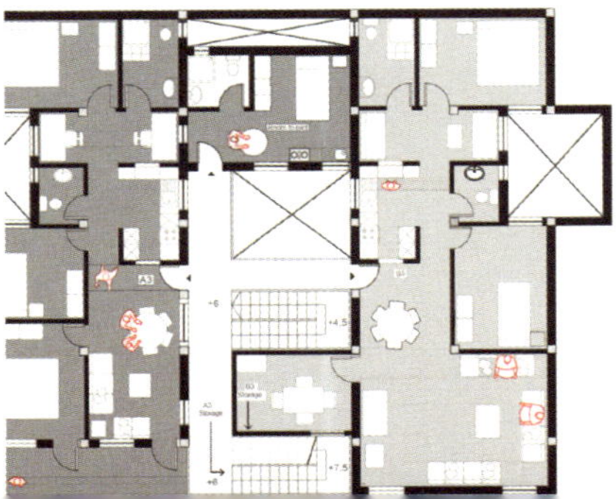

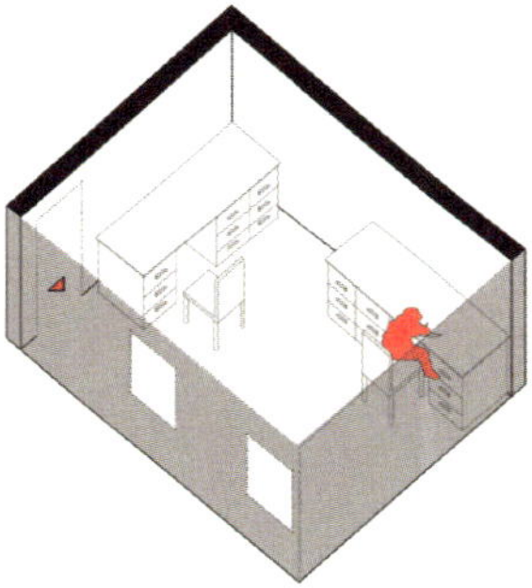

Addittional Study room
Extension of Apartment B

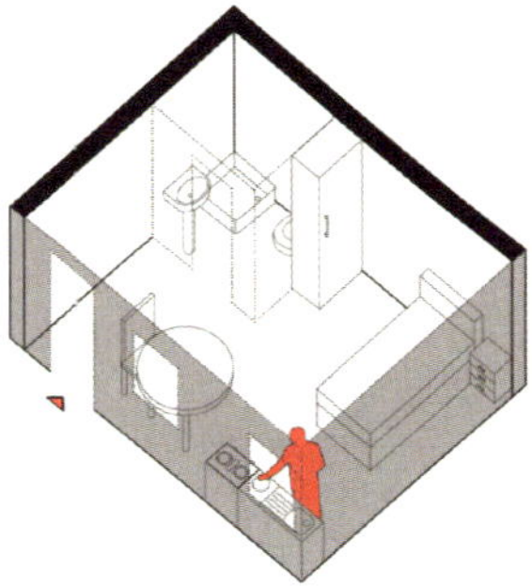

Room to rent with seperate entrances switch room between two apartments .

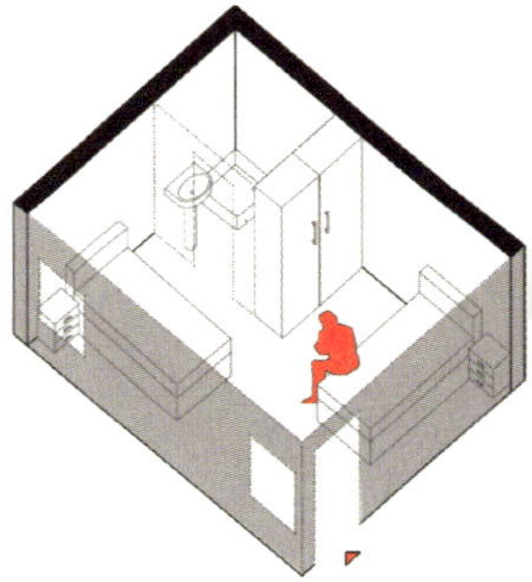

Additional bedroom
Extension of Apartment A

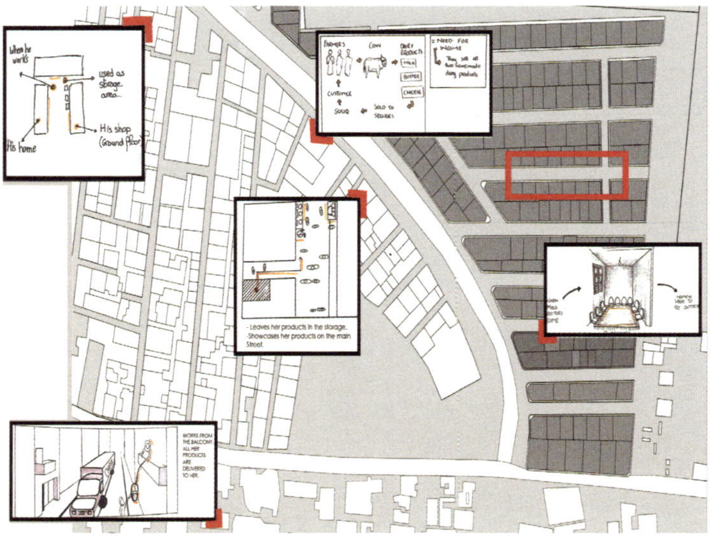

Residents customize the façade enclosure, traces of personalization is visible from the outside. This flexibility and openness are intended to restore Qalyoub's identity in a new skin.

661LOVGCM

SELECTED PROJECTS

5786R5W19

FANTASİSM CİTY SEEDS

Yihia Qandil
Egypt

A proposal, Fantasism city would be a step for humans to evolve and for the nature to recover. By focusing on three approaches which are Urban Platforms, Smart Transportation, and Living Upscend, these are the 3 main strategies for Fantasism City to be achieved. Starting with the urban platform, showing a case study of selected location and extracting the potentials, architectural language and elements to create urban platforms consisting of sky gardens, elevated parks and fixin urban behavior of humans.

ECOVERD

Phase Z
NATURE WINS

URBAN PLATFORM FOR CONNECTION = EXPERIENC

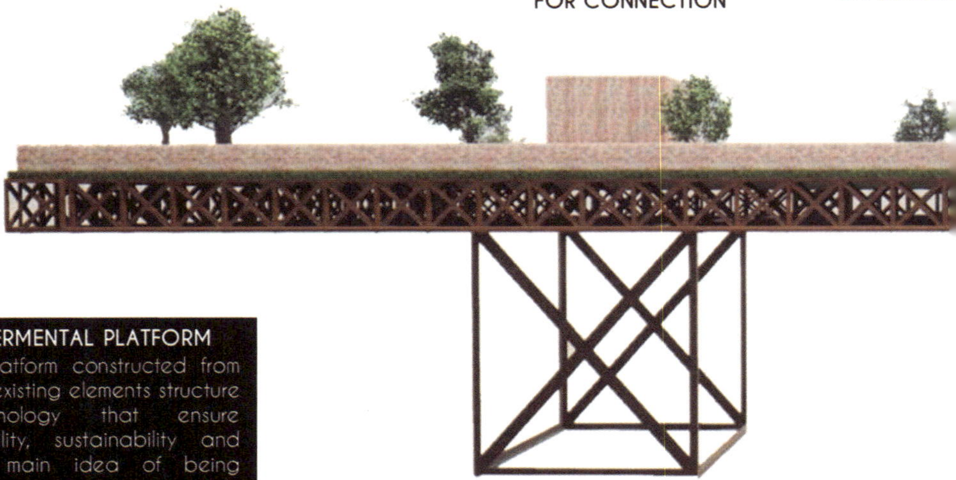

EXPERMENTAL PLATFORM

A platform constructed from the existing elements structure technology that ensure stability, sustainability and the main idea of being resilience.

INTIAL DIAGRAMS

PLATFORM THAT CREATE REMARKABLE SKY GARDENS "PARKS" THROUGH EXISTING RAPID URBAN SOLID MASSES GROWTH

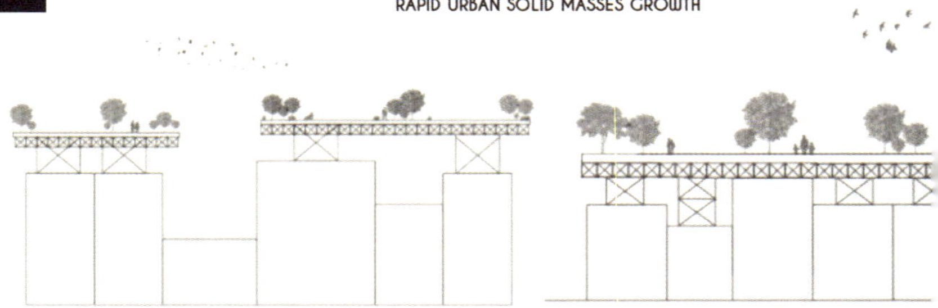

GREEN RESTORATION

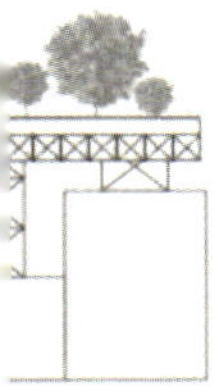

The project is located in Saft El Laban in Imbaba in a selected site showing the result of rapid urban growth (Urban Cancer) and the wound made by ring road separating the city into a coin with two faces showing the decreased in the green lands

SELECTED PROJECTS

617TKV5UB

MiZZi ViLLAGE

Jeremiah Oonyu
Zani Gichuki
Rwanda

MIZIZI VILLAGE Gender based violence is a not problem that can be fixed simply by good design. Structural change to our society is needed, meaning that as designers we will need to collaborate with social scientists, activists and governments to change the lives of the victims. We present the integration of rehabilitation spaces for them into urban planning. Drawing on inspiration from the matriarchal 'Umoja village' in northern Kenya, founded by women who have escaped gender based violence, this integrated village aims to provide not only a refuge but also a space for healing, learning and self actualization for the residents

SINGLE MOTHER UNIT

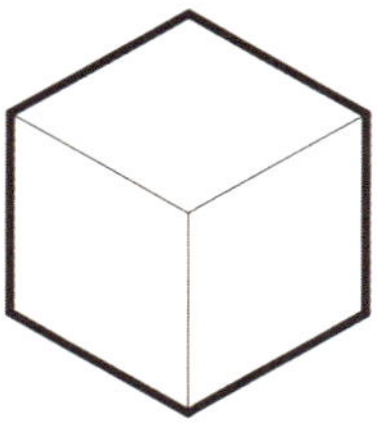

SHARED UNIT 2 WOMEN

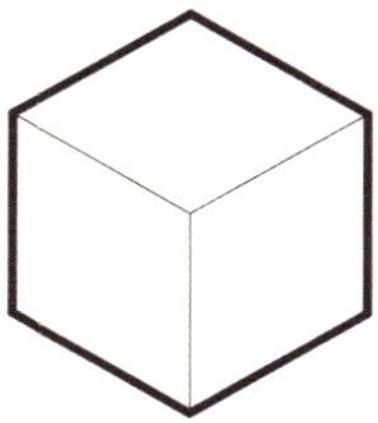

SELF CONTAINED UNIT

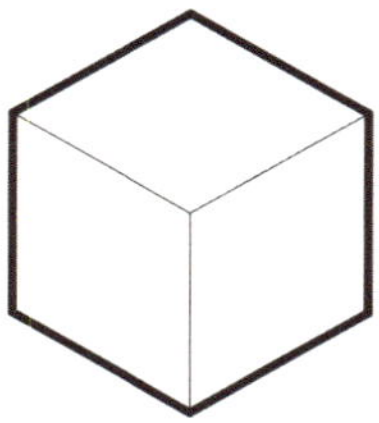

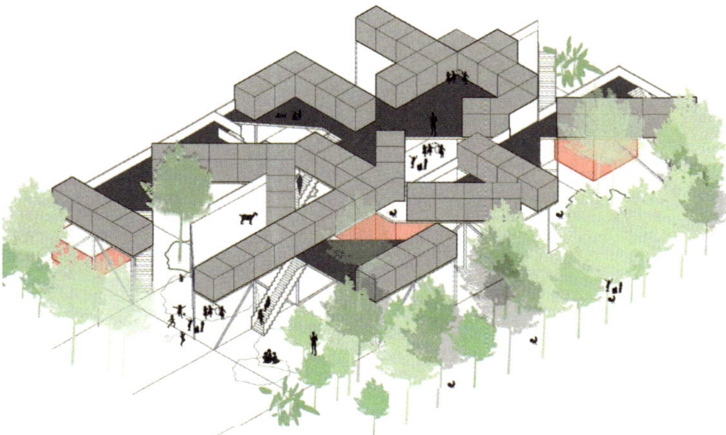

The design is based on this 2.5 x 2.5 module, that can be a self contained pod for one woman with her kids, or shared by 2 women, or as a pod for just one woman.

617TKV5UB

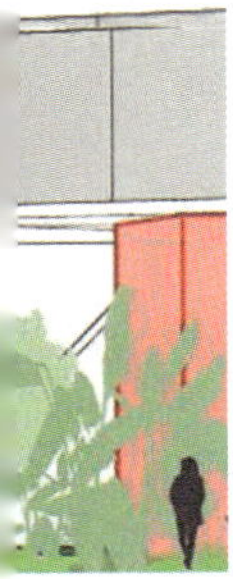

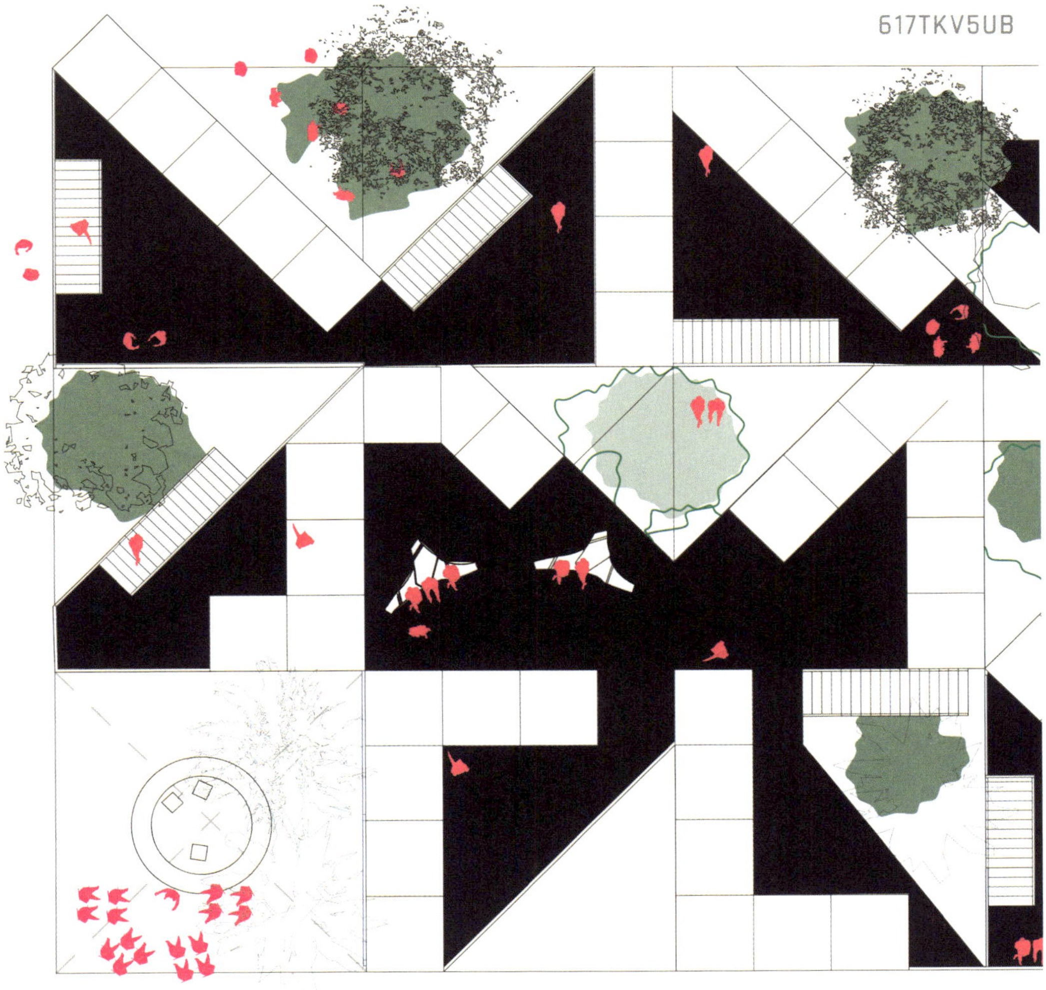

SELECTED PROJECTS

717WJ8SFN

URBAN BİCYCLE PARKİNG BENCH

Haole Zhang
Minjie Liang
China

This urban furniture provides both bicycle parking and rest bench for pedestrians. On the top is a groove for installing green plants and a solar panel for powering the LED under the canopy. Its modular allows people to combined freely. For example, in combination 1, furniture is mixed arranged, and bicycle parking and rest benches both face the street at the same time, making the street interface more fun. In combination 2, doubled furniture keeps the side of benches facing the street mainly meets the needs of pedestrians to have a rest.

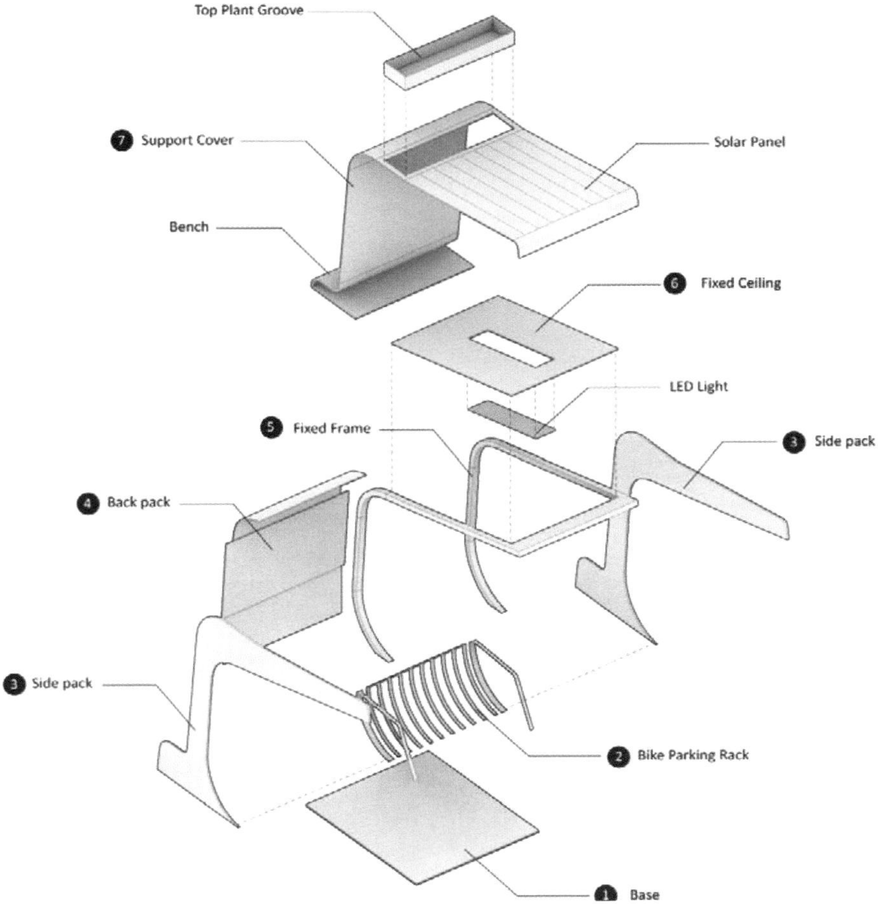
Top Plant Groove
7 Support Cover
Solar Panel
Bench
6 Fixed Ceiling
LED Light
5 Fixed Frame
3 Side pack
4 Back pack
3 Side pack
2 Bike Parking Rack
1 Base

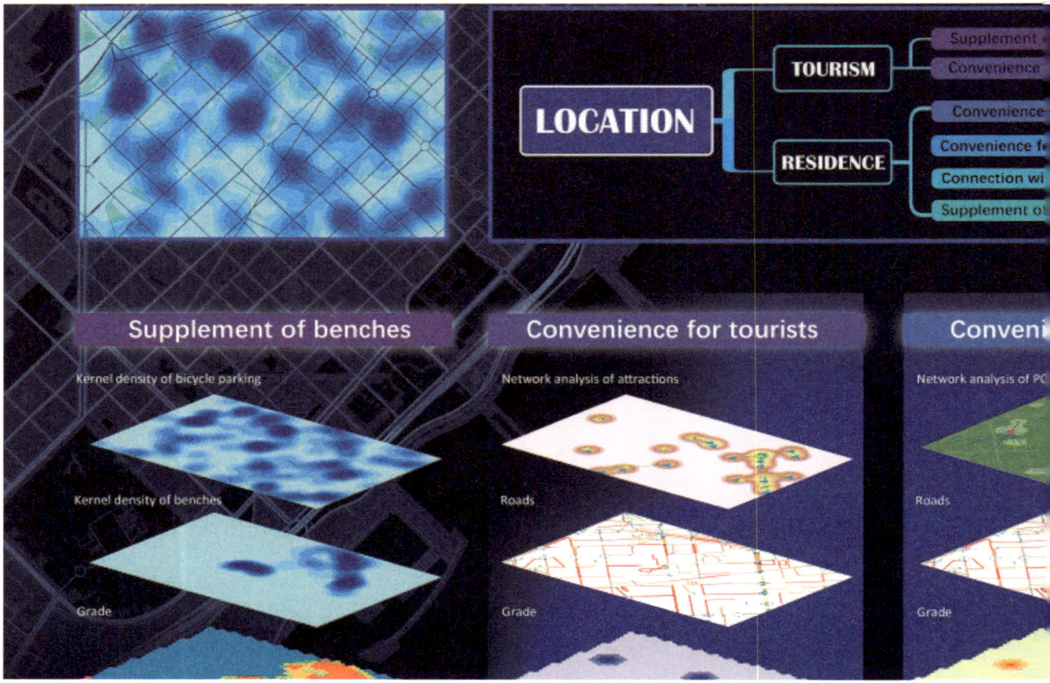
LOCATION
TOURISM
RESIDENCE
Supplement of benches
Convenience for tourists
Kernel density of bicycle parking
Kernel density of benches
Grade
Network analysis of attractions
Roads
Grade
Roads
Grade

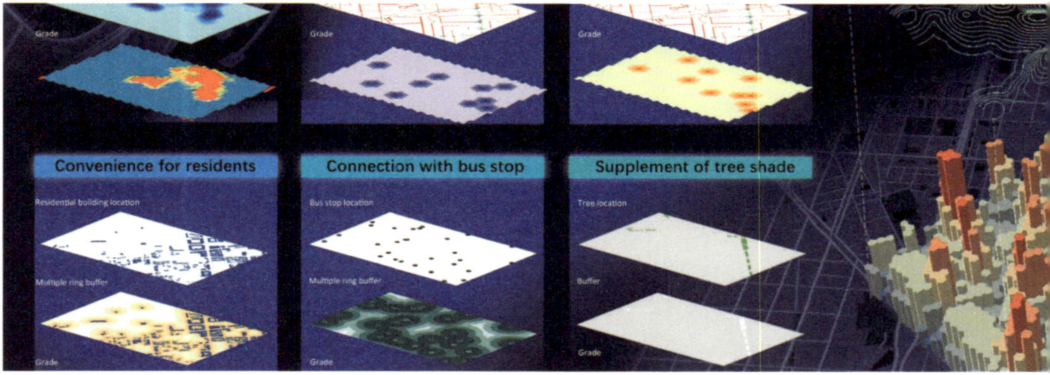
Grade
Grade
Grade
Convenience for residents
Connection with bus stop
Supplement of tree shade
Residential building location
Multiple ring buffer
Grade
Bus stop location
Multiple ring buffer
Grade
Tree location
Buffer
Grade

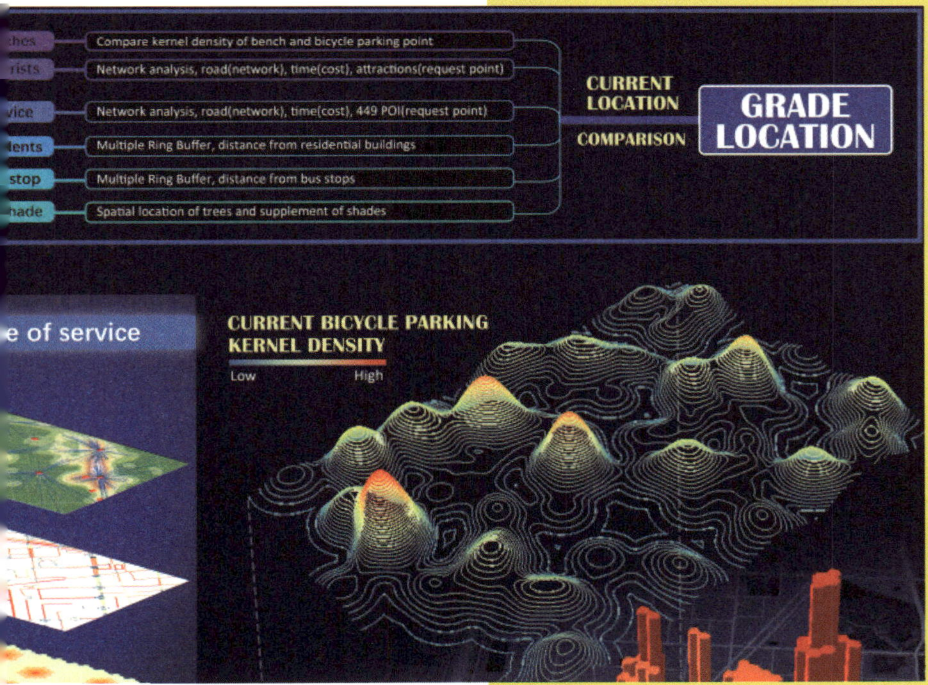

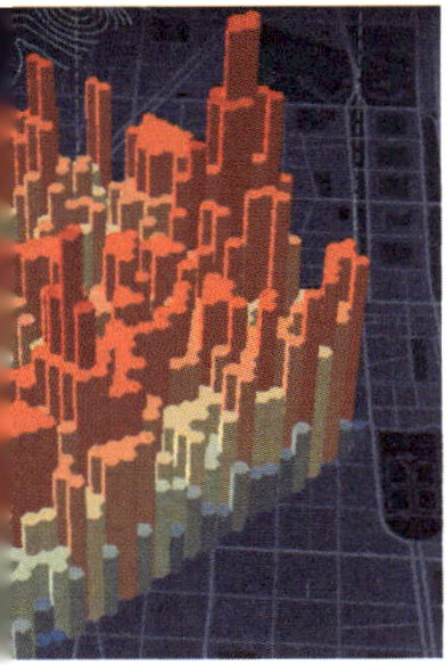

Recommended bicycle parking location general grades

SELECTED PROJECTS 529GRTZP7

SPİKEMOSS

THE ROSE OF RESURRECTİON

Ziyad Wassef
Egypt

Spikemoss brings the qualities of the ultimate survivors of the desert, with the ability to catch rainwater by instantly blooming, and extracting groundwater by piercing the sand and pressuring water upwards. Reviving the tradition of using fabric to ventilate the interior spaces and as a natural air purifier. The shell creates a better environment to host new plants for food, grown locally for self-sufficiency. The waste is stored in biogas generators, along with the solar panels, mounted on the roof, together they provide clean zero-emissions energy.

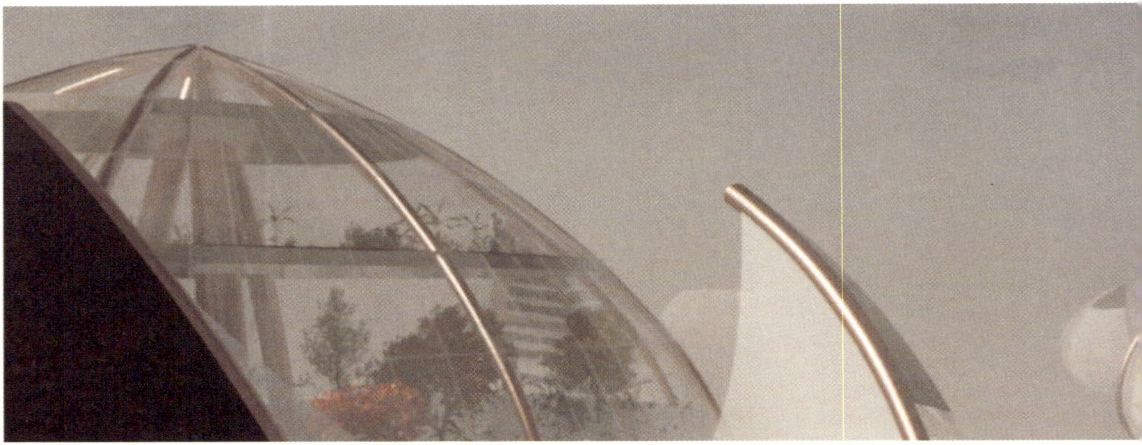

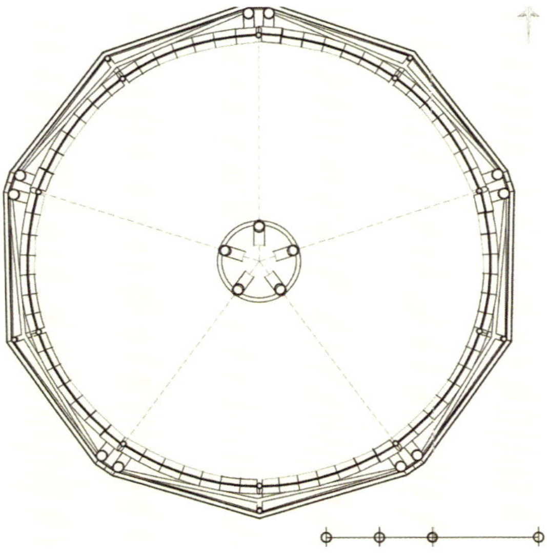

This project represents a future vision for living. Imagining a sustainable contemporary community, in a desert with unseen potential, in a modular form that can expand and be applied in many areas

529GRTZP7

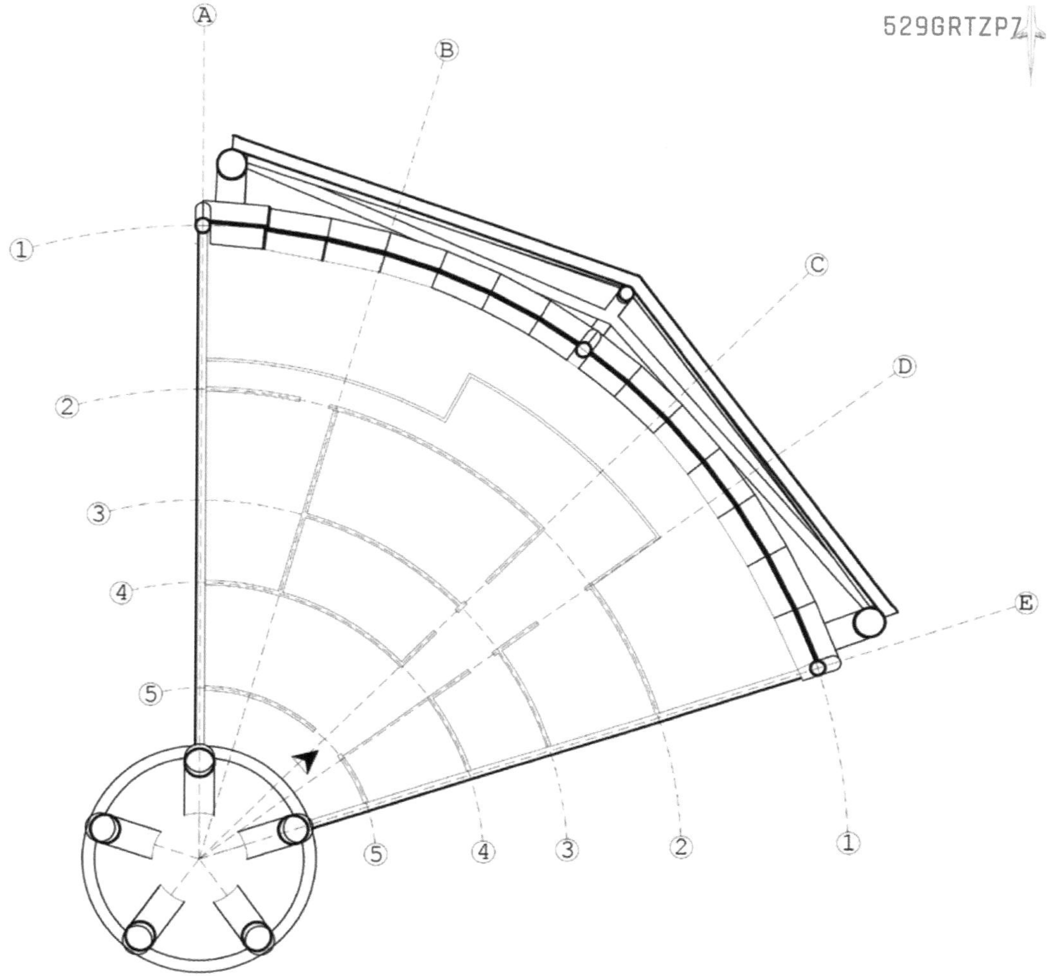

SELECTED PROJECTS

213UXIPAP

BRİNG COUNTRYSİDE İNTO THE CİTY

MAKE EXİSTİNG MATTER ECO

Zuzanna Montwill
Poland

My idea is focued on touching city and rural matter and connect it. We have to take into consideration living as a whole. Life has not only physical aspect but also metaphysical. In my opinion we have to begin with our commitemtent for an environment, we have to take part in creating the city to feel responsible.

SELECTED PROJECTS

5254NWIY4

UNTITLED

Xue Yang
China

The traditional way of communication is mainly neighborhood communication, the distance between cities and villages is far, the transportation is not convenient, the information is not developed. Public space and private space equilibrium empty. With the modern developed transportation system and information technology, the distance between people is getting shorter and shorter. With the diversification and openness of people's communication methods, private space has been crushed by the public space.

In ancient times, our ancestors built nests to escape wild animals and natural disasters, they often live alone.

Later, people learned how to use tools and drilled wood for fire.

SELECTED PROJECTS

329YTH6ZE

HA LONG BAY

Jędrzej Napierała
Poland

Developing cities towards water saves nature. Water provides food, transport, electricity. Let the house be a stable yacht to live and work. Use the yacht to travel for supplies, entertainment, anything. Now take a future water city structure as a mechanism, instead a fixed plan. Let houses move periodically, so each one touches the coast once a while. Change any street, change any neighbors, move a square, move home. Go work, go shopping, go sport, meet friends, go traveling by the house. Dynamic urbanism of floating eco houses, buildings, life.

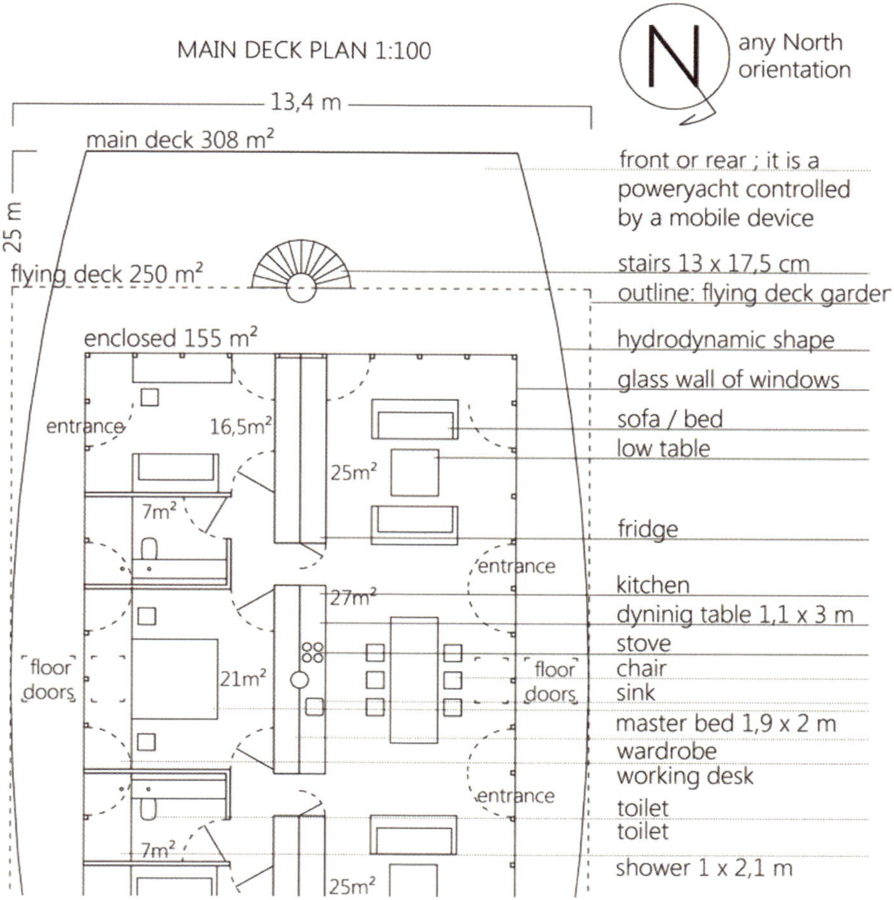
MAIN DECK PLAN 1:100
N
any North orientation
13,4 m
main deck 308 m²
25 m
flying deck 250 m²
enclosed 155 m²
entrance
16,5m²
25m²
7m²
entrance
27m²
floor doors
21m²
floor doors
entrance
7m²
25m²
front or rear ; it is a poweryacht controlled by a mobile device
stairs 13 x 17,5 cm
outline: flying deck garder
hydrodynamic shape
glass wall of windows
sofa / bed
low table
fridge
kitchen
dyninig table 1,1 x 3 m
stove
chair
sink
master bed 1,9 x 2 m
wardrobe
working desk
toilet
toilet
shower 1 x 2,1 m

SELECTED PROJECTS

6765BCHH3

LİFE CYCLES AND TRANSFORMATİON OF HOUSES

Ferenc Posta
Liliána Posta
Hungary

SINGLE FAMILY HOUSES COUNTRYSIDE

DETACHED HOUSES SUBURBAN AREAS

The 6×12 m units are designed with 1 m modules, each built-in furniture fits into this. When transformation is needed, these panels can be interchanged or replaced by new types. The electrical and mechanical installations take place in the suspended ceiling and raised floor. The housing units may be built as single-family houses or as part of urban development, such as detached houses in the suburbs or high-rise residential complexes in city centers. Since the eco-friendly units are designed identically, they are highly suitable to build up a modular system.

STANDARD
TRANSFORMATION PROCESS
FLEXIBLE
TRANSFORMATION PROCESS

SELECTED PROJECTS

691QJQVYI

FROM BODY PARTS TO THE LİVİNG UNİVERSE

Sasan Bahrami
Iman Sheikhansari
Iran

With tactile decentralization and the node-based approach to units of living, we could achieve a higher quality of life within the current state. Controlling units and nodes with the accompaniment of peer to peer blockchain network and use of algorithms to collect data, and manned by units/nodes and blocks themselves would lead to digital twins that make our lives more peaceful. Depicted illustrations are based on sufficing humans' demands-based novelty of needs in the current era, aligned with the future of life. The rising notion to open agriculture and organic foods, in-house manufacturing and workspace, open source healthcare and regenerative lifecycle with tangible and intangible interfaces could bring a new age of the Anthropocene.

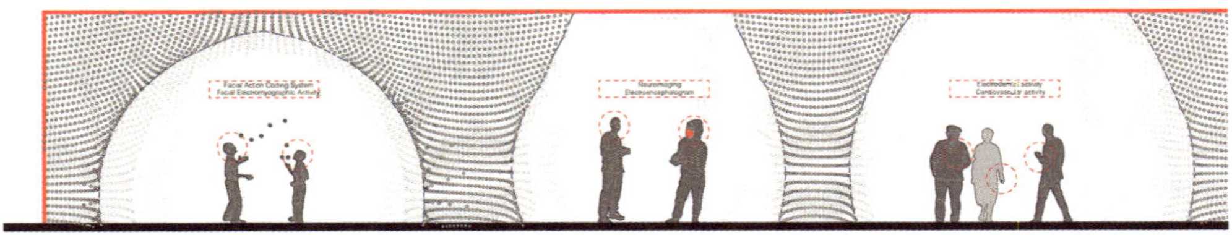

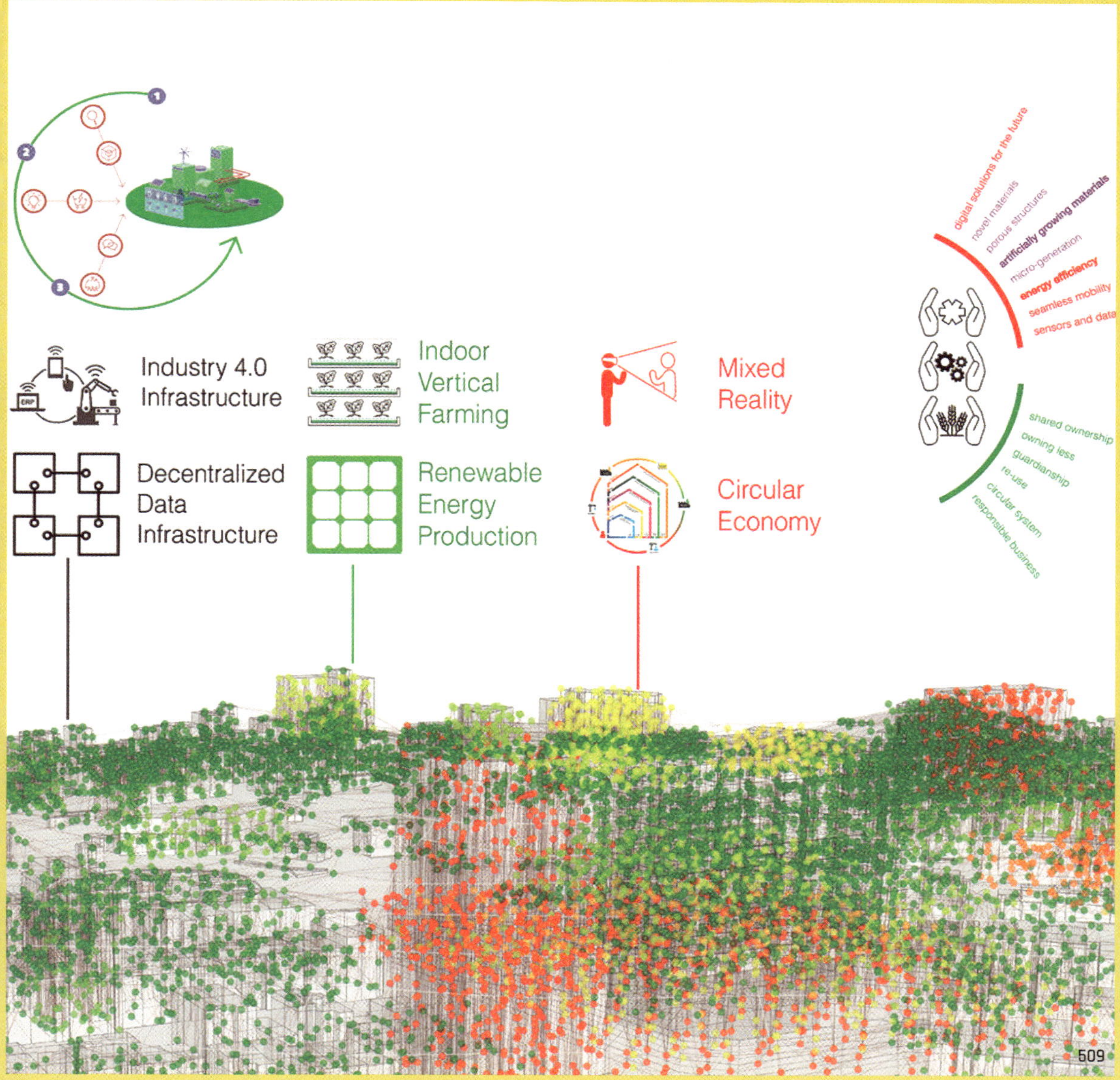
Industry 4.0
Infrastructure
Indoor
Vertical
Farming
Mixed
Reality
Decentralized
Data
Infrastructure
Renewable
Energy
Production
Circular
Economy
digital solutions for the future
novel materials
porous structures
artificially growing materials
micro-generation
energy efficiency
seamless mobility
sensors and data
shared ownership
owning less
guardianship
re-use
circular system
responsible business

SELECTED PROJECTS

698AQ5I08

HABİTABLE BALLON

Yuliia Surova
Germany

The idea came after water/land invers map. Our blue planet mainly covered with oceans, seas and rivers. That was the way to travel. Portable, floating house, that can be used through all over the world. But how? The answer is in the structure of it. Inflatable construction is supported by air, which can be any temperature according to the place where the dwelling is. When in some point it appeared in polar climate, the air inside it will be already warm, so heating is not necessary. And reverse, it trobical climate the cool air will be a supporter.

Here you can see palm tree
(tropical climate)

Snow load
Snow load
Wind load
Internal pressure
Wind load
Intern
Air supported structure
Air inflatable structure
Temperature of the air inside habitable balloon according to the climate of presence

SELECTED PROJECTS

686SIOUJ1

UNTITLED

Yumo Wu
Diya Seepaul
United Kingdom

EVENTS

2020

Land Pier, Peter Cook, Dennis Cromptom, Ron Herron, Archigram Features Monte Carlo, 1969

As a stage for discussion prior to the contest, a series of conferences and debates were organized around the issues raised. Being the eighth edition of the contest, this initiative made it possible to connect various generations of people who in one way or another have been linked to the activities organized around the IAAC. The conversations covered topics of interest, projects carried out and visions about the future that served as inspiration to those who would become the participants of the contest.

Exchanges like these made it possible to show the networks that have been created around the IAAC, many of the ideas that have been incubated and how these ideas and people have influenced the world around them. Some examples showed that goals are not always achieved quickly and that perseverance is important. Similarly, other cases showed that sometimes the consequences of our actions can go much further than we think.

Combining these conversations with the contest and its results, it is possible to conclude that one of the benefits of IAAC is its ability to react and adapt quickly to changes, proposing a contest on a current and necessary topic. At times like these, the institution becomes a catalyst for the proposals that are generated around it.

DESİGN FOR LİVİNG

Launching Event - May 4th - 2020

A global event to rethink our habitat

Global Event to launch the 8th Advanced Architecture Contest, connecting simultaneously 7 jurors from all continents, to talk about their experience of lockdown and how they imagine how we can rethink our human habitat, from the body to the city at a time when we fight for the life and climate.

Donald Bates
Melbourne

Mu Shao Hui
Shenzhen

Anupama Kundoo
Auroville (from Berlin)

Melat Assefa
Adis Abebba

Carlo Ratti
Torino

Marcela Sabino
Rio de Janeiro

Florencia Pita
Los Angeles

MAKİNG & DESİGNİNG X LİVİNG

Moderated by: Tomas Diez - May 12th - 2020

The power of making (and makers) has demonstrated that resilient and skillful people, with access to open source technology, can be game-changers during a crisis. Designers, engineers, medical doctors, makers, mostly everyone, contributed with a fast response to what society needed in an agile and collaborative way. The world that is about to come is not determined yet, we can take the best from extreme situations and make it foundational of the futures we want to create. We will gather a group of leaders in the field of design, technology, engineering, and social impact, in order to share with the world what it means to be able to make almost anything together.

Nadya Peek
Seattle
University of Washington

Alejandra Diaz de León
Mexico
ITESM Campus Monterrey

Tomas Vivanco Larrain
Chile
Pontificia Universidad Católica de Chile

Anastasia Pistofidou
Barcelona
Fab Lab Fabricademy

Oscar Tomico
Barcelona
Elisava

James Tooze
Brighton
University of Brighton & FAB City Collective

A WiNNERS CONVERSATiON

*Moderated by: **Vicente Guallart - May 15th 2020***

Three of the winners in past editions of the Advanced Architecture contest from Boston, Montreal and Barcelona participate in this event to share how studying at the IAAC transformed their lives and allowed them to do research and projects, as the last winner of the city of Barcelona award, as best building of the year.

Daniel Ibañez
Boston
Harvard GSD / Co-director MAEBB IAAC

Ji Won Jun
Montreal
Senior Architectural / Urban Designer

Javier Fernández Ponce
Barcelona
J2J Architects

CONFERENCIA - COLOQUIO

Moderated by: Nuria Moliner - June 11th 2020

Barcelona, in the face of the climate and life crisis

In this conference-colloquium, moderated by Nuria Moliner, presenter of the TVE program Escala Humana. The chief architect of Barcelona will offer his vision on how to address the challenges facing Barcelona and cities around the world and will debate with the founder of IAAC on the potential of new digital technologies and natural resources to define new paradigms for architecture and the city.

Barcelona, frente a la crisis por el clima y la vida

En esta conferencia-coloquio, moderada por Nuria Moliner, presentadora del programa Escala Humana de TVE. El arquitecto jefe de Barcelona ofrecera su vision sobre como abordar los retos que se presentan en Barcelona y en la ciudades del mundo y debatirá con el fundador del IAAC sobre el potencial de las nuevas tecnologías digitales y los recursos naturales para definir nuevos paradigmas para la arquitectura y la ciudad.

Xavier Matilla
Barcelona
Arquitecte en Cap Ajuntament de Barcelona

Nuria Moliner
Barcelona
Escala Humana de TVE

Vicente Guallart
Barcelona / Moscow
Cofundador del IAAC, Ex-Arquitecte en Cap Ajuntament de Barcelona (2011-2015)

URBAN LİFE MATTERS

*Moderated by: **Marziah Zad - June 26th - 2020***

This conference brings together architects and urban planners to talk about how pandemics and the climate crises will impact, in the near future, the design of cities.

These selecte group of architects will debate on a global and local scale in urban design from their diverse cultural backgrounds.

Caroline Bos
Netherlands
Co-founder / Principal Urban Planner UNStudio

Nasrine Seraji
Iran - UK - France - Hong Kong
Founder Atelier Seraji

Dana Behrman
UK - Israel - Netherlands
Urban Planner

Marziah Zad
Iran - USA
Architect / Moderator

Aziza Chaouni
Morocco - Canada
Architect

CROSS-REFERENCES FOR A DESİGNED POST-PANDEMİC FUTURE.

REFLECTİONS AROUND OVER 100 PROPOSALS SENT TO THE IAAC DESİGN FOR LİVİNG CONTEST.

by **Fabio Capra Ribeiro**

Although humanity has gone through various periods of crisis, it does not take long to rebuild the idea of abundance, of infinite resources, of exploiting the planet for generations and generations without consequences. Recently, the intense process of globalization strengthened this feeling,[1] expanding the reach of people and opening the possibilities of consumption to a global market. Thanks to the distance, the consequences of the exploitation of people and resources are almost imperceptible and require a certain level of consciousness. It is not easy to digest that the mobile phone we buy contains metals extracted from all corners of the planet, has been transported for thousands of kilometres and has involved people in poor working conditions.

With the arrival of the pandemic, these almost invisible relationships became evident when they began to fail, demonstrating consequences far beyond the borders of the affected place.[2] This fact triggered an intense process of fragmentation. The territories that seemed to be in constant expansion began to shrink,1 limiting their scope as well as the possibilities of displacement. Quickly, the global illusion of abundance was exposed,[3] manifesting the delicate balance that tries to keep societies functioning today. In concrete terms, "[u]rban areas produce over 80% of global economic output, but with over 95% of COVID-19 cases located in these areas, much of the economic activities in cities have been placed at a standstill due to the measures needed to control the pandemic."[4] Designing during this false abundance has degraded the planet[3] and drastically reduced our chances of survival.

As the pandemic raged around the world, the economic recession made its way, investments to combat climate change were severely curtailed, threats to public health that resulted in lockdowns and shutdowns increased, and inequality intensified as the world was trying to migrate to a system of digital education and work.[5] The consequences are still unknown, but for the moment we know that "80% youth whose mental health deteriorated during the pandemic,"[6] "70% of working women across nine of the world's largest economies believe their careers will be slowed by the pandemic's disruption,"[7] "while 51% of youth from 112 countries believe their educational progress has been delayed."[8] Fear seized a large part of the population; meeting spaces were lost and there was even the risk of losing control over one's own body when falling victim to the disease.[1]

Although the general situation was similar around the world, important differences could also be observed. In China, cities were fragmenting into communities seeking to contain the spread of the virus.[9] In Germany, responsible behaviour was common, not requiring attention from the forces of order, even children showed behaviour according to the new demands.[10] In Morocco, the measures were extremely strict from the beginning and people risked up to three days in prison for not obeying controls.[11] In cities like Los Angeles, individuality prevailed, large houses and wide spaces for vehicular circulation facilitated isolation.[12] In Brazil, the president encouraged people to go out, underestimating the danger, although many favelas decided to isolate themselves, implemented their own controls, monitored the sick, and tried to respond to the needs of their neighbours.[13] While in India or Ethiopia many people did not have a home to spend the quarantine and also had to move around the city in daily basis to find ways to survive.[10-14] The central question opens within this contextual framework: "How can architecture and urban design contribute to better lives?"[15]

One of the most visible consequences of the pandemic was the widespread confinement. Many societies got used to their daytime life unfolding through the city, while the house was only a place to sleep, but that situation changed rapidly with the confinement.[16] With the confinement it became clear how homes have been increasingly disconnected from the city, a typical process of the twentieth century. Balconies became more visible than ever, starring in all kinds of scenes. At the same time, the roofs took on a new prominence, places to take a breath or rest from the confinement without the police having access.[11] Living this process surely made us appreciate the public space and the possibility of going out much more, which before was perfectly normal and could even be overlooked.

Even faced with the consequences of the pandemic, it is clear that "we are not giving up the urban life."[15] The issue is not to leave the city, but to change it. The city is originally understood as a space of welcome, protection, prosperity, and it is these same axes that should be at the centre of development.[17] Build a governance system where the individual and the collective are synchronized instead of facing each other.[10] Although these concepts seem to be far from the reality that exists today, there are many resources that are not being used and that could represent an important contribution to bring us closer to this balance. For example, in urban areas there is a huge need for housing, while they are thousands of empty homes[13] and large empty spaces are forgotten in key points of the cities. There are even invisible resources that can be harnessed. As the pandemic progressed, the need to isolate oneself highlighted the logistical capabilities of delivery services, as well as the service possibilities associated with web and mobile applications.

Many of the contradictions are associated with the problems and costs of displacement, in addition to the way in which urban dynamics is capable of consuming land area. Probably, urban centres should not grow without limit. Proximity has been a subject in constant discussion in recent years and recent events underscore its importance. Those who could walk to the market, to the pharmacy, even to work, were surely able to adapt more easily to the restrictions imposed around the pandemic.

While it is true that the problems are large and complex, there is also a consensus that special attention should be paid to the most vulnerable populations. From there the changes must begin. Considering the elderly population, gender differences, minorities, economic and social inequalities in general, the logic of balance must be imposed.[17] All the more so now that "[t]he COVID-19 pandemic is exacerbating urban inequality" affecting mostly informal workers.[2] This fact puts at the centre of the debate the existing slums around the world, but which are home to most of the population in the Global South. These sectors were particularly affected by infections and the consequences of confinement, further increasing inequality,[11] but rethinking the conditions of populations with fewer resources, potentially represents an improvement for the entire social fabric.

While reflecting on how to deal with the pandemic and its consequences, at the same time it must be borne in mind that there is "[n]o vaccine for environmental degradation."[18] The abrupt emergency that recently unfolded cannot make us forget an even greater danger: the degradation of the environment. In addressing this issue, urban areas play a fundamental role. Being part of nature, restoring the natural wild life in cities will also favour people's lives and the conditions of their surroundings.[19] In the same way, it is necessary to change the direction that urban space is following on a global scale in order to improve the survival possibilities of the world as we know it.[20] Currently, most of the population understands this phenomenon, just as there is significant consensus on some of the actions that should be taken. For example, large, paved areas should be turned into green areas, which would require resources in addition to a different management system that includes different sectors of society in their maintenance, because the current system would not be enough.[17] As the example indicates, although there are agreements in the objectives, there are significant obstacles to their implementation.

In the same way, it is understood that we need to neutralize polluting emissions. In this sense, the pandemic showed a photo of what could be the future since "COVID-19-induced lockdowns led to a sudden fall in carbon emissions and improvements in air quality in cities, providing the world a brief window into the decarbonized, sustainable future environmental advocates have championed for decades."[2] Obviously, the situation that has been experienced recently is not the solution, but at least it allows us to see a horizon. Hopefully, some of the environmental benefits will continue, but it is equally likely that as the pandemic is brought under control, habits will be the same again.[16]

Faced with attention to the environment in urban space, one of the most common proposals has to do with the activation of spaces, buildings, and landscapes. In this sense, there is talk of the incorporation of a diverse vegetation that enriches people's lives, but also promotes biodiversity. Green is thought of as a filter for greenhouse gases, sequestering carbon from the air during its growth, but also in spaces to generate food, integrated into buildings, where the community can participate. Participation also becomes learning and thus increases the value we place on the environment. Without forgetting that integration with the environment considers the sustainable use of its renewable resources and waste management.

Addressing the restoration of the environment includes, among other things, changing production processes. This fact includes a change in the concept of value, where value is determined by the possibility of meeting a need or even a desire,[21] without being tied only to an economic condition. Likewise, it requires thinking about local production processes, improving the possibilities of becoming aware of the environmental wear and tear that the exploitation of resources entails and reducing transportation needs. This without forgetting the other end of the cycle, from production to the end of its useful lifepan. Include in the designs the possibility of sharing information, so that it can be produced in other places, in other laboratories, adapting them to local particularities. At the same time, it is necessary to design the process of disassembly, decomposition, recycling, etc. Consider the complete life cycle of materials and designs, while thinking about ways to reuse existing ones. Returning to the resources of urban areas, it is necessary to think about how empty spaces are activated, how factories and structures that are not in operation evolve, how the limits between different sectors of the city are managed, how housing is adapted to life on a planet in ecological, economic and social imbalance.

Acting on these and other imbalances requires information. If the pandemic has shown one thing, it is the importance of data and its representation to better understand the real situation.[22] Precisely, "[e]arly response efforts were hampered by the lack of robust data-sharing systems."[23] This same fact occurs with our relationship with the environment, where it is difficult to understand and transfer the scale of the problem to the general population. Information is key to reducing costs, improving production efficiency and including the most vulnerable populations; which is why the current crisis is accelerating the massification of digital data analysis tools.[4] Just as the virus has a code that reproduces and attacks us, designers can generate codes to spread, opportunities to replicate our ideas and fight back.[24] Information management, care for the environment and vulnerable populations, everything seems to be framed in the need to share needs, resources, ideas.

As a result of the pandemic, a sense of community has been strengthened, of knowing your neighbour better and helping him, that is something not to be missed.[25] This type of structure "enabled cities to minimize the negative economic impact of COVID-19 and increased the potential for accelerated recovery, which is an essential characteristic of urban resilience."[4] This fact reinforces the idea of thinking in communities with greater autonomy. Change the centralized structure that characterizes many governments and societies today, for a network structure that improves resilience.[3] This greater local stability does not pose isolation, but rather the organization of networks that can collaborate directly at the local level, while creating other types of relationships at the regional and global levels.[22] "Collaborating to create joint value."[15] Sharing to allow linking research with practice to generate innovative solutions. In other words, the organization of the decentralized community that can be more easily sustained,[9] while it is structured as an "open system, located in a territorial context that includes other human settlements such as rural areas, in between which there exist interdependent relations"[26]

Regarding the consequences of the pandemic, some changes may be considered for the future. In the last century, world wars, the oil crisis and the great depression were some of the phenomena that generated changes in the development of societies.[22] In this sense, it is necessary to question the possibilities of changes that the pandemic could create and the role of the designer in its formulation.[21] In the same way, since the world we want does not exist and some things that have changed recently should not return to the previous normality, we have the task of imagining a new future and making the most of the spaces for debate and interaction.[13] In the best of cases, the pandemic will have accelerated innovation and change. Issues that were pending and that progressed slowly have been accelerated by this situation. Perhaps the best example is online education, which had been growing, but has now been shown as a powerful possibility to multiply the scope of knowledge.

Currently, the most important thing is how we use our skills to contribute to the process of evolving into the future.[24] Some would say that it is early to draw conclusions about how the confinement and other consequences of the pandemic will affect society and what we can do about it, but that is precisely the role of the designer, to think and plan ahead. Find formulas to strengthen commitments between community members and the environment to build healthier and more sustainable spaces. Faced with this crisis, we cannot go back to the past because we will have lost the opportunity to innovate that this important challenge imposes on us.[27]

Working for the future means planning, but also concrete actions. It requires "dedicated task forces engaged in the development of not only recovery plans, including financial and economic dimensions, but also strategies for doing better than they were before the crisis."[4] It will be necessary to establish plans that define concrete objectives, time frames, value of actions, pace of implementation, verification and evaluation of results, but acting as soon as possible;[22] there is no time to waste. The problems we are facing are too great and have been growing for a long time. For this, a fundamental question that we must ask ourselves is: Is the future a post-pandemic life or a with-pandemic life?

In short, a complex thought is built that is in constant transformation and where society, technology and nature are intercepted in a constant search for a balance that allows improving the probabilities of the beings that currently populate the planet. It requires a dynamic understanding that evolves faster than the challenges we face. Contemporary cities are eminently open, diverse and complex systems, composed by multiple actors with very heterogeneous objectives,[28] which is why complex and flexible reasoning is required to adapt to unstable reality.

The paradox is that we naturally tend to rely on the structures of thought and the most widespread technologies today to build different scenarios, which imposes important challenges and generates the need to innovate. From there, one could surely defend the fact that many of the solutions already exist, have even begun to be applied. This affirmation is reinforced by the fact that we remain sorry not for doing what we know we have and can do, living in a constant process of consolation.[22] This being the case, the problem is how to achieve a significant change in the trends that currently move the world. In this regard, part of the solution seems to lie in designing formulas that allow expanding those pilot projects or small initiatives that seem to point in the right direction. To do this, you have to be aware that every action, small or large, is significant, but more important is to build networks of activities that multiply ideas.

The pandemic has created a vacuum that we should take care of,[17] but "there is no need for a refoundation, restart or revolution but for an evolution that learns from both good and bad."[29] As activities normalize, "there is an opportunity to embed greater societal equality and sustainability into the recovery, accelerating rather than delaying progress towards the 2030."[5] Even so, it is necessary to understand: first, it is not a short or simple process; second, it is neither the only nor the first call to implement the necessary changes; third, it is about moving against the current. Individual actions are important, but they will become exponentially more important and effective to the extent that they are structured through formal and informal networks that multiply results and scope; in addition to spreading with words and deeds a different path that allows us to extend the presence of life as we know it on this planet.

REFERENCES

[1] N. Seraji, 'Urban Life Matter', Jun. 2020.
[2] UN Habitat, World Cities Report 2020 The Value of Sustainable Urbanization. 2020.
[3] T. Vivanco Larrain, 'Making & Designing X Living', May 2020.
[4] UN Habitat, 'Global Compendium of Practices on Local Economic and Financial Recovery. Building Urban Economic Resilience during and after COVID-19', 2021. Accessed: Mar. 10, 2021.
[5] World Economic Forum, 'COVID-19 Risks Outlook: A Preliminary Mapping and its Implications', Switzerland, 2020. Accessed: Mar. 13, 2021.
[6] P. Jefferies and M. Ungar, 'Social anxiety in young people: A prevalence study in seven countries', PLOS ONE, vol. 15, no. 9, Sep. 2020, doi: 10.1371/journal.pone.0239133.
[7] 'Understanding the Pandemic's Impact on Working Women', Deloitte Switzerland.
[8] 'Youth & COVID-19: Impacts on jobs, education, rights and mental well-being', Report, Aug. 2020. Accessed: Mar. 11, 2021.
[9] M. Shao Hui, '8th Advanced Architecture Contest: Design for Living Launch', May 2020.
[10] A. Kundoo, '8th Advanced Architecture Contest: Design for Living Launch', May 2020.
[11] A. Chaouni, 'Urban Life Matter', Jun. 2020.
[12] F. Pita, '8th Advanced Architecture Contest: Design for Living Launch', May 2020.
[13] M. Riquet Sabino, '8th Advanced Architecture Contest: Design for Living Launch', May 2020.
[14] M. Assefa, '8th Advanced Architecture Contest: Design for Living Launch', May 2020.
[15] C. Bos, 'Urban Life Matter', Jun. 2020.
[16] D. Bates, '8th Advanced Architecture Contest: Design for Living Launch', May 2020.
[17] X. Matilla, 'Conferencia, frente a la crisis por el clima y la vida', Jun. 2020.
[18] World Economic Forum, 'The Global Risks Report 2021. 16th Edition'.
[19] A. Wlodarczyk and J. Mascarenhas, 'Nature in cities. Renaturalization of riverbanks in urban areas', Open Eng., vol. 6, Jan. 2016, doi: 10.1515/eng-2016-0095.
[20] K. Barbey, 'Nature-Based Urban Space Transformation', presented at the SBE2016 Towards Post-Carbon Cities, Turin, 2016.
[21] J. Tooze, 'Making & Designing X Living', May 2020.
[22] V. Guallart, 'Conferencia, frente a la crisis por el clima y la vida', Jun. 2020.
[23] C. V. Cosgriff, D. K. Ebner, and L. A. Celi, 'Data sharing in the era of COVID-19', Lancet Digit. Health, vol. 2, no. 5, p. e224, May 2020, doi: 10.1016/S2589-7500(20)30082-0.
[24] C. Ratti, '8th Advanced Architecture Contest: Design for Living Launch', May 2020.
[25] D. Behrman, 'Urban Life Matter', Jun. 2020.
[26] N. CEPAL, 'Latin America and the Caribbean: Challenges, dilemmas and commitments of a common urban agenda. Executive summary', Oct. 2016, Accessed: Mar. 7, 2021.
[27] D. Ibañez, 'A winners conversation', May 2020.
[28] J. M. Fernández Güell, 'Ciudades Inteligentes: La mitificación de las nuevas tecnologías como respuesta a los retos de las ciudades contemporáneas', Econ. Ind., no. 395, Art. no. 395, 2015.
[29] F. Capra Ribeiro, Uncertain Regional Urbanism in Venezuela: Government, Infrastructure and Environment. Routledge, 2020.

Design For Living

Published by
Actar Publishers, New York, Barcelona
www.actar.com

Edited by
Vicente Guallart

Award Contest Coordinator
Laia Pifarre
Content Coordinator
Fabio Capra Ribeiro

Distribution
Actar D, Inc. New York, Barcelona.

New York
440 Park Avenue South, 17th Floor
New York, NY 10016, USA
T +1 2129662207
salesnewyork@actar-d.com

Barcelona
Roca i Batlle 2
08023 Barcelona, Spain
T +34 933 282 183
eurosales@actar-d.com

Publication date: 2021

Graphic Design
Lina Salamanca
Dayana González

The editorial office can be contacted at
designforliving@iaac.net

Content team
Rebecca Baierwick
Fatemeh Nejatisalout
Yangchuan Tian
Paulina Sevilla

Web Development
Miquel Martinez - Mad Systems

Indexing
English ISBN: 978-1-948765-97-8
PCN: Library of Congress Control Number: 2021935592

https://advancedarchitecturecontest.org/